Readings in
Philosophy of Psychology

The Language and Thought Series

Series Editors
Jerrold J. Katz
D. Terence Langendoen
George A. Miller

Readings in Philosophy of Psychology, Volume 1
NED BLOCK,

Editor

Readings in Philosophy of Psychology, Volume 2
NED BLOCK,

Editor

Surface Structure: The Interface of Autonomous Components
ROBERT FIENGO

Semantics: Theories of Meaning in Generative Grammar
JANET DEAN FODOR

The Language of Thought
JERRY A. FODOR

Propositional Structure and Illocutionary Force
JERROLD J. KATZ

Relevance: Communication and Cognition
DAN SPERBER AND DEIRDRE WILSON

An Integrated Theory of Linguistic Ability
THOMAS BEVER, JERROLD J. KATZ, AND D. TERENCE LANGENDOEN,

Editors (Distributed by Harper & Row, Publishers)

Readings in
Philosophy of Psychology

Volume 1

Edited by Ned Block

HARVARD UNIVERSITY PRESS
Cambridge, Massachusetts

Library of Congress Cataloging in Publication Data

Main entry under title:

Readings in philosophy of psychology.

  (Language and thought series)
  Includes index.
  1. Psychology—Philosophy—Addresses, essays,
lectures.   I. Block, Ned Joel, 1942-
BF38.R35   150'.1   79-25593
ISBN 0-674-74875-1 (v. 1, cloth)
ISBN 0-674-74876-X (v. 1, paper)

Preface

IT IS INCREASINGLY CLEAR that progress in philosophy of mind is greatly facilitated by knowledge of many areas of psychology and also that progress in psychology is facilitated by knowledge of philosophy. What makes this interrelationship most obvious to practitioners in these fields is that in order to keep up with the current literature on the problems on which they work, they find that they must be able to read the technical literature of one another's fields. The simple fact is that lines of research in many areas of philosophy and psychology have tended to converge on the same clusters of issues.

This convergence reflects a deeper mesh of the fields. A host of crucial issues do not "belong" to either philosophy or psychology, but rather fall equally well in both disciplines because they reflect the traditional concerns or require the traditional methods of both fields. The problems will yield only to philosophically sophisticated psychologists or to psychologically sophisticated philosophers.

The interest and viability of approaching these problems from the joint perspective of philosophy and psychology are widely acknowledged, as is indicated by the number of people engaged in joint research, by the existence of journals wholly or partly devoted to it, by the existence of at least one learned society and a number of less formal discussion groups, and by conferences too numerous to mention. Although there have been a number of books of proceedings of philosophy of psychology conferences, until now there has been no general anthology intended as a text in philosophy of psychology. It is this gap that the present book, which appears in two volumes, is intended to fill.

This is the first volume of *Readings in Philosophy of Psychology*. The second volume covers mental representation, imagery, the subject matter of grammar, and innate ideas—topics that are closely related to current psychological research. The topics covered in this volume—mainly the chief "isms" of contemporary theory of the nature of the mind—deal with the conceptual foundations of psychology and are rather distant from the day-to-day empirical concerns of psychology. Since the anthology has been divided into two volumes, I want to stress that neither volume on its own gives a picture of the field.

It should be said, moreover, that this anthology is *not* intended to survey the field. No single book could be comprehensive and at the same time present its topics in any depth. The topics covered here were chosen because they are especially interesting, because they have been a focus of current activity, because they allowed the selection of high-caliber articles, and because they fit together in a coherent way.

For articles that have been previously published, details of the original publication appear at the foot of the first page. The others (all the introductions, Fred Feldman's "Identity, Necessity, and Events," and David Lewis's "Mad Pain and Martian Pain") appear here for the first time. Throughout the anthology, nonstandard symbols have been used instead of common symbols such as the arrow, double arrow, backward "E," upside-down "A," square, and diamond. Explanations of the notation are repeated in each chapter where they appear.

Contents

Introduction. What Is Philosophy of Psychology?   1
  Ned Block

Part One. Behaviorism

Introduction: Behaviorism   11
  Harris Savin

1. The Logical Analysis of Psychology   14
  Carl G. Hempel

2. Brains and Behavior   24
  Hilary Putnam

3. Selections from *Science and Human Behavior*   37
  B. F. Skinner

4. A Review of B. F. Skinner's *Verbal Behavior*   48
  Noam Chomsky

Part Two. Reductionism and Physicalism

Materialism without Reductionism: What Physicalism
Does Not Entail   67
  Richard Boyd

5. Mental Events   107
  Donald Davidson

6. Special Sciences, or The Disunity of Science as a
Working Hypothesis   120
  Jerry A. Fodor

7. Philosophy and Our Mental Life   134
  Hilary Putnam

8. Excerpt from "Identity and Necessity"   144
  Saul A. Kripke

9. Identity, Necessity, and Events   148
   Fred Feldman
10. Anomalous Monism and Kripke's Cartesian Intuitions   156
    Colin McGinn
11. What Is It Like to Be a Bat?   159
    Thomas Nagel

Part Three. Functionalism
    Introduction: What Is Functionalism?   171
        Ned Block

Functional Analysis
12. Functional Analysis   185
    Robert Cummins

Functional Specification
13. The Nature of Mind   191
    D. M. Armstrong
14. Armstrong on the Mind   200
    Thomas Nagel
15. Psychophysical and Theoretical Identifications   207
    David Lewis
16. Mad Pain and Martian Pain   216
    David Lewis

Functional State Identity Theory
17. The Nature of Mental States   223
    Hilary Putnam
18. Review of Putnam   232
    David Lewis
19. Physicalism and the Multiple Realizability of Mental States   234
    Jaegwon Kim
20. What Psychological States Are Not   237
    Ned Block and Jerry A. Fodor
21. Functionalism and Qualia   251
    Sydney Shoemaker
22. Troubles with Functionalism   268
    Ned Block
    Index   307

Introduction

What Is Philosophy of Psychology?

Ned Block

PHILOSOPHY OF PSYCHOLOGY is the study of conceptual issues in psychology. For the most part, these issues fall equally well in psychology as in philosophy. But this is not to say these issues are always on the *borderline* between philosophy and psychology, peripheral to both fields.

How can it be that a set of issues falls in the mainstream of two such different disciplines? Part of the answer is that progress in science involves the solution of various sorts of conceptual puzzles, often requiring substantial conceptual articulation and sometimes the ferreting out of serious conceptual confusions. For example, Aristotelian physics conflated instantaneous velocity with average velocity, creating paradoxes and contradictions—as Galileo showed (see Kuhn, 1964). Newton's mechanics required resolving the ordinary notion of weight into force and mass, and Cannizzaro's breakthrough in chemistry involved distinguishing among atomic weight, molecular weight, and equivalent weight. Normally, the scien-

An earlier version of this introduction appeared as "Philosophy of Psychology" in Peter D. Asquith and Henry E. Kyburg, Jr., eds., *Current Research in Philosophy of Science* (East Lansing: Philosophy of Science Association, 1979) pp. 450-462. Reprinted by permission.

tists themselves solve conceptual problems in science. Although the skills involved are of the sort in which philosophers are trained (and in which scientists are typically not trained), only those at the frontiers of scientific knowledge are in a position to see the issues with the requisite degree of clarity.

What is different about conceptual issues in psychology is mainly that the frontiers of knowledge in the field are so close to the heartland of folk psychology that the conceptual issues about the mind that philosophers have long discussed are very nearly the same as the issues that impede theoretical progress in psychology. Indeed, the majority of topics of concern to contemporary philosophers of psychology would have been intelligible and, in many cases, even familiar to philosophers who lived long before the rise of modern psychology. Consider for example such topics of current controversy as the nature of mental representation in general and mental images in particular; whether there are innate ideas; whether perception is inferential; what it is to have a concept; the subject matter of grammar; and what the difference is between rule-governed and rule-described action (all discussed in this anthology). It is worth noting by contrast that a philosopher who lived before the rise of modern physics (albeit long before the rise of modern psychology) would be utterly baffled by most of the issues of concern to contemporary philosophers of physics. (Imagine Aristotle being asked whether the psi function of quantum mechanics is a probability wave.) The difference is that advances in physics have involved strikingly new concepts, and thus new conceptual issues, while advances in psychology have not.

This being said, it should also be conceded that the old issues typically appear in new and often more tractable forms. Indeed, some of the old issues are hardly recognizable in their new forms. For example, the issue of whether the subject matter of grammar is rules in the mind has been considerably altered by the advances in transformational-generative grammar and Chomsky's distinction between competence and performance. Moreover, since psychology does contain *some* new theoretical apparatus, new conceptual questions arise in connection with that apparatus: for example, the philosophical issues concerning Freudian theory (Wollheim, 1974). Also, new experimental techniques sometimes reveal previously unrecognized human capacities whose nature involves recognizably philosophical difficulties. For example, the experimental techniques of psychophysics reveal that people can make a series of judgments of relative brightness of lights that are stable and coherent and that allow experimenters to conclude that brightness is a certain function of a physical parameter (intensity). But this result raises the question of what brightness is, and what it means for one light to be twice as bright as another (see Savage, 1970). The claims of psychometricians to measure intelligence, personality, and so on, have attracted the attention of philosophers of psychology (Block and Dworkin, 1974; Block, 1976). What makes this issue of interest to philosophers (aside from its moral and political implications) is, first, that arguments

for the claims made on behalf of the tests have gone unformulated and unexamined, and it is a typically philosophical task to formulate arguments and examine them, and, second, that psychometric practice and ideology presuppose dubious philosophical doctrines.

The sort of problem described in the last paragraph is the exception rather than the rule, however. As I said, the problems of philosophy of psychology are, by and large, traditional problems in new guises. In some cases, hindsight reveals that an old philosophical problem was largely empirical: for example, the question of whether the differences between different emotions are differences of feeling or attitude. Current work by psychologists (Schachter and Singer, 1962), though flawed, suggests that while all emotions involve states of physiological arousal, the differences between them are indeed cognitive differences. Similarly, the old issue of inference in perception seems (to me at least) to have been resolved in the affirmative (Neisser, 1967; Gregory, 1974; but see Anscombe, 1974; Neisser, 1976). Even in this case, some of the old disputes are played out once again among psychologists of different stripes. Thus we have J. J. Gibson and his followers adducing empirical considerations supplemented by traditional philosophical arguments against inferential views.

To illustrate how old issues take on new forms, I shall briefly sketch some of the issues having to do with what is currently philosophy of psychology's hottest topic: mental representation. Issues of current interest include the following: how mental representations refer; how representations that express concepts combine to form representations that have truth value; whether mental representation requires a system of mental representations; whether the meaning of a mental representation is a matter of its role in inference, decision making, and other mental processes (and, if not, what the meaning of a mental representation does consist in); whether natural languages (such as English) are the major systems of mental representation, or whether we have to translate from English into our internal systems; whether the processes that manipulate mental representations take account of their meaning or of their shape only; what the identity conditions on mental representations are; what the difference is between discursive representations and imagistic or pictorial representations; whether images exist and, if so, whether they can refer, and if so, whether they can refer in virtue of resemblance to their causes (as William of Ockham apparently thought). (These issues are discussed in volume 2, part one, "Mental Representation," and volume 2, part two, "Imagery.")

Difficulties about imagery provide a good example of issues that have been changed not one iota by new theory; rather, they have been altered (in the direction of intractability, I fear) by striking new evidence. Roger Shepard and his students (see Shepard and Metzler, 1971) have put together an impressive array of evidence that people perform certain tasks by generating mental images (a process that can be timed) and rotating them at constant angular velocity. For example, when subjects are presented with two figures that clearly differ in their orientation and then are asked whether the figures have identical shapes, the time it takes subjects to answer is proportional to the angular displacement of the figures—independently of whether the rotation is in the plane of the page or at right angles to it.

In another experiment (described in volume 2, part two), subjects were asked to form an image of a map of an (imaginary) island containing seven small pictured objects (a house, a well, a tree, and so forth). Subjects were asked to "zoom in" on (as it might be) their image of the tree, and then answer, *by consulting their image*, the question "Does the island contain a house?" It was found that the time it took to answer was highly correlated with the distance between the tree and the house. Distances between objects varied considerably, and all of the pairs of objects (21) were used. These and many other results make it seem for all the world as if subjects are secretly manipulating drawings or models. Compelling as these experiments are, they do not cast much light on the traditional philosophical issues about images. We still want to know: What are images? Are the images of perception the same sort of thing as the images we "conjure up"? Are images like pictures in the head? If so, in what respects? How can an image be the end product in perception, for then there would have to be a perceiver of the image, and who would perceive *his* images? But what other role could an image have in perception? How can it be that an image of a tiger has no definite number of stripes? Is an image a neural entity? If so, what about the traditional Leibniz's Law problems—for instance, that images can be pink and green striped while the brain is mainly gray.

Another familiar issue having to do with mental representation is the question of what the difference is between behavior being rule-described and behavior being rule-governed. This distinction is at least as old as Aristotle and is also a major issue with respect to Kant's Categorical Imperative: "Act only according to a maxim which can at the same time be willed a universal law." Is a maxim of your action one that merely describes it, or one that governs it as well?

One major issue is whether behavior can be rule-governed, even in cases where one is not conscious of acting in accordance with a rule. Many philosophers of psychology are convinced that in an important class of rule-governed behaviors, we have no conscious knowledge of the rule. Here is an example of the sort of case that provides evidence for that view.

Speakers of most dialects of English pronounce the 'g' differently in 'finger' and 'singer'. The first 'g' might be described as "hard," the second as "soft."[1] There is a regularity here: roughly, the 'g' in 'nger' words formed from verbs is soft; otherwise, it is hard. What is the explanation of the fact that the rule "use soft 'g' in 'nger' words formed from verbs—otherwise use hard 'g' " describes our pronunciation behavior? One possible explanation is that we have in effect memorized the pronunciation of each 'nger' word. Another explanation is that the rule mentioned above (or some other rule—a possibility I will ignore) governs the behavior as well as describing it. Here is one item of evidence that rules out the former hypothesis and thus makes the latter more plausible. Let us coin the word 'ming': to ming is to look to the east. Someone who habitually looks to the east is a minger—with a *soft* 'g'. Since the rule applies to new cases, we have some reason to think the behavior is rule-governed.

It has been suggested (Fodor, 1975) that what the distinction between rule-governed and rule-described behavior comes to is that behavior is governed by a rule just in case a mental representation of the rule causally influences the behavior so as to make it described by the rule. This proposal raises a traditional bogeyman, described below.

Carroll (1895) pointed out that principles of logic cannot be applied without the use of reasoning that itself embodies logical principles. This fact creates difficulties for a view that says that all reasoning is rule-governed—that is, causally controlled by mentally represented rules. For example, suppose one reasons as follows:

The Argument: All men are mortal; Socrates is a man; therefore Socrates is mortal.

If all reasoning is causally controlled by mentally represented rules, it is plausible that the rule involved in this case is something like this:

The Rule: If an argument is of the form 'for any x, if x is F, then x is G; a is F; therefore a is G', then the argument is valid.

But how could The Rule play a causal role in one's reaching The Argument's conclusion that Socrates is mortal? It is hard to see how The Rule could be involved here if not in something like the following reasoning. The Rule says every argument of a certain specified form is valid; The Argument is of that form; so The Argument is valid. But this bit of reasoning *itself involves the application of The Rule*. (This can be made explicit by putting the reasoning so that it is clear that it fits the specified form, with F = being of the specified form, and G = validity: for any x, if x is of a certain form then x is valid; a is of that form; therefore, a is valid.) Thus it seems that in order to apply our mental representation of The Rule to The Argument, we require *another* application of a mental representation of The Rule. And so on. It is hard to see how a mental representation of The Rule can be applied at all. This traditional puzzle can be seen as a serious problem for the foundations of psychology.[2]

I described this puzzle partly to illustrate the traditional aspect of issues of contemporary philosophy of psychology, but partly also to indicate a way in which new approaches often differ from the old. The way the new approach differs here has perhaps as much to do with new technology as with new theory (though this distinction is of less note with regard to psychology than to some other fields). The new technology is that of the digital computer; the new theoretical concept is that of the Turing machine. The example of the digital computer shows us the rough outlines of a solution to this problem (and also suggests a way out of the problem of the infinite regress of image perceivers mentioned above. A digital computer is a device one knows to be rule-governed, for the rules are inserted by us as part of the program. In the digital computer, some operations are accomplished "automatically," by hard-wired circuitry, and not via the application of any represented rules. Minsky (1967) describes two primitive operations 'add 1' and 'subtract 1 or if register $= 0$, jump to the nth (where n is indicated) instruction'; he then shows that these two operations will suffice for the power of a universal Turing machine. In a commercial digital computer, the operations referred to in the rules that one programs into the computer are ultimately defined in terms of such primitive operations, the terms for which constitute a "machine language" that the machine is *built* to use, in the sense that when a primitive instruction appears in the appropriate register, the hard-wired circuitry accomplishes the operation. There is no regress because the machine's primitive operations are not rule-governed. The claimed solution, then, is that there are mental operations analogous to the primitive operations of the computer, and also mental operations analogous to the programmed operations, the latter being composed of the former in the mind as in the computer.

The fallacy in the argument in the paragraph before last can be blamed on the assumption that all reasoning is rule-governed (causally controlled by mentally represented rules). Some reasoning is "automatic" in the manner of the primitive operations of digital computers. Alternatively, one could hold on to the claim that all reasoning is rule-governed and blame the unsoundness of the argument on the premise (implicit in the sentence "It is hard to see how The Rule could be involved here . . .") that a rule can govern reasoning only via an application that itself involves reasoning. Sometimes a rule causally controls reasoning "automatically," in the way the machine lan-

guage command "ADD 1" causes the representation in a register to change, by the operation of hard-wired circuitry, and not by any process involving reasoning.

I have left out many issues that are closely related to those described above, among them perception, memory, attention, intentionality, innate ideas, conceptual development (such as issues arising from the work of Jean Piaget and Lawrence Kohlberg) and the foundations of artificial intelligence. But had these been described in more detail, the picture of philosophy of psychology sketched here would be even more skewed toward cognitive psychology. Psychology is a very fragmented field—cognitive psychology, mathematical psychology, and social psychology, for example, have little in common; those who work in or know about one rarely have much expertise in the other. I have given little indication of the interest and activity in topics on the borderline of psychology with physiology, such as split brains (Nagel, 1971; Puccetti, 1973); mathematical psychology; traits (Alston, 1976); noncognitive states of mind; and the foundations of social psychology (Harre and Secord, 1973). The emotions, especially, have been the topic of a veritable flurry of books and articles (Solomon, 1976; Thalberg, 1977; Rorty, forthcoming) on such topics as the intentionality of the emotions; whether emotions are voluntary; whether the expression of an emotion is part of the emotional state; the relation of emotions to character traits; and problems in the cross-cultural identification of the emotions.

The discussion above is also misleading in that it scants what might be called traditional philosophy of mind, including such topics as mind-body identity, other minds, privacy, consciousness, and the like. Some philosophers might consider this omission fortunate, appealing to the idea that philosophy of mind has as little to do with philosophy of psychology as metaphysics has to do with philosophy of physics. On the contrary, however, I see good reason to count philosophy of mind as part of philosophy of psychology (rather than conversely, as is commonly supposed). For one thing, as I have argued above, most of the problems in philosophy of psychology simply *are* versions of traditional problems. Second, even rather rarefied problems in philosophy of mind such as the status of "qualia" often have rather more direct relations to central conceptual issues in psychology than one might think at first glance. For example, functionalism (the view that mental states are functional states, states defined by their causal role) is currently the dominant view of the nature of mind. While some philosophers regard functionalism as providing a foundation for representational theories of belief (Harman, 1973; Fodor, 1979); others think functionalism counts against representational theories of belief (Stalnaker, 1976). The latter group regards the claim that belief is a functional state as a *rival* of the claim that belief is a relation to a sentence in the language of thought (see Field, 1978, for a critique of such arguments). At least there is wide agreement among philosophers of radically different points of view that functionalism is *relevant* to the foundations of psychology. The problems of qualia are in turn relevant to functionalism because there is reason to think that two states can be functionally identical, even though one lacks and the other has qualitative character (Block and Fodor, chapter 20; Block, chapter 22); hence qualia are the basis for an argument that functionalism is false. Of course, there is a great deal of disagreement about this matter (Shoemaker, chapter 21; Block, 1980). Dennett has gone so far as to argue that qualia can be explained by psychological models of the sort currently in vogue in cognitive psychology (Dennett, 1978).

Traditional philosophy of mind is often taken to include issues that more properly belong in metaphysics (personal identity) or epistemology (some issues about sense data), but the other issues in philosophy of mind, the ones that are genuinely about the mind, seem best classified as part of philosophy of psychology, even though some of them are related to empirical issues in a very abstract way.

The variety of problems in the philosophy of psychology is sufficiently great that no single anthology on the subject could possibly be comprehensive. The best one can do is pick a few topics and cover them in moderate depth. Inevitably, many major issues must be entirely omitted. Thus, for example, this anthology has no part devoted to problems of perception or to whether children's conceptual systems differ from those of adults. I have tried to pick disparate topics that at the same time fit together coherently.

All of the parts have something to do with empirical psychology, although part one, "Behaviorism," part two, "Reductionism and Physicalism," and part three, "Functionalism," could as easily fit into a book on traditional philosophy of mind. The first two parts overlap considerably with the third; indeed, Putnam's "Brains and Behavior" (chapter 2) and "Philosophy and Our Mental Life" (chapter 7) and much of Boyd's introduction to part two and Field's "Mental Representation" (see volume 2, part one) could have been included in "Functionalism" with some justice. The issues raised there lead naturally into those in "Mental Representation" (volume 2, part one), since one of the plausible answers to the question of what makes mental representations represent is their functional role. Although they are not all in the same part, the articles by Nagel (chapter 11), Shoemaker (chapter 21), and Block (chapter 22) are a natural group, since they are all concerned with problems of consciousness. "Mental Representation" and "Imagery" (volume 2, parts one and two) go naturally together, images and mental language being the leading candidate mental representations. The issues discussed in "Mental Representation" have natural applications in "The Subject Matter of Grammar" and "Innate Ideas" (volume 2, parts three and four). The former is about the issue of whether grammars are theories of mental representations, and the latter is about the issue of whether (or to what degree) our mental representations of grammar are innate.

Notes

1. Actually, the 'g' in the "soft" cases is deleted, and the 'n' is velar.
2. I am indebted to a discussion with Hartry Field and David Hills.

References

Alston, W. 1976. "Traits, Consistency, and Conceptual Alternatives for Personality Theory." *Journal for the Theory of Social Behavior* 5, no. 1: 17-48.

Anscombe, G. E. M. 1974. "Comment on Professor R. L. Gregory's Paper." In S. C. Brown, ed., *Philosophy of Psychology.* New York: Barnes and Noble.

Block, N. 1976. "Fictionalism, Functionalism, and Factor Analysis." In R. S. Cohen, C. A. Hooker, and A. C. Michalos, eds., *PSA 1974. Boston Studies in Philosophy of Science*, vol. 32. Dordrecht: Reidel.

—— 1978. "Troubles With Functionalism." In C. W. Savage, ed., *Minnesota Studies in the Philosophy of Science.* Vol. 9. Minneapolis: University of Minnesota Press. Reprinted as chapter 22, this volume.

—— 1980. "Are Absent Qualia Impossible?" *Philosophical Review* 89.

Block, N., and G. Dworkin. 1974. "IQ, Heritability and Inequality." *Philosophy and Public Affairs* 3, no. 4: 331-409; 4, no. 1: 40-99.

Block, N., and J. A. Fodor. 1972. "What Psychological States Are Not." *Philosophical Review* 81: 159-181. Reprinted as chapter 20, this volume.

Brown, S. C., ed. 1974. *Philosophy of Psychology.* New York: Barnes and Noble.

Carroll, L. 1895. "What the Tortoise Said to Achilles." *Mind* 4: 278-280.

Cummins, R. 1975. "Functional Analysis." *Journal of Philosophy* 72: 741-764. Reprinted in part as chapter 12, this volume.

Dennett, D. 1969. *Content and Consciousness.* London: Routledge & Kegan Paul.

—— 1977. "Review of Fodor's *The Language of Thought.*" *Mind* 86: 265-280.

—— 1978. "A Cognitive Theory of Consciousness." In C. W. Savage, ed., *Minnesota Studies in the Philosophy of Science.* Vol. 9. Minneapolis: University of Minnesota Press.

—— In press. "Why a Computer Can't Feel Pain." *Synthese.*

Field, H. 1978. "Mental Representation." *Erkenntniss* 13: 19-61.

Fodor, J. A. 1975. *The Language of Thought.* New York: Crowell.

—— 1978. "Computation and Reduction." In C. W. Savage, ed., *Minnesota Studies in the Philosophy of Science.* Vol. 9. Minneapolis: University of Minnesota Press.

—— 1979. "Propositional Attitudes." *Monist.*

—— 1980. "Methodological Solipsism." *Behavioral and Brain Sciences.*

Gregory, R. L. 1974. "Perceptions as Hypotheses." In S. C. Brown, ed., *Philosophy of Psychology.* New York: Barnes and Noble.

Harman, G., 1973. *Thought.* Princeton: Princeton University Press.

—— 1975. "Language, Thought and Communication." In K. Gunderson, ed., *Language, Mind, and Knowledge. Minnesota Studies in Philosophy of Science.* Vol. 7. Minneapolis: University of Minnesota Press.

Harre, R., and P. Secord. 1973. *The Explanation of Social Behavior.* Oxford: Blackwell.

Kosslyn, S., and J. Pomerantz. 1977. "Imagery, Propositions, and the Form of Internal Representations." *Cognitive Psychology* 9: 52-76.

Kuhn, T. S. 1964. "A Function for Thought Experiments." In *Mélanges Alexandre Koyré, II, L'aventure de l'esprit.* Paris: Herman.

Minsky, M. 1967. *Computation.* Englewood Cliffs, N.J.: Prentice-Hall.

Nagel, T. 1971. "Brain Bisection and the Unity of Consciousness." *Synthese* 22: 396-413.

Neisser, U. 1967. *Cognitive Psychology.* New York: Appleton-Century-Crofts.

—— 1976. *Cognition and Reality.* San Francisco: Freeman.

Puccetti, R. 1973. "Brain Bisection and Personal Identity." *British Journal for the Philosophy of Science* 24: 339-355.

Rorty, A. Forthcoming. *A Natural History of the Emotions.*

Savage, C. W. 1970. *The Measurement of Sensation.* Berkeley and Los Angeles: University of California Press.

Savage, C. W., ed. 1978. *Perception and Cognition: Issues in the Foundations of Psychology. Minnesota Studies in the Philosophy of Science.* Vol. 9. Minneapolis: University of Minnesota Press.

Schachter, S., and Singer, J. E. 1962. "Cognitive, Social and Physiological Determinants of Emotional States." *Psychological Review* 69: 379-399.

Shepard, R., and J. Metzler. 1971. "Mental Rotation of Three-Dimensional Objects." *Science* 171: 701-703.

Shoemaker, S. 1975. "Functionalism and Qualia." *Philosophical Studies* 22: 291-313. Reprinted as chapter 21, this volume.

Sober, E. 1976. "Mental Representations." *Synthese* 33: 101-148.

Solomon, R. 1976. *The Passions.* New York: Doubleday, Anchor.

Stalnaker, R. 1976. "Propositions." In A. McKay and D. Merrill, eds., *Issues in the Philosophy of Language.* New Haven: Yale University Press.

Thalberg, I. 1977. *Perception, Emotion and Action.* Oxford: Blackwell.

Wollheim, R., ed. 1974. *Freud.* New York: Doubleday, Anchor.

Part One

Behaviorism

Introduction: Behaviorism

Harris Savin

ON FIRST READING, the behaviorist conclusions of Carl G. Hempel and of B.F. Skinner, who exemplify the two main currents of behaviorist thought, have utterly different bases. Hempel's is an epistemological thesis, purporting to show that, insofar as psychological sentences are intelligible, they describe "physical behavior." For Hempel, that is to say, there is nothing psychology *could* be about except behavior. Skinner, on the contrary, has not an epistemological thesis but advice about the most expedient way to do psychology. He assumes without argument that the only interesting objective for psychology is the prediction of behavior, and he argues that it is fruitless, if that is one's objective, to consider mental states or mental processes: "The objection to inner states is not that they do not exist but that they are not relevant to a functional analysis."

Note that neither position entails the other. On the one hand, Skinner, unlike Hempel, is open to the possibility that there are psychological sentences that are not translatable into physical language. He insists only that he does not need them for his science of behavior. Hempel, on the other hand, has no quarrel with such psychological notions as purposes and beliefs, nor does he deny that there may be psychological laws whose most illuminating formulation will refer to such psychological entities. His only claim is that it is always possible in principle, even if far too tedious for the everyday purposes of scientific psychology, to translate such laws into physical language. In short, Hempel's thesis about the ultimate foundations of psychology has no obvious bearing on the day-to-day activity of psychologists, while Skinner's advice about how psychologists can best spend their time has no obvious epistemological content.

Hempel is most vulnerable to attack when he claims that "the meaning of a proposition is established by its conditions of verification." "Conditions of verification," he supposes, must be physical conditions; any psychological sentence, therefore, must have the same meaning as some physical sentence. In reply, one might try (as Hilary Putnam does in chapter 2) to show that, however closely mental events and behavioral events may, as a matter of empirical fact, be correlated with one another, mind statements cannot, in general, be *translated* by behavior statements.

There are two obvious ways to challenge Skinner: by questioning his assumption that the only interesting goal for psychology is the prediction of behavior, and by showing that, even for the prediction of behavior, it is expedient on occasion to consider mental states. Skinner notwithstanding, it surely needs no argument to establish that some of us look to psychology for descriptions of mental states and for knowledge about how to modify those states. As for Skinner's lack of interest in such topics, it is a mere idiosyncrasy, warranting no discussion here. More interesting is the question whether or not consideration of mental states may help in the prediction of behavior. Skinner says not, and gives the following argument. Either we know what a person's mental state is by virtue of what we know of his history of stimulation and behavior (knowing he is hungry, for example, because we know he has not eaten today), or else we do not have such evidence for his mental state. In the former case, we may as well forget about the mental state and relate subsequent behavior directly to history (predicting, for example, that the subject of our experiment will eat on the basis not of his inferred hunger but of his observed history of deprivation. If, on the contrary, we have not inferred our subject's mental state from his prior history, then (ignoring such far-fetched possibilities as telepathy) we do not know what his mental state is and therefore can make no predictive use of any putative law relating behavior to mental states.

The latter half of this argument is sound enough, but Skinner's dismissal of mental states that are inferred from a subject's history is unconvincing. Consider, for a moment, the variety of mental states that, on different occasions, might figure in explanations of eating: we may eat because we are hungry, because we do not want to offend our hostess, because the doctor has ordered us to eat, because we think it imprudent to drink on an empty stomach, or for any number of other rea-

sons. Such distinctions among states of mind are obviously crucial for predicting subsequent behavior—for predicting, for example, whether we will stop eating when the hostess leaves the room, when the doctor pronounces us cured, or when we learn there is no whiskey in the house. Skinner would urge that we can nonetheless dispense with these motives for eating and relate the differences in behavior directly to differences in previous history.

It takes only a moment's reflection to see that such a program for psychology is only plausible to the extent that discoverable principles relate past history to future behavior. There are, obviously, far too many significantly different human histories for anyone to propose that a practicable psychological theory could consist of an exhaustive enumeration of histories, each one paired with a prediction of subsequent behavior. Skinner, of course, recognizes this need for principles and, indeed, claims to have discovered the necessary principles in his work on operant conditioning. How widely these principles of operant conditioning apply outside the laboratory remains a matter of controversy among psychologists. It suffices for the purposes of the present discussion to note that Skinner believes, as does everyone else, that we need principles if we want to predict behavior from past history, yet his argument omits to consider the possibility that mental states will occur as theoretical constructs in some such successful system of principles.

Notwithstanding the differences between Skinner's thesis and Hempel's, their two behaviorisms evidence a shared conviction that people are in no important respect different from inanimate aggregates of matter. Now, what is important depends on one's interests and one's point of view. From certain limited but perfectly valid points of view, a man may usefully be regarded as a mass of matter concentrated at a single point. For other purposes, his description may consist of what he does in a factory, an army, or an artist's studio. I do not wish to quarrel with the decision to study man from any of these special points of view, nor with anyone who chooses to see to what extent it is possible to carry out Hempel's program, or Skinner's. But it is a remarkable and distressing fact that, for much of the present century, the scientific study of man has been so largely in the hands of those who wished to study him from one or the other of these two points of view and that the human sciences have taken so little serious interest in man as artist, as lover, as moral or political theorist, or, indeed, as creator of scientific knowledge. Even more remarkable and more distressing, most of those who have developed the behaviorist point of view in the human sciences have believed that their particular point of view was not the result of a largely arbitrary choice. On the contrary, they have supposed, for reasons such as those discussed here, that behaviorism was the only possible basis for the scientific study of man.

One need not impugn the motives of the founders of behaviorism to note the compatibility between their view of the proper study of man and the interests of those—generals, politicians, advertisers, and so forth—whose business it is to predict or control the behavior of masses of anonymous humanity. Of late, behaviorist fervor has greatly diminished, owing in part perhaps to growing disenchantment with these nonacademic purposes and in part also to the examples of Jean Piaget and Noam Chomsky, who, in their rather different ways, have made striking advances in the scientific study of the nature of human knowledge—advances that, moreover, cannot plausibly be construed as advances in the study of human behavior.

1

The Logical Analysis of Psychology

Carl G. Hempel

Author's prefatory note, 1977. The original French version of this article was published in 1935. By the time it appeared in English, I had abandoned the narrow translationist form of physicalism here set forth for a more liberal reductionist one, referred to in note 1, which presents psychological properties and states as partially characterized, but not defined, by bundles of behavioral dispositions. Since then, I have come to think that this conception requires still further broadening, and that the introduction and application of psychological terms and hypotheses is logically and methodologically analogous to the introduction and application of the terms and hypotheses of a physical theory.* The considerations that prompt-

ed those changes also led me long ago to abandon as untenable the verificationist construal of the "empirical meaning" of a sentence—a construal which plays such a central role in the arguments set forth in this article.

Since the article is so far from representing my present views, I was disinclined to consent to yet another republication, but I yielded to Dr. Block's plea that it offers a concise account of an early version of logical behaviorism and would thus be a useful contribution to this anthology.

In an effort to enhance the closeness of translation and the simplicity of formulation, I have made a number of small

An earlier version of this paper appeared in Ausonio Marras., ed., *Intentionality, Mind, and Language* (Urbana: University of Illinois Press, 1972), pp. 115-131, and in Herbert Feigl and Wilfrid Sellars, eds., *Readings in Philosophical Analysis* (New York: Appleton-Century-Crofts, 1949), pp. 373-384, translated from the French by W. Sellars. Reprinted, with revisions by the author, by permission of the author, Herbert Feigl, Wilfrid Sellars, and the editors of *Revue de Synthese*.

*My reasons are suggested in some of my more recent articles, among them "Logical Positivism and the Social Sciences," in P. Achinstein and S. F. Barker, eds., *The Legacy of Legal Posi-*

tivism (Baltimore: Johns Hopkins University Press, 1969); "Reduction: Ontological and Linguistic Facets," in S. Morgenbesser, P. Suppes, and M. White, eds., *Philosophy, Science, and Method. Essays in Honor of Ernest Nagel* (New York: St. Martin's Press, 1969); "Dispositional Explanation and the Covering-Law Model: Response to Laird Addis," in A. C. Michalos and R. S. Cohen, eds., *PSA 1974: Proceedings of the 1974 Biennial Meeting of the Philosophy of Science Association* (Dordrecht: Reidel, 1976), pp. 369-376.

changes in the text of the original English version; none of these affects the substance of the article.

I

One of the most important and most discussed problems of contemporary philosophy is that of determining how psychology should be characterized in the theory of science. This problem, which reaches beyond the limits of epistemological analysis and has engendered heated controversy in metaphysics itself, is brought to a focus by the familiar alternative, "Is psychology a natural science, or is it one of the sciences of mind and culture (*Geisteswissenschaften*)?"

The present article attempts to sketch the general lines of a new analysis of psychology, one which makes use of rigorous logical tools, and which has made possible decisive advances toward the solution of the above problem.[1] This analysis was carried out by the "Vienna Circle" (*Weiner Kreis*), the members of which (M. Schlick, R. Carnap, P. Frank, O. Neurath, F. Waismann, H. Feigl, etc.) have, during the past ten years, developed an extremely fruitful method for the epistemological examination and critique of the various sciences, based in part on the work of L. Wittgenstein.[2] We shall limit ourselves essentially to the examination of psychology as carried out by Carnap and Neurath.

The method characteristic of the studies of the Vienna Circle can be briefly defined as a *logical analysis of the language of science*. This method became possible only with the development of a subtle logical apparatus which makes use, in particular, of all the formal procedures of modern symbolic logic.[3] However, in the following account, which does not pretend to give more than a broad orientation, we shall limit ourselves to setting out the general principles of this new method, without making use of strictly formal procedures.

II

Perhaps the best way to characterize the position of the Vienna Circle as it relates to psychology, is to say that it is the exact antithesis of the current epistemological thesis that there is a fundamental difference between experimental psychology, a natural science, and introspective psychology; and in general, between the natural sciences on the one hand, and the sciences of mind and culture on the other.[4] The common content of the widely different formulations used to express this contention, which we reject, can be set down as follows. Apart from certain aspects clearly related to physiology, psychology is radically different, both in subject matter and in method, from physics in the broad sense of the term. In particular, it is impossible to deal adequately with the subject matter of psychology by means of physical methods. The subject matter of physics includes such concepts as mass, wave length, temperature, field intensity, etc. In dealing with these, physics employs its distinctive method which makes a combined use of description and causal explanation. Psychology, on the other hand, has for its subject matter notions which are, in a broad sense, mental. They are *toto genere* different from the concepts of physics, and the appropriate method for dealing with them scientifically is that of empathetic insight, called "introspection," a method which is peculiar to psychology.

One of the principal differences between the two kinds of subject matter is generally believed to consist in the fact that the objects investigated by psychology—in contradistinction to those of physics—are specifically endowed with meaning. Indeed, several proponents of this idea state that the distinctive method of psychology consists in "understanding the sense of meaningful structures" (*sinnvolle Gebilde verstehend zu erfassen*). Take, for example, the case of a man who speaks. Within the framework of physics, this process is considered to be completely explained once the movements which make up the utterance have been traced to their causes, that is to say, to certain physiological processes in the organism, and, in particular, in the central nervous system. But, it is said, this does not even broach the psychological problem. The latter begins with understanding the sense of what was said, and proceeds to integrate it into a wider context of meaning.

It is usually this latter idea which serves as a principle for the fundamental dichotomy that is introduced into the classification of the sciences. There is taken to be an *absolutely impassable gulf* between the *natural sciences* which have a subject matter devoid of meaning and the *sciences of mind and culture*, which have an intrinsically meaningful subject matter, the appropriate methodological instrument for the scientific study of which is "comprehension of meaning."

III

The position in the theory of science which we have just sketched has been attacked from several different points of view.[5] As far as psychology is concerned, one of the principal countertheses is that formulated by behaviorism, a theory born in America shortly before the war. (In Russia, Pavlov has developed similar ideas.) Its principal methodological postulate is that a scientific psychology should limit itself to the study of the bodily behavior with which man and the animals respond to changes in their physical environment, and should proscribe as nonscientific any descriptive or explanatory step which makes use of terms from introspective or "understanding" psychology, such as 'feeling', 'lived experience', 'idea', 'will', 'intention', 'goal', 'disposition', 'repression'.[6] We find in behaviorism, consequently, an attempt to construct a scientific psychology which would show by its success that even in psychology we have

to do with purely physical processes, and that therefore there can be no impassable barrier between psychology and physics. However, this manner of undertaking the critique of a scientific thesis is not completely satisfactory. It seems, indeed, that the soundness of the behavioristic thesis expounded above depends on the possibility of fulfilling the program of behavioristic psychology. But one cannot expect the question as to the scientific status of psychology to be settled by empirical research in psychology itself. To achieve this is rather an undertaking in epistemology. We turn, therefore, to the considerations advanced by members of the Vienna Circle concerning this problem.

IV

Before addressing the question whether the subject matters of physics and psychology are essentially the same or different in nature, it is necessary first to clarify the very concept of the subject matter of a science. The theoretical content of a science is to be found in statements. It is necessary, therefore, to determine whether there is a fundamental difference between the statements of psychology and those of physics. Let us therefore ask what it is that determines the content—one can equally well say the "meaning"—of a statement. When, for example, do we know the meaning of the following statement: "Today at one o'clock, the temperature of such and such a place in the physics laboratory was 23.4° centigrade"? Clearly when, and only when, we know under what conditions we would call the statement true, and under what circumstances we would call it false. (Needless to say, it is not necessary to know whether or not the statement is true.) Thus, we understand the meaning of the above statement since we know that it is true when a tube of a certain kind filled with mercury (in short, a thermometer with a centigrade scale), placed at the indicated time at the location in question, exhibits a coincidence between the level of the mercury and the mark of the scale numbered 23.4. It is also true if in the same circumstances one can observe certain coincidences on another instrument called an "alcohol thermometer"; and, again, if a galvanometer connected with a thermopile shows a certain deviation when the thermopile is placed there at the indicated time. Further, there is a long series of other possibilities which make the statement true, each of which is described by a "physical test sentence," as we will call it. The statement itself clearly affirms nothing other than this: all these physical test sentences obtain. (However, one verifies only some of these physical test sentences, and then "concludes by induction" that the others obtain as well.) The statement, therefore, is nothing but an abbreviated formulation of all those test sentences.

Before continuing the discussion, let us sum up this result as follows:

1. A statement that specifies the temperature at a selected point in space-time can be "retranslated" without change of meaning into another statement—doubtless longer—in which the word "temperature" no longer appears. That term functions solely as an abbreviation, making possible the concise and complete description of a state of affairs the expression of which would otherwise be very complicated.

2. The example equally shows that *two statements which differ in formulation* can nevertheless have the *same meaning*. A trivial example of a statement having the same meaning as the above would be: "Today at one o'clock, at such and such a location in the laboratory, the temperature was 19.44° Réaumur."

As a matter of fact, the preceding considerations show—and let us set it down as another result—that *the meaning of a statement is established by the conditions of its verification*. In particular, two differently formulated statements have the same meaning or the same effective

content when, and only when, they are both true or both false in the same conditions. Furthermore, a statement for which one can indicate absolutely no conditions which would verify it, which is in principle incapable of confrontation with test conditions, is wholly devoid of content and without meaning. In such a case we have to do, not with a statement properly speaking, but with a "pseudo-statement," that is to say, a sequence of words correctly constructed from the point of view of grammar, but without content.[7]

In view of these considerations, our problem reduces to one concerning the difference between the circumstances which verify psychological statements and those which verify the statements of physics. Let us therefore examine a statement which involves a psychological concept, for example: "Paul has a toothache." What is the specific content of this statement, that is to say, what are the circumstances in which it would be verified? It will be sufficient to indicate some test sentences which describe these circumstances.

a. Paul weeps and makes gestures of such and such kinds.

b. At the question "What is the matter?," Paul utters the words "I have a toothache."

c. Closer examination reveals a decayed tooth with exposed pulp.

d. Paul's blood pressure, digestive processes, the speed of his reactions, show such and such changes.

e. Such and such processes occur in Paul's central nervous system.

This list could be expanded considerably, but it is already sufficient to bring out the fundamental and essential point, namely, that all the circumstances which verify this psychological statement are expressed by physical test sentences. [This is true even of test condition *b*, which merely expresses the fact that in specified physical circumstances (the propagation of vibra-

tions produced in the air by the enuncia-
tion of the words, "What is the matter?")
there occurs in the body of the subject a
certain physical process (speech behavior
of such and such a kind).]

The statement in question, which is
about someone's "pain," is therefore, just
like that concerning the temperature, simply an abbreviated expression of the fact
that all its test sentences are verified.[8]
(Here, too, one verifies only some of the
test sentences and then infers by way of
induction that the others obtain as well.)
It can be retranslated without loss of content into a statement which no longer contains the term "pain," but only physical
concepts. Our analysis has consequently
established that a certain statement belonging to psychology has the same content as a statement belonging to physics; a
result which is in direct contradiction to
the thesis that there is an impassable gulf
between the statements of psychology and
those of physics.

The above reasoning can be applied
to *any psychological statement*, even to
those which concern, as is said, "deeper
psychological strata" than that of our example. Thus, the assertion that Mr. Jones
suffers from intense inferiority feelings of
such and such kinds can be confirmed or
falsified only by observing Mr. Jones' behavior in various circumstances. To this
behavior belong all the bodily processes
of Mr. Jones, and, in particular, his gestures, the flushing and paling of his skin,
his utterances, his blood pressure, the
events that occur in his central nervous
system, etc. In practice, when one wishes
to test statements concerning what are
called the deeper layers of the psyche, one
limits oneself to the observation of external bodily behavior, and, particularly, to
speech movements evoked by certain
physical stimuli (the asking of questions).
But it is well known that experimental
psychology has also developed techniques
for making use of the subtler bodily states
referred to above in order to confirm the

psychological discoveries made by cruder
methods. The statement concerning the
inferiority feelings of Mr. Jones—whether
true or false—means only this: such and
such happenings take place in Mr. Jones'
body in such and such circumstances.

We shall call a statement which can
be translated without change of meaning
into the language of physics, a "physicalistic statement," whereas we shall reserve
the expression "statement of physics" to
those which are already formulated in the
terminology of physical science. (Since
every statement is in respect of content
equivalent to itself, every statement of
physics is also a physicalistic statement.)
The result of the preceding considerations
can now be summed up as follows: *All
psychological statements which are meaningful, that is to say, which are in principle verifiable, are translatable into statements which do not involve psychological
concepts, but only the concepts of physics. The statements of psychology are
consequently physicalistic statements.
Psychology is an integral part of physics.*
If a distinction is drawn between psychology and the other areas of physics, it is
only from the point of view of the practical aspects of research and the direction of
interest, rather than a matter of principle.
This logical analysis, the result of which
shows a certain affinity with the fundamental ideas of behaviorism, constitutes
the physicalistic conception of psychology.

V

It is customary to raise the following
fundamental objection against the above
conception. The physical test sentences of
which you speak are absolutely incapable
of formulating the intrinsic nature of a
mental process; they merely describe the
physical *symptoms* from which one infers, by purely psychological methods—
notably that of understanding—the presence of a certain mental process.

But it is not difficult to see that the

use of the method of understanding or of other psychological procedures is bound up with the existence of certain observable physical data concerning the subject undergoing examination. There is no psychological understanding that is not tied up physically in one way or another with the person to be understood. Let us add that, for example, in the case of the statement about the inferiority complex, even the "introspective" psychologist, the psychologist who "understands," can confirm his conjecture only if the body of Mr. Jones, when placed in certain circumstances (most frequently, subjected to questioning), reacts in a specified manner (usually, by giving certain answers). Consequently, even if the statement in question had to be arrived at, *discovered*, by "empathetic understanding," the only *information* it gives us is nothing more nor less than the following: under certain circumstances, certain specific events take place in the body of Mr. Jones. It is this which constitutes the meaning of the psychological statement.

The further objection will perhaps be raised that men can feign. Thus, though a criminal at the bar may show physical symptoms of mental disorder, one would nevertheless be justified in wondering whether his mental confusion was "real" or only simulated. One must note that in the case of the simulator, only some of the conditions are fulfilled which verify the statement "This man is mentally unbalanced," those, namely, which are most accessible to direct observation. A more penetrating examination—which should in principle take into account events occurring in the central nervous system— would give a decisive answer; and this answer would in turn clearly rest on a physicalistic basis. If, at this point, one wished to push the objection to the point of admitting that a man could show *all the* "*symptoms*" of a mental disease without being "really" ill, we reply that it would be absurd to characterize such a man as

"really normal"; for it is obvious that by the very nature of the hypothesis we should possess no criterion in terms of which to distinguish this man from another who, while exhibiting the same bodily behavior down to the last detail, would "in addition" be "really ill." (To put the point more precisely, one can say that this hypothesis contains a *logical contradiction*, since it amounts to saying, "It is possible that a statement should be false even when the necessary and sufficient conditions of its truth are fulfilled.")

Once again we see clearly that the meaning of a psychological statement consists solely in the function of abbreviating the description of certain modes of physical response characteristic of the bodies of men or animals. An analogy suggested by O. Neurath may be of further assistance in clarifying the logical function of psychological statements.[9] The complicated statements that would describe the movements of the hands of a watch in relation to one another, and relatively to the stars, are ordinarily summed up in an assertion of the following form: "This watch runs well (runs badly, etc.)." The term "runs" is introduced here as an auxiliary defined expression which makes it possible to formulate briefly a relatively complicated system of statements. It would thus be absurd to say, for example, that the movement of the hands is only a "physical symptom" which reveals the presence of a running which is intrinsically incapable of being grasped by physical means, or to ask, if the watch should stop, what has become of the running of the watch.

It is in exactly the same way that abbreviating symbols are introduced into the language of physics, the concept of temperature discussed above being an example. The system of physical test sentences *exhausts* the meaning of the statement concerning the temperature at a place, and one should not say that these sentences merely have to do with "symptoms" of the existence of a certain temperature.

Our argument has shown that it is necessary to attribute to the characteristic concepts of psychology the same logical function as that performed by the concepts of "running" and of "temperature." They do nothing more than make possible the succinct formulation of propositions concerning the states or processes of animal or human bodies.

The introduction of new psychological concepts can contribute greatly to the progress of scientific knowledge. But it is accompanied by a danger, that, namely, of making an excessive and, consequently, improper use of new concepts, which may result in questions and answers devoid of sense. This is frequently the case in metaphysics, notably with respect to the notions which we formulated in section II. Terms which are abbreviating symbols are imagined to designate a special class of "psychological objects," and thus one is led to ask questions about the "essence" of these objects, and how they differ from "physical objects." The time-worn problem concerning the relation between mental and physical events is also based on this confusion concerning the logical function of psychological concepts. Our argument, therefore, enables us to see that *the psycho-physical problem is a pseudo-problem*, the formulation of which is based on an inadmissible use of scientific concepts; it is of the same logical nature as the question, suggested by the example above, concerning the relation of the running of the watch to the movement of the hands.[10]

VI

In order to bring out the exact status of the fundamental idea of the physicalistic conception of psychology (or logical behaviorism), we shall contrast it with certain theses of psychological behaviorism and of classical materialism, which give the appearance of being closely related to it.[11]

1. Logical behaviorism claims neither that minds, feelings, inferiority complexes, voluntary actions, etc., do not exist, nor that their existence is in the least doubtful. It insists that the very question as to whether these psychological constructs really exist is already a pseudo-problem, since these notions in their "legitimate use" appear only as abbreviations in physicalistic statements. Above all, one should not interpret the position sketched in this paper as amounting to the view that we can know only the "physical side" of psychological processes, and that the question whether there are mental phenomena behind the physical processes falls beyond the scope of science and must be left either to faith or to the conviction of each individual. On the contrary, the logical analyses originating in the Vienna Circle, one of whose consequences is the physicalistic conception of psychology, teach us that every meaningful question is, in principle, capable of a scientific answer. Furthermore, these analyses show that what, in the case of the mind-body problem, is considered as an object of belief, is absolutely incapable of being expressed by a factual proposition. In other words, there can be no question here of an "article of faith." Nothing can be an object of faith which cannot, in principle, be an object of knowledge.

2. The thesis here developed, though related in certain ways to the fundamental idea of behaviorism, does not demand, as does the latter, that psychological research restrict itself methodologically to the study of the responses organisms make to certain stimuli. It by no means offers a theory belonging to the domain of psychology, but rather a logical theory about the statements of scientific psychology. Its position is that the latter are without exception physicalistic statements, by whatever means they may have been obtained.

Consequently, it seeks to show that if in psychology only physicalistic statements are made, this is not a limitation because it is logically *impossible* to do otherwise.

3. In order for logical behaviorism to be valid, it is not necessary that we be able to describe the physical state of a human body which is referred to by a certain psychological statement—for example, one dealing with someone's feeling of pain—down to the most minute details of the phenomena of the central nervous system. No more does it presuppose a knowledge of all the physical laws governing human or animal bodily processes; nor *a fortiori* is the existence of rigorously deterministic laws relating to these processes a necessary condition of the truth of the behavioristic thesis. At no point does the above argument rest on such a concrete presupposition.

VII

In concluding, I should like to indicate briefly the clarification brought to the problem of the division of the sciences into totally different areas, by the method of the logical analysis of scientific statements, applied above to the special case of the place of psychology among the sciences. The considerations we have advanced can be extended to the domain of sociology, taken in the broad sense as the science of historical, cultural, and economic processes. In this way one arrives at the result that every sociological assertion which is meaningful, that is to say, in principle verifiable, "has as its subject matter nothing else than the states, processes and behavior of groups or of individuals (human or animal), and their responses to one another and to their environment,"[12] and consequently that every sociological statement is a physicalistic statement. This view is characterized by Neurath as the thesis of "social behaviorism," which he adds to that of "individual behaviorism" which we have expounded

above. Furthermore, it can be shown[13] that every statement of what are called the "sciences of mind and culture" is a sociological statement in the above sense, provided it has genuine content. Thus one arrives at the "thesis of the unity of science":

The division of science into different areas rests exclusively on differences in research procedures and direction of interest; *one must not regard it as a matter of principle. On the contrary, all the branches of science are in principle of one and the same nature; they are branches of the unitary science, physics.*

VIII

The method of logical analysis which we have attempted to explicate by clarifying, as an example, the statements of psychology, leads, as we have been able to show only too briefly for the sciences of mind and culture, to a "physicalism" based on logic (Neurath): *Every statement of the above-mentioned disciplines, and, in general, of empirical science as a whole, which is not merely a meaningless sequence of words, is translatable, without change of content, into a statement containing only physicalistic terms, and consequently is a physicalistic statement.*

This thesis frequently encounters strong opposition arising from the idea that such analyses violently and considerably reduce the richness of the life of mind or spirit, as though the aim of the discussion were purely and simply to eliminate vast and important areas of experience. Such a conception comes from a false interpretation of physicalism, the main elements of which we have already examined in section VII above. As a matter of fact, nothing can be more remote from a philosophy which has the methodological attitude we have characterized than the making of decisions, on its own authority, concerning the truth or falsity of particular scientific statements, or the desire to eliminate any matters of fact whatsoever. *The subject matter of this philosophy is limited to the form of scientific statements, and the deductive relationships obtaining between them.* It is led by its analyses to the thesis of physicalism, and establishes on purely logical grounds that a certain class of venerable philosophical "problems" consists of pseudo-problems. It is certainly to the advantage of the progress of scientific knowledge that these imitation jewels in the coffer of scientific problems be known for what they are, and that the intellectual powers which have till now been devoted to a class of meaningless questions which are by their very nature insoluble, become available for the formulation and study of new and fruitful problems. That the method of logical analysis stimulates research along these lines is shown by the numerous publications of the Vienna Circle and those who sympathize with its general point of view (H. Reichenbach, W. Dubislav, and others).

In the attitude of those who are so bitterly opposed to physicalism, an essential role is played by certain psychological factors relating to individuals and groups. Thus the contrast between the constructs (*Gebilde*) developed by the psychologist, and those developed by the physicist, or, again, the question as to the nature of the specific subject matter of psychology and the cultural sciences (which present the appearance of a search for the essence and unique laws of "objective spirit") is usually accompanied by a strong emotional coloring which has come into being during the long historical development of a "philosophical conception of the world," which was considerably less scientific than normative and intuitive. These emotional factors are still deeply rooted in the picture by which our epoch represents the world to itself. They are protected by certain affective dispositions which surround them like a rampart, and for all these reasons appear to us to have genuine content

—something which a more penetrating analysis shows to be impossible.

A psychological and sociological study of the causes for the appearance of these "concomitant factors" of the metaphysical type would take us beyond the limits of this study,[14] but without tracing it back to its origins, it is possible to say that if the logical analyses sketched above are correct, the fact that they necessitate at least a partial break with traditional philosophical ideas which are deeply dyed with emotion can certainly not justify an opposition to physicalism—at least if one acknowledges that philosophy is to be something more than the expression of an individual vision of the world, that it aims at being a science.

Notes

1. I now consider the type of physicalism outlined in this paper as too restrictive; the thesis that all statements of empirical science are *translatable*, without loss of theoretical content, into the language of physics, should be replaced by the weaker assertion that all statements of empirical science are *reducible* to sentences in the language of physics, in the sense that for every empirical hypothesis, including, of course, those of psychology, it is possible to formulate certain test conditions in terms of physical concepts which refer to more or less directly observable physical attributes. But those test conditions are not asserted to exhaust the theoretical content of the given hypothesis in all cases. For a more detailed development of this thesis, cf. R. Carnap, "Logical Foundations of the Unity of Science," reprinted in A. Marras, ed., *Intentionality, Mind, and Language* (Urbana: Univ. of Illinois Press, 1972).

2. *Tractatus Logico-Philosophicus* (London, 1922).

3. A recent presentation of symbolic logic, based on the fundamental work of Whitehead and Russell, *Principia Mathematica*, is to be found in R. Carnap, *Abriss der Logistik* (Vienna: Springer, 1929; vol. 2 of the series *Schriften zur Wissenschaftlichen Weltauffassung*). It includes an extensive bibliography, as well as references to other logistic systems.

4. The following are some of the principal publications of the Vienna Circle on the nature of psychology as a science: R. Carnap, *Scheinprobleme in der Philosophie. Das Fremdpsychische und des Realismusstreit* (Leipzig: Meiner, 1928); *Der Logische Aufbau der Welt* (Leipzig: Meiner, 1928) [English trans.: *Logical Structure of the World* (Berkeley: Univ. of California Press, 1967)]; "Die Physikalische Sprache als Universalsprache der Wissenschaft," *Erkenntnis*, 2 (1931-32), 432-465 [English trans.: *The Unity of Science* (London: Kegan Paul, 1934)]; "Psychologie in physikalischer Sprache," *Erkenntnis*, 3 (1932-33), 107-142 [English trans.: "Psychology in Physical Language," in A. J. Ayer, ed., *Logical Positivism* (New York: Free Press, 1959)]; "Ueber Protokollsaetze," *Erkenntnis*, 3 (1932-33), 215-228; O. Neurath, "Protokollsaetze," *Erkenntnis*, 3 (1932-33), 204-214 [English trans.: "Protocol Sentences," in *Logical Positivism*]; *Einheitswissenschaft und Psychologie* (Vienna: Springer, 1933; vol. 1 of the series *Einheitswissenschaft*). See also the publications mentioned in the notes below.

5. P. Oppenheim, for example, in his book *Die Natuerliche Ordnung der Wissenschaften* (Jena: Fischer, 1926), opposes the view that there are fundamental differences between any of the different areas of science. On the analysis of "understanding," cf. M. Schlick, "Erleben, Erkennen, Metaphysik," *Kantstudien*, 31 (1926), 146.

6. For further details see the statement of one of the founders of behaviorism: J. B. Watson, *Behaviorism* (New York: Norton, 1930); also A. A. Roback, *Behaviorism and Psychology* (Cambridge, Mass.: Univ. Bookstore, 1923); and A. P. Weiss, *A Theoretical Basis of Human Behavior*, 2nd ed. rev. (Columbus, Ohio: Adams, 1929); see also the work by Koehler cited in note 11 below.

7. Space is lacking for further discussion of the logical form of test sentences (recently called "protocol sentences" by Neurath and Carnap). On this question see Wittgenstein, *Tractatus Logico-Philosophicus*, as well as the articles by Neurath and Carnap which have appeared in *Erkenntnis* (above, note 4).

8. Two critical comments, 1977: (a) This reference to verification involves a conceptual confusion. The thesis which the preceding considerations were intended to establish was clearly that the statement "Paul has a tooth-ache" is, in effect, an abbreviated expression of all its test sentences; not that it expresses the claim (let alone the "fact") that all those test sentences have actually been tested and verified. (b) Strictly speaking, none of the test sentences just mentioned is implied by the statement "Paul has a toothache": the latter may be true and yet any or all of those test sentences may be false. Hence, the preceding considerations fail to show that the given psychological statement can be "translated" into sentences which, in purely physical terms, describe macro-behavioral manifestations of pain. This failure of the arguments outlined in the text does not preclude the possibility, however, that sentences ascribing pain or other psychological characteristics to an individual might be "translatable," in a suitable sense, into physical sentences ascribing associated physical micro-states or micro-events to the nervous system or to the entire body of the individual in question.

9. "Soziologie im Physikalismus," *Erkenntnis*, 2 (1931-32), 393-431, particularly p. 411 [English trans.: "Sociology and Physicalism," in A. J. Ayer, ed., *Logical Positivism*].

10. Carnap, *Der Logische Aufbau der Welt*, pp. 231-236; id. *Scheinprobleme in der Philosophie*. See also note 4 above.

11. A careful discussion of the ideas of so-called "internal" behaviorism is to be found in *Psychologische Probleme* by W. Koehler (Berlin: Springer, 1933). See particularly the first two chapters.

12. R. Carnap, "Die Physikalische Sprache als Universalsprache," p. 451. See also: O. Neurath, *Empirische Soziologie* (Vienna: Springer, 1931; the fourth monograph in the series *Schriften zur wissenschaftlichen Weltauffassung*).

13. See R. Carnap, *Der Logische Aufbau der Welt*, pp. 22-34 and 185-211, as well as the works cited in the preceding note.

14. O. Neurath has made interesting contributions along these lines in *Empirische Soziologie* and in "Soziologie im Physikalismus" (see above, note 9), as has R. Carnap in his article "Ueberwindung der Metaphysik durch logische Analyse der Sprache," *Erkenntnis*, 2 (1931-32), 219-241 [English trans.: "The Elimination of Metaphysics through Logical Analysis of Language," in A. J. Ayer, ed., *Logical Positivism*].

Brains and Behavior

Hilary Putnam

Once upon a time there was a tough-minded philosopher who said, 'What is all this talk about "minds", "ideas", and "sensations"? Really—and I mean *really* in the real world—there is nothing to these so-called "mental" events and entities but certain processes in our all-too-material heads.'

And once upon a time there was a philosopher who retorted, 'What a masterpiece of confusion! Even if, say, *pain* were perfectly correlated with any particular event in my brain (which I doubt) that event would obviously have certain properties—say, a certain numerical intensity measured in volts—which it would be *senseless* to ascribe to the feeling of pain. Thus, it is *two* things that are correlated, not *one*—and to call *two* things *one* thing is worse than being mistaken; it is utter contradiction.'

For a long time dualism and material-

From R. J. Butler, ed., *Analytical Philosophy*, vol. 2 (Oxford: Blackwell, 1965). Reprinted by permission of the author. Notes have been renumbered for this edition. This paper was read as part of the program of the American Association for the Advancement of Science, Section L (History and Philosophy of Science), December 27, 1961.

ism appeared to exhaust the alternatives. Compromises were attempted ('double aspect' theories), but they never won many converts and practically no one found them intelligible. Then, in the mid-1930s, a seeming third possibility was discovered. This third possibility has been called *logical behaviorism*. To state the nature of this third possibility briefly, it is necessary to recall the treatment of the natural numbers (i.e. zero, one, two, three . . .) in modern logic. Numbers are identified with *sets*, in various ways, depending on which authority one follows. For instance, Whitehead and Russell identified zero with the set of all empty sets, one with the set of all one-membered sets, two with the set of all two-membered sets, three with the set of all three-membered sets, and so on. (This has the appearance of circularity, but they were able to dispel this appearance by defining 'one-membered set', 'two-membered set', 'three-membered set', etc., without using 'one', 'two', 'three', etc.) In short, numbers are treated as *logical constructions out of sets*. The number theorist is doing set theory without knowing it, according to this interpretation.

What was novel about this was the idea of getting rid of certain philosophically unwanted or embarrassing entities (numbers) without failing to do justice to the appropriate body of discourse (number theory) by treating the entities in question as logical constructions. Russell was quick to hold up this success as a model to all future philosophers. And certain of those future philosophers—the Vienna positivists, in their 'physicalist' phase (about 1930)—took Russell's advice so seriously as to produce the doctrine that we are calling *logical behaviorism*— the doctrine that, just as numbers are (allegedly) logical constructions out of *sets*, so *mental events* are logical constructions out of actual and possible *behavior events.*

In the set theoretic case, the 'reduction' of number theory to the appropriate part of set theory was carried out in detail and with indisputable technical success. One may dispute the philosophical significance of the reduction, but one knows exactly what one is talking about when one disputes it. In the mind-body case, the reduction was never carried out in even *one* possible way, so that it is not possible to be clear on just *how* mental entities or events are to be (identified with) logical constructions out of behavior events. But broadly speaking, it is clear what the view implies: it implies that all talk about mental events is translatable into talk about actual or potential overt behavior.

It is easy to see in what way this view differs from both dualism and classical materialism. The logical behaviorist agrees with the dualist that what goes on in our brains has no connection whatsoever with what we *mean* when we say that someone is in pain. He can even take over the dualist's entire stock of arguments against the materialist position. Yet, at the same time, he can be as 'tough-minded' as the materialist in denying that ordinary talk of 'pains', 'thoughts', and 'feelings' involves reference to 'Mind' as a Cartesian substance.

Thus it is not surprising that logical behaviorism attracted enormous attention —both pro and con—during the next thirty years. Without doubt, this alternative proved to be a fruitful one to inject into the debate. Here, however, my intention is not to talk about the fruitfulness of the investigations to which logical behaviorism has led, but to see if there was any upshot to those investigations. Can we, after thirty years, say anything about the rightness or wrongness of logical behaviorism? Or must we say that a third alternative has been added to the old two; that we cannot decide between three any more easily than we could decide between two; and that our discussion is thus half as difficult again as it was before?

One conclusion emerged very quickly from the discussion pro and con logical behaviorism: that the extreme thesis of logical behaviorism, as we just stated it (that all talk about 'mental events' is translatable into talk about overt behavior) is false. But, in a sense, this is not very interesting. An extreme thesis may be false, although there is 'something to' the way of thinking that it represents. And the more interesting question is this: what, if anything, can be 'saved' of the way of thinking that logical behaviorism represents?

In the last thirty years, the original extreme thesis of logical behaviorism has gradually been weakened to something like this:

(1) That there exist entailments between mind-statements and behavior-statements; entailments that are not, perhaps, analytic in the way in which 'All bachelors are unmarried' is analytic, but that nevertheless follow (in some sense) from the meanings of mind words. I shall call these *analytic entailments.*

(2) That these entailments may not provide an actual *translation* of 'mind talk' into 'behavior talk' (this 'talk' talk was introduced by Gilbert Ryle in his *Concept of Mind*), but that this is true for such superficial reasons as the greater ambiguity of mind talk, as compared with the rela-

tively greater specificity of overt behavior talk.

I believe that, although no philosopher would to-day subscribe to the older version of behaviorism, a great many philosophers[1] would accept these two points, while admitting the unsatisfactory imprecision of the present statement of both of them. If these philosophers are right, then there is much work to be done (e.g. the notion of 'analyticity' has to be made clear), but the direction of work is laid out for us for some time to come.

I wish that I could share this happy point of view—if only for the comforting conclusion that first-rate philosophical research, continued for some time, will eventually lead to a solution to the mind-body problem which is independent of troublesome empirical facts about brains, central causation of behavior, evidence for and against nonphysical causation of at least some behavior, and the soundness or unsoundness of psychical research and parapsychology. But the fact is that I come to bury logical behaviorism, not to praise it. I feel that the time has come for us to admit that logical behaviorism is a mistake, and that even the weakened forms of the logical behaviorist doctrine are incorrect. I cannot hope to establish this in so short a paper as this one;[2] but I hope to expose for your inspection at least the main lines of my thinking.

Logical Behaviorism

The logical behaviorist usually begins by pointing out what is perfectly true, that such words as 'pain' ('pain' will henceforth be our stock example of a mind word) are not taught by reference to standard examples in the way in which such words as 'red' are. One can point to a standard red thing, but one cannot point to a standard pain (that is, except by pointing to some piece of *behavior*) and say: 'Compare the feeling you are having with this one (say, Jones's feeling at time t_1). If the two feelings have the identical *quality*, then your

feeling is legitimately calle   feeling of *pain*.' The difficulty, of course, is that I cannot have Jones's feeling at time t_1—unless I *am* Jones, and the time *is* t_1.

From this simple observation, certain things follow. For example, the account according to which the *intension* of the word 'pain' is a certain *quality* which 'I know from my own case' must be wrong. But this is not to refute dualism, since the dualist need not maintain that I know the intension of the English word 'pain' from my own case, but only that I experience the referent of the word.

What then is the intension of 'pain'? I am inclined to say that 'pain' is a cluster-concept. That is, the application of the word 'pain' is controlled by a whole cluster of criteria, *all of which can be regarded as synthetic.*[3] As a consequence, there is no satisfactory way of answering the question 'What does "pain" mean?' except by giving an exact synonym (e.g. 'Schmerz'); but there are a million and one different ways of saying what pain *is*. One can, for example, say that pain is that feeling which is normally evinced by saying 'ouch', or by wincing, or in a variety of other ways (or often not evinced at all).

All this is compatible with logical behaviorism. The logical behaviorist would reply: 'Exactly. "Pain" is a cluster-concept —that is to say, it stands for *a cluster of phenomena.*' But that is not what I mean. Let us look at another kind of cluster-concept (cluster-concepts, of course, are not a homogeneous class): names of diseases.

We observe that, when a virus origin was discovered for polio, doctors said that certain cases in which all the symptoms of polio had been present, but in which the virus had been absent, had turned out not to be cases of polio at all. Similarly, if a virus should be discovered which normally (almost invariably) is the cause of what we presently call 'multiple sclerosis', the hypothesis that this virus is *the* cause of multiple sclerosis would not be falsified if, in some few exceptional circumstances, it was possible to have all the symptoms of multiple sclerosis for some other combination of reasons, or if this virus caused symptoms not presently recognized as symptoms of multiple sclerosis in some cases. These facts would certainly lead the lexicographer to *reject* the view that 'multiple sclerosis' means 'the simultaneous presence of such and such symptoms'. Rather he would say that 'multiple sclerosis' means 'that disease which is normally responsible for some or all of the following symptoms . . .'

Of course, he does not have to say this. Some philosophers would prefer to say that 'polio' *used to mean* 'the simultaneous presence of such-and-such symptoms'. And they would say that the *decision* to accept the presence or absence of a virus as a criterion for the presence or absence of polio represented a *change of meaning*. But this runs strongly counter to our common sense. For example, doctors used to say 'I believe polio is caused by a virus'. On the 'change of meaning' account, those doctors were *wrong*, not *right*. Polio, *as the word was then used*, was not always caused by a virus; it is only what *we* call polio that is always caused by a virus. And if a doctor ever said (and many did) 'I believe this may not be a case of polio', knowing that all of the textbook symptoms were present, that doctor must have been contradicting himself (even if we, to-day, would say that he was right) or, perhaps, 'making a disguised linguistic proposal'. Also, this account runs counter to good linguistic methodology. The definition we proposed a paragraph back—'multiple sclerosis' means 'the disease that is normally *responsible* for the following symptoms . . .' —has an exact analogue in the case of polio. This kind of definition leaves open the question whether there is a single cause or several. It is consonant with such a definition to speak of 'discovering a single origin for polio (or two or three or

four)', to speak of 'discovering X did not have polio' (although he exhibited all the symptoms of polio), and to speak of 'discovering X did have polio' (although he exhibited *none* of the 'textbook symptoms'). And, finally, such a definition does not require us to say that any 'change of meaning' took place. Thus, this is surely the definition that a good lexicographer would adopt. But this entails *rejecting* the 'change of meaning' account as a philosopher's invention.[4]

Accepting that this is the correct account of the names of diseases, what follows? There *may* be analytic entailments connecting diseases and symptoms (although I shall argue against this). For example, it looks plausible to say that:

'Normally people who have multiple sclerosis have some or all of the following symptoms . . .' is a necessary ('analytic') truth. But it does not follow that 'disease talk' is translatable into 'symptom talk'. Rather the contrary follows (as is already indicated by the presence of the word 'normally'): statements about multiple sclerosis are not translatable into statements about the symptoms of multiple sclerosis, not because disease talk is 'systematically ambiguous' and symptom talk is 'specific', but because *causes* are not logical constructions out of their *effects*.

In analogy with the foregoing, both the dualist and the materialist would want to argue that, although the meaning of 'pain' may be *explained* by reference to overt behavior, what we mean by 'pain' is not the presence of a cluster of responses, but rather the presence of an event or condition that normally causes those responses. (Of course the pain is not the whole cause of the pain behavior, but only a suitably invariant part of that cause,[5] but, similarly, the virus-caused tissue damage is not the whole cause of the individual symptoms of polio in some individual case, but a suitably invariant part of the cause.) And they would want to argue further, that even if it *were* a necessary truth that

'Normally, when one says "ouch" one has a pain'

or a necessary truth that

'Normally, when one has a pain one says "ouch" '

this would be an interesting observation about what 'pain' means, but it would shed no metaphysical light on what pain is (or isn't). And it certainly would not follow that 'pain talk' is translatable into 'response talk', or that the failure of translatability is only a matter of the 'systematic ambiguity' of pain talk as opposed to the 'specificity' of response talk: quite the contrary. Just as before, causes (pains) are not logical constructions out of their effects (behavior).

The traditional dualist would, however, want to go farther, and deny the necessity of the two propositions just listed. Moreover, the traditional dualist is right: there is nothing self-contradictory, as we shall see below, in talking of hypothetical worlds in which there are pains but no pain behavior.

The analogy with names of diseases is still preserved at this point. Suppose I identify multiple sclerosis as the disease that normally produces certain symptoms. If it later turns out that a certain virus is the cause of multiple sclerosis, using this newly discovered criterion I may then go on to find out that multiple sclerosis has quite different symptoms when, say, the average temperature is lower. I can then perfectly well talk of a hypothetical world (with lower temperature levels) in which multiple sclerosis does not normally produce the usual symptoms. It is true that if the words 'multiple sclerosis' are used in any world in such a way that the above lexical definition is a good one, then many victims of the disease must have had some or all of the following symptoms . . . And in the same way it is true that if the explanation

suggested of the word 'pain' is a good one (i.e. 'pain is the feeling that is normally being evinced when someone says "ouch", or winces, or screams, etc.'), then persons in pain must have at some time winced or screamed or said 'ouch'—but this does not imply that 'if someone ever had a pain, then someone must at some time have winced or screamed or said "ouch".' To conclude this would be to confuse preconditions for talking about pain as we talk about pain with preconditions for the existence of pain.

The analogy we have been developing is not an identity: linguistically speaking, mind words and names of diseases are different in a great many respects. In particular, first person uses are very different: a man may have a severe case of polio and not know it, even if he knows the word 'polio', but one cannot have a severe pain and not know it. At first blush, this may look like a point in favor of logical behaviorism. The logical behaviorist may say: it is because the premises 'John says he has a pain', 'John knows English', and 'John is speaking in all sincerity',[6] entail 'John has a pain', that pain reports have this sort of special status. But even if this is right, it does not follow that logical behaviorism is correct unless sincerity is a 'logical construction out of overt behavior'! A far more reasonable account is this: one can have a 'pink elephant hallucination', but one cannot have a 'pain hallucination', or an 'absence of pain hallucination', simply because any situation that a person cannot discriminate from a situation in which he himself has a pain counts as a situation in which he has a pain, whereas a situation that a person cannot distinguish from one in which a pink elephant is present does not necessarily count as the presence of a pink elephant.

To sum up: I believe that pains are not clusters of responses, but that they are (normally, in our experience to date) the causes of certain clusters of responses.

But response not precondition to pain.

Moreover, although this is an empirical fact, it underlies the possibility of talking about pains in the particular way in which we do. However, it does not rule out in any way the possibility of worlds in which (owing to a difference in the environmental and hereditary conditions) pains are not responsible for the usual responses, or even are not responsible for any responses at all.

Let us now engage in a little science fiction. Let us try to describe some worlds in which pains are related to responses (and also to causes) in quite a different way than they are in our world.

If we confine our attention to non-verbal responses by full grown persons, for a start, then matters are easy. Imagine a community of 'super-spartans' or 'super-stoics'—a community in which the adults have the ability to successfully suppress *all* involuntary pain behavior. They may, on occasion, admit that they feel pain, but always in pleasant well-modulated voices —even if they are undergoing the agonies of the damned. They do *not* wince, scream, flinch, sob, grit their teeth, clench their fists, exhibit beads of sweat, or otherwise act like people in pain or people suppressing the unconditioned responses associated with pain. However, they do feel pain, and they dislike it (just as we do). They even admit that it takes a great effort of will to behave as they do. It is only that they have what they regard as important ideological reasons for behaving as they do, and they have, through years of training, learned to live up to their own exacting standards.

It may be contended that children and not fully mature members of this community will exhibit, to varying degrees, normal unconditioned pain behavior, and that this is all that is necessary for the ascription of pain. On this view, the *sine qua non* for significant ascription of pain to a species is that its immature members should exhibit unconditioned pain responses.

One might well stop to ask whether this statement has even a clear meaning. Supposing that there are Martians: do we have any criterion for something being an 'unconditioned pain response' for a Martian? Other things being equal, one *avoids* things with which one has had painful experiences: this would suggest that *avoidance* behavior might be looked for as a universal unconditioned pain response. However, even if this were true, it would hardly be specific enough, since avoidance can also be an unconditioned response to many things that we do not associate with pain—to things that disgust us, or frighten us, or even merely bore us.

Let us put these difficulties aside, and see if we can devise an imaginary world in which there are not, even by lenient standards, any unconditioned pain responses. Specifically, let us take our 'super-spartans', and let us suppose that after millions of years they begin to have children who are born fully acculturated. They are born speaking the adult language, knowing the multiplication table, having opinions on political issues, and *inter alia* sharing the dominant spartan beliefs about the importance of not evincing pain (except by way of verbal report, and even that in a tone of voice that suggests indifference). Then there would not *be* any 'unconditioned pain responses' in this community (although there might be unconditioned *desires* to make certain responses—desires which were, however, always suppressed by an effort of will). Yet there is a clear absurdity to the position that one cannot ascribe to these people a capacity for feeling pain.

To make this absurdity evident, let us imagine that we succeed in converting an adult 'super-spartan' to *our* ideology. Let us suppose that he begins to evince pain in the normal way. Yet he reports that the pains he is feeling are not more *intense* than are the ones he experienced prior to conversion—indeed, he may say that giving expression to them makes them *less* intense. In this case, the logical behaviorist would have to say that, through the medium of this one member, we had demonstrated the existence of unconditioned pain responses in the whole species, and hence that ascription of pain to the species is 'logically proper'. But this is to say that had this one man never lived, and had it been possible to demonstrate only indirectly (via the use of *theories*) that these beings feel pain, then pain ascriptions *would* have been improper.

We have so far been constructing worlds in which the relation of pain to its nonverbal *effects* is altered. What about the relation of pain to *causes*? This is even more easy for the imagination to modify. Can one not imagine a species who feel pain only when a magnetic field is present (although the magnetic field causes no detectable damage to their bodies or nervous systems)? If we now let the members of such a species become converts *to* 'super-spartanism', we can depict to ourselves a world in which pains, in our sense, are clearly present, but in which they have neither the normal causes nor the normal effects (apart from verbal reports).

What about verbal reports? Some behaviorists have taken these as the characteristic form of pain behavior. Of course, there is a difficulty here: If 'I am in pain' means 'I am disposed to utter this kind of verbal report' (to put matters crudely), then how do we tell that any particular report is 'this kind of verbal report'? The usual answer is in terms of the unconditioned pain responses and their assumed supplantation by the verbal reports in question. However, we have seen that there are no *logical* reasons for the existence of unconditioned pain responses in all species capable of feeling pain (there *may* be logical reasons for the existence of avoidance desires, but avoidance *desires* are not themselves behavior any more than pains are).

Once again, let us be charitable to the

extent of waiving the first difficulty that comes to mind, and let us undertake the task of trying to imagine a world in which there are not even pain *reports*. I will call this world the 'X-world'. In the X-world we have to deal with 'super-super-spartans'. These have been super-spartans for so long, that they have begun to suppress even *talk* of pain. Of course, each individual X-worlder may have his private way of thinking about pain. He may even have the *word* 'pain' (as before, I assume that these beings are born fully acculturated). He may *think* to himself: 'This pain is intolerable. If it goes on one minute longer I shall scream. Oh No! I mustn't do that! That would disgrace my whole family . . .' But X-worlders do not even admit to *having* pains. They pretend not to know either the word or the phenomenon to which it refers. In short, if pains are 'logical constructs out of behavior', then our X-worlders behave so as not to have pains!—Only, of course, they do have pains, and they know perfectly well that they have pains.

If this last fantasy is not, in some disguised way, self-contradictory, then logical behaviorism is simply a mistake. Not only is the second thesis of logical behaviorism—the existence of a near-translation of pain talk into behavior talk—false, but so is even the first thesis—the existence of 'analytic entailments'. Pains *are* responsible for certain kinds of behavior—but only in the context of our beliefs, desires, ideological attitudes, and so forth. From the statement 'X has a pain' by itself *no* behavioral statement follows—not even a behavioral statement with a 'normally' or a 'probably' in it.

In our concluding section we shall consider the logical behaviorist's stock of counter-moves to this sort of argument. If the logical behaviorist's positive views are inadequate owing to an oversimplified view of the nature of cluster words—amounting, in some instances, to an open denial that it is *possible* to have a word governed by a cluster of indicators, *all* of which are synthetic—his negative views are inadequate owing to an oversimplified view of empirical reasoning. It is unfortunately characteristic of modern philosophy that its problems should overlap three different areas—to speak roughly, the areas of linguistics, logic, and 'theory of theories' (scientific methodology)—and that many of its practitioners should try to get by with an inadequate knowledge of at least two out of the three.

Some Behaviorist Arguments

We have been talking of 'X-worlders' and 'super-spartans'. No one denies that, in *some* sense of the term, such fantasies are 'intelligible'. But 'intelligibility' can be a superficial thing. A fantasy may be 'intelligible', at least at the level of 'surface grammar', although we may come to see, on thinking about it for a while, that some absurdity is involved. Consider, for example, the supposition that last night, just on the stroke of midnight, all distances were instantaneously doubled. Of course, we did not notice the change, for *we* ourselves also doubled in size! This story may seem intelligible to us at first blush, at least as an amusing possibility. On reflection, however, we come to see that logical contradiction is involved. For 'length' means nothing more nor less than a relation to a standard, and it is a contradiction to maintain that the length of everything doubled, while the relations to the standards remained unchanged.

What I have just said (speaking as a logical behaviorist might speak) is false, but not totally so. It is false (or at least the last part is false), because 'length' does *not* mean 'relation to a standard'. If it did (assuming a 'standard' has to be a macroscopic material object, or anyway a material object), it would make no sense to speak of distances in a world in which there were only gravitational and electromagnetic fields, but no material objects. Also, it would make no sense to speak of

the *standard* (whatever it might be) as having changed its length. Consequences so counter-intuitive have led many physicists (and even a few philosophers of physics) to view 'length' not as something operationally defined, but as a theoretical magnitude (like electrical charge), which can be measured in a virtual infinity of ways, but which is not explicitly and exactly definable in terms of any of the ways of measuring it. Some of these physicists —the 'unified field' theorists—would even say that, far from it being the case that 'length' (and hence 'space') depends on the existence of suitably related material bodies, material bodies are best viewed as local variations in the curvature of space —that is to say, local variations in the intensity of a certain magnitude (the tensor g_{ik}), one aspect of which we experience as 'length'.

Again, it is far from true that the hypothesis 'last night, on the stroke of midnight, everything doubled in length' has no testable consequences. For example, if last night everything did double in length, and the velocity of light did not also double, then this morning we would have experienced an apparent halving of the speed of light. Moreover, if g (the gravitational constant) did not double, then we would have experienced an apparent halving in the intensity of the gravitational field. And if h (Planck's constant) did not change, then . . . In short, our world would have been bewilderingly different. And if we could survive at all, under so drastically altered conditions, no doubt some clever physicist would figure out what had happened.

I have gone into such detail just to make the point that in philosophy things are rarely so simple as they seem. The 'doubling universe' is a favorite classroom example of a 'pseudo-hypothesis'—yet it is the worst possible example if a 'clear case' is desired. In the first place, what is desired is a hypothesis with no testable consequences—yet *this* hypothesis, as it is always stated, *does* have testable consequences (perhaps some more complex hypothesis does not; but then we have to see this more complex hypothesis stated before we can be expected to discuss it). In the second place, the usual argument for the absurdity of this hypothesis rests on a simplistic theory of the meaning of 'length' —and a full discussion of *that* situation is hardly possible without bringing in considerations from unified field theory and quantum mechanics (the latter comes in connection with the notion of a 'material standard'). But, the example aside, one can hardly challenge the point that a superficially coherent story may contain a hidden absurdity.

Or can one? Of course, a superficially coherent story may contain a hidden contradiction, but the whole point of the logical behaviorist's sneering reference to 'surface grammar' is that *linguistic coherence, meaningfulness of the individual terms*, and *logical consistency*, do not by themselves guarantee freedom from another kind of absurdity—there are 'depth absurdities' which can only be detected by more powerful techniques. It is fair to say that to-day, after thirty years of this sort of talk, we lack both a single *convincing* example of such a depth absurdity, and a technique of detection (or alleged technique of detection) which does not reduce to 'untestable, *therefore* nonsense'.

To come to the case at hand: the logical behaviorist is likely to say that our hypothesis about 'X-worlders' is untestable in principle (if there *were* 'X-worlders', by hypothesis we couldn't distinguish them from people who really didn't know what pain is); and *therefore* meaningless (apart from a certain 'surface significance' which is of no real interest). If the logical behaviorist has learned a little from 'ordinary language philosophy', he is likely to shy away from saying 'untestable, therefore *meaningless*', but he is still likely to say or at least think: 'untestable, therefore in *some* sense absurd'. I shall try to meet

this 'argument' *not* by challenging the premiss, be it overt or covert, that 'untestable synthetic statement' is some kind of contradiction in terms (although I believe that premiss to be mistaken), but simply by showing that, on any but the most naive view of testability, our hypothesis *is* testable.

Of course, I could not do this if it were true that 'by hypothesis, we couldn't distinguish X-worlders from people who *really* didn't know what pain is'. But that isn't true—at any rate, it isn't true 'by hypothesis'. What is true by hypothesis is that we couldn't distinguish X-worlders from people who really didn't know what pain is *on the basis of overt behavior alone*. But that still leaves many other ways in which we might determine what is going on 'inside' the X-worlders—in both the figurative and literal sense of 'inside'. For example, we might examine their *brains*.

It is a fact that when pain impulses are 'received' in the brain, suitable electrical detecting instruments record a characteristic 'spike' pattern. Let us express this briefly (and too simply) by saying that 'brain spikes' are one-to-one correlated with experiences of pain. If our X-worlders belong to the human species, then we can verify that they do feel pains, notwithstanding their claim that they don't have any idea what pain is, by applying our electrical instruments and detecting the tell-tale 'brain spikes'.

This reply to the logical behaviorist is far too simple to be convincing. 'It is true,' the logical behaviorist will object, 'that experiences of pain are one-to-one correlated with "brain spikes" in the case of normal human beings. But you don't know that the X-worlders are normal human beings, in this sense—in fact, you have every reason to suppose that they are *not* normal human beings'. This reply shows that no *mere* correlation, however carefully verified in the case of normal human beings, can be used to verify ascriptions of pain to X-worlders. Fortunately, we do not have to suppose that our knowledge will always be restricted to mere correlations, like the pain-'brain spike' correlation. At a more advanced level, considerations of simplicity and coherence can begin to play a role in a way in which they cannot when only crude observational regularities are available.

Let us suppose that we begin to detect waves of a new kind, emanating from human brains—call them 'V-waves'. Let us suppose we develop a way of 'decoding' V-waves so as to reveal people's unspoken thoughts. And, finally, let us suppose that our 'decoding' technique also works in the case of the V-waves emanating from the brains of X-worlders. How does this correlation differ from the pain-'brain spike' correlation?

Simply in this way: it is reasonable to say that 'spikes'—momentary peaks in the electrical intensity in certain parts of the brain—could have almost any cause. But waves which go over into coherent English (or any other language), under a relatively simple decoding scheme, could not have just any cause. The 'null hypothesis'—that this is just the operation of 'chance'—can be dismissed at once. And if, in the case of human beings, we verify that the decoded waves correspond to what we are in fact thinking, then the hypothesis that this same correlation holds in the case of X-worlders will be assigned an immensely high probability, simply because no other likely explanation readily suggests itself. But 'no other likely explanation readily suggests itself' isn't verification, the logical behaviorist may say. On the contrary. How, for example, have we verified that cadmium lines in the spectrographic analysis of sunlight indicate the presence of cadmium in the sun? Mimicking the logical behaviorist, we might say: 'We have verified that under normal circumstances, cadmium lines only occur when heated cadmium is present. But we don't know that circumstances on the sun are normal

in this sense'. If we took this seriously, we would have to *heat cadmium on the sun* before we could say that the regularity upon which we base our spectrographic analysis of sunlight had been verified. In fact, we have verified the regularity under 'normal' circumstances, and we can *show* (deductively) that *if* many other laws, that have also been verified under 'normal' circumstances and *only* under 'normal' circumstances (i.e. never on the surface of the sun), hold on the sun, *then* this regularity holds also under 'abnormal' circumstances. And if someone says, 'But perhaps *none* of the usual laws of physics hold on the sun', we reply that this is like supposing that a random process always produces coherent English. The fact is that the 'signals' (sunlight, radio waves, etc.) which we receive from the sun cohere with a vast body of theory. Perhaps there is some other explanation than that the sun obeys the usual laws of physics; but *no other likely explanation suggests itself*. This sort of reasoning *is* scientific verification; and if it is not reducible to simple Baconian induction—well, then, philosophers must learn to widen their notions of verification to embrace it.

The logical behaviorist might try to account for the decodability of the X-worlders' 'V-waves' into coherent English (or the appropriate natural language) without invoking the absurd 'null hypothesis'. He might suggest, for example, that the 'X-worlders' are having fun at our expense—they are able, say, to produce misleading V-waves at will. If the X-worlders have brains quite unlike ours, this may even have some plausibility. But once again, in an advanced state of knowledge, considerations of coherence and simplicity may quite conceivably 'verify' that this is false. For example, the X-worlders may have brains quite like ours, rather than unlike ours. And we may have built up enough theory to say how the brain of a human being should 'look' if that human being were pretending not to be in pain when he was, in fact, in pain. Now consider what the 'misleading V-waves' story requires: it requires that the X-worlders produce V-waves in quite a different way than we do, without specifying what that different way is. Moreover, it requires that this be the case, although the reverse hypothesis—that X-worlders' brains function *exactly* as human brains do—in fact, that they *are* human brains—fits all the data. Clearly, this story is in serious methodological difficulties, and any other 'counter-explanation' that the logical behaviorist tries to invoke will be in similar difficulties. In short, the logical behaviorist's argument reduces to this: 'You cannot verify "psycho-physical" correlations in the case of X-worlders (or at least, you can't verify ones having to do, directly or indirectly, with *pain*), because, by hypothesis, X-worlders won't tell you (or indicate behaviorally) when they are in pain'. 'Indirect verification'— verification using theories which have been 'tested' only in the case of human beings—is not verification at all, because X-worlders *may* obey different laws than human beings. And it is not incumbent upon *me* (the logical behaviorist says) to suggest what those laws might be: it is incumbent upon *you* to rule out *all* other explanations. And this is a silly argument. The scientist does not have to rule out all the ridiculous theories that someone *might* suggest; he only has to show that he has ruled out any reasonable alternative theories that one might put forward on the basis of present knowledge.

Granting, then, that we might discover a technique for 'reading' the unspoken thoughts of X-worlders: we would then be in the same position with respect to the X-worlders as we were with respect to the original 'super-spartans'. The super-spartans were quite willing to tell us (and each other) about their pains; and we could see that their pain talk was linguistically coherent and situationally appropriate (e.g. a super-spartan will tell you

that he feels intense pain when you touch him with a red hot poker). On this basis, we were quite willing to grant that the super-spartans did, indeed, feel pain—all the more readily, since the deviancy in their behavior had a perfectly convincing ideological explanation. (Note again the role played here by considerations of coherence and simplicity.) But the X-worlders also 'tell' us (and, perhaps, each other), exactly the same things, albeit *un*willingly (by the medium of the involuntarily produced 'V-waves'). Thus we have to say— at least, we have to say as long as the 'V-wave' theory has not broken down—that the X-worlders are what they, in fact, are —just 'super-super-spartans'.

Let us now consider a quite different argument that a logical behaviorist might use. 'You are assuming,' he might say, 'the following principle:

If someone's brain is in the same state as that of a human being in pain (not just at the moment of the pain, but before and after for a sufficient interval), then he is in pain. Moreover, this principle is one which it would never be reasonable to give up (on your conception of 'methodology'). Thus, you have turned it into a tautology. But observe what turning this principle into a tautology involves: it involves changing the meaning of 'pain'. What 'pain' means for *you* is: the presence of pain, in the colloquial sense of the term, *or* the presence of a brain state identical with the brain state of someone who feels pain. Of course, in that sense we can verify that your 'X-worlders' experience 'pain'—but that is not the sense of 'pain' at issue.

The reply to this argument is that the premiss is simply false. It is just not true that, on my conception of verification, it would *never* be reasonable to give up the principle stated. To show this, I have to beg your pardons for engaging in a little more science fiction. Let us suppose that scientists discover yet another kind of waves—call them 'W-waves'. Let us suppose that W-waves do not emanate from human brains, but that they are detected emanating from the brains of X-worlders. And let us suppose that, once again, there exists a simple scheme for decoding W-waves into coherent English (or whatever language X-worlders speak), and that the 'decoded' waves 'read' like this: 'Ho, ho! are we fooling those Earthians! They think that the V-waves they detect represent our thoughts! If they only knew that instead of pretending not to have pains when we really have pains, we are really pretending to pretend not to have pains when we really do have pains when we really don't have pains!' Under these circumstances, we would 'doubt' (to put it mildly) that the same psycho-physical correlations held for normal humans and for X-worlders. Further investigations might lead us to quite a number of different hypotheses. For example, we might decide that X-worlders don't think with their brains at all—that the 'organ' of thought is not just the brain, in the case of X-worlders, but some larger structure—perhaps even a structure which is not 'physical' in the sense of consisting of elementary particles. The point is that what is necessarily true is not the principle stated in the last paragraph, but rather the principle:

If someone (some organism) is in the same state as a human being in pain in all relevant respects, then he (that organism) is in pain.

—And *this* principle *is* a tautology by anybody's lights! The only *a priori* methodological restriction I am imposing here is this one:

If some organism is in the same state as a human being in pain in all respects *known* to be relevant, and there is no reason to suppose that there exist unknown relevant respects, then don't postulate any.

—But this principle is not a 'tautology'; in fact, it is not a *statement* at *all*, but a methodological directive. And deciding to conform to this directive is not (as hardly needs to be said) changing the meaning of the word 'pain', or of *any* word.

There are two things that the logical behaviorist can do: he can claim that ascribing pains to X-worlders, or even super-spartans, involves a 'change of meaning',[7] or he can claim that ascribing pains to super-spartans, or at least to X-worlders, is 'untestable'. The first thing is a piece of unreasonable linguistics; the second, a piece of unreasonable scientific method. The two are, not surprisingly, mutually supporting: the unreasonable scientific method makes the unreasonable linguistics appear more reasonable. Similarly, the normal ways of thinking and talking are mutually supporting: reasonable linguistic field techniques are, needless to say, in agreement with reasonable conceptions of scientific method. Madmen sometimes have consistent delusional systems; so madness and sanity can both have a 'circular' aspect. I may not have succeeded, in this paper, in breaking the 'delusional system' of a committed logical behaviorist; but I hope to have convinced the uncommitted that that system need not be taken seriously. If we have to choose between 'circles', the circle of reason is to be preferred to any of the many circles of unreason.

Notes

1. E.g. these two points are fairly explicitly stated in Strawson's *Individuals*. Strawson has told me that he no longer subscribes to point (1), however.

2. An attempted fourth alternative—i.e. an alternative to dualism, materialism, *and* behaviorism—is sketched in "The Mental Life of Some Machines," which appeared in the Proceedings of the Wayne Symposium on the Philosophy of Mind. This fourth alternative is materialistic in the wide sense of being compatible with the view that organisms, including human beings, are physical systems consisting of elementary particles and obeying the laws of physics, but does not require that such 'states' as *pain* and *preference* be defined in a way which makes reference to either overt behavior or physical-chemical constitution. The idea, briefly, is that predicates which apply to

Selections from *Science and Human Behavior*

B. F. Skinner

Inner "Causes"

Every science has at some time or other looked for causes of action inside the things it has studied. Sometimes the practice has proved useful, sometimes it has not. There is nothing wrong with an inner explanation as such, but events which are located inside a system are likely to be difficult to observe. For this reason we are encouraged to assign properties to them without justification. Worse still, we can invent causes of this sort without fear of contradiction. The motion of a rolling stone was once attributed to its *vis viva*. The chemical properties of bodies were thought to be derived from the *principles* or *essences* of which they were composed. Combustion was explained by the *phlogiston* inside the combustible object. Wounds healed and bodies grew well because of a *vis medicatrix*. It has been especially tempting to attribute the behavior of a living organism to the behavior of an inner agent, as the following examples may suggest.

From *Science and Human Behavior* (New York: Macmillan, 1953), pp. 27-35, 62-66, 87-90. Copyright © 1953 by Macmillan Publishing Co., Inc. Reprinted with the permission of Macmillan Publishing Co., Inc.

Neural causes. The layman uses the nervous system as a ready explanation of behavior. The English language contains hundreds of expressions which imply such a causal relationship. At the end of a long trial we read that the jury shows signs of *brain fag*, that the *nerves* of the accused are *on edge*, that the wife of the accused is on the verge of a *nervous breakdown*, and that his lawyer is generally thought to have lacked the *brains* needed to stand up to the prosecution. Obviously, no direct observations have been made of the nervous systems of any of these people. Their "brains" and "nerves" have been invented on the spur of the moment to lend substance to what might otherwise seem a superficial account of their behavior.

The sciences of neurology and physiology have not divested themselves entirely of a similar practice. Since techniques for observing the electrical and chemical processes in nervous tissue had not yet been developed, early information about the nervous system was limited to its gross anatomy. Neural processes could only be inferred from the behavior which was said to result from them. Such inferences were legitimate enough as scientific theories, but they could not justifiably be used to explain the very behavior upon which they were based. The hypotheses of the early physiologist may have been sounder than those of the layman, but until independent evidence could be obtained, they were no more satisfactory as explanations of behavior. Direct information about many of the chemical and electrical processes in the nervous system is now available. Statements about the nervous system are no longer necessarily inferential or fictional. But there is still a measure of circularity in much physiological explanation, even in the writings of specialists. In World War I a familiar disorder was called "shell shock." Disturbances in behavior were explained by arguing that violent explosions had damaged the structure of the nervous system, though no direct evidence of such damage was available. In World War II the same disorder was classified as "neuropsychiatric." The prefix seems to show a continuing unwillingness to abandon explanations in terms of hypothetical neural damage.

Eventually a science of the nervous system based upon direct observation rather than inference will describe the neural states and events which immediately precede instances of behavior. We shall know the precise neurological conditions which immediately precede, say, the response, "No, thank you." These events in turn will be found to be preceded by other neurological events, and these in turn by others. This series will lead us back to events outside the nervous system and, eventually, outside the organism. In the chapters which follow we shall consider external events of this sort in some detail. We shall then be better able to evaluate the place of neurological explanations of behavior. However, we may note here that we do not have and may never have this sort of neurological information at the moment it is needed in order to predict a specific instance of behavior. It is even more unlikely that we shall be able to alter the nervous system directly in order to set up the antecedent conditions of a particular instance. The causes to be sought in the nervous system are, therefore, of limited usefulness in the prediction and control of specific behavior.

Psychic inner causes.   An even more common practice is to explain behavior in terms of an inner agent which lacks physical dimensions and is called "mental" or "psychic." The purest form of the psychic explanation is seen in the animism of primitive peoples. From the immobility of the body after death it is inferred that a spirit responsible for movement has departed. The *enthusiastic* person is, as the etymology of the word implies, energized by a "god within." It is only a modest refinement to attribute every feature of the behavior of the physical organism to a corresponding feature of the "mind" or of some inner "personality." The inner man is regarded as driving the body very much as the man at the steering wheel drives a car. The inner man wills an action, the outer executes it. The inner loses his appetite, the outer stops eating. The inner man wants and the outer gets. The inner has the impulse which the outer obeys.

It is not the layman alone who resorts to these practices, for many reputable psychologists use a similar dualistic system of explanation. The inner man is sometimes personified clearly, as when delinquent behavior is attributed to a "disordered personality," or he may be dealt with in fragments, as when behavior is attributed to mental processes, faculties, and traits. Since the inner man does not occupy space, he may be multiplied at will. It has been argued that a single physical organism is controlled by several psychic agents and that its behavior is the resultant of their several wills. The Freudian concepts of the ego, superego, and id are often used in this way. They are frequently regarded as nonsubstantial creatures, often in violent conflict, whose defeats or victories lead to the adjusted or maladjusted behavior of the physical organism in which they reside.

Direct observation of the mind comparable with the observation of the nervous system has not proved feasible. It is true that many people believe that they observe their "mental states" just as the physiologist observes neural events, but another interpretation of what they observe is possible, as we shall see in Chapter XVII. Introspective psychology no longer pretends to supply direct information about events which are the causal antecedents, rather than the mere accompaniments, of behavior. It defines its "subjective" events in ways which strip them of any usefulness in a causal analysis. The events appealed to in early mentalistic explanations of behavior have remained beyond the reach of observation. Freud insisted upon this by emphasizing the role of the unconscious—a frank recognition that important mental processes are not directly observable. The Freudian literature supplies many examples of behavior from which unconscious wishes, impulses, instincts, and emotions are inferred. Unconscious thought-processes have also been used to explain intellectual achievements. Though the mathematician may feel that he knows "how he thinks," he is often unable to give a coherent account of the mental processes leading to the solution of a specific problem. But any mental event which is unconscious is necessarily inferential, and the explanation is therefore not based upon independent observations of a valid cause.

The fictional nature of this form of inner cause is shown by the ease with which the mental process is discovered to have just the properties needed to account for the behavior. When a professor turns up in the wrong classroom or gives the wrong lecture, it is because his *mind* is, at least for the moment, *absent*. If he forgets to give a reading assignment, it is because it has slipped his *mind* (a hint from the class may re*mind* him of it). He begins to tell an old joke but pauses for a moment, and it is evident to everyone that he is trying to make up his *mind* whether or not he has already used the joke that term. His

lectures grow more tedious with the years, and questions from the class confuse him more and more, because his *mind* is failing. What he says is often disorganized because his *ideas* are confused. He is occasionally unnecessarily emphatic because of the force of his *ideas*. When he repeats himself, it is because he has an *idée fixe;* and when he repeats what others have said, it is because he borrows his *ideas*. Upon occasion there is nothing in what he says because he lacks *ideas*. In all this it is obvious that the mind and the ideas, together with their special characteristics, are being invented on the spot to provide spurious explanations. A science of behavior can hope to gain very little from so cavalier a practice. Since mental or psychic events are asserted to lack the dimensions of physical science, we have an additional reason for rejecting them.

Conceptual inner causes. The commonest inner causes have no specific dimensions at all, either neurological or psychic. When we say that a man eats *because* he is hungry, smokes a great deal *because* he has the tobacco habit, fights *because* of the instinct of pugnacity, behaves brilliantly *because* of his intelligence, or plays the piano well *because* of his musical ability, we seem to be referring to causes. But on analysis these phrases prove to be merely redundant descriptions. A single set of facts is described by the two statements: "He eats" and "He is hungry." A single set of facts is described by the two statements: "He smokes a great deal" and "He has the smoking habit." A single set of facts is described by the two statements: "He plays well" and "He has musical ability." The practice of explaining one statement in terms of the other is dangerous because it suggests that we have found the cause and therefore need search no further. Moreover, such terms as "hunger," "habit," and "intelligence" convert what are essentially the properties of a process or relation into what appear to be things. Thus we are unprepared for the properties eventually to be discovered in the behavior itself and continue to look for something which may not exist.

The Variables of Which Behavior Is a Function

The practice of looking inside the organism for an explanation of behavior has tended to obscure the variables which are immediately available for a scientific analysis. These variables lie outside the organism, in its immediate environment and in its environmental history. They have a physical status to which the usual techniques of science are adapted, and they make it possible to explain behavior as other subjects are explained in science. These independent variables are of many sorts and their relations to behavior are often subtle and complex, but we cannot hope to give an adequate account of behavior without analyzing them.

Consider the act of drinking a glass of water. This is not likely to be an important bit of behavior in anyone's life, but it supplies a convenient example. We may describe the topography of the behavior in such a way that a given instance may be identified quite accurately by any qualified observer. Suppose now we bring someone into a room and place a glass of water before him. Will he drink? There appear to be only two possibilities: either he will or he will not. But we speak of the *chances* that he will drink, and this notion may be refined for scientific use. What we want to evaluate is the *probability* that he will drink. This may range from virtual certainty that drinking will occur to virtual certainty that it will not. The very considerable problem of how to measure such a probability will be discussed later. For the moment, we are interested in how the probability may be increased or decreased.

Everyday experience suggests several possibilities, and laboratory and clinical observations have added others. It is decidedly not true that a horse may be led to water but cannot be made to drink. By arranging a history of severe deprivation we could be "absolutely sure" that drinking would occur. In the same way we may be sure that the glass of water in our experiment will be drunk. Although we are not likely to arrange them experimentally, deprivations of the necessary magnitude sometimes occur outside the laboratory. We may obtain an effect similar to that of deprivation by speeding up the excretion of water. For example, we may induce sweating by raising the temperature of the room or by forcing heavy exercise, or we may increase the excretion of urine by mixing salt or urea in food taken prior to the experiment. It is also well known that loss of blood, as on a battlefield, sharply increases the probability of drinking. On the other hand, we may set the probability at virtually zero by inducing or forcing our subject to drink a large quantity of water before the experiment.

If we are to predict whether or not our subject will drink, we must know as much as possible about these variables. If we are to induce him to drink, we must be able to manipulate them. In both cases, moreover, either for accurate prediction or control, we must investigate the effect of each variable quantitatively with the methods and techniques of a laboratory science.

Other variables may, of course, affect the result. Our subject may be "afraid" that something has been added to the water as a practical joke or for experimental purposes. He may even "suspect" that the water has been poisoned. He may have grown up in a culture in which water is drunk only when no one is watching. He may refuse to drink simply to prove that we cannot predict or control his behavior. These possibilities do not disprove the relations between drinking and the variables listed in the preceding paragraphs; they simply remind us that other variables may have to be taken into account. We must know the history of our subject with respect to the behavior of drinking water, and if we cannot eliminate social factors from the situation, then we must know the history of his personal relations to people resembling the experimenter. Adequate prediction in any science requires information about all relevant variables, and the control of a subject matter for practical purposes makes the same demands.

Other types of "explanation" do not permit us to dispense with these requirements or to fulfill them in any easier way. It is of no help to be told that our subject will drink provided he was born under a particular sign of the zodiac which shows a preoccupation with water or provided he is the lean and thirsty type or was, in short, "born thirsty." Explanations in terms of inner states or agents, however, may require some further comment. To what extent is it helpful to be told, "He drinks because he is thirsty"? If to be thirsty means nothing more than to have a tendency to drink, this is mere redundancy. If it means that he drinks because of a state of thirst, an inner causal event is invoked. If this state is purely inferential —if no dimensions are assigned to it which would make direct observation possible—it cannot serve as an explanation. But if it has physiological or psychic properties, what role can it play in a science of behavior?

The physiologist may point out that several ways of raising the probability of drinking have a common effect: they increase the concentration of solutions in the body. Through some mechanism not yet well understood, this may bring about a corresponding change in the nervous system which in turn makes drinking more probable. In the same way, it may be argued that all these operations make the organism "feel thirsty" or "want a drink" and that such a psychic state also acts upon the nervous system in some unexplained way to induce drinking. In each case we have a causal chain consisting of three links: (1) an operation performed upon the organism from without—for example, water deprivation; (2) an inner condition—for example, physiological or psychic thirst; and (3) a kind of behavior —for example, drinking. Independent information about the second link would obviously permit us to predict the third without recourse to the first. It would be a preferred type of variable because it would be nonhistoric; the first link may lie in the past history of the organism, but the second is a current condition. Direct information about the second link is, however, seldom, if ever, available. Sometimes we infer the second link from the third: an animal is judged to be thirsty if it drinks. In that case, the explanation is spurious. Sometimes we infer the second link from the first: an animal is said to be thirsty if it has not drunk for a long time. In that case, we obviously cannot dispense with the prior history.

The second link is useless in the *control* of behavior unless we can manipulate it. At the moment, we have no way of directly altering neural processes at appropriate moments in the life of a behaving organism, nor has any way been discovered to alter a psychic process. We usually set up the second link through the first: we make an animal thirsty, in either the physiological or the psychic sense, by depriving it of water, feeding it salt, and so on. In that case, the second link obviously does not permit us to dispense with the first. Even if some new technical discovery were to enable us to set up or change the second link directly, we should still have to deal with those enormous areas in which human behavior is controlled through manipulation of the first link. A technique of operating upon the second link would increase our control of behavior, but the techniques which have already been developed would still remain to be analyzed.

The most objectionable practice is to follow the causal sequence back only as far as a hypothetical second link. This is a serious handicap both in a theoretical science and in the practical control of behavior. It is no help to be told that to get an organism to drink we are simply to "make it thirsty" unless we are also told how this is to be done. When we have obtained the necessary prescription for thirst, the whole proposal is more complex than it need be. Similarly, when an example of maladjusted behavior is explained by saying that the individual is "suffering from anxiety," we have still to be told the cause of the anxiety. But the external conditions which are then invoked could have been directly related to the maladjusted behavior. Again, when we are told that a man stole a loaf of bread because "he was hungry," we have still to learn of the external conditions responsible for the "hunger." These conditions would have sufficed to explain the theft.

The objection to inner states is not that they do not exist, but that they are not relevant in a functional analysis. We cannot account for the behavior of any system while staying wholly inside it; eventually we must turn to forces operating upon the organism from without. Unless there is a weak spot in our causal chain so that the second link is not lawfully determined by the first, or the third by the second, then the first and third links must be lawfully related. If we must always go back beyond the second link for prediction and control, we may avoid many tiresome and exhausting digressions by examining the third link as a function of the first. Valid information about the second link may throw light upon this relationship but can in no way alter it.

* * *

Operant Conditioning

To get at the core of Thorndike's Law of Effect, we need to clarify the notion of "probability of response." This is an extremely important concept; unfortunately, it is also a difficult one. In discussing

human behavior, we often refer to "tendencies" or "predispositions" to behave in particular ways. Almost every theory of behavior uses some such term as "excitatory potential," "habit strength," or "determining tendency." But how do we observe a tendency? And how can we measure one?

If a given sample of behavior existed in only two states, in one of which it always occurred and in the other never, we should be almost helpless in following a program of functional analysis. An all-or-none subject matter lends itself only to primitive forms of description. It is a great advantage to suppose instead that the *probability* that a response will occur ranges continuously between these all-or-none extremes. We can then deal with variables which, unlike the eliciting stimulus, do not "cause a given bit of behavior to occur" but simply make the occurrence more probable. We may then proceed to deal, for example, with the combined effect of more than one such variable.

The everyday expressions which carry the notion of probability, tendency, or predisposition describe the frequencies with which bits of behavior occur. We never observe a probability as such. We say that someone is "enthusiastic" about bridge when we observe that he plays bridge often and talks about it often. To be "greatly interested" in music is to play, listen to, and talk about music a good deal. The "inveterate" gambler is one who gambles frequently. The camera "fan" is to be found taking pictures, developing them, and looking at pictures made by himself and others. The "highly sexed" person frequently engages in sexual behavior. The "dipsomaniac" drinks frequently.

In characterizing a man's behavior in terms of frequency, we assume certain standard conditions: he must be able to execute and repeat a given act, and other behavior must not interfere appreciably. We cannot be sure of the extent of a man's interest in music, for example, if he is necessarily busy with other things. When we come to refine the notion of probability of response for scientific use, we find that here, too, our data are frequencies and that the conditions under which they are observed must be specified. The main technical problem in designing a controlled experiment is to provide for the observation and interpretation of frequencies. We eliminate, or at least hold constant, any condition which encourages behavior which competes with the behavior we are to study. An organism is placed in a quiet box where its behavior may be observed through a one-way screen or recorded mechanically. This is by no means an environmental vacuum, for the organism will react to the features of the box in many ways; but its behavior will eventually reach a fairly stable level, against which the frequency of a selected response may be investigated.

To study the process which Thorndike called stamping in, we must have a "consequence." Giving food to a hungry organism will do. We can feed our subject conveniently with a small food tray which is operated electrically. When the tray is first opened, the organism will probably react to it in ways which interfere with the process we plan to observe. Eventually, after being fed from the tray repeatedly, it eats readily, and we are then ready to make this consequence contingent upon behavior and to observe the result.

We select a relatively simple bit of behavior which may be freely and rapidly repeated, and which is easily observed and recorded. If our experimental subject is a pigeon, for example, the behavior of raising the head above a given height is convenient. This may be observed by sighting across the pigeon's head at a scale pinned on the far wall of the box. We first study the height at which the head is normally held and select some line on the scale which is reached only infrequently. Keeping our eye on the scale we then be-

gin to open the food tray very quickly whenever the head rises above the line. If the experiment is conducted according to specifications, the result is invariable: we observe an immediate change in the frequency with which the head crosses the line. We also observe, and this is of some importance theoretically, that higher lines are now being crossed. We may advance almost immediately to a higher line in determining when food is to be presented. In a minute or two, the bird's posture has changed so that the top of the head seldom falls below the line which we first chose.

When we demonstrate the process of stamping in in this relatively simple way, we see that certain common interpretations of Thorndike's experiment are superfluous. The expression "trial-and-error learning," which is frequently associated with the Law of Effect, is clearly out of place here. We are reading something into our observations when we call any upward movement of the head a "trial," and there is no reason to call any movement which does not achieve a specified consequence an "error." Even the term "learning" is misleading. The statement that the bird "learns that it will get food by stretching its neck" is an inaccurate report of what has happened. To say that it has acquired the "habit" of stretching its neck is merely to resort to an explanatory fiction, since our only evidence of the habit is the acquired tendency to perform the act. The barest possible statement of the process is this: we make a given consequence contingent upon certain physical properties of behavior (the upward movement of the head), and the behavior is then observed to increase in frequency.

It is customary to refer to any movement of the organism as a "response." The word is borrowed from the field of reflex action and implies an act which, so to speak, answers a prior event—the stimulus. But we may make an event contingent upon behavior without identifying, or being able to identify, a prior stimulus.

We did not alter the environment of the pigeon to *elicit* the upward movement of the head. It is probably impossible to show that any single stimulus invariably precedes this movement. Behavior of this sort may come under the control of stimuli, but the relation is not that of elicitation. The term "response" is therefore not wholly appropriate but is so well established that we shall use it in the following discussion.

A response which has already occurred cannot, of course, be predicted or controlled. We can only predict that *similar* responses will occur in the future. The unit of a predictive science is, therefore, not a response but a class of responses. The word "operant" will be used to describe this class. The term emphasizes the fact that the behavior *operates* upon the environment to generate consequences. The consequences define the properties with respect to which responses are called similar. The term will be used both as an adjective (operant behavior) and as a noun to designate the behavior defined by a given consequence.

A single instance in which a pigeon raises its head is a *response*. It is a bit of history which may be reported in any frame of reference we wish to use. The behavior called "raising the head," regardless of when specific instances occur, is an *operant*. It can be described, not as an accomplished act, but rather as a set of acts defined by the property of the height to which the head is raised. In this sense an operant is defined by an effect which may be specified in physical terms; the "cutoff" at a certain height is a property of behavior.

The term "learning" may profitably be saved in its traditional sense to describe the reassortment of responses in a complex situation. Terms for the process of stamping in may be borrowed from Pavlov's analysis of the conditioned reflex. Pavlov himself called all events which strengthened behavior "reinforcement"

and all the resulting changes "conditioning." In the Pavlovian experiment, however, a reinforcer is paired with a *stimulus*; whereas in operant behavior it is contingent upon a *response*. Operant reinforcement is therefore a separate process and requires a separate analysis. In both cases, the strengthening of behavior which results from reinforcement is appropriately called "conditioning." In operant conditioning we "strengthen" an operant in the sense of making a response more probable or, in actual fact, more frequent. In Pavlovian or "respondent" conditioning we simply increase the magnitude of the response elicited by the conditioned stimulus and shorten the time which elapses between stimulus and response. (We note, incidentally, that these two cases exhaust the possibilities: an organism is conditioned when a reinforcer [1] accompanies another stimulus or [2] follows upon the organism's own behavior. Any event which does neither has no effect in changing a probability of response.) In the pigeon experiment, then, food is the *reinforcer* and presenting food when a response is emitted is the *reinforcement*. The *operant* is defined by the property upon which reinforcement is contingent— the height to which the head must be raised. The change in frequency with which the head is lifted to this height is the process of *operant conditioning*.

While we are awake, we act upon the environment constantly, and many of the consequences of our actions are reinforcing. Through operant conditioning the environment builds the basic repertoire with which we keep our balance, walk, play games, handle instruments and tools, talk, write, sail a boat, drive a car, or fly a plane. A change in the environment—a new car, a new friend, a new field of interest, a new job, a new location—may find us unprepared, but our behavior usually adjusts quickly as we acquire new responses and discard old. We shall see in the following chapter that operant reinforcement does more than build a behavioral repertoire. It improves the efficiency of behavior and maintains behavior in strength long after acquisition or efficiency has ceased to be of interest.

* * *

Goals, Purposes, and Other Final Causes

It is not correct to say that operant reinforcement "strengthens the response which precedes it." The response has already occurred and cannot be changed. What is changed is the future probability of responses in the same *class*. It is the operant as a class of behavior, rather than the response as a particular instance, which is conditioned. There is, therefore, no violation of the fundamental principle of science which rules out "final causes." But this principle is violated when it is asserted that behavior is under the control of an "incentive" or "goal" which the organism has not yet achieved or a "purpose" which it has not yet fulfilled. Statements which use such words as "incentive" or "purpose" are usually reducible to statements about operant conditioning, and only a slight change is required to bring them within the framework of a natural science. Instead of saying that a man behaves because of the consequences which *are* to follow his behavior, we simply say that he behaves because of the consequences which *have* followed similar behavior in the past. This is, of course, the Law of Effect or operant conditioning.

It is sometimes argued that a response is not fully described until its purpose is referred to as a current property. But what is meant by "describe"? If we observe someone walking down the street, we may report this event in the language of physical science. If we then add that "his purpose is to mail a letter," have we said anything which was not included in our first report? Evidently so, since a man may walk down the street "for many purposes" and in the same physical way in each case. But the distinction which needs

to be made is not between instances of behavior; it is between the variables of which behavior is a function. Purpose is not a property of the behavior itself; it is a way of referring to controlling variables. If we make our report after we have seen our subject mail his letter and turn back, we attribute "purpose" to him from the event which brought the behavior of walking down the street to an end. This event "gives meaning" to his performance, not by amplifying a description of the behavior as such, but by indicating an independent variable of which it may have been a function. We cannot see his "purpose" before seeing that he mails a letter, unless we have observed similar behavior and similar consequences before. Where we have done this, we use the term simply to predict that he will mail a letter upon this occasion.

Nor can our subject see his own purpose without reference to similar events. If we ask him why he is going down the street or what his purpose is and he says, "I am going to mail a letter," we have not learned anything new about his behavior but only about some of its possible causes. The subject himself, of course, may be in an advantageous position in describing these variables because he has had an extended contact with his own behavior for many years. But his statement is not therefore in a different class from similar statements made by others who have observed his behavior upon fewer occasions. As we shall see in Chapter XVII, he is simply making a plausible prediction in terms of his experiences with himself. Moreover, he may be wrong. He may report that he is "going to mail a letter," and he may indeed carry an unmailed letter in his hand and may mail it at the end of the street, but we may still be able to show that his behavior is primarily determined by the fact that upon past occasions he has encountered someone who is important to him upon just such a walk. He may not be "aware of this purpose" in the sense of being able to say that his behavior is strong for this reason.

The fact that operant behavior seems to be "directed toward the future" is misleading. Consider, for example, the case of "looking for something." In what sense is the "something" which has not yet been found relevant to the behavior? Suppose we condition a pigeon to peck a spot on the wall of a box and then, when the operant is well established, remove the spot. The bird now goes to the usual place along the wall. It raises its head, cocks its eye in the usual direction, and may even emit a weak peck in the usual place. Before extinction is very far advanced, it returns to the same place again and again in similar behavior. Must we say that the pigeon is "looking for the spot"? Must we take the "looked for" spot into account in explaining the behavior?

It is not difficult to interpret this example in terms of operant reinforcement. Since visual stimulation from the spot has usually preceded the receipt of food, the spot has become a conditioned reinforcer. It strengthens the behavior of looking in given directions from different positions. Although we have undertaken to condition only the pecking response, we have in fact strengthened many different kinds of precurrent behavior which bring the bird into positions from which it sees the spot and pecks it. These responses continue to appear, even though we have removed the spot, until extinction occurs. The spot which is "being looked for" is the spot which has occurred in the past as the immediate reinforcement of the behavior of looking. In general, looking for something consists of emitting responses which in the past have produced "something" as a consequence.

The same interpretation applies to human behavior. When we see a man moving about a room opening drawers, looking under magazines, and so on, we may describe his behavior in fully objective terms: "Now he is in a certain part of the room; he has grasped a book between the thumb and forefinger of his right hand; he is lifting the book and bending his head so that any object under the book can be seen." We may also "interpret" his behavior or "read a meaning into it" by saying that "he is looking for something" or, more specifically, that "he is looking for his glasses." What we have added is not a further description of his behavior but an inference about some of the variables responsible for it. There is no *current* goal, incentive, purpose, or meaning to be taken into account. This is so even if we ask him what he is doing and he says, "I am looking for my glasses." This is not a further description of his behavior but of the variables of which his behavior is a function; it is equivalent to "I have lost my glasses," "I shall stop what I am doing when I find my glasses," or "When I have done this in the past, I have found my glasses." These translations may seem unnecessarily roundabout, but only because expressions involving goals and purposes are abbreviations.

Very often we attribute purpose to behavior as another way of describing its biological adaptability. This issue has already been discussed, but one point may be added. In both operant conditioning and the evolutionary selection of behavioral characteristics, consequences alter future probability. Reflexes and other innate patterns of behavior evolve because they increase the chances of survival of the *species*. Operants grow strong because they are followed by important consequences in the life of the *individual*. Both processes raise the question of purpose for the same reason, and in both the appeal to a final cause may be rejected in the same way. A spider does not possess the elaborate behavioral repertoire with which it constructs a web because that web will enable it to capture the food it needs to survive. It possesses this behavior because similar behavior on the part of spiders in the past has enabled *them* to capture the food *they* needed to survive. A series of events have been relevant to the behavior of web-making in its earlier evolutionary history. We are wrong in saying that we observe the "purpose" of the web when we observe similar events in the life of the individual.

A Review of B. F. Skinner's *Verbal Behavior*

Noam Chomsky

1

A great many linguists and philosophers concerned with language have expressed the hope that their studies might ultimately be embedded in a framework provided by behaviorist psychology, and that refractory areas of investigation, particularly those in which meaning is involved, will in this way be opened up to fruitful exploration. Since this volume [*Verbal Behavior* (New York: Appleton-Century-Crofts, 1957)—*Ed.*] is the first large-scale attempt to incorporate the major aspects of linguistic behavior within a behaviorist framework, it merits and will undoubtedly receive careful attention. Skinner is noted for his contributions to the study of animal behavior. The book under review is the product of study of linguistic behavior extending over more than twenty years. Earlier versions of it have been fairly widely circulated, and there are quite a few references in the psychological literature to its major ideas.

The problem to which this book is

From *Language* 35, no. 1 (1959): 26-58. Reprinted by permission of the Linguistic Society of America and the author. Sections 5-10 have been omitted (the notes are therefore not numbered consecutively).

addressed is that of giving a "functional analysis" of verbal behavior. By functional analysis, Skinner means identification of the variables that control this behavior and specification of how they interact to determine a particular verbal response. Furthermore, the controlling variables are to be described completely in terms of such notions as *stimulus, reinforcement, deprivation*, which have been given a reasonably clear meaning in animal experimentation. In other words, the goal of the book is to provide a way to predict and control verbal behavior by observing and manipulating the physical environment of the speaker.

Skinner feels that recent advances in the laboratory study of animal behavior permit us to approach this problem with a certain optimism, since "the basic processes and relations which give verbal behavior its special characteristics are now fairly well understood . . . the results [of this experimental work] have been surprisingly free of species restrictions. Recent work has shown that the methods can be extended to human behavior without serious modification (3).[1]

It is important to see clearly just what it is in Skinner's program and claims that makes them appear so bold and remarkable. It is not primarily the fact that he has set functional analysis as his problem, or that he limits himself to study of *observables*, i.e., input-output relations. What is so surprising is the particular limitations he has imposed on the way in which the observables of behavior are to be studied, and, above all, the particularly simple nature of the *function* which, he claims, describes the causation of behavior. One would naturally expect that prediction of the behavior of a complex organism (or machine) would require, in addition to information about external stimulation, knowledge of the internal structure of the organism, the ways in which it processes input information and organizes its own behavior. These characteristics of the organism are in general a complicated product of inborn structure, the genetically determined course of maturation, and past experience. Insofar as independent neurophysiological evidence is not available, it is obvious that inferences concerning the structure of the organism are based on observation of behavior and outside events. Nevertheless, one's estimate of the relative importance of external factors and internal structure in the determination of behavior will have an important effect on the duration of research on linguistic (or any other) behavior, and on the kinds of analogies from animal behavior studies that will be considered relevant or suggestive.

Putting it differently, anyone who sets himself the problem of analyzing the causation of behavior will (in the absence of independent neurophysiological evidence) concern himself with the only data available, namely the record of inputs to the organism and the organism's present response, and will try to describe the function specifying the response in terms of the history of inputs. This is nothing more than the definition of his problem. There are no possible grounds for argument here, if one accepts the problem as legitimate, though Skinner has often advanced

and defended this definition of a problem as if it were a thesis which other investigators reject. The differences that arise between those who affirm and those who deny the importance of the specific "contribution of the organism" to learning and performance concern the particular character and complexity of this function, and the kinds of observations and research necessary for arriving at a precise specification of it. If the contribution of the organism is complex, the only hope of predicting behavior even in a gross way will be through a very indirect program of research that begins by studying the detailed character of the behavior itself and the particular capacities of the organism involved.

Skinner's thesis is that external factors consisting of present stimulation and the history of reinforcement (in particular, the frequency, arrangement, and withholding of reinforcing stimuli) are of overwhelming importance, and that the general principles revealed in laboratory studies of these phenomena provide the basis for understanding the complexities of verbal behavior. He confidently and repeatedly voices his claim to have demonstrated that the contribution of the speaker is quite trivial and elementary, and that precise prediction of verbal behavior involves only specification of the few external factors that he has isolated experimentally with lower organisms.

Careful study of this book (and of the research on which it draws) reveals, however, that these astonishing claims are far from justified. It indicates, furthermore, that the insights that have been achieved in the laboratories of the reinforcement theorist, though quite genuine, can be applied to complex human behavior only in the most gross and superficial way, and that speculative attempts to discuss linguistic behavior in these terms alone omit from consideration factors of fundamental importance that are, no doubt, amenable to scientific study, although their specific character cannot at present be precisely formulated. Since Skinner's work is the most extensive attempt to accommodate human behavior involving higher mental faculties within a strict behaviorist schema of the type that has attracted many linguists and philosophers, as well as psychologists, a detailed documentation is of independent interest. The magnitude of the failure of this attempt to account for verbal behavior serves as a kind of measure of the importance of the factors omitted from consideration, and an indication of how little is really known about this remarkably complex phenomenon.

The force of Skinner's argument lies in the enormous wealth and range of examples for which he proposes a functional analysis. The only way to evaluate the success of his program and the correctness of his basic assumptions about verbal behavior is to review these examples in detail and to determine the precise character of the concepts in terms of which the functional analysis is presented. Section 2 of this review describes the experimental context with respect to which these concepts are originally defined. Sections 3 and 4 deal with the basic concepts—*stimulus, response,* and *reinforcement*—Sections 6 to 10 with the new descriptive machinery developed specifically for the description of verbal behavior. In Section 5 we consider the status of the fundamental claim, drawn from the laboratory, which serves as the basis for the analogic guesses about human behavior that have been proposed by many psychologists. The final section (Section 11) will consider some ways in which further linguistic work may play a part in clarifying some of these problems.

2

Although this book makes no direct reference to experimental work, it can be understood only in terms of the general framework that Skinner has developed for the description of behavior. Skinner divides the responses of the animal into two main categories. *Respondents* are purely reflex responses elicited by particular stimuli. *Operants* are emitted responses, for which no obvious stimulus can be discovered. Skinner has been concerned primarily with operant behavior. The experimental arrangement that he introduced consists basically of a box with a bar attached to one wall in such a way that when the bar is pressed, a food pellet is dropped into a tray (and the bar press is recorded). A rat placed in the box will soon press the bar, releasing a pellet into the tray. This state of affairs, resulting from the bar press, increases the *strength* of the bar-pressing operant. The food pellet is called a *reinforcer;* the event, *a reinforcing event.* The strength of an operant is defined by Skinner in terms of the rate of response during extinction (i.e., after the last reinforcement and before return to the pre-conditioning rate).

Suppose that release of the pellet is conditional on the flashing of a light. Then the rat will come to press the bar only when the light flashes. This is called *stimulus discrimination.* The response is called a *discriminated operant* and the light is called the *occasion* for its emission: this is to be distinguished from elicitation of a response by a stimulus in the case of the respondent.[2] Suppose that the apparatus is so arranged that bar-pressing of only a certain character (e.g., duration) will release the pellet. The rat will then come to press the bar in the required way. This process is called *response differentiation.* By successive slight changes in the conditions under which the response will be reinforced, it is possible to shape the response of a rat or a pigeon in very surprising ways in a very short time, so that rather complex behavior can be produced by a process of successive approximation.

A stimulus can become reinforcing by repeated association with an already reinforcing stimulus. Such a stimulus is called a *secondary reinforcer.* Like many contemporary behaviorists, Skinner considers money, approval, and the like to be secondary reinforcers which have become reinforcing because of their association with food, etc.[3] Secondary reinforcers can be *generalized* by associating them with a variety of different primary reinforcers.

Another variable that can affect the rate of the bar-pressing operant is drive, which Skinner defines operationally in terms of hours of deprivation. His major scientific book, *Behavior of Organisms*, is a study of the effects of food-deprivation and conditioning on the strength of the bar-pressing response of healthy mature rats. Probably Skinner's most original contribution to animal behavior studies has been his investigation of the effects of intermittent reinforcement, arranged in various different ways, presented in *Behavior of Organisms* and extended (with pecking of pigeons as the operant under investigation) in the recent *Schedules of Reinforcement* by Ferster and Skinner (1957). It is apparently these studies that Skinner has in mind when he refers to the recent advances in the study of animal behavior.[4]

The notions *stimulus, response, reinforcement* are relatively well defined with respect to the bar-pressing experiments and others similarly restricted. Before we can extend them to real-life behavior, however, certain difficulties must be faced. We must decide, first of all, whether any physical event to which the organism is capable of reacting is to be called a stimulus on a given occasion, or only one to which the organism in fact reacts; and correspondingly, we must decide whether any part of behavior is to be called a response, or only one connected with stimuli in lawful ways. Questions of this sort pose something of a dilemma for the experimental psychologist. If he accepts the broad definitions, characterizing any physical event impinging on the organism as a stimulus and any part of the organism's behavior as a response, he must con-clude that behavior has not been demonstrated to be lawful. In the present state of our knowledge, we must attribute an overwhelming influence on actual behavior to ill-defined factors of attention, set, volition, and caprice. If we accept the narrower definitions, then behavior is lawful by definition (if it consists of responses); but this fact is of limited significance, since most of what the animal does will simply not be considered behavior. Hence, the psychologist either must admit that behavior is not lawful (or that he cannot at present show that it is—not at all a damaging admission for a developing science), or must restrict his attention to those highly limited areas in which it is lawful (e.g., with adequate controls, bar-pressing in rats; lawfulness of the observed behavior provides, for Skinner, an implicit definition of a good experiment).

Skinner does not consistently adopt either course. He utilizes the experimental results as evidence for the scientific character of his system of behavior, and analogic guesses (formulated in terms of a metaphoric extension of the technical vocabulary of the laboratory) as evidence for its scope. This creates the illusion of a rigorous scientific theory with a very broad scope, although in fact the terms used in the description of real-life and of laboratory behavior may be mere homonyms, with at most a vague similarity of meaning. To substantiate this evaluation, a critical account of his book must show that with a literal reading (where the terms of the descriptive system have something like the technical meanings given in Skinner's definitions) the book covers almost no aspect of linguistic behavior, and that with a metaphoric reading, it is no more scientific than the traditional approaches to this subject matter, and rarely as clear and careful.[5]

3

Consider first Skinner's use of the notions *stimulus* and *response*. In *Behavior of Organisms* (9) he commits himself to the narrow definitions for these terms. A part of the environment and a part of behavior are called *stimulus* (eliciting, discriminated, or reinforcing) and *response*, respectively, only if they are lawfully related; that is, if the *dynamic laws* relating them show smooth and reproducible curves. Evidently, stimuli and responses, so defined, have not been shown to figure very widely in ordinary human behavior.[6] We can, in the face of presently available evidence, continue to maintain the lawfulness of the relation between stimulus and response only by depriving them of their objective character. A typical example of *stimulus control* for Skinner would be the response to a piece of music with the utterance *Mozart* or to a painting with the response *Dutch*. These responses are asserted to be "under the control of extremely subtle properties" of the physical object or event (108). Suppose instead of saying *Dutch* we had said *Clashes with the wallpaper, I thought you liked abstract work, Never saw it before, Tilted, Hanging too low, Beautiful, Hideous, Remember our camping trip last summer?*, or whatever else might come into our minds when looking at a picture (in Skinnerian translation, whatever other responses exist in sufficient strength). Skinner could only say that each of these responses is under the control of some other stimulus property of the physical object. If we look at a red chair and say *red*, the response is under the control of the stimulus *redness*; if we say *chair*, it is under the control of the collection of properties (for Skinner, the object) *chairness* (110), and similarly for any other response. This device is as simple as it is empty. Since properties are free for the asking (we have as many of them as we have nonsynonymous descriptive expressions in our language, whatever this means exactly), we can account for a wide class of responses in terms of Skinnerian functional analysis by identifying the *controlling stimuli*. But the word *stimulus* has

lost all objectivity in this usage. Stimuli are no longer part of the outside physical world; they are driven back into the organism. We identify the stimulus when we hear the response. It is clear from such examples, which abound, that the talk of *stimulus control* simply disguises a complete retreat to mentalistic psychology. We cannot predict verbal behavior in terms of the stimuli in the speaker's environment, since we do not know what the current stimuli are until he responds. Furthermore, since we cannot control the property of a physical object to which an individual will respond, except in highly artificial cases, Skinner's claim that his system, as opposed to the traditional one, permits the practical control of verbal behavior[7] is quite false.

Other examples of *stimulus control* merely add to the general mystification. Thus, a proper noun is held to be a response "under the control of a specific person or thing" (as controlling stimulus, 113). I have often used the words *Eisenhower* and *Moscow*, which I presume are proper nouns if anything is, but have never been *stimulated* by the corresponding objects. How can this fact be made compatible with this definition? Suppose that I use the name of a friend who is not present. Is this an instance of a proper noun under the control of the friend as stimulus? Elsewhere it is asserted that a stimulus controls a response in the sense that presence of the stimulus increases the probability of the response. But it is obviously untrue that the probability that a speaker will produce a full name is increased when its bearer faces the speaker. Furthermore, how can one's own name be a proper noun in this sense? A multitude of similar questions arise immediately. It appears that the word *control* here is merely a misleading paraphrase for the traditional *denote* or *refer*. The assertion (115) that so far as the speaker is concerned, the relation of reference is "simply the probability that the speaker will emit a response of a given form in the presence of a stimulus having specified properties" is surely incorrect if we take the words *presence, stimulus,* and *probability* in their literal sense. That they are not intended to be taken literally is indicated by many examples, as when a response is said to be "controlled" by a situation or state of affairs as "stimulus." Thus, the expression *a needle in a haystack* "may be controlled as a unit by a particular type of situation" (116); the words in a single part of speech, e.g., all adjectives, are under the control of a single set of subtle properties of stimuli (121); "the sentence *The boy runs a store* is under the control of an extremely complex stimulus situation" (335); "*He is not at all well* may function as a standard response under the control of a state of affairs which might also control *He is ailing*" (325); when an envoy observes events in a foreign country and reports upon his return, his report is under "remote stimulus control" (416); the statement *This is war* may be a response to a "confusing international situation" (441); the suffix *-ed* is controlled by that "subtle property of stimuli which we speak of as action-in-the-past" (121) just as the *-s* in *The boy runs* is under the control of such specific features of the situation as its "currency" (332). No characterization of the notion *stimulus control* that is remotely related to the bar-pressing experiment (or that preserves the faintest objectivity) can be made to cover a set of examples like these, in which, for example, the *controlling stimulus* need not even impinge on the responding organism.

Consider now Skinner's use of the notion *response.* The problem of identifying units in verbal behavior has of course been a primary concern of linguists, and it seems very likely that experimental psychologists should be able to provide much-needed assistance in clearing up the many remaining difficulties in systematic identification. Skinner recognizes (20) the fundamental character of the problem of identification of a unit of verbal behavior, but is satisfied with an answer so vague and subjective that it does not really contribute to its solution. The unit of verbal behavior—the verbal operant—is defined as a class of responses of identifiable form functionally related to one or more controlling variables. No method is suggested for determining in a particular instance what are the controlling variables, how many such units have occurred, or where their boundaries are in the total response. Nor is any attempt made to specify how much or what kind of similarity in form or *control* is required for two physical events to be considered instances of the same operant. In short, no answers are suggested for the most elementary questions that must be asked of anyone proposing a method for description of behavior. Skinner is content with what he calls an *extrapolation* of the concept of operant developed in the laboratory to the verbal field. In the typical Skinnerian experiment, the problem of identifying the unit of behavior is not too crucial. It is defined, by fiat, as a recorded peck or bar-press, and systematic variations in the rate of this operant and its resistance to extinction are studied as a function of deprivation and scheduling of reinforcement (pellets). The operant is thus defined with respect to a particular experimental procedure. This is perfectly reasonable and has led to many interesting results. It is, however, completely meaningless to speak of extrapolating this concept of operant to ordinary verbal behavior. Such "extrapolation" leaves us with no way of justifying one or another decision about the units in the "verbal repertoire."

Skinner specifies "response strength" as the basic datum, the basic dependent variable in his functional analysis. In the bar-pressing experiment, response strength is defined in terms of rate of emission during extinction. Skinner has argued[8] that this is "the only datum that varies significantly and in the expected direction under conditions which are relevant to the 'learning process.'" In the book under review, response strength is defined as "probability of emission" (22). This definition provides a comforting impression of objectivity, which, however, is quickly dispelled when we look into the matter more closely. The term *probability* has some rather obscure meaning for Skinner in this book.[9] We are told, on the one hand, that "our evidence for the contribution of each variable [to response strength] is based on observation of frequencies alone" (28). At the same time, it appears that frequency is a very misleading measure of strength, since, for example, the frequency of a response may be "primarily attributable to the frequency of occurrence of controlling variables" (27). It is not clear how the frequency of a response can be attributable to anything BUT the frequency of occurrence of its controlling variables if we accept Skinner's view that the behavior occurring in a given situation is "fully determined" by the relevant controlling variables (175, 228). Furthermore, although the evidence for the contribution of each variable to response strength is based on observation of frequencies alone, it turns out that "we base the notion of strength upon several kinds of evidence" (22), in particular (22-28): emission of the response (particularly in unusual circumstances), energy level (stress), pitch level, speed and delay of emission, size of letters etc. in writing, immediate repetition, and—a final factor, relevant but misleading—over-all frequency.

Of course, Skinner recognizes that these measures do not co-vary, because (among other reasons) pitch, stress, quantity, and reduplication may have internal linguistic functions.[10] However, he does not hold these conflicts to be very important, since the proposed factors indicative of strength are "fully understood by everyone" in the culture (27). For example, "if we are shown a prized work of art and exclaim *Beautiful!*, the speed and energy of the response will not be lost on the owner." It does not appear totally obvious that in this case the way to impress the owner is to shriek *Beautiful* in a loud, high-pitched voice, repeatedly, and with no delay (high response strength). It may be equally effective to look at the picture silently (long delay) and then to murmur *Beautiful* in a soft, low-pitched voice (by definition, very low response strength).

It is not unfair, I believe, to conclude from Skinner's discussion of response strength, the *basic datum* in functional analysis, that his *extrapolation* of the notion of probability can best be interpreted as, in effect, nothing more than a decision to use the word *probability*, with its favorable connotations of objectivity, as a cover term to paraphrase such low-status words as *interest, intention, belief*, and the like. This interpretation is fully justified by the way in which Skinner uses the terms *probability* and *strength*. To cite just one example, Skinner defines the process of confirming an assertion in science as one of "generating additional variables to increase its probability" (425), and more generally, its strength (425-29). If we take this suggestion quite literally, the degree of confirmation of a scientific assertion can be measured as a simple function of the loudness, pitch, and frequency with which it is proclaimed, and a general procedure for increasing its degree of confirmation would be, for instance, to train machine guns on large crowds of people who have been instructed to shout it. A better indication of what Skinner probably has in mind here is given by his description of how the theory of evolution, as an example, is confirmed. This "single set of verbal responses . . . is made more plausible—is strengthened—by several types of construction based upon verbal responses in geology, paleontology, genetics, and so on" (427). We are no doubt to interpret the terms *strength* and *probability* in this context as paraphrases of more familiar locutions such as "justified belief" or "warranted assertability," or something of the sort. Similar latitude of interpretation is presumably expected when we read that "frequency of effective action accounts in turn for what we may call the listener's 'belief' " (88) or that "our belief in what someone tells us is similarly a function of, or identical with, our tendency to act upon the verbal stimuli which he provides" (160).[11]

I think it is evident, then, that Skinner's use of the terms *stimulus, control, response,* and *strength* justify the general conclusion stated in the last paragraph of Section 2. The way in which these terms are brought to bear on the actual data indicates that we must interpret them as mere paraphrases for the popular vocabulary commonly used to describe behavior and as having no particular connection with the homonymous expressions used in the description of laboratory experiments. Naturally, this terminological revision adds no objectivity to the familiar *mentalistic* mode of description.

4

The other fundamental notion borrowed from the description of bar-pressing experiments is *reinforcement.* It raises problems which are similar, and even more serious. In *Behavior of Organisms,* "the operation of reinforcement is defined as the presentation of a certain kind of stimulus in a temporal relation with either a stimulus or response. A reinforcing stimulus is defined as such by its power to produce the resulting change [in strength]. There is no circularity about this: some stimuli are found to produce the change, others not, and they are classified as reinforcing and nonreinforcing accordingly" (62). This is a perfectly appropriate definition[12] for the study of schedules of reinforcement. It is perfectly useless, however, in the discussion of real-life behavior, unless we can somehow characterize the stimuli which are reinforcing (and the sit-

uations and conditions under which they are reinforcing). Consider first of all the status of the basic principle that Skinner calls the "law of conditioning" (law of effect). It reads: "if the occurrence of an operant is followed by presence of a reinforcing stimulus, the strength is increased" (*Behavior of Organisms,* 21). As *reinforcement* was defined, this law becomes a tautology.[13] For Skinner, learning is just change in response strength.[14] Although the statement that presence of reinforcement is a sufficient condition for learning and maintenance of behavior is vacuous, the claim that it is a necessary condition may have some content, depending on how the class of reinforcers (and appropriate situations) is characterized. Skinner does make it very clear that in his view reinforcement is a necessary condition for language learning and for the continued availability of linguistic responses in the adult.[15] However, the looseness of the term *reinforcement* as Skinner uses it in the book under review makes it entirely pointless to inquire into the truth or falsity of this claim. Examining the instances of what Skinner calls *reinforcement*, we find that not even the requirement that a reinforcer be an identifiable stimulus is taken seriously. In fact, the term is used in such a way that the assertion that reinforcement is necessary for learning and continued availability of behavior is likewise empty.

To show this, we consider some examples of *reinforcement.* First of all, we find a heavy appeal to automatic self-reinforcement. Thus, "a man talks to himself . . . because of the reinforcement he receives" (163); "the child is reinforced automatically when he duplicates the sounds of airplanes, streetcars . . ." (164); "the young child alone in the nursery may automatically reinforce his own exploratory verbal behavior when he produces sounds which he has heard in the speech of others" (58); "the speaker who is also an accomplished listener 'knows when he has correctly echoed a response' and is reinforced thereby" (68); thinking is "behaving which automatically affects the behaver and is reinforcing because it does so" (438; cutting one's finger should thus be reinforcing, and an example of thinking); "the verbal fantasy, whether overt or covert, is automatically reinforcing to the speaker as listener. Just as the musician plays or composes what he is reinforced by hearing, or as the artist paints what reinforces him visually, so the speaker engaged in verbal fantasy says what he is reinforced by hearing or writes what he is reinforced by reading" (439); similarly, care in problem solving, and rationalization, are automatically self-reinforcing (442-43). We can also reinforce someone by emitting verbal behavior as such (since this rules out a class of aversive stimulations, 167), by not emitting verbal behavior (keeping silent and paying attention, 199), or by acting appropriately on some future occasion (152: "the strength of [the speaker's] behavior is determined mainly by the behavior which the listener will exhibit with respect to a given state of affairs"; this Skinner considers the general case of "communication" or "letting the listener know"). In most such cases, of course, the speaker is not present at the time when the reinforcement takes place, as when "the artist . . . is reinforced by the effects his works have upon . . . others" (224), or when the writer is reinforced by the fact that his "verbal behavior may reach over centuries or to thousands of listeners or readers at the same time. The writer may not be reinforced often or immediately, but his net reinforcement may be great" (206; this accounts for the great "strength" of his behavior). An individual may also find it reinforcing to injure someone by criticism or by bringing bad news, or to publish an experimental result which upsets the theory of a rival (154), to describe circumstances which would be reinforcing if they were to occur (165), to avoid repetition (222), to "hear" his own

name though in fact it was not mentioned or to hear nonexistent words in his child's babbling (259), to clarify or otherwise intensify the effect of a stimulus which serves an important discriminative function (416), and so on.

From this sample, it can be seen that the notion of reinforcement has totally lost whatever objective meaning it may ever have had. Running through these examples, we see that a person can be reinforced though he emits no response at all, and that the reinforcing *stimulus* need not impinge on the *reinforced person* or need not even exist (it is sufficient that it be imagined or hoped for). When we read that a person plays what music he likes (165), says what he likes (165), thinks what he likes (438-39), reads what books he likes (163), etc., BECAUSE he finds it reinforcing to do so, or that we write books or inform others of facts BECAUSE we are reinforced by what we hope will be the ultimate behavior of reader or listener, we can only conclude that the term *reinforcement* has a purely ritual function. The phrase "X is reinforced by Y (stimulus, state of affairs, event, etc.)" is being used as a cover term for "X wants Y," "X likes Y," "X wishes that Y were the case," etc. Invoking the term *reinforcement* has no explanatory force, and any idea that this paraphrase introduces any new clarity or objectivity into the description of wishing, liking, etc., is a serious delusion. The only effect is to obscure the important differences among the notions being paraphrased. Once we recognize the latitude with which the term *reinforcement* is being used, many rather startling comments lose their initial effect—for instance, that the behavior of the creative artist is "controlled entirely by the contingencies of reinforcement" (150). What has been hoped for from the psychologist is some indication how the casual and informal description of everyday behavior in the popular vocabulary can be explained or clarified in terms of the notions developed in careful experiment and observation, or perhaps replaced in terms of a better scheme. A mere terminological revision, in which a term borrowed from the laboratory is used with the full vagueness of the ordinary vocabulary, is of no conceivable interest.

It seems that Skinner's claim that all verbal behavior is acquired and maintained in "strength" through reinforcement is quite empty, because his notion of reinforcement has no clear content, functioning only as a cover term for any factor, detectable or not, related to acquisition or maintenance of verbal behavior.[16] Skinner's use of the term *conditioning* suffers from a similar difficulty. Pavlovian and operant conditioning are processes about which psychologists have developed real understanding. Instruction of human beings is not. The claim that instruction and imparting of information are simply matters of conditioning (357-66) is pointless. The claim is true, if we extend the term *conditioning* to cover these processes, but we know no more about them after having revised this term in such a way as to deprive it of its relatively clear and objective character. It is, as far as we know, quite false, if we use *conditioning* in its literal sense. Similarly, when we say that "it is the function of predication to facilitate the transfer of response from one term to another or from one object to another" (361), we have said nothing of any significance. In what sense is this true of the predication *Whales are mammals?* Or, to take Skinner's example, what point is there in saying that the effect of *The telephone is out of order* on the listener is to bring behavior formerly controlled by the stimulus *out of order* under control of the stimulus *telephone* (or the telephone itself) by a process of simple conditioning (362)? What laws of conditioning hold in this case? Furthermore, what behavior is *controlled* by the stimulus *out of order*, in the abstract? Depending on the object of which this is predicat-

ed, the present state of motivation of the listener, etc., the behavior may vary from rage to pleasure, from fixing the object to throwing it out, from simply not using it to trying to use it in the normal way (e.g., to see if it is really out of order), and so on. To speak of "conditioning" or "bringing previously available behavior under control of a new stimulus" in such a case is just a kind of play-acting at science (cf. also 43n).

* * *

11

The preceding discussion covers all the major notions that Skinner introduces in his descriptive system. My purpose in discussing the concepts one by one was to show that in each case, if we take his terms in their literal meaning, the description covers almost no aspect of verbal behavior, and if we take them metaphorically, the description offers no improvement over various traditional formulations. The terms borrowed from experimental psychology simply lose their objective meaning with this extension, and take over the full vagueness of ordinary language. Since Skinner limits himself to such a small set of terms for paraphrase, many important distinctions are obscured. I think that this analysis supports the view expressed in Section 1, that elimination of the independent contribution of the speaker and learner (a result which Skinner considers of great importance, cf. 311-12) can be achieved only at the cost of eliminating all significance from the descriptive system, which then operates at a level so gross and crude that no answers are suggested to the most elementary questions.[46] The questions to which Skinner has addressed his speculations are hopelessly premature. It is futile to inquire into the causation of verbal behavior until much more is known about the specific character of this behavior; and there is little point in speculating about the process of acquisition without much better understanding of what is acquired.

Anyone who seriously approaches the study of linguistic behavior, whether linguist, psychologist, or philosopher, must quickly become aware of the enormous difficulty of stating a problem which will define the area of his investigations, and which will not be either completely trivial or hopelessly beyond the range of present-day understanding and technique. In selecting functional analysis as his problem, Skinner has set himself a task of the latter type. In an extremely interesting and insightful paper,[47] K. S. Lashley has implicitly delimited a class of problems which can be approached in a fruitful way by the linguist and psychologist, and which are clearly preliminary to those with which Skinner is concerned. Lashley recognizes, as anyone must who seriously considers the data, that the composition and production of an utterance is not simply a matter of stringing together a sequence of responses under the control of outside stimulation and intraverbal association, and that the syntactic organization of an utterance is not something directly represented in any simple way in the physical structure of the utterance itself. A variety of observations lead him to conclude that syntactic structure is "a generalized pattern imposed on the specific acts as they occur" (512), and that "a consideration of the structure of the sentence and other motor sequences will show . . . that there are, behind the overtly expressed sequences, a multiplicity of integrative processes which can only be inferred from the final results of their activity" (509). He also comments on the great difficulty of determining the "selective mechanisms" used in the actual construction of a particular utterance (522).

Although present-day linguistics cannot provide a precise account of these integrative processes, imposed patterns, and selective mechanisms, it can at least set itself the problem of characterizing

these completely. It is reasonable to regard the grammar of a language L ideally as a mechanism that provides an enumeration of the sentences of L in something like the way in which a deductive theory gives an enumeration of a set of theorems. (*Grammar*, in this sense of the word, includes phonology.) Furthermore, the theory of language can be regarded as a study of the formal properties of such grammars, and, with a precise enough formulation, this general theory can provide a uniform method for determining, from the process of generation of a given sentence, a structural description which can give a good deal of insight into how this sentence is used and understood. In short, it should be possible to derive from a properly formulated grammar a statement of the integrative processes and generalized patterns imposed on the specific acts that constitute an utterance. The rules of a grammar of the appropriate form can be subdivided into the two types, optional and obligatory; only the latter must be applied in generating an utterance. The optional rules of the grammar can be viewed, then, as the selective mechanisms involved in the production of a particular utterance. The problem of specifying these integrative processes and selective mechanisms is nontrivial and not beyond the range of possible investigation. The results of such a study might, as Lashley suggests, be of independent interest for psychology and neurology (and conversely). Although such a study, even if successful, would by no means answer the major problems involved in the investigation of meaning and the causation of behavior, it surely will not be unrelated to these. It is at least possible, furthermore, that such a notion as *semantic generalization*, to which such heavy appeal is made in all approaches to language in use, conceals complexities and specific structure of inference not far different from those that can be studied and exhibited in the case of syntax, and that consequently the general character of the results of syntactic investigations may be a corrective to oversimplified approaches to the theory of meaning.

The behavior of the speaker, listener, and learner of language constitutes, of course, the actual data for any study of language. The construction of a grammar which enumerates sentences in such a way that a meaningful structural description can be determined for each sentence does not in itself provide an account of this actual behavior. It merely characterizes abstractly the ability of one who has mastered the language to distinguish sentences from nonsentences, to understand new sentences (in part), to note certain ambiguities, etc. These are very remarkable abilities. We constantly read and hear new sequences of words, recognize them as sentences, and understand them. It is easy to show that the new events that we accept and understand as sentences are not related to those with which we are familiar by any simple notion of formal (or semantic or statistical) similarity or identity of grammatical frame. Talk of generalization in this case is entirely pointless and empty. It appears that we recognize a new item as a sentence not because it matches some familiar item in any simple way, but because it is generated by the grammar that each individual has somehow and in some form internalized. And we understand a new sentence, in part, because we are somehow capable of determining the process by which this sentence is derived in this grammar.

Suppose that we manage to construct grammars having the properties outlined above. We can then attempt to describe and study the achievement of the speaker, listener, and learner. The speaker and the listener, we must assume, have already acquired the capacities characterized abstractly by the grammar. The speaker's task is to select a particular compatible set of optional rules. If we know, from grammatical study, what choices are available

to him and what conditions of compatibility the choices must meet, we can proceed meaningfully to investigate the factors that lead him to make one or another choice. The listener (or reader) must determine, from an exhibited utterance, what optional rules were chosen in the construction of the utterance. It must be admitted that the ability of a human being to do this far surpasses our present understanding. The child who learns a language has in some sense constructed the grammar for himself on the basis of his observation of sentences and nonsentences (i.e., corrections by the verbal community). Study of the actual observed ability of a speaker to distinguish sentences from nonsentences, detect ambiguities, etc., apparently forces us to the conclusion that this grammar is of an extremely complex and abstract character, and that the young child has succeeded in carrying out what from the formal point of view, at least, seems to be a remarkable type of theory construction. Furthermore, this task is accomplished in an astonishingly short time, to a large extent independently of intelligence, and in a comparable way by all children. Any theory of learning must cope with these facts.

It is not easy to accept the view that a child is capable of constructing an extremely complex mechanism for generating a set of sentences, some of which he has heard, or that an adult can instantaneously determine whether (and if so, how) a particular item is generated by this mechanism, which has many of the properties of an abstract deductive theory. Yet this appears to be a fair description of the performance of the speaker, listener, and learner. If this is correct, we can predict that a direct attempt to account for the actual behavior of speaker, listener, and learner, not based on a prior understanding of the structure of grammars, will achieve very limited success. The grammar must be regarded as a component in the behavior of the speaker and listener which can only be inferred, as Lashley has put it, from the resulting physical acts. The fact that all normal children acquire essentially comparable grammars of great complexity with remarkable rapidity suggests that human beings are somehow specially designed to do this, with data-handling or "hypothesis-formulating" ability of unknown character and complexity.[48] The study of linguistic structure may ultimately lead to some significant insights into this matter. At the moment the question cannot be seriously posed, but in principle it may be possible to study the problem of determining what the built-in structure of an information-processing (hypothesis-forming) system must be to enable it to arrive at the grammar of a language from the available data in the available time. At any rate, just as the attempt to eliminate the contribution of the speaker leads to a "mentalistic" descriptive system that succeeds only in blurring important traditional distinctions, a refusal to study the contribution of the child to language learning permits only a superficial account of language acquisition, with a vast and unanalyzed contribution attributed to a step called *generalization* which in fact includes just about everything of interest in this process. If the study of language is limited in these ways, it seems inevitable that major aspects of verbal behavior will remain a mystery.

Notes

1. Skinner's confidence in recent achievements in the study of animal behavior and their applicability to complex human behavior does not appear to be widely shared. In many recent publications of confirmed behaviorists there is a prevailing note of skepticism with regard to the scope of these achievements. For representative comments, see the contributions to *Modern Learning Theory* (by W. K. Estes et al.; New York: Appleton-Century-Crofts, Inc., 1954); B. R. Bugelski, *Psychology of Learning* (New York: Holt, Rinehart & Winston, Inc., 1956); S. Koch, in *Nebraska Symposium on Motivation*, 58 (Lincoln, 1956); W. S. Verplanck, "Learned and Innate Behavior," *Psych. Rev.*, 52 (1955), 139. Perhaps the strongest view is that of H. Harlow, who has asserted ("Mice, Monkeys, Men, and Motives," *Psych. Rev.*, 60 [1953], 23-32) that "a strong case can be made for the proposition that the importance of the psychological problems studied during the last 15 years has decreased as a negatively accelerated function approaching an asymptote of complete indifference." N. Tinbergen, a leading representative of a different approach to animal-behavior studies (comparative ethology), concludes a discussion of *functional analysis* with the comment that "we may now draw the conclusion that the causation of behavior is immensely more complex than was assumed in the generalizations of the past. A number of internal and external factors act upon complex central nervous structures. Second, it will be obvious that the facts at our disposal are very fragmentary indeed"—*The Study of Instinct* (Toronto: Oxford Univ. Press, 1951), p. 74.

2. In *Behavior of Organisms* (New York: Appleton-Century-Crofts, Inc., 1938), Skinner remarks that "although a conditioned operant is the result of the correlation of the response with a particular reinforcement, a relation between it and a discriminative stimulus acting prior to the response is the almost universal rule" (178-79). Even emitted behavior is held to be produced by some sort of "originating force" (51) which, in the case of operant behavior, is not under experimental control. The distinction between eliciting stimuli, discriminated stimuli, and "originating forces" has never been adequately clarified and becomes even more confusing when private internal events are considered to be discriminated stimuli (see below).

3. In a famous experiment, chimpanzees were taught to perform complex tasks to receive tokens which had become secondary reinforcers because of association with food. The idea that money, approval, prestige, etc. actually acquire their motivating effects on human behavior according to this paradigm is unproved, and not particularly plausible. Many psychologists within the behaviorist movement are quite skeptical about this (cf. 23n). As in the case of most aspects of human behavior, the evidence about secondary reinforcement is so fragmentary, conflicting, and

complex that almost any view can find some support.

4. Skinner's remark quoted above about the generality of his basic results must be understood in the light of the experimental limitations he has imposed. If it were true in any deep sense that the basic processes in language are well understood and free of species restriction, it would be extremely odd that language is limited to man. With the exception of a few scattered observations (cf. his article, "A Case History in Scientific Method," *The American Psychologist*, 11 [1956], 221-33), Skinner is apparently basing this claim on the fact that qualitatively similar results are obtained with bar pressing of rats and pecking of pigeons under special conditions of deprivation and various schedules of reinforcement. One immediately questions how much can be based on these facts, which are in part at least an artifact traceable to experimental design and the definition of *stimulus* and *response* in terms of *smooth dynamic curves* (see below). The dangers inherent in any attempt to *extrapolate* to complex behavior from the study of such simple responses as bar pressing should be obvious and have often been commented on (cf., e.g., Harlow, *op. cit.*). The generality of even the simplest results is open to serious question. Cf. in this connection M. E. Bitterman, J. Wodinsky, and D. K. Candland, "Some Comparative Psychology," *Am. Jour. of Psych.*, 71 (1958), 94-110, where it is shown that there are important qualitative differences in solution of comparable elementary problems by rats and fish.

5. An analogous argument, in connection with a different aspect of Skinner's thinking, is given by M. Scriven in "A Study of Radical Behaviorism," *Univ. of Minn. Studies in Philosophy of Science*, I. Cf. Verplanck's contribution to *Modern Learning Theory, op. cit.* pp. 283-88, for more general discussion of the difficulties in formulating an adequate definition of *stimulus* and *response*. He concludes, quite correctly, that in Skinner's sense of the word, stimuli are not objectively identifiable independently of the resulting behavior, nor are they manipulable. Verplanck presents a clear discussion of many other aspects of Skinner's system, commenting on the untestability of many of the so-called "laws of behavior" and the limited scope of many of the others, and the arbitrary and obscure character of

Skinner's notion of *lawful relation*; and, at the same time, noting the importance of the experimental data that Skinner has accumulated.

6. In *Behavior of Organisms*, Skinner apparently was willing to accept this consequence. He insists (41-42) that the terms of casual description in the popular vocabulary are not validly descriptive until the defining properties of stimulus and response are specified, the correlation is demonstrated experimentally, and the dynamic changes in it are shown to be lawful. Thus, in describing a child as hiding from a dog, "it will not be enough to dignify the popular vocabulary by appealing to essential properties of *dogness* or *hidingness* and to suppose them intuitively known." But this is exactly what Skinner does in the book under review, as we will see directly.

7. 253f. and elsewhere, repeatedly. As an example of how well we can control behavior using the notions developed in this book, Skinner shows here how he would go about evoking the response *pencil*. The most effective way, he suggests, is to say to the subject, "Please say *pencil*" (our chances would, presumably, be even further improved by use of "aversive stimulation," e.g., holding a gun to his head). We can also "make sure that no pencil or writing instrument is available, then hand our subject a pad of paper appropriate to pencil sketching, and offer him a handsome reward for a recognizable picture of a cat." It would also be useful to have voices saying *pencil* or *pen and* . . . in the background; signs reading *pencil* or *pen and* . . . ; or to place a "large and unusual pencil in an unusual place clearly in sight." "Under such circumstances, it is highly probable that our subject will say *pencil*." "The available techniques are all illustrated in this sample." These contributions of behavior theory to the practical control of human behavior are amply illustrated elsewhere in the book, as when Skinner shows (113-14) how we can evoke the response *red* (the device suggested is to hold a red object before the subject and say, "Tell me what color this is").

In fairness, it must be mentioned that there are certain nontrivial applications of *operant conditioning* to the control of human behavior. A wide variety of experiments have shown that the number of plural nouns (for example) produced by a subject will increase if the experimenter says "right" or "good" when one is produced (similarly, positive attitudes on a certain issue, stories with particular content, etc.; cf. L. Krasner, "Studies of the Conditioning of Verbal Behavior," *Psych. Bull.*, 55 [1958], for a survey of several dozen experiments of this kind, mostly with positive results). It is of some interest that the subject is usually unaware of the process. Just what insight this gives into normal verbal behavior is not obvious. Nevertheless, it is an example of positive and not totally expected results using the Skinnerian paradigm.

8. "Are Theories of Learning Necessary?", *Psych. Rev.*, 57 (1950), 193-216.

9. And elsewhere. In his paper "Are Theories of Learning Necessary?" Skinner considers the problem how to extend his analysis of behavior to experimental situations in which it is impossible to observe frequencies, rate of response being the only valid datum. His answer is that "the notion of probability is usually extrapolated to cases in which a frequency analysis cannot be carried out. In the field of behavior we arrange a situation in which frequencies are available as data, but we use the notion of probability in analyzing or formulating instances of even types of behavior which are not susceptible to this analysis" (199). There are, of course, conceptions of probability not based directly on frequency, but I do not see how any of these apply to the cases that Skinner has in mind. I see no way of interpreting the quoted passage other than as signifying an intention to use the word *probability* in describing behavior quite independently of whether the notion of probability is at all relevant.

10. Fortunately, "In English this presents no great difficulty" since, for example, "relative pitch levels . . . are not . . . important" (25). No reference is made to the numerous studies of the function of relative pitch levels and other intonational features in English.

11. The vagueness of the word *tendency*, as opposed to *frequency*, saves the latter quotation from the obvious incorrectness of the former. Nevertheless, a good deal of stretching is necessary. If *tendency* has anything like its ordinary meaning, the remark is clearly false. One may believe strongly the assertion that Jupiter has four moons, that many of Sophocles' plays have been irretrievably lost, that the earth will burn to a crisp in ten million years, and so on, without experiencing the slightest

tendency to act upon these verbal stimuli. We may, of course, turn Skinner's assertion into a very unilluminating truth by defining "tendency to act" to include tendencies to answer questions in certain ways, under motivation to say what one believes is true.

12. One should add, however, that it is in general not the stimulus as such that is reinforcing, but the stimulus in a particular situational context. Depending on experimental arrangement, a particular physical event or object may be reinforcing, punishing, or unnoticed. Because Skinner limits himself to a particular, very simple experimental arrangement, it is not necessary for him to add this qualification, which would not be at all easy to formulate precisely. But it is of course necessary if he expects to extend his descriptive system to behavior in general.

13. This has been frequently noted.

14. See, for example, "Are Theories of Learning Necessary?", *op. cit.*, p. 199. Elsewhere, he suggests that the term *learning* be restricted to complex situations, but these are not characterized.

15. "A child acquires verbal behavior when relatively unpatterned vocalizations, selectively reinforced, gradually assume forms which produce appropriate consequences in a given verbal community" (31). "Differential reinforcement shapes up all verbal forms, and when a prior stimulus enters into the contingency, reinforcement is responsible for its resulting control. . . . The availability of behavior, its probability or strength, depends on whether reinforcements *continue* in effect and according to what schedules" (203-4); elsewhere, frequently.

16. Talk of schedules of reinforcement here is entirely pointless. How are we to decide, for example, according to what schedules covert reinforcement is *arranged*, as in thinking or verbal fantasy, or what the scheduling is of such factors as silence, speech, and appropriate future reactions to communicated information?

46. E.g., what are in fact the actual units of verbal behavior? Under what conditions will a physical event capture the attention (be a stimulus) or be a reinforcer? How do we decide what stimuli are in "control" in a specific case? When are stimuli "similar"? And so on. (It is not interesting to be told, e.g., that we

say *Stop* to an automobile or billiard ball because they are sufficiently similar to reinforcing people [46].)

The use of unanalyzed notions like *similar* and *generalization* is particularly disturbing, since it indicates an apparent lack of interest in every significant aspect of the learning or the use of language in new situations. No one has ever doubted that in some sense, language is learned by generalization, or that novel utterances and situations are in some way similar to familiar ones. The only matter of serious interest is the specific "similarity." Skinner has, apparently, no interest in this. Keller and Schoenfeld, *op. cit.*, proceed to incorporate these notions (which they identify) into their Skinnerian "modern objective psychology" by defining two stimuli to be similar when "we make the same sort of *response* to them" (124; but when are responses of the "same sort"?). They do not seem to notice that this definition converts their "principle of generalization" (116), under any reasonable interpretation of this, into a tautology. It is obvious that such a definition will not be of much help in the study of language learning or construction of new responses in appropriate situations.

47. "The Problem of Serial Order in Behavior," in L. A. Jeffress, ed., *Hixon Symposium on Cerebral Mechanisms in Behavior* (New York: John Wiley & Sons Inc., 1951). Reprinted in F. A. Beach, D. O. Hebb, C. T. Morgan, H. W. Nissen, eds., *The Neuropsychology of Lashley* (New York: McGraw-Hill Book Company, 1960). Page references are to the latter.

48. There is nothing essentially mysterious about this. Complex innate behavior patterns and innate "tendencies to learn in specific ways" have been carefully studied in lower organisms. Many psychologists have been inclined to believe that such biological structure will not have an important effect on acquisition of complex behavior in higher organisms, but I have not been able to find any serious justification for this attitude. Some recent studies have stressed the necessity for carefully analyzing the strategies available to the organism, regarded as a complex "information-processing system" (cf. J. S. Bruner, J. J. Goodnow, and G. A. Austin, *A Study of Thinking* [New York, 1956]; A. Newell, J. C. Shaw, and H. A. Simon, "Elements of a Theory of Human Problem Solving," *Psych. Rev.*, 65 [1958], 151-66), if anything significant is to be said about the character of human learning. These may be largely innate, or developed by early learning processes about which very little is yet known. (But see Harlow, "The Formation of Learning Sets," *Psych. Rev.*, 56 (1949), 51-65, and many later papers, where striking shifts in the character of learning are shown as a result of early training; also D. O. Hebb, *Organization of Behavior*, 109 ff.). They are undoubtedly quite complex. Cf. Lenneberg, *op. cit.*, and R. B. Lees, review of N. Chomsky's *Syntactic Structures* in *Language*, 33 (1957), 406f, for discussion of the topics mentioned in this section.

Part Two

Reductionism and Physicalism

Materialism without Reductionism: What Physicalism Does Not Entail

Richard Boyd

IN A RECENT WORK of substantial importance, Saul A. Kripke (1972) offers an alternative to the received accounts of reference, necessity, and essential properties. In a small section of the paper Kripke applies his account of necessity to certain traditional "essentialist" objections to mind-body identity—objections according to which mind and body cannot be identical because they have different essential properties. According to Kripke, standard materialist rebuttals to these

Copyright © 1980 by Richard Boyd. An early version of this paper was presented to the Philosophy Discussion Club of the Sage School of Philosophy at Cornell University. I am grateful for many helpful comments on that version, especially for the detailed comments of Carl Ginet and Norman Malcolm. I am indebted to a large number of other colleagues for helpful criticism and discussion of the positions defended here. I especially want to thank Rogers Albritton, Ned Block, Oswaldo Chateaubriand, Alex Goldstein, Barbara Koslowski, Norman Kretzmann, Richard Miller, Hilary Putnam, Sydney Shoemaker, Robert Stalnaker, Nicholas Sturgeon, and William Wimsatt. [Editor's note: This paper was solicited as a discussion of nonreductionist materialism and its relation to "essentialist" critiques of mind-body identity theses. The author kindly agreed to expand the paper to include an introduction to the central linguistic issues raised by materialism.]

objections rest on a mistaken account of essential properties. He suggests that, in fact, no rebuttal is possible.

In this paper I hope to accomplish two things. First, I intend to show that Kripke's discussion of reference and necessity constitutes a significant contribution to our understanding of the mind-body problem, not only because his account explicates better certain objections to materialism but also because something like Kripke's account of reference is required for a satisfactory defense of materialism. Second, I intend to show that the particular essentialist arguments Kripke directs against materialist theories of mind are, though ingenious, entirely unsuccessful.

1. "Essentialist" Objections to Materialism

A striking thing about materialist solutions to the mind-body problem is the strong and conflicting philosophical intuitions they seem to elicit. On the one hand, it has seemed to a great many philosophers and scientists that the doctrine that mental phenomena are really a species of the physical is an almost unavoidable conclusion in the light of the increasing success with which physical scientists

have explained complex biological phenomena. It seems to them overwhelmingly unlikely that physical explanations for
features of our mental life will not also be
forthcoming.[1] On the other hand, many
of the same thinkers, some of the time,
and a great many others, all of the time,
share the contrary intuition that it is absurd and incoherent (or, perhaps, even
mad) to assert that mental phenomena are
physical. Mental phenomena are simply
the wrong *kind* of thing to be physical;
they are *essentially* nonphysical.

At least since Descartes, such intuitions have been understood in terms of a
putative contrast between the essential
properties of mental and physical phenomena. Mental phenomena are said to
have as *essential* properties certain properties (like privacy or introspectability)
that are not possessed or, at any rate, are
not possessed *essentially* by physical phenomena; alternatively, physical phenomena are said to have certain *essential* properties (like spatial location or publicity)
that are not *essential* properties of mental
phenomena. It is sometimes maintained
that mental and physical phenomena have
contradictory essential properties (that
physical events are essentially spatial, for
instance, while mental events are essentially nonspatial). In all these cases, antimaterialist intuitions are understood as
intuitions that the properties that are logically possible (logically necessary, logically impossible) for mental phenomena are
different from those properties that are
logically possible (logically necessary,
logically impossible) for physical phenomena, and therefore that mental phenomena must not be physical. It might be
maintained, for example, that pain cannot
be a physical phenomenon, since it is logically possible for there to be pain without
matter, but logically impossible for there
to be any physical phenomenon without
matter.

2. The Standard Materialist Rebuttal

Against the objection that mental
and physical phenomena have different
essential properties, modern materialists
have typically replied along roughly the
following lines.

Materialism affirms that each mental
state (event, process) is identical to some
physical state (event, process); it affirms
identity statements like "Pain = C-fiber-
firings." Such identities are supposed to be
contingent rather than necessary identities;
they are supposed to be like "Water =
H_2O," which is a contingent identity statement reflecting an empirical discovery.

From such a contingent identity statement it does not follow that the identified
expressions have the same meaning. Water
is identical to H_2O even though the terms
"water" and "H_2O" have different meanings. From the identity "Water = H_2O," it
does follow, of course, that water and H_2O
have the same properties. However, a
property that is an essential property of
water *under the description "H_2O"* (like
containing hydrogen) need not be an essential property of water *under the description
"water."* Provided that the identity "Water
= H_2O" is only contingently true (that is,
that "water" and "H_2O" have different
meanings), it is quite unremarkable that
water and H_2O should have different essential properties (under these two different
descriptions). This state of affairs guaran-
tees that the identity "Water = H_2O" cannot be necessarily true, but it does not preclude its contingent truth.

Similarly, if "Pain = C-fiber-firings" is
a contingent identity statement, then it is
certainly unremarkable that pain should
have some property (such as, for example,
introspectability) essentially under the description "pain" but only contingently
under the description "C-fiber-firings." It is
part of the meaning of "pain" that pains are
introspectable, but not part of the meaning
of "C-fiber-firings" that C-fiber-firings are
introspectable. But this no more precludes
the possibility that pain is identical to C-

fiber-firings, than the fact that "water" and "H₂O" differ in meaning precludes the possibility that water is identical to H₂O. Contingent identity statements entail that the identified entities have the same properties, but (since essential properties are description-dependent) they do not entail that the identified entities have the same essential properties.²

Against the claim that mental and physical phenomena have contradictory essential properties, the typical materialist rebuttal involves insisting that a seemingly necessary statement is refutable, and is therefore actually contingent. Thus, for example, against the claim that mental phenomena are necessarily nonspatial, whereas spatial location is essential to physical phenomena, it is typically replied that we do not know a priori that mental phenomena lack definite spatial location and, consequently, that suitable experimental results could establish that thoughts, for instance, do have location in space. Lack of spatial location is thus shown (so the argument goes) to be at best a contingent property of thoughts, and the claim that thoughts have essential properties inconsistent with those of physical phenomena is thus refuted.

3. The Lockean Account of Essential Properties

The rebuttals just described depend crucially on an account of essential properties and logical necessity according to which logical necessity is always verbal necessity—that is, an account according to which necessarily true statements are just those whose truth follows from the meanings of their constituent terms. Such accounts have two important features. First, they entail that the essential properties of an entity are *relative to a description*, so that something may have a property essentially with respect to one description and contingently with respect to

another. Second, they entail that necessity and apriority coincide and thus that a statement may be shown to be contingent by showing that it is refutable. It is just these two consequences that are essential to the cogency of the standard materialist rebuttal to Cartesian criticisms of materialism.

Such accounts of necessity have been the received empiricist accounts ever since Locke, and such accounts rest upon an account of the meaning of natural kind terms that—in various versions—has been the standard empiricist account since its introduction by Locke.³ According to these empiricist accounts, the meaning of a natural kind term, or of general terms of any sort, is given by conventionally adopted criteria for telling which things fall under the term. According to such an account, for example, a term like "gold," "bachelor," "H₂O," "water," or "pain" would have *as its meaning* a set consisting of one or more properties by which gold, bachelors, H₂O, water, and pain are recognized. These properties are essential properties of gold, bachelor, H₂O, water, and pain just because they are part of the meanings of "gold," "bachelor," "H₂O," "water," "pain." Which properties should be grouped together to form the meaning of a general term is not a question of fact; it is entirely a matter of linguistic choice or decision that we associate one set of properties with each other as the meaning of a general term. ". . . our distinct species are nothing but complex ideas with distinct names attached to them"; ". . . Each abstract idea with a name to it makes a distinct species" (Locke, 1690, book III, chap. vi, secs. 8, 38).

Following Locke and Hume, the motivation for these accounts of necessity and of general terms has been antimetaphysical: the essence of a natural kind is said to consist of its "nominal essence," the conventional meaning of the term that describes it, precisely to rule out of court metaphysical questions about the real essence of natural kinds. Thus, for example, Locke holds that the question whether bats are birds is a purely verbal question (1690, book III, chap. xi, sec. 7). Bats are birds if and only if the criteria conventionally adopted for applying the term "bird" apply to bats. According to such a view, it would have been literally nonsense for a seventeenth-century biologist, living in a linguistic community that considered bats to be among the paradigm cases of birds, to claim to have discovered that bats really were not birds, that they lacked the essential features shared by other birds. He could propose to change the meaning of "bird" to *make it true* that bats did not fall under that term, but there is no such thing as a fundamental principle governing the application of a general term's being mistaken: such principles are true by definition and are the basis for all necessary truths about natural kinds.

Such empiricist positions regarding general terms and necessity, particularly in their modern (and most plausible) forms, derive their plausibility from verificationist considerations. Questions regarding the real essence of natural kinds are held to lie beyond the range of possible empirical investigation and thus to involve unscientific and pointless speculation. It is impossible, according to such a view, for us to know the real essence of anything.

4. The Importance of Non-Lockean Accounts of Language and Necessity

Such accounts of necessity *de dicto*—of necessity as resting on meaning and linguistic conventions—have been accepted by the great majority of recent authors on the mind-body problem. In particular, antimaterialists who find essentialist objections to materialist theories of mind convincing typically accept the analysis of necessity upon which the rebuttals cited rest, and attack those rebuttals on other

grounds. In many respects, however, a Lockean account of necessity and of essential properties seems inadequate for a full understanding both of the issues raised by the essentialist objections and of the position of materialists themselves.

Whatever their merit may ultimately be, the essentialist intuitions in question do not seem to be fairly captured by a Lockean account of essential properties. The views that physical events are essentially spatial, or that H_2O contains hydrogen essentially, or that consciousness is an essential feature of the experience of pain, do not—at first glance anyway—seem to be judgments about meanings or linguistic usage. The philosopher to whom it seems obvious that—whatever the atomic components of water may be—these components are *essential* to water—seems, at least at first glance, to hold a position about the substance of water *itself*, not about water under some particular description ("H_2O"). Water just *is* H_2O, no matter how it is described; being H_2O is *its* essence—so the intuition goes—not merely the essence of the linguistic expression "H_2O".

If, as Kripke maintains, an account of necessity that justifies these judgments is available, then it will not merely better reflect the intuitions of antimaterialists. It will, as well, effectively disarm the standard materialist rebuttals to their essentialist objections. For, if the intuitions indicated above can be made coherent, we would have an account of necessity *de re* (not *de dicto*): an account according to which the essential properties of a thing do not depend on a particular description of it. Such an account of necessity would also preclude the strategy of showing that a statement is not necessary by showing that it represents an empirical claim that is refutable. The claim that water contains hydrogen is certainly a refutable empirical claim, but—on a *de re* account of necessity—it might be a necessary truth as well.

It is clear, therefore, that if (as, of

course, many philosophers doubt) a coherent account of necessity *de re* can be successfully defended, such an account would provide the basis for a more faithful formulation of essentialist objections to materialism than does a Lockean account. What is equally true—but less obvious—is that a Lockean account of necessity and of general terms poses difficulties for materialists as well as for their opponents. This claim may seem strange. After all, materialists typically insist that the entire body of materialist doctrines concerning mental phenomena (and other phenomena as well) are contingent empirical truths. The materialist, it seems, need not affirm that any of his doctrines are necessary truths; his interest in necessity is solely in rebutting essentialist objections to materialism and for that purpose the Lockean account of necessity is ideal.

The difficulty that the Lockean account poses arises not because materialists must defend their doctrines as necessary truths (although, as we shall see, Kripke believes that they must), but rather because the antimetaphysical philosophy of language—and, in particular, the account of natural kind terms—upon which the Lockean account rests, itself poses difficulties to the defender of materialism.

It is a crucial feature of empiricist accounts of language that questions regarding the classification of entities under general terms are always questions regarding *existing* linguistic *conventions*. The question whether a particular entity falls under a general term is nothing more than the question whether its properties satisfy the criteria conventionally associated with the term. What is *not* possible, according to this account, is that some entity should lack the criterial properties associated with a term by current convention, but be properly classified under that term nevertheless. It might seem that such a state of affairs is possible: the entity might possess qualities really essential to the kind referred to by the general term,

but might lack the properties by which the kind is generally identified. But this possibility is just what the Lockean account of general terms precludes. Only the nominal essence of the term is at issue in classification. We do not—because we cannot—classify things according to their own real essences or according to the real essences of the species into which they fall.[4]

In a similar way, relations of containment and identity between natural kinds turn out to be matters of current convention. The question whether two general terms name the same property, substance, or state, is merely the question whether these two terms are conventionally associated with the same criterial properties (or, perhaps with sets of criterial properties between which there is a relation of mutual meaning-entailment). It is not possible, according to a Lockean account, for two general terms with different nominal essences to refer to what is really the same property, substance, or state. If general terms referred to real essences, of course, such a situation could obtain, but since only nominal essences are involved, "each abstract idea with a name to it makes a distinct species" (Locke, 1690, book III, chap. vi, sec. 38).

The upshot of all this is that a Lockean account of necessity—and the account of general terms upon which it rests—has the effect of enshrining the *status quo* in matters of classification: it portrays the most basic standards that we employ in applying general terms as fixed by linguistic convention and immune from refutation. There is simply no such thing as discovering that our fundamental standards of classifications are wrong. We can change standards, of course (by changing the meanings of our terms). It can, perhaps, even be rational to do so—but the rationality cannot be the rationality of correcting a mistaken belief in the face of new evidence.[5]

It will now be evident why a Lockean account of general terms poses such an acute challenge to materialism. A Lockean account of meaning enshrines our most fundamental principles of classification as definitional truths not amenable to revision. Dualism—and the principles of classification that traditional dualism supports—are among the most entrenched of our classificatory principles. Thus a Lockean materialist runs the risk of having to hold (because of his philosophy of language) that, for instance, the statement that pains are physical states of the central nervous system is not merely false but self-contradictory. After all, pains are among the paradigm cases of states that we now classify as nonphysical; if there are classificatory conventions at all (and the Lockean account insists that there are), then surely it must be a truth by convention that pains are nonphysical.

What is ruled out, it must be remembered, by a Lockean account of general terms—and by the associated empiricist epistemological outlook—is the view that, although we do not now classify pains as physical, nevertheless pain poses the same essential features as do paradigmatically physical states, and we could eventually discover that they are really physical. According to a Lockean analysis, all there is —or could be—to being physical is having the properties conventionally taken to be marks of the physical.

The view that a Lockean account of general terms, together with certain commonplace facts about current usage, is logically incompatible with materialism is not, of course, held by materialists who accept a basically Lockean account of general terms. It does not even appear to be defended—in exactly the terms presented above—by any critic of materialism. Nevertheless, closely related objections to materialism do occur in the literature, and —what is even more important to the current issue—many materialists modify their accounts of materialism to accommodate them to a Lockean account of general terms and, in doing so, substantially weaken their own position.

Thus, for example, as we have seen, many materialists (and many of their critics) hold that materialism is committed to the truth of identity statements of the form "$M = P$" where "M" is a general term of classification for mental states ("M" might be "pain") and "P" is some general description of a physical state, couched in obviously physical (or physiological) terms ("P" might be, for example, "The firing of C-fibers," to use a now standard imaginary example). (It will be recalled that it is just statements of this sort that play so prominent a role in the essentialist objections I am considering.)

It is conceded by materialists—in fact they typically insist on it—that "M" and "P" here have different meanings, and are associated with different criteria. The identity is supposed to be contingent, not a priori. But, according to a Lockean account of general terms, this is just the sort of identity statement that cannot be true. Each distinct set of criteria—each distinct "meaning"—gives rise to a distinct species. If "M" and "P" are general terms, different in meaning, then, it would appear, the statement "$M = P$" is necessarily false! Now, this potential criticism of materialism is—in various guises—seriously treated in the literature. Many materialist authors are at pains to insist that contingent, non-a priori identity statements are sometimes true and known to be true. "Water = H_2O" is, indeed, the standard example.

Of course, the fact that it is possible to be a materialist, a Lockean about general terms, and a believer that water is contingently identical to H_2O does not show that it is possible to hold all these views consistently. The tension between them is revealed in the writings of recent materialists not by the admission that they are inconsistent, but rather by a special sort of exegesis offered for contingent identity statements like "Water = H_2O," "Pain = C-fiber firings." Such identities, "theoretical identities" they are sometimes called, are not, strictly speaking, the ordinary garden-variety identities—so this sort of account goes.[6] When, for theoretical reasons, we *identify* two terms whose ordinary rules of usage are so different, it is not strict identity we are talking about. For example, it does not follow from the theoretical identification of pain with C-fiber firings and from the fact that some pains feel vaguely cold, that some C-fiber firings feel vaguely cold.

Although proponents of this view are not always clear about the matter, their treatment of the "identity theses" really amounts to this: we do not ask, for example, "Are pains identical to C-fiber firings?"[7] The answer to that question is "No," and the negative answer is dictated by linguistic convention. We ask instead, "Would it be reasonable, in the light of current scientific discoveries, to change our conventions so that we *can* say, 'Pain = the firing of C-fibers' without fear of self-contradiction?" This is the real issue of "theoretical identification." It is revealing that the verb for "to identify with" is so often employed in discussions of this view. We are really seen as facing the question whether or not *we* should identify pain with C-fiber firings, that is, whether or not we should adopt a new linguistic *convention*, to *identify* the expressions "pain" and "C-fiber firing." The issue is one of *linguistic choice*.[8] In treating the issue this way, modern materialists continue the Lockean tradition of treating disputes over classification as "purely verbal" rather than as factual. In positivist terminology, they treat the issue whether pains are C-fiber firings as the issue whether or not to *adopt* the "meaning convention" expressed by the axiom "Pain = C-fiber firing."

Although the practice of treating ontological issues as though they were issues of free linguistic choice, thus reformulating them as issues expressible in the "formal mode of speech," has an honorable history,[9] the fact remains that such a gloss on materialism fundamentally distorts its claims. For better or worse, the materialist claims that mental states, events, and processes are really physical. He does not claim *merely* that we could *adopt the convention* of saying that they are. He claims they are already, anyway! If he says that pain is identical to C-fiber firings, he means it. He does not mean that *we* could *identify* the one *term* with the other *term* —he does not even mean that it would be rational to *adopt* such a *convention*. He certainly does not mean that, even though it is analytically false that pains are C-fiber firings, it would be convenient to change the meanings of our terms to *make* it true. What he means—for better or worse—is that pains simply *are* C-fiber firings. In his view it could, of course, be rational and (probably) convenient to say "Pain = C-fiber firings," but the rationality involved would be the rationality of accepting an important discovery in the light of new evidence, not the pragmatic rationality of *adopting* a simpler language. A "Lockean" gloss makes materialism into a mere shadow of its former self.

Worse things yet happen. As we have seen, one of those problems that face materialists is that there seem to be properties that physical states possess and mental states essentially lack, or vice versa. Thus physical states possess special locations, whereas mental states may seem to be essentially nonspatial. Similarly, some thoughts are dim, fading, or nagging,[10] whereas it would seem that physical states essentially lack these properties. How is the materialist to deal with these difficulties? The "standard rebuttal" discussed in section 2 replies that, for example, it is not a necessary truth that brain states lack the property naggingness and that this can be seen by realizing that suitable experimental results (presumably those which confirm a materialist theory of mind) could show that some brain states *are* nagging, however queer that may now sound. Similarly, this rebuttal requires a defense of the claim that we could discover that, for instance, thoughts are located in the head, however queer that may sound.

As we have seen, such rebuttals depend for their cogency on a Lockean account of necessity. They proceed to establish that a statement is not necessary by demonstrating that it is not a priori. What several defenders of materialism have recognized is that this rebuttal seems to run afoul of the very Lockean account of general terms on which it rests. If there is a problem about attributing nagginess to brain states or location to thoughts, then the problem arises because such attributions are linguistically deviant enough to be counted as violating current rules of linguistic usage. If—as the Lockean account requires—there are linguistic conventions governing general terms like "has location" or "is nagging," then linguistic normalcy and linguistic deviance must be reflections of *just those conventions*. So, there is a philosophical problem about predicating location of thoughts or nagginess of brain states if and only if such predications *violate conventions of language*, that is, if and only if the denials of such predications are, after all, really a priori, and the standard rebuttal, therefore, unsuccessful. The rebuttal works only if it is not needed.[11]

As a substitute, many defenders of materialism have made proposals that emphasize their (perhaps unintentional) commitment to the view that the issue of materialism is (at least substantially) a question of *linguistic decision*. Thus, for example, Shaffer (1961) suggests that it would be reasonable to *change* our conventions so as to *allow* predicating location of thoughts, and Feyerabend (1963) urges that materialists recognize that they are committed to proposing such meaning

changes in order to avoid a "dualism of features."

Where materialists ought to say that since mental events *are* physical events, they certainly *do* have locations in space, these philosophers are led by their Lockean conception of general terms to assert merely that we could *decide* to change the language to *make* materialism true. But this retreat to conventionalism is not by any means the most heroic measure taken by defenders of materialism who find themselves in this Lockean bind. Rorty (1965) concerns himself with the problem of predicating mental properties like nagginess of brain processes, which seems unavoidable if one acknowledges that some thoughts are nagging and also insists that each thought is identical to a brain process. His solution is to treat the relevant identity statements, those of the form "$M = P$" where "M" is a mental term and "P" a physical term, as expressing a "disappearance" form of the identity thesis. In this view, such expressions do not express ordinary identity, but rather express identity between "to put it crudely —existent entities and non-existent entities." The statement "My thought at $t =$ brain state B" really says that there is no such thing as my thought at t but that brain state B is what we should talk about instead. Since there are no thoughts—and hence no nagging thoughts—the problem of predicating nagginess of brain state does not arise. And, similarly, for other difficult cases of mental-physical identity.

Although ingenious, this cure may be worse than the disease. It places our materialist in the unenviable position of denying that there are thoughts, pains, feelings of joy or anguish, and so forth. It places him in an essentially untenable position. It must be pointed out that not all materialists whose philosophy of language is empiricist advocate these particular positions. Indeed, some do not even recognize the difficulties that their account of language poses to their materialism. What is important is that it *does* pose such problems and that the available solutions (within a Lockean framework) all weaken the claims of materialists to the point that their doctrine is either untenable or not very interesting.

We have, therefore, a very interesting situation. *Both sides* in the dispute between materialists and "essentialist" dualists seem to be misrepresented if their positions are explicated in terms of a Lockean account of general terms. The materialists' position is trivialized and the essentialists' intuitions regarding necessity seem altogether misunderstood. It is for this reason that Kripke's efforts to find an alternative account of reference and necessity—and to apply it to the mind-body problem—is of such great importance for philosophy of mind.

5. "Rigid Designators" and Kripke's Account of Necessity

Kripke's discussion of materialism, with which we are primarily concerned in this essay, takes only eight of the ninety pages that constitute his development of a theory of necessity. Although it will be necessary here to provide a broad outline of the main features of Kripke's theory, I am not going to attempt to summarize all of the important aspects of its development, nor am I going to adopt a position regarding its soundness. What I do intend to show is that, assuming Kripke's account of necessity to be sound, his criticisms of materialism are not successful. I shall also indicate why the sort of account of reference that forms the foundation for his account of necessity is crucial to the defense of materialism. Although Kripke's account of necessity touches the issue of materialism primarily with respect to the issue of essential properties of natural kinds, and that of the way in which natural kind terms function in language, his exposition of necessity begins with a treatment of proper names. Since his doctrines are clearest with respect to this issue, I shall begin there, too.

Consider the question how proper names (of people, countries, towns, and so on) refer. In certain situations, when someone uses the word "Moses," by his use of the name "Moses" he refers to the leader of the Israelite exodus. Other uses of the name "Moses" refer to other men, as when someone now says, "My neighbor, Moses, is on vacation in Vienna." Many people are, or have been, named "Moses." What is it, about, for instance, a use of the term "Moses" that *does* refer to the Israelite leader that makes it refer to him and not to someone else, or no one at all?

One influential answer (defended in various forms by both Gottlob Frege and Bertrand Russell) is closely analogous to a Lockean account of general terms. In this view, proper names like "Moses" (or any other proper name) are "disguised definite descriptions"; when someone uses a proper name, he means by the name some description or other that (if the utterance in question refers at all) holds of one and only one person. Thus, for example, if I use the name "Quine" in saying "Quine's attack on analyticity was crucial to the development of early postpositivist philosophy of science," my use of the term "Quine" refers to the philosopher at Harvard of that name because I use the name "Quine" as shorthand for some definite description of him, for example, "the philosopher who teaches at Harvard and who is the author of 'Two Dogmas of Empiricism.' " My use of the name "Quine" refers to the Quine at Harvard just because the definite description in question is true only of him. My success in communicating to a listener, in this case, depends, somehow, on a recognition of the fact that it is this (or roughly this) definite description that I have in mind (rather than, perhaps, "the man who owns the bakery on Seventh Street and Feigl Avenue"). The man who says "Quine makes good cream puffs," and refers to Quine the baker, does so because he uses "Quine" as shorthand for just such an alternative definite description.

In the case of most proper names, it is not entirely clear just how—on this theory's account—the listeners come to understand a definite description relevantly like that intended by the speaker. In the case of historical figures like Moses, however, the solution is easier. On most "disguised definite description" accounts of such names there is a general linguistic convention that associates the term "Moses" (at least when it is used in discussing biblical history) with a definite set, or, perhaps, a "cluster" of the most important properties by which historians recognize him: male, Israelite leader, lived for a while in Egypt, led the exodus, died in Canaan, and so on. It is, according to these views, a matter of *linguistic convention* that the name "Moses" (used in the right sort of contexts) refers if and only if there is one person who has all (or, in some versions, most) of these properties. If there is such a person, "Moses" refers to him. The similarity between this sort of account and Lockean accounts of general terms is obvious. Like the Lockean account of general terms, this Russellian account of proper names has the consequence that necessity and apriority coincide with respect to certain statements involving proper names. Thus, Moses has a property essentially if and only if that property is entailed by the properties that make up the "definition" of the name "Moses." It is logically possible that Moses had brown hair (or that he had red hair) because his hair color is not mentioned in the definition of "Moses," whereas it is necessarily true (and a priori) that if there was a Moses he performed all (or, by some accounts, most) of the historical acts attributed to him in the definition. Likewise, it is logically impossible, and a priori refutable, that Moses should have

been, for instance, an officer in the Egyptian army who opposed the exodus.

Aside from any other difficulties that it may face, such an account of proper names has some provocative consequences regarding the essential properties of people. It is not surprising that Moses is not essentially brown-haired. What may seem counterintuitive is that it is both true and known a priori that there could be no possible world in which Moses sought and received a commission in the Egyptian army, became an opponent of the exodus, and died in Thebes. We have strong intuitions that such a state of affairs is logically possible, and that empirical evidence forms the only basis for our acceptance of the account that we actually believe.

Against the Russellian account of proper names—and in defense of these central intuitions—Kripke offers an alternative "causal" theory of reference for proper names. On the Russellian view, a proper name is associated with exactly the same "cluster" of defining properties in every possible world (and refers to their unique bearer, if there is one). On Kripke's view, a proper name should be seen as referring to exactly the same *individual* in every possible world in which it refers at all, whatever properties the individual may have in that world. In his view, my employment of the name "Moses" refers to Moses not because I am participating in a linguistic convention that associates with the term "Moses" some definite description, but rather because my employment of that name bears the right sort of causal connection to the historical events surrounding the giving of the name "Moses" (or whatever name it is from which the name "Moses" derives) to the man Moses. When I use the name "Moses" I, in effect, "point" back in time toward the relevant first employments of the name, and I refer to whatever was named "Moses" in these initial "dubbing" uses of the name. In this respect—according to Kripke's account—my referring to Moses by the term "Moses" is more like ostensive reference—reference by pointing, for example—than it is like referring via a definite description. Similarly, when I use the name "Moses" to refer instead to Moses the literature teacher down the hall, I refer to him rather than to the historical figure not because I use his name as a disguised definite description but because my use of the name "Moses" bears the appropriate, causal relation to, for example, the events surrounding his parents' naming him "Moses," and my use of the name does not bear the right causal relation to the "dubbing" of the Israelite Moses. Certain social and linguistic conventions are involved in our use of names, no doubt. But, Kripke maintains, whatever conventionality is involved in naming, it does not result in statements about people that are true by definition.

It might seem that, according to this account, Moses, for instance, would have no nontrivial essential properties (that is, no essential properties except those that are dictated by principles of formal logic like being either living or nonliving). Indeed, such a view is compatible with the account of reference for proper names just presented. Kripke maintains, however, the plausible view that a person's parents are essential to him: that a man who, in some possible world, had different parents from those Moses had in the actual world, would not *be* Moses, whatever other properties he had. Although his account of proper names does not entail it, it does make possible such an account of description-independent (*de re*) essential properties of persons.

Here we can also see how Kripke's account of reference and necessity makes necessity and apriority distinct. Suppose that Moses' parents were Philip and Samantha. Then it would be a *necessary* truth (it would be true in all possible worlds in which Moses exists) that Moses'

parents were Philip and Samantha; and this sort of necessity obtains in the case of every person and his/her parents. But, of course, we do not know a priori who someone's parents are; it is not part of the *meaning* of the name "Moses" that Moses' parents were Philip and Samantha. Thus, "Moses' parents were Philip and Samantha," if true, is an a posteriori (indeed, a refutable) necessary truth.

Thus Kripke's account of reference and necessity (which I have examined so far only with respect to clear-cut cases of proper names) provides for the existence of a posteriori necessary truths. At least in the case of proper names, it shows how a necessary truth might be unknown to us (as when we do not know who the parents of a historical figure were) and even contrary to our most fundamental convictions (as when we are *very* sure we have correctly identified the parents of a historical figure, but we are wrong). An illustrative example of the sort of a posteriori necessary truth that plays a role in Kripke's revitalized essentialist objections to physicalism is provided by the identity statement "Cicero = Tully." Suppose that there is a man who was called "Cicero" and also called "Tully"—that each of these proper names was "given" to him. Suppose I say "Cicero is identical to Tully," and that the causal antecedents of my usages of the names "Cicero" and "Tully" are such that each of them refers to this man. Then in any possible world the referent of the terms "Cicero" and "Tully" is *that very man*, and the statement "Cicero = Tully" is, therefore, a necessary truth: it is true in every possible world in which its constituent terms refer.

For our purposes, the interest of Kripke's work arises from the extension of his account of proper names to certain other referring expressions. Kripke introduces the expression "rigid designator" for those terms that, like proper names, refer to the same thing in every possible world in which they refer at all. Kripke suggests that various natural kind terms and terms for natural phenomena are also rigid designators, for instance, "gold," "water," "heat," "hydrogen," "pain," and so forth. Kripke denies the standard Lockean account according to which the reference of these terms is fixed by criterial attributes or defining characteristics that are "part of the meaning" of these terms. Thus, for example, a Lockean might offer an analysis of the term "heat" according to which the property by which "heat" is defined is the capacity to make us feel warm. "Heat" might be said to mean "that natural phenomenon that is present in all things that make us feel warm and that causes them to make us feel warm" or something of this sort. According to a view of this sort, the statement "Heat makes (most) people feel warm" would be both a priori and (therefore) *necessary.*

In Kripke's view, however, there is no difficulty in accepting the claim that there is a possible world in which, for instance, no animals ever developed a sensitivity to heat and in which heat produces no sensation at all in any person. Heat need not possess the analytic definition "that which warms us," *nor any other analytic definition at all.* As is the case with proper names, there may well have been some particular sensible characteristics by which people recognized heat when they first started calling it "heat"—just as there may have been some particular description by which Moses' parents referred to him when they named him "Moses," but these are not defining criteria for "heat" established by linguistic convention. Heat might come to lack these characteristics, or—in some possible world—might never have had them.

Of equal importance (from our point of view), the fact that "heat" possesses no analytic definition makes certain fundamental beliefs of ours about heat—which a Lockean might believe to be true by convention—refutable in principle. Thus, for example, there would be no logical impossibility to our discovering that there were kinds of heat that, although quite intense, produced no sensation in us at all. It will be appreciated that this sort of treatment of natural kind terms represents just the sort of non-Lockean view of these terms required by the materialist who wishes to say, without self-contradiction, that certain of our most basic principles of classification associated with the terms "mental" and "physical" are (and will be shown to be) fundamentally mistaken.[12]

If rigid designators are just those terms that have the very same referent in every possible world in which they refer at all, then, it must be noticed, *some* rigid designators *may be* definite descriptions. Suppose (as is plausible) that "hydrogen" and "oxygen" are rigid designators. Consider the expression "H_2O." It is reasonable to hold that "H_2O" *means* "the compound whose molecules consist of two hydrogen atoms and one oxygen atom." Thus it is a definite description. But, since the terms "hydrogen" and "oxygen" are both rigid designators, the description "the compound whose molecules consist of two hydrogen atoms and one oxygen atom" refers to exactly the same compound in every possible world in which it refers at all. Thus, by this analysis of its meaning, "H_2O" is a rigid designator.

6. Rigid Designators and Surprisingly Necessary Identities

"Cicero = Tully," it will be recalled, is necessary if true, and this is the case for all identities of the same form involving proper names. Evidently the same is true of all identities in which the identity sign is flanked by rigid designators.

This consequence of Kripke's theory has, itself, some surprising consequences. As we have seen, philosophers who defend materialist theories of mind, and are looking for noncontroversial examples of identity statements between natural kinds, often cite the identity "Water = H_2O" as an especially clear example. Of course, "Water = H_2O" is not an a priori truth, so, if apriority and necessity coincide (as empiricists claim), it is not necessary either. But according to Kripke's account, if, *in the actual world*, water really is identical to H_2O, then this identity is necessary: it holds in every possible world in which water (or H_2O) exists. Water, if it *is* H_2O, is H_2O *essentially*. Similarly, every chemical compound, whatever atomic constitution it has, has that constitution essentially, even if its constitution is not merely not known a priori, but not known at all. Likewise, if heat is identical to molecular vibrational kinetic energy (another standard example of an a posteriori, "contingent" identity), then heat is *essentially* molecular vibrational kinetic energy. All of these examples—if Kripke's account is sound—are cases in which a substance or natural phenomenon has an essential property independently of any linguistic convention *or choice of description*.

Furthermore, all of these are cases of a posteriori, *refutable* necessary truths; they provide concrete illustrations of the fact that Kripke's account of necessity—because it does not rest on a Lockean account of language—divorces apriority from necessity. In particular, they show how Kripke's account of necessity blocks any attempt to show that a statement is not necessary that proceeds by showing that it is refutable.

These features of Kripke's account—it will be recognized—make it (at least apparently) more suitable than the Lockean account for the defense of the essentialist arguments against materialism that I have been considering. Kripke's account treats essential properties of things as description-independent (thereby blocking one feature of standard materialist rebuttal) and allows for a posteriori but necessary truths (thus blocking the other). It accords with the intuition that a substance itself may have its constituents as essential features—because without just those con-stituents it would not exist—even though the features are not specified in some analytic definition of a term referring to the substance. Thus, just as Kripke's sketch of a non-Lockean account of reference is particularly well suited to a faithful exegesis of materialist theories of mind, the corresponding account of necessity seems particularly well suited to a faithful exegesis of essentialist criticisms of those theories.

7. Essentialist Criticisms Revisited

It remains to be seen what the force of essentialist criticisms of materialism is, if they are understood according to Kripke's non-Lockean account of necessity and are, therefore, invulnerable to the standard materialist rebuttals. In order to see what the force of such criticisms is, let us first consider the case of a less controversial "theoretical" identity: "Water is H_2O."

Imagine a defender of this water/hydrogen oxide "identity thesis," who describes his position according to the standard analysis offered by materialists. He maintains that, although "water" and "H_2O" differ in meaning, the identity "Water = H_2O" is nevertheless an empirical discovery and an example of a *purely contingent* identity statement. On Kripke's account of necessity, our "identity theorist" has already adopted an untenable position. "Water" and "H_2O" are rigid designators. Therefore the identity "Water = H_2O," if it is true at all, must be a *necessary* truth. It *cannot* be contingently true. Thus the "identity theorist" must retract the claim that his identity thesis is contingent. He must live with—and, more important, he must defend—the claim that water is *essentially* H_2O, if he is to claim that water *is* H_2O at all.

This consequence of the identity "Water = H_2O" has, itself, additional consequences with which the "identity theorist" must live. The expression "H_2O" is not just a rigid designator. It is also what might be called a composition-specifying term (this terminology is not Kripke's). Whatever is H_2O must—in any possible world—be made of hydrogen and oxygen. If "Water = H_2O" is true in the actual world—and hence in all possible worlds—it then follows that having the particular molecular composition specified by "H_2O" is an *essential* feature of water. The identity theorist must, therefore, defend this claim. He must, for example, be prepared to deny the seemingly plausible claim that there is a possible world in which water does not have a molecular structure at all, because matter in that world is continuous and does not have a discrete microstructure. Similarly, the defender of the "theoretical" identity "Heat = molecular vibrational kinetic energy" must hold that there is no possible world in which heat is not, for instance, dependent on molecular motions. A possible world in which matter has no molecular microstructure is *ipso facto* a world in which *there is no heat!*

It should be emphasized that defending these claims is by no means the hopeless task that it would be if one adopted a Lockean account of necessity. Part of the point of Kripke's account is that necessary truths need not be a priori. Thus the defender of these "identity theses" does not face the hopeless task of trying, for example, to show that being made of molecules is "part of the meaning" of the word "water." The identity theorist does, however, face an important essentialist challenge: in taking the identity statements "Water = H_2O" and "Heat = molecular vibrational kinetic energy" to be contingent, rather than necessary, our "identity theorist" was not merely following current fashion. We (or, at any rate, many of those who consider such issues) have strong intuitions that, for example, water is only contingently identical to H_2O or that there could be heat in a possible world in which heat lacks a molecular microstructure. The identity theorist must provide us with

sufficiently good reasons for rejecting these strong philosophical intuitions.

The same challenge, of course, faces the materialist regarding his account of mental phenomena. If, for example, he claims that some identity statement like "Pain = C-fiber firings" is true, then he must claim that it is necessarily true. Since "C-fiber firings" is a composition-specifying term that names a kind of physical phenomenon, he must defend, for example, the claim that there could be no pains in any possible world in which there is no matter (indeed, there could only be pain in possible worlds in which matter is organized into C-fibers that fire). Similarly, he must defend the claim that it is impossible for there to be a world in which some C-fibers fire without a pain's being felt. In these cases, the identity theorist's claims run afoul of very strong philosophical intuitions indeed. As we shall see, Kripke's view is that—while the defenders of "Water = H_2O" and "Heat = molecular vibrational kinetic energy" can overcome these difficulties—mind-brain identity theorists cannot.

8. The Standard Materialist Rebuttal (New Version)

Each of the "identity theses," "Water = H_2O," "Heat = molecular vibrational kinetic energy," "Pain = C-fiber firings," faces, at the outset, the same essentialist challenges: each asserts the identity of entities that appear to have different essential properties. The standard materialist rebuttals, which we examined earlier, depend on a Lockean account of necessity: on the doctrine that the essential properties of a thing are description-dependent, and on the doctrine that refutable statements cannot be necessarily true.

If Kripke's account of necessity and essential properties is correct, these rebuttals are ruled out. The identity theorist must hold that the identities in question represent a posteriori *necessary* truths and that the identified entities do have (description-independently) the same essential properties. It remains then for the identity theorist to undermine philosophical criticisms of these views—to explain away the tendency to hold, for example, that water is only contingently H_2O or that heat might, in some possible world, be a nonmolecular fluid.

In order to show how this may be done, Kripke introduces what we may think of as the standard strategy for explaining away the apparent contingency of necessary a posteriori statements. The strategy involves finding a genuinely contingent statement that corresponds in the right way to the apparently contingent necessary statement, and attributing the apparent contingency of the second to the recognition of the actual contingency of the first. An example will make the strategy clear.

In the case of the apparently contingent (but necessary) identity statement "Water = H_2O," the corresponding contingent statement might be "The cooling, tasteless, odorless, wetting liquid that quenches thirst = H_2O." This statement *is* contingent, since there could be a possible world in which some other liquid than water satisfies the definite description on the left of the identity sign. The contingency of this statement, furthermore, can be adduced to explain the apparent contingency of "Water = H_2O." The definite description "the cooling, tasteless . . ." is true of water in the actual world, and is chosen so that it describes water in terms of the properties by which it is usually recognized. If a Lockean account of terms like "water" were true, this definite description would be a candidate for the definition of "water," and would refer to water in every possible world. The intuition that "Water = H_2O" is contingent is explained as resulting from the correct judgment that the corresponding contingent sentence is contingent, together with

the mistaken belief that the definite description in it is the definition of "water" and refers to water in every possible world.

In general, in the case where the apparently contingent but necessary statement is an identity statement involving rigid designators, "$R_1 = R_2$," this strategy requires that one find referring expressions "D_1" and "D_2" such that, in the actual world, "D_1" and "D_2" are coreferential with "R_1" and "R_2," but where at least one of "D_1" and "D_2" is a nonrigid designator that describes the properties that, in the actual world, are appropriate to the detection of the referent of the corresponding rigid designator. "$D_1 = D_2$" will be contingent and its contingency will (together with a mistaken Lockean account of the rigid designators "R_1" and "R_2") explain the apparent contingency of "$R_1 = R_2$."

In the case of apparently contingent necessary statements that are not identities, the strategy is similar. The defender of the identity statement "Heat = molecular vibrational kinetic energy" must maintain that it is a necessary truth that if there is heat, there are molecules present. The intuition that this is a merely contingent statement can be explained by adducing the corresponding genuinely contingent statement "If there is a natural phenomenon whose presence makes us feel warm, then there are molecules present." As before, the contingency of this statement, coupled with the mistaken belief that "the natural phenomenon whose presence makes us feel warm" is the definition of the term "heat" explain the apparent contingency of the necessary truth in question. In all of these cases, the apparent contingency of an a posteriori necessary statement is explained by finding a corresponding genuinely contingent statement in which one or more rigid designators are replaced by qualitative descriptions of the sort a Lockean would offer as analyses of the meaning of the rigid designators in question. What Kripke suggests is that this standard rebuttal does not work in the case of the necessary-if-true statements to which a materialist theory of mind is committed.

9. Kripke's Argument against Materialism

According to the strategy of the standard materialist rebuttal (new version), the apparent contingency of a necessary a posteriori statement "S" is explained by finding a corresponding genuinely contingent statement "S*" in which (at least typically) one or more rigid designators occurring in "S" are replaced by definite descriptions in terms of sensible properties. In every possible world these descriptions refer (if they refer at all) to some thing or property that has in that world the same sensible properties that the rigidly designated thing or property has in the actual world. In any possible world we would be in an "appropriate qualitatively identical evidential situation" with respect to the referents of these descriptions, as we are in the actual world with respect to the referents of the rigid designators. Kripke's claim that the standard strategy fails for statements that follow from a materialist account of mental phenomena rests on the (very plausible) claim that certain mental states have as essential properties the way they feel. In any possible world, something that feels like a pain is a pain, and no pain fails to feel painful. If, in some world W, someone bears to an entity e a relation qualitatively identical to the relation we bear, in the actual world, to a pain, then e is a pain in W.

Consider, now, the materialist who defends a type-type version of the identity thesis. He holds, let us say, that each mental state is identical to a physical state of the central nervous system. In particular, he holds that pain is identical to a physical state of the central nervous system. Let us assume that the state of the central ner-

vous system in question is the firing of the mythical "C-fibers." Our materialist, then, defends the identity "Pain = C-fiber firing." If he is a typical materialist (and has not read Kripke) he will explain that this is a contingent identity statement. He will agree with the Cartesian intuition that it is logically possible that there might be C-fiber firings but no felt pain, and that it is logically possible that someone might experience a pain even though there are no C-fibers (and no other material objects, for that matter). These logical possibilities would be excluded—he will maintain—if "Pain = C-fiber firings" were a necessary identity; but it is a posteriori and hence contingent.

Of course, this position is one that Kripke's account of necessity (if it is sound, as we assume here) rules out. "Pain" and "C-fiber firings" are rigid designators of natural kinds and, therefore, "Pain = C-fiber firings" is necessary if true. The "essentialist" challenge to the materialist is to explain its apparent contingency. What he must explain, for example, are the intuitions that there is a possible world in which there are pains but no C-fiber firings and that there is a possible world in which there are C-fiber firings but no one feels any painful sensation.

This is just what Kripke says cannot be done. In the case of the identity "Water = H_2O," the corresponding problem is to explain the intuitions (a) that there is a possible world in which there is water but no H_2O, and (b) that there is a possible world in which there is H_2O but no water. The problem is soluble. To solve it, all we need to establish is that there are possible worlds W_1 and W_2 such that (a) in W_1, there is a liquid that is not H_2O but that has all the qualitative properties water possesses in the actual world and (b) in W_2, H_2O exists but fails to have the qualitative properties by which we detect water in the actual world. But, of course, it is quite reasonable to insist that such possible worlds as W_1 and W_2 exist while maintaining that "Water = H_2O" is true in every possible world.

In the case of the identity "Pain = C-fiber firings," we might expect analogous maneuvers to provide us with explanations for the intuitions (a) that there is a possible world in which there are pains but no C-fiber firings and (b) that there is a possible world in which there are C-fiber firings but no pains. By analogy to the case of "Water = H_2O," we might expect to explain these intuitions by finding possible worlds W_1^* and W_2^* such that (a) in W_1^* there are entities that have the sensible properties that pains have in the actual world but they are not C-fiber firings, and (b) in W_2^* there are C-fiber firings but they do not have the sensible properties that pains have in the actual world.

This is the sort of explanation of the apparent contingency of "Pain = C-fiber firings" that Kripke claims is impossible. If such possible worlds as W_1^* and W_2^* exist, then the natural phenomena in W_1^* that, in W_1^*, have the sensible properties that pains have in the actual world, are not C-fiber firings, and, therefore, are not pains. The C-fiber firings in W_2^* that, in W_2^*, do not feel like pain, nevertheless are pains. But this is absurd. The sensible qualities of pains are essential to pains and definitive of them. In any possible world, anything that feels like a pain is a pain, and, thus, there is no such possible world as W_1^*. Similarly, in any possible world a natural phenomenon that is a pain must feel the way pains feel in the actual world, and thus there is no such possible world as W_2^*.

On the basis of these considerations, Kripke concludes that the standard materialist rebuttal (new version), although adequate to the defense of identities like "Water = H_2O," must fail for those identities like "Pain = C-fiber firings" that are advanced by philosophers who defend a materialist theory of mental phenomena. Unless an entirely new sort of rebuttal can be devised, which Kripke doubts, we must reject identities like "Pain = C-fiber firings" and the mind-brain "identity thesis" in general.

Some "identity theorists" deny that a materialist account of mental phenomena entails "type" identities like "Pain = C-fiber firings." They hold that all an identity theorist must maintain are "token" identities, which identify each particular occurrence of a mental state, event, or process with some specific physical state, event, or process. In such a view, a materialist account of mental phenomena would entail the existence of true identity statements of the form "Jones's having a pain at $T = \ldots$," where the right-hand expression describes some quite specific physiological or molecular configuration. The defender of such token identity statements, Kripke observes, faces exactly the same sort of essentialist challenges as the defender of "type" identities. In either of these cases, if Kripke is right, the materialist cannot defend the required identity theses against essentialist criticisms, and materialism seems to be unworkable as an account of the nature of those mental phenomena that, like pains, seem entirely defined by their sensible properties.

10. Reply to Kripke, I:
The New Standard Rebuttal Does Work

As we shall see, the greatest weakness of Kripke's criticisms lies in the fact that— protests of its defenders notwithstanding —a materialist account of mental phenomena does not entail the sort of identity statements to which Kripke's argument applies. I shall develop this theme in section 11.

What is striking is that Kripke's arguments have an additional defect: he has underestimated the potential of the (new) standard materialist rebuttal to essentialist criticisms. Recall that, given a necessary but apparently contingent identity statement "$R_1 = R_2$," where "R_1" and "R_2" are rigid designators, the new standard rebuttal requires forming a contingent identity statement "$D_1 = D_2$," where at least one of "D_1" and "D_2" is a description of the referent of "R_1" and "R_2" in terms of the symptoms typically associated with the replaced rigid designator.

The gist of Kripke's argument is that this strategy will fail if we attempt to explain the contingency of a statement of the form "Pain = R_2" by finding a contingent statement of the form "$D_1 = R_2$," because if "D_1" is an expression that designates pain in terms of just the sensible qualities that pains have in the actual world, then "D_1" designates pain in every possible world. "D_1" is itself a rigid designator. If we agree with Kripke (as I have for the sake of this discussion) that the sensible qualities that pains have in the actual world are essential to pain and definitive of it, then this must be right.

What seems to have been overlooked is that the successful employment of this strategy does not require that it be the less "technical" or "scientific" term in the identity that is replaced by a nonrigid designator. As we have seen earlier, we can explain the apparent contingency of "Water = H_2O" by insisting on the existence of a possible world in which the corresponding contingent sentence "The cooling, tasteless . . . liquid . . . = H_2O" is false. This employment of the new standard strategy relies on the fact that the sensible properties by which we typically recognize water are not essential properties of water. But neither are the standard chemical tests appropriate to the term "H_2O" logically definitive of water. It is certainly logically possible that there should be a world in which a liquid that is not H_2O satisfies all the chemical tests that—in the actual world—are reliable indicators of H_2O. Thus we could equally well have explained the apparent contingency of "Water = H_2O" by appealing to the contingency of the corresponding qualitative statement "Water = the liquid that ***," where "***" describes the standard chemical

tests appropriate (in the actual world) to the detection of H_2O.

Thus the employment of a corresponding contingent qualitative statement to explain away the apparent contingency of "Pain = C-fiber firings" does not depend on the existence of a possible world in which pain does not feel like (actual world) pain or in which some nonpain feels like an actual world pain: it does not depend on a purely phenomenal description of pain not being a rigid designator. All that is required is that *either* the expression "pain" or the description "C-fiber firings" can be replaced by an appropriate purely qualitative description that does not designate rigidly.

Of course, this can be done. For any physiological or anatomical description like the imaginary "C-fiber firings" there is certainly a possible world in which something has the qualitative properties typically associated with the term in the actual world, but really is not, in this case, an instance of "C-fiber firings." Some other sort of nerve cell might, in a different possible world, look just the way C-fibers do in the actual world, or there might be specious indications that C-fibers are firing when they are really dormant. Thus we must conclude that, contrary to Kripke's suggestions, the new standard materialist rebuttal does permit one to explain the apparent contingency of mind-body identity statements like "Pain = C-fiber firings," and also to explain the apparent contingency of token-token identity statements like "His pain at t = such and such molecular event."

It is evident that the same strategy allows the explanation of the apparent possibility of worlds in which there are pains but no C-fibers, or in which C-fibers fire but no pain is felt. The apparent possibility of a world in which there are pains but no matter at all can be explained by the real possibility of a world in the following sentence is true: "There are pains but there is nothing that + + +," where

"+ + +" describes all the ways in which matter makes itself evident to the senses. A possible world in which this sentence is true would not (if pain is identical to C-fiber firings) be a world without matter, but it would be a world in which the senses functioned in such a way that nothing produced the symptoms that we typically take to indicate the presence of matter.

It would appear, then, that the (new) standard rebuttal to essentialism provides the materialist with a more powerful defense than Kripke recognizes. The materialist who insists that he is committed to the truth of identity statements like "Pain = C-fiber firings" or "Jones's pain at t = such and such molecular configuration" can successfully employ the strategy of the (new) standard rebuttal against essentialist criticisms of his doctrine. What is even more striking is that materialists are mistaken in believing that they are committed to the existence of true identity statements of either of these forms.

11. Reply to Kripke, II: Materialism without Reductionism

The materialist asserts that all natural phenomena, all events, processes, objects, and so forth, are in fact physical: all objects are composed solely of matter and all events and processes consist solely in interactions between material things. Mental events, states, and processes, in particular, differ from uncontroversially physical events, states, and processes only in the particular arrangements or configurations of matter and material forces that realize them. Pains are quite different from, for instance, earthquakes; but the difference is configurational, not constitutional. They are made of the same sorts of stuff. The strategy of essentialist objections to this claim is to insist that if true in fact, materialism must be true necessarily, and then to attempt a refutation of this latter claim.

The position that materialism must, if true, be necessarily true, rests on the conviction that materialists are committed to the identity thesis, that is, to the truth of mind-body identity statements like "Pain = C-fiber firings," which involve rigid designators. As we have seen, the (new) standard materialist rebuttal is effective in defending these "identity theses" against essentialist criticisms. It is not, however, necessary to invoke this rebuttal. Materialism, properly understood, does not entail the sort of mind-body identity statements against which the essentialist criticisms are directed. Indeed, as we shall see, materialism poses no difficulties for most of our intuitions regarding possible relations between mental phenomena and physical phenomena. In particular, a materialist account of mental phenomena is quite compatible with the view that there are possible worlds in which mental phenomena exist but are nonphysical.

This conclusion, if sound, is significant for two reasons. First, the intuitions about necessity and possibility that underlie the essentialist criticisms of materialism are very strong ones, and the new standard materialist rebuttal does not establish that these intuitions are unfounded. It merely offers a possible explanation for them. The case for materialism is greatly strengthened if it can be shown that materialism does not even entail the sort of mind-body identity statements against which these criticisms are directed.

Second, the claim that materialism does not entail the existence of true mind-body identity statements contradicts the standard empiricist analyses of materialism. According to such analyses, materialism asserts the syntactic reducibility of the vocabulary and laws of all the sciences to the vocabulary and laws of physics. In particular, a materialist account of mental phenomena, according to such analyses, entails the definability of all mental and psychological states (or, on some accounts, all token mental and psychological states) in the vocabulary of physics.

But definitions of the sort required by such an analysis are just the sorts of identity statements linking mental and physical states that I claim materialism does *not* entail. Indeed, I shall show that the version of materialist psychology best supported by available evidence entails that mental and psychological states are *not* definable in physical terms.

The reductionist analysis of materialism shares with the empiricist account of natural kind terms discussed earlier the same verificationist and antimetaphysical motivation: it represents an attempt to "rationally reconstruct" a metaphysical question as a formal question about language. If, as I am arguing here, each of these empiricist interpretations results in a misleading account of the philosophical consequences and evidential status of materialist psychology, then we have even greater evidence for the claim made earlier that the nonverificationist treatment of natural kind terms of the sort proposed by Kripke is essential to a sound understanding of the issue of materialism, and, presumably, of other scientific issues as well.

A variety of different considerations dictate the conclusions outlined above. I shall consider them in stages.

Mind-Body Identity, Mind-Body Identity Statements, and the Apparent Necessity of Materialist Doctrines

Part of the motivation for attempts to formulate materialist psychology as an "identity thesis," aside from the empiricist reductionistic analyses, has been the desire to distinguish materialism from "epiphenomenalism," the view that mental states are not physical, but are universally correlated with distinct physical states whose causal powers explain the effects normally attributed to the corresponding mental states. Materialists, quite rightly, have been careful to insist that each mental state is identical to, not merely correlated with, some physical state.

This "identity thesis" does not, however, entail the existence of true mind-body identity statements of the sort Kripke considers, nor does it entail that materialism must be necessarily true if it is true at all. To see the distinction between these two sorts of "identity theses," consider the case of water. "Water contains hydrogen" and "Water is rare in the Gobi Desert" are both true statements, and they entail, respectively, the "identity theses" "Water is identical to a substance that contains hydrogen" and "Water is identical to a substance rare in the Gobi Desert."

Yet (assuming as I do here that Kripke's account of necessity is correct), water contains hydrogen essentially, but water is only contingently rare in the Gobi Desert. It is relatively easy to see why this is so. In the first place, neither of the "identity theses" just discussed has the form of identity statements that link rigid designators; neither is, as it stands, the sort of identity claim which must be necessary if true. Instead, each has the form "(Ex) (water $= x$ and Px)" where "P" is ". . . is a substance containing hydrogen" or ". . . is a substance that is rare in the Gobi Desert." [*Editor's note:* In this anthology, the ordinary "E" is used instead of the backward "E" as the existential quantifier.]

In the first of these cases, we can conclude that water contains hydrogen necessarily only because we can find a rigid designator "R" such that (i) the identity statement "Water $= R$" is true in the actual world, and hence in all possible worlds, and (ii) "R" is such that anything it designates must (in any possible world) contain hydrogen. The rigid designator "H_2O" is such an "R." The corresponding situation does not obtain in the second case. Water is identical to a substance (water itself) that is, in the actual world, rare in the Gobi Desert, but (since being rare in the Gobi Desert is not an essential property of water), there is no rigid designator "R" such that (i) the identity statement "Water $= R$" is true in the actual world, and hence in all possible worlds, and (ii) "R" is such that anything it designates must (in any possible world) be rare in the Gobi Desert.

We are able to show that water contains hydrogen essentially not just because water is identical to a substance that contains hydrogen, but because we are able to find another rigid designator for water (besides "water") that is formulated in a particular vocabulary (in this case, the vocabulary of chemical formulae) and that is such that whatever it names must contain hydrogen in every possible world. As we have seen, however, it is not always the case that when a statement of the form "(Ex) (x is R_1 and Px)" is true, where "R_1" is a rigid designator, there is a second rigid designator "R_2" such that (i) "$R_1 = R_2$" is true and (ii) "R_2" is such that whatever it names must have P, in every possible world.

The point is that the essentialist argument that purports to show that if mental phenomena (such as pains) are physical then they must be necessarily physical depends for its cogency on a quite specific kind of analysis of materialism. It depends on an analysis of materialism according to which, for example, the claim that pain is a physical process entails that there is a rigid designator "R_2" that is such that (i) "Pain = R_2" is true and (ii) "R_2" is such that whatever it designates, in any possible world, must be a physical process.

As we have just seen, in the case of essential and contingent properties of water, the doctrine that pains are physical processes trivially entails that pains are identical to physical process, but this, by itself, provides no guarantee that (i) and (ii) are satisfied. It is thus perfectly consistent to affirm the "identity thesis" that pain is identical to a physical process and to deny the existence of a rigid designator "R_2," satisfying (i) and (ii). The philosopher who understands materialism to entail the stronger sort of "identity theses" represented by (i) and (ii) must maintain that the required rigid designators satisfy-

ing (i) and (ii) always exist. It is this claim that I deny.

Plasticity: Compositional and Configurational

Let us turn now to the main issue: whether the doctrine that mental phenomena are physical phenomena entails the existence of true mind-body identity statements linking rigid designators, that is, whether it entails the truth of statements like "Pain = C-fiber firings." I shall concentrate first on the issue of whether a materialist account of mental phenomena entails the existence of true type-type identity statements of this kind—that is, whether materialism entails that each mental type event, state, or process is definable (by a rigidly designating expression) in a physical vocabulary. I shall turn to the issue of token-token identity statements after considering the type-type case.

My strategy is this: I shall introduce a notion of "plasticity" for type events, states, or processes, and I shall argue that the version of materialism best supported by available evidence entails that mental states admit sufficient plasticity in the way in which they are realized that it is logically possible for mental states to be nonphysically realized, even though in the actual world all mental phenomena are physically realized. By plasticity of a type of event, state, or process I understand its capacity to be realized in more than one way; the plasticity of a type of event, state, or process is indicated by the degree of variability in the particular (token) events, states, or processes that could realize it. Thus, for example, the (type) process of starting a car displays more plasticity than the (type) process of starting a 1949 Ford, because the possible token processes that could realize the first type process display greater variation (in brand of the constituent car, for example) than do the possible processes that could realize the latter.

At least roughly, we may distinguish two dimensions of plasticity (there may be more, but these are particularly relevant to the issue at hand), compositional plasticity and configurational plasticity. Compositional plasticity is displayed by a type of state, event, or process to the extent that there are possible realizations of that state, event, or process that differ in the sorts of substances or causal factors that constitute them. Configurational plasticity, in contrast, is displayed by a type of state, event, or process to the extent that its possible token realizations differ in the structural configuration or arrangement of their constituent parts, events, substances, or causal factors.

Thus, for example, the smelting of iron displays considerable configurational plasticity, since there are realizations of iron smelting involving quite different kinds and geometrical arrangements of equipment and different temporal sequences of constituent processes. Iron smelting is importantly limited, however, in its compositional plasticity: all instances of iron smelting must involve a quantity of iron. By contrast, the state of being an inscription of the English sentence "Heritability is a population-relative statistic" displays very substantial compositional plasticity: such an inscription can be written in ink on paper, carved on wood, cast in bronze, chiseled into marble, pressed into plastic, and so on. Yet the state of being an inscription of this important English sentence displays quite limited configurational plasticity: any two inscriptions of this sentence will have fundamentally similar structures; indeed, except for misspelled inscriptions, they will be isomorphic at the level of constituent letters.

An important class of states seems to possess unlimited compositional plasticity, but relatively limited configurational plasticity. "Computational states," such as being a realization of a computation of e^x for input $x = 9$, or (what is a different computational state) being a realization of a computation of e^x for input $x = 9$ according to machine-language program P (for some definite P), or (still different) being a realization of a computation of e^x for input $x = 9$ according to a machine-language program that is a member of some definite set S of machine-language programs, all seem to possess maximal compositional plasticity: in any particular possible world, only the causal laws governing that world limit the possible composition of realizations of such computational states; such states have no essential properties that constrain the sorts of substances or causal factors that can be constituents of their realizations.

What I shall argue here—following those philosophers and psychologists who have defended the view that mental and psychological states are "functional" states of organisms—is that mental events, states, and processes are like computational states in being entirely configurational, that is, in possessing maximal compositional plasticity. It will follow that—even though mental states may always be physically realized in the actual world—there is no logical impossibility of their being nonphysically realized in some other possible world. Before turning to a defense of this claim, I must clarify some details of the notion of plasticity that are crucial to a correct assessment of the plasticity of mental states.

What is crucial to this discussion is the way in which plasticity is assessed in the case of events, states, or processes that are essentially relational. The problem can be illustrated by reconsidering the issue of the plasticity of computational states, like the state of being a calculation of e^x according to machine-language program P, for the input $x = 9$. I have said that this is a purely configurational state, and that the only properties essential to its (token) realizations are those configurational properties that are dictated by the program P. In a perfectly clear sense this is true: in any possible world W, a computer capable of embodying program P, and acting on input 9 can be made of whatever arrangement of causal factors are capable—given the causal laws governing W—of realizing the required configuration of machine states and the required transitions between them.

At the same time, more is required in order for a computational state of the sort in question to be actually realized than the existence of a machine of the right sort, operating on the right sort of input, and functioning normally. It is perfectly possible for there to be one computer C_1, which is in the state of computing e^x according to machine language program P, for input $x = 9$, and for there to be another computer C_2, which goes through *exactly the same* succession of physical states (and, therefore, exactly the same sequence of configurational internal states) such that C_2 is *not* in the state of computing e^x according to machine language P for input $x = 9$. This state of affairs is possible because the same computer program can be used to compute quite different mathematical functions depending on the interpretation given to the language in which its inputs and outputs are represented.

The state of being a computation of e^x according to machine-language program P for input $x = 9$ has essentially a relational component. It is realized in a possible world W if and only if there is in W some arrangement of causal factors that realizes the program P and the input 9 *and* that is suitably related to users of its programming language whose conventions for its use are such that, with respect to them, the program P should be interpreted as computing e^x. This sort of relation to user(s) is an essential property of the computational state in question.

The existence of states, events, and processes that are essentially relational in this way forces one to refine the notion of plasticity. When one assesses the plasticity of a type of state, event, or process,

one assesses the variability in the sorts of particular (token) states, events, or processes that can realize it. The outcome of this assessment will, in the case of essentially relational states, depend on whether one adopts a narrow or broad construal of what might be termed the "scope" of the particular states, events, or processes whose variability is to be assessed.[13]

By a narrow-scope construal I understand one according to which a particular realization of a type of state, event, or process is understood to consist of those natural phenomena that actually go together to constitute the occurrence of the state, event, or process, at the time, and in the place, where it occurs, even if there are other phenomena such that if they had not occurred the particular state, event, or process would not have had whatever relational properties are essential to the type of state, event, or process in question. By a broad-scope construal, I understand one according to which a realization of a type of state, event, or process consists of the occurrence of those phenomena that constitute it according to the narrow-scope construal, together with all those occurrences by virtue of which the particular state, event, or process has the relational properties essential to the type of state, event, or process in question.

What is important to my purposes here is that plasticity can be assessed with respect to either construal, and that the results may differ according to the construal chosen. Thus, for example, the computational state I have been discussing might seem to have more configurational plasticity on the broad-scope construal than on the narrow. On the narrow-scope construal all realizations are isomorphic (actually, since a computation of a real-valued function may be nonterminating, what is really true is that any two equally long computations are isomorphic on the narrow-scope construal), whereas on the broad-scope construal there may be significant structural variety among realizations, since there may be structurally quite different social processes that result in the adoption of the same interpretation for a programming language. More important for my purposes, the choice of broad- or narrow-scope construal will often affect assessments of compositional plasticity.

It is uncontroversial in that there are some mental states that are essentially relational in a way that precludes their being purely configurational when their scope is construed in the broad sense. For example, the state of having a vivid visual memory of the Eiffel Tower is realized by some mental processes (physical or not) only if they bear the right sort of causal relation to the Eiffel Tower (roughly, they must be caused by the subject's having in the past seen the Eiffel Tower, and the intervening causal mechanisms involved must be such that they constitute storage of visual information). Arguably, the Eiffel Tower is necessarily physical (and certainly, by Kripke's account of necessity, it is a necessary truth that the Eiffel Tower was physical when it was created). Arguably, then, every realization in the broad sense of the state of having a vivid visual memory of the Eiffel Tower must involve some physical object, and certainly there can be no realization of this mental state in any possible world in which there are and never were any physical objects.

Furthermore, as we shall see, according to certain functionalist analyses of pain a similar situation obtains. Pain (at least in the interspecific sense) is held to have as an essential feature the property of being the psychological state that is, in the species in question, typically a response to tissue damage, and typically an intermediate step in the mechanisms that lead from tissue damage to avoidance behavior. If such an account of pain is sound, and if, as seems plausible, tissues are necessarily physical, then there is an important limitation to the compositional plasticity of the state of being in pain, if

that state is given a broad-scope construal: there could be no pains in a possible world in which there has never been matter.

It will be recalled that I set out to show that, according to the best available materialist account of mental phenomena, mental states, events, and processes are entirely configurational: that is, they have no compositional properties essentially. I can now state my claim more precisely in the light of refinement in the notion of plasticity: what I shall defend is the view that, on the best available materialist account of mental phenomena, mental states are entirely configurational when they are given a narrow-scope construal and, furthermore, purely phenomenal states—states characterized solely by the quality of the experiences involved and not by their relational properties—are purely configurational on either construal of their scope.[14]

Let us turn now to the main task of this section. I want to show that, according to the materialist account of mental phenomena that is best supported by available evidence, mental states are entirely configurational on a narrow-scope construal and that phenomenal states are entirely configurational on any construal of their scope. I shall defend this position in a series of stages—which present evidence favoring increasingly high degrees of compositional plasticity for mental states. I shall consider the question whether materialism (in its most plausible version) entails the existence of true mind-body identity statements like "pain = . . ." where ". . ." is a rigid designator for a necessarily physical state, or, in other words, the question whether materialism entails that mental events, states, and processes are physically definable. Successive stages in my presentation correspond to the consideration of this question with respect to increasingly complex sorts of physical definitions, until, at the last stage, I conclude that the compositional plasticity of mental states rules out all possible physical definitions, however complex. The argument presented represents a rehearsal and an extension of the considerations that have led philosophers to defend "functionalist" theories of mental phenomena. For a fuller discussion of the considerations that support functionalism the reader should consult the many important recent papers defending it.[15]

Compositional Plasticity, I: Interspecific Psychological States and Central Nervous System Plasticity

Consider first the question whether the most plausible version of materialist psychology entails the truth of mind-body identity statements that are like "Pain = C-fiber firings" in that they identify each mental state with the operation of some quite specific neuroanatomical structure. The fact that animals of quite different species may be in the same psychological or mental state provides good reason to deny that any plausible psychology should entail such identities. It is highly unlikely that there is any quite specific neurophysiological state common to, for example, all animals that are in pain, and it is even less plausible that there is a single neuroanatomical structure whose operation is definitive of pain in all logically possible animals as well (as identities of the sort in question would entail).

Instead, what functionalists claim is essential to a mental or psychological state is not the particular physiological mechanisms that realize it, but rather the "computational" or "information-processing" role that these mechanisms play with respect to the animal's nervous system and body generally. A physiological state of an animal that plays the right sort of role in a particular animal's processing of information, and the regulation of its behavior, is a pain, on this view, even though other quite different physiological states play the same role (and, therefore, realize pain) in animals of other species. It is by no means uncontroversial just how this functionalist position should be worked out in the case of particular mental and psychological states. It might be argued, for example, that pain has certain relational properties essentially—its causal connections to certain typical behaviors, for example; whereas, on the contrary, it might be maintained that its phenomenal qualities alone are essential to and definitive of pain (as Kripke appears to hold, at least in the case of pain in persons).

Nevertheless, it seems reasonable that the most plausible materialist response to the issue of interspecific occurrences of mental and psychological states is to adopt some sort of functionalist account: to claim that for each type of mental or psychological state, event, or process there are certain configurations of information-processing systems, or internal "programs," such that their manifestation in the body of an animal is (together with the realization of whatever essential relational properties the mental or psychological state may have) sufficient to constitute a manifestation of the mental or psychological event, state, or process in question. Functionalism of this sort entails a degree of compositional plasticity (on the narrow-scope construal) for mental and psychological states, and it rules out the claim that they possess very simple physiological definitions. Nevertheless, these considerations by themselves do not entail that mental and psychological events, states, and processes have maximal compositional plasticity. They do not rule out the possibility of a species-by-species physiological definition of mental and psychological states, nor do they rule out the possibility that mental and psychological states possess physical definitions more complex than those just considered.

The issue of species-by-species definability is important because it is quite plausible that the debate between materialists and dualists has really been concerned only with mental and psychological states in man. Dualists since Descartes have often seemed to maintain the position that the attribution of mental and psychological states to animals represents a significant extension of those mental and psychological concepts that we employ in describing the states of men and have adopted, or at least been prepared to tolerate, a materialist account of mental and psychological states in nonhuman animals. An understanding of mental terms according to which they involve a certain ambiguity between their human and non-human employments is particularly appropriate to an account of Kripke's anti-materialist arguments. Kripke holds that the phenomenal qualities of pain are essential to them. Such a position is plausible if it is understood to apply to pain in man, but it is utterly implausible if it is understood to apply to pain as an interspecific mental state. Even though it is undoubtedly true that having a phenomenal quality of some sort (probably, even, having an unpleasant phenomenal quality) is essential to the interspecific state pain, it is wildly implausible that in order to be a pain, a mental state of a guppy must have the *same* phenomenal quality as a pain in man.

It is, therefore, reasonable to inquire whether the most plausible version of materialist psychology entails the existence of true identity statements each of which links a mental or psychological state in man with one quite specific physiological state: that is, whether it entails statements like "Pain in man = C-fiber firings." Once again, the considerations which support functionalism suggest that the answer is no. Identities of the sort in question would entail that it is logically impossible for any particular mental state to be realized (in man) by other than the quite specific physiological state that typically realizes it (since it is this state, presumably, with which it would be linked by the relevant mind-body identity state-

ment). There is, however, substantial evidence that such atypical realizations are not only possible but actual. For example, the most plausible accounts of certain cases of recovery from aphasia induced by brain lesions seem to be that the relevant information-processing function of the damaged tissue is taken over by parts of the nervous system that do not typically perform this function. There is no reason to doubt the logical possibility (indeed, the practical possibility in many cases) that mental and psychological states other than linguistic capacities also display a similar plasticity.

Considerations such as these make it clear that the version of materialist psychology that is most plausible in the light of available evidence does not entail the existence of true identity statements linking human mental and psychological states with quite specific neurophysiological states. They provide evidence as well for the functionalist position that mental and psychological states are closely analogous to computational states of machines. The question remains whether more complicated physiological or other physical definitions exist for mental and psychological states. Although for most philosophical and scientific purposes only finite definitions are worth considering in answering this question, for the purposes of this inquiry into the modal consequences of materialism we must consider this question with respect to infinite definitions of a sort that would have no explanatory value, and would otherwise have limited philosophical importance.

Compositional Plasticity, II:
Realization by Mechanical Computers
and by Nonphysical Systems

Let "Q" rigidly designate the set of all those physiological states that, in some possible world, realize pain in man. Q may well be infinite. Nevertheless we can inquire whether the most plausible version of materialism entails the identity statement "Pain in man = the state of being in a state that is itself a member of Q." This statement represents the most general possible *physiological* definition of pain in man. If materialism entails the physiological definability of pain in man, and of other mental and psychological events, states, and processes, even via definitions of this complexity, then materialism does entail that mental events, states, and processes in men are necessarily physical.

Before I turn to a discussion of this issue, there is a technical question that must be resolved. In the last section I turned my attention to the question of species-by-species physiological definitions for mental and psychological states, and in particular to the question of physiological definability of such states in man. There is a possible confusion introduced when one considers the issue of the physiological definability of, say, pain *"in man."* If by "man" one intends a *biological* species, the complex physiological definition I am considering may well define pain, at least on a materialist account of mental phenomena. It is entirely plausible that creatures in some possible world, who, however much they are very like us, are nevertheless sufficiently different from us that their mental and psychological states are not physically manifested, would not be members of the same biological species as ourselves. The materialist who—setting himself up for the new essentialist challenge—affirms that even though our mental states are physical there is a possible world in which men's mental states are nonphysical is not (unless he is very careless) thereby adopting the position that such possible men would be members of the same biological species as ourselves. All he need maintain, in being faithful to our strong philosophical intuitions, is that it is logically possible that there be beings whose mental and psychological capacities are the same as ours, and whose conscious mental states are phenomenally just like ours, but

whose mental states are nonphysical. In what follows, I shall adopt the convention that in talking about mental and psychological events, states, and processes I shall be understood to be discussing events, states, and processes phenomenally just like those that occur in ordinary humans, occurring in beings whose mental and psychological capacities are those of human beings. I now turn to the issue of the physiological definability of mental events, states, and processes.

Against the definability of mental events, states, and processes in physiological terms (via even possibly infinite definitions) I argue that, according to the most plausible materialist understanding of mental phenomena, it is logically possible—indeed, even physically possible—for these phenomena to be realized by entirely inorganic mechanical computers, and, thus, that they can be realized by systems that possess no *physiological* definition whatsoever.

Two considerations indicate that machine realization of mental states is possible. In the first place, the most plausible explanation for the compositional plasticity that mental events, states, and processes seem to display in the actual world is that they can be realized in different anatomical structures because what is essential to them is their role in information processing, and their relations to other computational or information-processing structures in the same organism. Thus their compositional plasticity has the same explanation as the compositional plasticity that is displayed by what I earlier called "computational" states of computing machines. Indeed, analogies between mental states and computational states have been suggested by almost every defender of functionalism. The point is that there is no evidence to suggest that the analogy is not exact, no evidence that mental and psychological states should not be viewed as computational states of organisms. There is no reason to doubt, therefore, that the same computational or information-processing structures could be realized in nonorganic matter as well as in animal tissue.

The second consideration concerns the available evidence for a materialist account of mental phenomena. I am inquiring here about the consequences of the version(s) of materialist psychology that are best supported by available evidence. Now, many philosophers who defend materialist theories of mind, for reasons of modesty, timidity, or methodological confusion, maintain that they defend the mere logical possibility that scientists will eventually confirm materialism, but insist that there is no currently available evidence that strongly supports a materialist account of mental phenomena. Their modesty is misplaced. It is plain that the upsurge of recent interest in materialist theories of mind reflects growing—though by no means conclusive—evidence favoring materialism. The evidence is not as "direct" as some theorists seem to require: no one has identified the particular brain mechanisms that realize a particular mental or psychological state in any higher animal. But there is substantial "indirect" evidence that favors a materialist account of mental phenomena, and materialism generally. This evidence is of three sorts: the variety of cases (brain lesions, electrode-implantation experiments, drugs with highly specific psychological effects) in which different physical and chemical changes produce different and highly specific changes in mental or psychological state; the success of modern biochemistry in the elucidation the chemistry of heredity and of other cellular processes; and the limited success of "artificial-intelligence" programs in simulating certain intellectual processes on mechanical (that is, nonorganic) computers.

The first sort of evidence is relevant because the most plausible explanation for these effects is that the various physical and chemical agents interfere with or alter the physical realizations of quite specific mental and psychological states. The second is relevant because such cases provide evidence for materialism generally, and because they serve to refute vitalism, which is closely linked to dualism by its insistence that certain directed, purposeful, or organized structures, of the sort characteristic of living things, cannot possess a physical realization.

It is tempting to dismiss "artificial intelligence" as evidentially irrelevant. After all, only in science fiction, or in the press releases of the most boastful of its practitioners, does artificial intelligence achieve the computer simulation of the more difficult sorts of human intellectual activity. One should resist the temptation.

It must be remembered that one of the most serious objections to materialist theories of mind is the difficulty one has in even conceiving of how they might be true. We are unable to imagine exactly how an arrangement of physical parts could interact so as to manifest a feeling of pain, or so as to make a decision. Indeed, we (most of us anyway) have strong intuitions (at least some of the time) that physical realization of mental phenomena is impossible. Such "intuitions" are not to be dismissed lightly, as Kripke would be the first to insist. They should be taken seriously as prima facie evidence against materialism, not because "intuition" has some privileged epistemic status (it does not), nor because conceivability and possibility are the same thing (certainly they are not, at least if Kripke is right about modal logic), nor because "intuitions," linguistic or otherwise, are the subject matter of philosophy (they are not, and philosophy is much more nearly continuous with the sciences than we ordinarily recognize). Rather, such strong intuitions should be taken seriously because what we misleadingly call "intuitions" are, quite often, instances of scientifically reasonable inductive judgments, based on observations, informed by theoretical considerations, and amenable to revision in the light of new evidence. They are, indeed, perfectly typical examples of "theory-mediated" inductive judgments of the sort that are commonplace and essential in the proper conduct of scientific inquiry (see Boyd, 1973, forthcoming).

What this means is that the fact that a great many scientifically informed people are unable even to imagine how an ensemble of the sorts of physical systems with which they are familiar could realize a pain or a thought is itself some evidence that physical systems cannot realize such mental states. Of course, in any such case, an alternative explanation of the intuitions of impossibility is always available: failure of imagination (not necessarily culpable failure, but rather failure resulting from inadequate information or inadequate theoretical understanding). Such an explanation seems to account for the conviction shared by many eminent early twentieth-century biologists that there would not be a purely physical explanation for heredity (see, for example, Haldane, 1914).

It is, presumably, the business of materialists to offer and defend a similar explanation for the "intuition" that mental phenomena cannot be physical. Of course, the best way to do this (analogous to the discovery of DNA in the realm of cellular biology) would be actually to discover the details of the physical realization of some mental state in man. Lacking this triumph, however, it is still possible to offer less direct evidence against the reliability of these intuitions. In the first place, one can undermine the foundations upon which the intuitions of the impossibility of materialism rest. In large measure these foundations seem to consist in the conviction that certain traits characteristic of mental and psychological states— rationality, self-directedness, purposefulness, ingenuity, self-organization, adaptability, and the like—cannot be realized by a purely "mechanical" system. Against

this conviction, materialists must claim that it rests on an unduly narrow conception of the range of possible mechanical systems. Evidence for this materialist rebuttal is provided by every case in which it is established that physical systems can realize some traits of this sort, which would previously have been thought to lie in the realm of the necessarily nonphysical. This consideration explains the central importance of advances in biochemical explanation of cellular phenomena as evidence for a materialist account of mental phenomena: the organized, self-reproducing, and adaptive cellular processes that now have been chemically explained are precisely the sorts of processes about which antimaterialist intuitions would have led (indeed, did lead) philosophers and scientists to doubt their physical realizability. Advances in "artificial intelligence" have also made a crucial contribution along the same lines to the defense of materialism. Although there has certainly not yet been machine realization of anything like human consciousness or problem-solving capacity (small wonder, given the puny size of modern computers when compared with the brains of even nonhuman mammals), it is still true that "artificial-intelligence" programs have realized the simulation of many problem-solving capacities of just the sort that would have been (were!) thought to lie in the exclusive realm of the nonphysical. It would be a mistake to underestimate the effect these achievements have had, *and ought to have had*, in undermining the prima facie force of antimaterialist intuitions.

The foundation of antimaterialist intuitions can be undermined from a different direction: one can advance theoretical understanding so that what was inconceivable becomes conceivable. We are still not at the stage where we can imagine exactly how human intelligence, for instance, or painful feelings, could be physically realized. Nevertheless, our capacity to imagine that they could be so realized has been considerably increased by the success, even the partial success, of cognitive psychologists in offering "information-processing" accounts of cognitive functions. Such accounts (even those of psychologists who are extremely doubtful about the fruitfulness of actual computer "modeling" of human cognitive functions) rely heavily on analogies between human cognition and "information processing" by machines, as the prevalence of computer-derived terminology ("feedback," "memory-limitation," "parallel processing," "subroutine," "information retrieval," and so on) in the working vocabularies of cognitive psychologists shows. Whenever a mental or psychological phenomenon is explained by a theory that rests on an analogy to the operation of physical mechanisms, as information-processing theories do, it becomes more reasonable to attribute the seeming impossibility of physically realized mental life to a lack of sufficient theoretical understanding.

Both of these rebuttals to antimaterialist intuitions, it will be noted, turn on the assumption that human mental and cognitive processes are "computational" or "information-processing" processes of the sort that can be, in principle, realized by nonorganic systems. Thus not only does the positive evidence of actual plasticity of the human nervous system indicate that mental events, states, and processes are machine realizable, but the most plausible materialist rebuttals of antimaterialist intuitions also rest on this assumption. I conclude, therefore, that the most plausible materialist psychology entails the machine-realizability of mental events, states, and processes, and thus that it entails that such events, states, and processes *do not* possess physiological definitions, however complex.

One important point must be made about the conclusion drawn here that mental and psychological states are "computational" states or organisms. There is no single notion of "computational state"; as we have seen, such states may be thought of as characterized merely by the function they compute—by input-output relations—or they may be thought of as characterized by one or more aspects of the particular "program" or arrangement of causal factors that realizes the computation. Most emphatically, it is with respect to the latter understanding that I mean to defend the view that mental events, states, and processes are computational. In the literature cited earlier, there have been objections raised to various versions of functionalism on the grounds that they did not acknowledge the fact that certain mental states, such as pain, have their qualitative features as essential properties. This criticism is certainly warranted if functionalism is understood to assert that mental states are characterized —as computational states—by the "function" they compute, that is, by just the role they play in linking sensory stimulation to behavior. What the materialist must maintain is that, for each sort of mental or psychological event, state, or process, there exists a definite class of possible (temporarily extended) patterns of interaction, or "programs," such that the realization of a member of this class by a physical system is a necessary and sufficient condition for the physical realization of all the nonrelational properties essential to the mental state, event, or process in question. According to this view, for example, there are certain configurations such that whenever they are realized by a physical system, whatever substances compose it, the qualitative feeling of pain is manifested. This is a very bold claim, and the evidence for it is not entirely conclusive. It is, nevertheless, dictated by the version of materialist psychology that is best supported by available evidence and it is probably one of the important grains of truth in various formulations of functionalism.

We will now inquire whether the most

plausible version of materialism entails that mental and psychological events, states, and processes in man possess physical definitions of any sort, physiological or not. As before, we may formulate the most general possible physical definition for any mental or psychological state. In the case of pain, for example, let W be the set of all those physical states that, in some possible world, realize pain. We will inquire whether the most plausible version of materialism entails the identity "Pain in man = the state that is realized by all and only members of W," and similar identities for other mental and psychological states in man.

By way of an answer, we are now in a position to see that materialism (in its most plausible version) entails that mental states are purely configurational, on a narrow-scope construal—that is, that their nonrelational essential features place no logical limitations whatsoever on the sorts of causal factors that may realize them. This conclusion is virtually dictated by what I have said so far. If all that is required to realize the nonrelational essential properties of any particular mental state is the physical realization of a certain configuration by any sort of matter whatsoever, and if this is true because mental states are computational or information-processing states, then there is no good reason for supposing that the same mental state would not be realized if the same configuration were realized by nonphysical causal factors. I conclude, therefore, that the most plausible materialist psychology entails that mental and psychological events, states, and processes are purely configurational on their narrow-scope construal, and that purely phenomenal events, states, and processes are, therefore, purely configurational on a broad-scope construal as well.

Possibilities, Possibilities . . .

We are now in a position to offer a new reply to certain essentialist challenges to materialism. The essentialist critic challenges the materialist to explain the strong philosophical intuitions that we have that materialism is only contingently true, and that there are possible worlds in which mental phenomena are not physical. The reply I now offer is that this claim is compatible with the most plausible version of materialist psychology, which itself entails just the right sort of compositional plasticity for mental events, states, and processes. It is, indeed, fully compatible with a plausible materialist psychology that there should be a possible world in which there is no matter at all, but in which there are events, states, and processes that have all the nonrelational properties essential to the mental events, states, and processes manifested in the actual world.

There is one essentialist challenge that I must consider here (before turning to the issues raised by token-token identity statements). Kripke, in moving against the materialist who asserts an identity statement like "Pain = C-fiber firings" maintains not only that we have strong intuitions that there could be pains without C-fiber firings, but also that we have strong intuitions to the effect that there could be C-fiber firings (or any other physical events) but no pains. He challenges the materialist to explain away this intuition as well. Of course, this particular form of the essentialist's objection does not apply to the most plausible versions of materialism, which do not entail the truth of such mind-body identity statements. But a closely related version of the same objection can still be formulated. The plausible materialist maintains that there are certain types of physical event (C-fiber firings, for instance) that have all the nonrelational properties essential to pains (in Kripke's view, these are all the essential properties of pain). In particular, the materialist maintains that it is impossible to have C-fibers fire without a pain being felt. But the same intuitions to which Kripke appeals in criticizing the identity statement "Pain = C-fiber firings" operates in this new case as well: we have strong intuitions that—contrary to the dictates of the most plausible materialism—it is possible to have C-fibers fire without a pain being felt.

As I have noted earlier, this challenge can be met by the standard materialist rebuttal (new version) whose strength Kripke has underestimated. In this case, however, one cannot reply, as I did in the case of the strong intuition that pains are possible in a world without matter, by accepting the intuitions as sound. What can be done, however, is to show that this particular application of the new standard materialist rebuttal is entirely unproblematical. To see this, consider a simpler case of the physical realizations of functional states, ordinary electronic computers. Suppose that one considers the circuits of a simple computer that, in fact, computes the square of whatever input is entered. Unless one happens to have previously studied circuits just like the one in question, one will have the strong intuition that the mess of wires could be turned on, the input 9 entered, the whole thing operate normally, and the result 15 be displayed subsequently. One cannot tell by looking (at least not easily) just what function a particular circuit will compute, or, even, that it is the circuit capable of realizing a computation at all. It is difficult to deduce the function computed by a computing device just from a specification of its internal structure (indeed, if one considers the generalized question of computers with unlimited memory, there is no generally effective procedure for recognizing computers that compute the square of their inputs). One has the intuition that the circuit in question could operate normally and still compute something other than the function that—in fact—it must compute, because it is quite easy to visualize the circuit while visualizing successive states of the display that are in-

compatible with the computations it in fact performs. Only if the functional capacity of a circuit leaped right out at us when we reflected on its physical appearance would we not have these intuitions. Yet it is unproblematically logically impossible for a circuit of the sort I am considering to operate normally (for an input of sufficiently small size) and not compute the square of its input. We have mistaken intuitions in cases of this sort because it is possible to visualize the structure of a computer without becoming aware of the function it computes, so that we can visualize the structure of the computer, think of it as operating normally, and visualize a behavior of its input-output systems that it cannot possibly realize, without any sense of contradiction. There is nothing odd or problematical about such an analysis of mistaken modal intuitions.

Of course, according to a functionalist account of the sort I am defending here, mental states like pain are computational and are subject to the same potential mistakes regarding their essential features. We can, indeed, visualize any anatomical configuration we like, and think of it as functioning normally, without recognizing in it the realization of any mental state whatsoever. But this is just what we should expect if mental states are computational states, and there is no reason to doubt that the (new) standard materialist rebuttal fully explains our mistaken intuitions in this case.

Thus I conclude that, insofar as intuitions concerning the essential properties of types of mental events, states, and processes are concerned, the materialist who adopts a functionalist position can—because he is not committed to any mind-body identity statements—accept the central Cartesian claim that it is logically possible for there to be mental life without matter, and—because his analysis of mental states is functional—he can offer an extremely plausible explanation for the seeming possibility that the physical systems that in fact realize mental states could exist without these mental states being realized. I turn now to the issue of the essential properties of token mental events, states, and processes.

Token States and Quite Specific Molecular Configurations

Kripke raises another class of essentialist criticisms against the materialist. The materialist must, he suggests, hold that each individual ("token") mental event, state, or process is identical to some quite specific physiological or molecular event. Thus, for example, it might be true to say "Jones's pain at t = the firing of fibers F_1, F_2 . . ." Yet, for any particular pain, for example, and any particular specific set of molecular motions, we have the intuition that each could occur without the other. Kripke suggests that what I have been calling the standard materialist rebuttal (new version) is inadequate to explain these intuitions, which are, of course, incompatible with the token-token identity statement in question. What should the functionalist materialist have to say regarding these intuitions?

In the first place, of course, we have already seen that the (new) standard rebuttal is sufficient to explain these intuitions. Furthermore, the compositional plasticity of type mental states that the functionalist analysis entails allows us to agree with the intuitions to the extent of saying that a pain phenomenally just like Jones's pain at t could indeed have been realized even though fibers F_1, F_2, and so forth, had not fired; indeed, a pain phenomenally just like Jones's pain at t could have been realized in a world with no matter at all. Apparently, we must deny the possibility that those very fibers could have fired at t without realizing Jones's pain at t, but the discussion in the previous section shows that, in this case, application of the (new) standard rebuttal is profoundly unproblematical.

Although the responses just indicated rebut the antimaterialist intuitions in a fashion perfectly adequate to the defense of materialism, there are plausible arguments that seem to support an even more satisfactory resolution of the challenge they represent. In the first place, it is a mistake to understand materialism as entailing that each token mental event, state, or process is identical to some quite specific molecular or physiological event, state, or process. The compositional plasticity that types of mental events, states, and processes display is mirrored in a corresponding transworld compositional plasticity for token mental events, states, and processes. Furthermore, it is plausible that this compositional plasticity is sufficient to make it logically possible that a token mental event, state, or process that is physically realized in the actual world could be nonphysically realized in some alternative possible world.

Some philosophers seem to have understood transworld identification of physical events, states, and processes to require microscopically identical molecular realizations, or something very close to it. They may reason as follows: an actual world physical event is nothing over and above the motions of the molecules that constitute it (ignoring the issue of essential relational properties, at least). Thus it is identical to those motions, and in any possible world in which it occurs it must be nothing over and above those very motions. The same conclusion can be reached as a consequence of the seemingly innocuous doctrine that if events in two possible worlds are identical they must have *exactly* the same causes. After all, each molecular motion that is part of the physical realization of an event is one of its causes, albeit perhaps a very minor one.

A number of examples show that this view is mistaken, and that it is, therefore, mistaken to affirm that physical events are typically identical to those smaller constituent motions (such as molecular motions) that constitute them. In the first place, such a transworld criterion of identity is strikingly at variance with the actual world criteria of identity for physical objects. A car remains the same car in the actual world if its generator (a constituent part) is replaced, and it is hard to see why the same plasticity should not obtain across possible worlds. The man who says, "Jim replaced the generator in his car yesterday, but he might not have replaced it at all," certainly seems to be—correctly—describing a possible but not actual state of the very car that Jim owns in the actual world. Similarly when he says (perhaps in response to the question whether the new generator caused Jim's actual world accident), "Jim's accident could have occurred even if he had not replaced the generator," he certainly seems to be describing a possible world in which the very same accident occurs but in which no replacement of the generator has occurred previously. But this will be a possible world in which the molecular constituents of the accident are different, since these constituents certainly include the motions of all the engine parts including the generator.

Finally, historical events certainly seem to admit a corresponding plasticity. The historian who says, "World War II would have ended earlier had the Allied powers not adopted the 'Unconditional surrender' slogan," certainly seems to be talking about a possible outcome for the very same war which, in the actual world, ended in August 1945. It would be absurd to insist that the materialist should resist this conclusion on the ground that World War II, like all other events, is entirely physical and therefore must have *exactly the same* physical realization in each possible world. Instead, the materialist should maintain that many kinds of physical events are like physical objects in displaying transworld plasticity.

Nevertheless, there are some sorts of physical events that do not admit this sort of plasticity. Let m be a particular molecule, and t be a particular trajectory (understood as a function from historical times to spatial locations). The token event m's moving along t is an example of a physical event that has exactly the same physical realization in every possible world in which it occurs. Let us be sure that token mental events, states, and processes do admit the plasticity typical of physical events, states, and processes.

Let P be an actual world person with a normal lifespan. Consider a possible world W in which clever Martians slowly but systematically replace parts of P's nervous system with nonorganic structures that bear to the remaining parts of his nervous system the same functional relations the replaced parts bore (they produce, for example, the same electrical potentials, and the same chemical substances), without interrupting in any way P's phenomenal states, or affecting in any way his behavior or the way in which his (increasingly nonorganic) nervous system processes information. Eventually, we can imagine, this process is completed and P now has a nervous system that is entirely artificial and we can imagine that he lives out his life with no change whatsoever in his phenomenal life, behavior, or information-processing states. The compositional plasticity already established for type mental states ensures that such a state of affairs is logically possible (even though it may be technically or physically impossible). For every token mental event, state, or process of P in the actual world, there is a corresponding token mental event, state, or process of P in W that has the same phenomenal features and is connected in exactly the same way with P's behavior, his other mental states, and plays the same role in P's information processing. Are these corresponding mental events, states, and processes identical?

It seems extremely plausible to say that they are. We (or at any rate, I) have strong intuitions that what is essential to the transworld identification of token mental events, states, and processes are the roles they play in the whole history of the subject's phenomenal experience, behavior, and cognitive processes. Token events (or states, or processes) that, in two different possible worlds, play exactly the same role, in this sense, in the mental life of the same person are identical. The difference in their physical realization is as irrelevant here as the difference in generators is irrelevant to the transworld identification of cars. The compositional plasticity of types of mental events, states, and processes produces transworld compositional plasticity in token events, states, and processes.

If this position is sound, as it seems to be, then the functionalist materialist can accept the intuition that any particular actual world mental event, state, or process could exist in a possible world in which the physical events that manifest it in the actual world do not occur. Indeed, there seems to be no barrier to the functionalist materialist's asserting that any particular actual world mental event, state, or process could be—in some other possible world—nonphysically realized. All one need do is to invoke a possible world in which the systematic replacement of parts of the central nervous system involves their replacement by nonphysical causal factors with the capacity to influence the other parts of the central nervous system in a way that exactly simulates the function of the replaced part (which we can imagine becomes deactivated). Finally, the same considerations appear to admit the possibility that certain kinds of actual world token mental events, states, or processes might be realized in some other possible world even if the body of the subject no longer exists.

All of these latter considerations are speculative: perhaps they push the notion of a possible world to the breaking point. Their soundness is not essential to a defense of materialism, but the very fact that they can be plausibly defended shows the extent to which functionalist versions of materialism avoid the sort of essentialist criticisms that Kripke offers.

Identity and Composition

The conclusions (not merely the most speculative ones) of the last section depend on a claim that merits further consideration. Let p be a particular pain and let c be the particular molecular process that realizes it in the actual world. Then, although it certainly makes sense to say that p is nothing over and above c, it is a mistake to claim that p and c are identical. Furthermore, although functional states, events, and processes seem to provide especially clear examples of this phenomenon, it is generally true that particular physical events, states, and processes, and physical things, of course, are not identical to the molecular arrangements that realize them.

Although this claim is widely accepted with respect to physical things, many philosophers find it much less plausible with respect to events, states, and processes. In the case of mental events, states, and processes, their conviction is partly explained by the vocabulary that has come to be used in formulating key issues in the mind-body problem. Part of the evidence for materialism consists in observed correlations between symptoms of various physical and chemical changes in the body and symptoms of corresponding changes in mental states. Indeed, some philosophers have thought that convincing evidence for materialism would rest on the establishment of correlations between symptoms of quite particular mental states and symptoms of the physical states that realize them. Regarding this sort of evidence, the question has been raised whether this correlation of symptoms, if it were observed, could not be explained in a fashion compatible with dualism by attributing the correlation of symptoms to a universal and lawlike correlation between nonphysical mental states and corresponding physical states of the central nervous system. The issue between this interpretation of the data and the materialist interpretation has come to be described as the issue of whether the corresponding mental and physical states are identical or (as the dualist suggests) merely correlated.

As we have seen, this way of putting the question is fundamentally misleading. The issue is not identity versus correlation, but composition versus correlation. The issue is whether the physical state associated with a mental state constitutes or realizes the mental state in question, or whether, on the contrary, it merely correlates with it. The tendency to put the issue in terms of identity rather than composition may rest to some extent on an ambiguity of the English verb "to be." Suppose that Jones's pain at t were realized by the firing of fiber f. In a perfectly good sense, it would be correct to say "Jones's pain at t was just the fiber f's firing at t." This is correct in just the same sense that it is correct to say "In the early days, Fort Dingbat was just a circular pile of stone and rubble; only under the administration of Colonel Graft did it grow into the imposing edifice we see today." In neither case is the "was" the past tense of the "is" of identity; if it were, then Fort Dingbat could not have been added to and remained the same fort, nor could Jones's pain at t have been realized in some other structure than the fiber f. Neither are these "was"s instances of the past tense of the "is" of predication. Instead, they represent what might be called the "is" of composition (or of realization or constitution). There is nothing dubious about this use of the verb "to be," but it has nothing significant to do with identity.

An additional reason for rejecting the identity of a token event, state, or process with its actual realization is provided by the observation that the same set of molecular motions may realize several different token events, states, or processes, as well as several different types of events, states, or processes. For example, suppose that the set of molecular motions that realizes Jim's pain at t constitute the firing of a particular C-fiber f. Then these motions realize at least three different token states: Jim's pain at t, the firing at t of f, and the token event that satisfies the description "the motion of m_1 along t_1, and the motion of m_2 along t_2, and the motion . . ." where the enumeration describes the precise trajectory for each of the molecules involved in the actual world of Jim's pain at t. These token states are not identical (as one can easily see by reflecting on the fact that, for any pair of them, there is a possible world in which only one is manifested), so they could hardly all be identical to the particular set of molecular motions in question (the third token state is, of course, identical to just that set of motions).

These considerations have the effect of making token events, states, and processes seem less like stereotypical "individuals" and more like type events, states, or processes—more like "universals"—in that a token event, for example, may have more than one instance (although in different possible worlds), to none of which it need be identical. This would be worrisome were it not for the fact that consideration of the issue of reidentification of individuals (physical things, for example, and people) over time shows that individuals are not very much like the convenient philosophical stereotype of individuals either.

Some philosophers (for instance, Geach, 1957) have suggested shifting whatever mystery there is in these facts about token events, states, and processes (and objects, as well) from the realm of metaphysics (physics?) to the realm of language by maintaining that some or all identity statements are incomplete unless they involve a sortal that specifies the sort of sameness relation in question. Thus, a particular set of molecular motions might be the *same mental state* as Jones's pain at *t*, the *same physiological state* as the firing of fiber *f* at *t*, the *same chemical state* as something else, but it would be a misuse of language to say that it was the same state (*simpliciter*) as any of these since the expression "the same state as" is incomplete and without definite meaning unless qualified by some such adjective as "mental," "physiological," or "chemical." There is, in other words, no such thing as identity *simpliciter* between states.

Such a solution has, in my view, little merit since it leaves to be explained what the various qualified sameness relations have in common, and the only sound answer to that seems to be that the sentence "*a* is the same *F* as *b*" is true just in case the *F* that *a* realizes is identical (*simpliciter*) to the *F* that *b* realizes. At any rate, whatever the merits of this linguistic maneuver, it does illustrate a tendency that provides the historical basis (and much of the current plausibility) for the view that materialism entails mind-body identity statements of the sorts I have been discussing. I have in mind the tendency to formulate or "rationally reconstruct" "metaphysical" statements as non-"metaphysical" statements regarding syntactic features of appropriate terms and sentences. It is this tendency that underlies both the "Lockean" conceptions of language and necessity and the view that the claims of materialist psychology are to be analyzed as claims about the syntactic reducibility of the terms and laws of psychology to the terms and laws of physics. The results of this paper should provide additional evidence—assuming such evidence is needed—of the bankruptcy of such "antimetaphysical" positivist positions in the philosophy of language and the philosophy of science.

12. Conclusion

I remarked earlier that Kripke's account of natural kind terms not only served to clarify essentialist criticisms of materialism, but also provided the foundations of an account of language that is crucial to the defense of materialism. The rival Lockean account of general terms, I argued, had the effect of treating as unrefutable linguistic conventions whatever principles of classification into natural kinds are most fundamental to current practice. Such an account makes any theoretical claims that involve fundamental change in classification (of the sort materialist psychology proposes) false by definition! Thus the Lockean account of natural kind terms appears to be incompatible with (or at least to pose very serious difficulties for) the view that materialist psychology is even logically possible, much less confirmable. Understanding natural kind terms as referring ostensively, as Kripke proposed, makes it possible to hold that some or all such terms are used to refer to kinds whose essential properties are to be discovered by scientific (or other) investigation, but not by reflection on linguistic conventions. Such an account of natural kind terms seems essential to a satisfactory account of the many cases in which research on a particular natural kind may turn up facts that are at variance with the most fundamental earlier beliefs regarding that kind, and such an account is therefore essential to a satisfactory understanding of the claims of materialist psychology. The implications for the philosophy of science of this ostensive view of reference of general terms are only now being investigated (see, for example, Goldstein, 1977; Putnam, 1975b), and much work in this area has yet to be done.

It must be remarked that in holding, with Kripke, that there is an ostensive aspect to the way in which the reference of natural kind terms and other scientific terms is fixed one need not necessarily hold, as Kripke seems to, that there is *no* descriptive component to the reference-fixing "apparatus" of such terms, nor need one hold that the scientifically relevant notion of essential property has sufficiently clear application outside the actual world to support the account of logical necessity offered in Kripke's work. Nevertheless, such an account of logical necessity does seem to be necessary in order to capture the force of essentialist criticisms of materialism, and some sort of ostensive account of the reference of general terms seems essential to any account of the possibility of genuinely novel scientific discoveries.

Thus, if Kripke's criticisms of materialism fail, they nevertheless provide us with the opportunity to examine the strongest versions of the sort of essentialist criticisms they represent, and the account of language on which they rest will undoubtedly play an important role in the development of postpositivist philosophy of science.

Notes

1. An especially clear and compelling expression of this optimism regarding the eventual physical explicability of mental phenomena is given by Smart (1970).

2. For argumentation of this sort, see Place, 1970, and Smart, 1970.

3. See Locke, 1690, book III, especially chap. iv. I do not mean to suggest that Locke, among the traditional empiricists, has had the most direct influence on the philosophy of language of contemporary logical empiricism. That honor certainly falls to Hume. Locke has priority, nevertheless, and his especial concern for the issue of essential properties makes it only fair to cite him in a discussion of Kripke's views. See Kretzmann, 1968, for an interesting discussion of Locke's semantic theory.

4. See Locke, book III, chap. vi, especially sections 8, 9, 10. This discussion does not deviate importantly from contemporary empiricist accounts.

5. The reader will recognize the similarity between this empiricist doctrine regarding change of classificatory principles and T. S. Kuhn's treatment of change of "paradigm." Despite his intention to be antiempiricist, Kuhn's relativistic treatment of paradigm change depends on just the sort of empiricist conception of language and conceptual change that I am discussing here (see Kuhn, 1962).

6. The term "theoretical identity" appears in Putnam, 1960. The best explicated version of this doctrine seems to be that defended by Nagel (1965). His "postscript" (Nagel, 1971) repudiates this particular view, but Nagel, 1965, remains the clearest exposition of it. Cornman (1962) speaks of a kind of "cross-category identity" immune from some applications of Leibniz's Law. The doctrine that the "identity thesis" is not really an *identity* thesis is also implied by various treatments of the issue of predicating mental predicates of brain states and physical predicates of mental states; see Cornman, 1962; Feyerabend, 1963; Rorty, 1965; Shaffer, 1961.

7. Rorty (1965) does insist that "language changes as empirical discoveries are made," but he does not discuss in detail the relation between this fact and empiricist theories meaning. Similarly, Putnam (1967) talks about "not wholly unmotivated extension of ordinary language" as underlying theoretical identifications.

8. For an explicit version of this view, see Feyerabend, 1963.

9. See, for example, Carnap, 1937, 1956; Schlick, 1959.

10. These examples are from Cornman, 1962.

11. Many philosophers propose to cope with this difficulty, and related difficulties regarding the issue of discovery versus "meaning change," by adopting a modification of the Lockean account of general terms according to which the meaning (and the reference) of a general term is fixed by a cluster (often a "law-cluster") of criteria a sufficient number, *but not all*, of which must remain unchanged if meaning is to be preserved. These "clusters" consist of the most deeply entrenched of the criteria actually employed in the typical usage of the term.

It is by no means clear that this strategy succeeds any better than those discussed later in this section. In the first place, it has proven remarkably difficult to spell out just which subsets of criteria in a "cluster" are sufficient for meaning-preservation (indeed, it is hard to say just what goes into the "cluster" and what does not). The issue seems so sensitive to conflicting intuitions and judgments that one wonders if any doctrine along these lines is available except that we decide by convention *after the fact* what changes in criteria we *will* take to have preserved meaning. This solution would hardly help the beleaguered Lockean materialist.

Finally, even if a satisfactory account of sufficiency were available, it is by no means clear that materialism could escape the charge that it involves unacceptable changes in the "clusters" associated with both physical and mental terms. Consistent materialism would—as everyone recognizes—require us to say a very large number of things that now seem so strange that many would consider them sense-less.

12. Strictly speaking, we may distinguish two features of Kripke's account of natural kind terms, *both* of which are required for an adequate defense of the revisability of fundamental principles of classification. In the first place, of course, a non-Lockean causal theory of reference for natural kind terms is a prerequisite for any account according to which natural kinds are not defined by conventionally fixed criteria of classification. A causal account of the mechanism of reference for natural kind terms, of the sort Kripke offers, *does not*, however, by itself preclude the view that natural kinds are defined by conventionally fixed (and logically necessary) criteria of classification. It is perfectly consistent to maintain—following Locke—that natural kinds are defined in just that way while adopting a causal theory of reference for the terms that refer to them. According to such a modified Lockean account, the first users of a natural kind term *T* would establish (by arbitrary convention) a set of logically necessary and sufficient defining properties for the kind referred to by *T*. A subsequent use of the term *T* would refer to the same natural (artificial?) kind if and only if it bore the right sort of causal relation to the original "dubbing" use of *T*.

Such an account accepts Locke's understanding of what a natural kind is (roughly, the extension of a conventionally fixed set of criteria) but a Kripkean account of the way in which terms refer to these kinds. This account is essentially Lockean. Indeed, it is probably the most plausible version of the Lockean account since it makes it easy to explain how someone can use a natural kind term to refer to a conventionally defined natural kind even though he does not himself know what the conventional definition is. "I especially want to see the gnus. I haven't the foggiest idea what

they are like." It remains, in particular, an account according to which the essence of a natural kind is its "nominal essence": according to which logical necessity is always verbal necessity.

The second component, then, in Kripke's account of natural kind terms is the claim that they refer to real rather than to nominal essences. Kripke's achievement is to show how such an account can be integrated into a plausible theory of reference. He does not, however, offer a fully developed non-Lockean account of natural kinds themselves. Such accounts will be required before the relevance of Kripke's work to the philosophy of science can be fully appreciated.

13. I am grateful to William Wimsatt and Sydney Shoemaker for helpful discussions regarding this point. I use the term "scope" at Wimsatt's suggestion.

14. It is, of course, arguable that there are no purely phenomenal states: that certain relations to bodily behavior are essential for every sort of mental state. It is beyond the scope of this paper to explore that issue. I here accept, for the sake of argument, Kripke's view that their qualitative character is essential to, and definitive of, for example, pains in man.

15. For discussions (pro and con) of functionalism see Armstrong, 1968; Block, 1978; Block and Fodor, 1972; Fodor, 1965, 1968; Putnam, 1975a, 1975c, 1975d, 1975e; Shoemaker, 1975. Block (1978) makes the interesting observation that, although functionalism entails that mental states cannot be identified with particular states of the central nervous system (since functionalism entails that mental states could be realized by nonbiological states), many authors nevertheless take functionalism to *support* the view that mental states are identical to physical states of the central nervous system. The discussion that follows, together with the earlier parts of section 11, can be taken as a resolution of the puzzle that Block raises. What materialists should claim is that mental states are *in fact* central-nervous-system states but that their having a central nervous system realization is not essential to them. Such an account is exactly like the one defended here: that mental states are identical to contingently physical states.

References

Armstrong, D. M. 1968. *A Materialist Theory of Mind.* London: Routledge and Kegan Paul.

Block, N. 1978. "Troubles with Functionalism." In C. W. Savage, ed., *Perception and Cognition. Issues in the Foundations of Psychology. Minnesota Studies in the Philosophy of Science,* vol. 9. Minneapolis: University of Minnesota Press.

Block, N., and J. A. Fodor. 1972. "What Psychological States Are Not." *Philosophical Review* 81, no. 2 (April):159-181.

Boyd, R. 1973. "Realism, Underdetermination and a Causal Theory of Evidence." *Nous* 7, no. 1 (March):1-12.

―――― Forthcoming. *Realism and Scientific Epistemology.* London: Cambridge University Press.

Carnap, R. 1937. *The Logical Syntax of Language.* London: Routledge and Kegan Paul.

―――― 1956. "Empiricism, Semantics and Ontology." In *Meaning and Necessity.* Chicago: University of Chicago Press.

Castañeda, H.-N. 1967. *Intentionality, Minds, and Perception.* Detroit: Wayne State University Press.

Cornman, J. 1962. "The Identity of Mind and Body." *Journal of Philosophy* 59 (August 30):486-492.

Feyerabend, P. 1963. "Mental Events and the Brain." *Journal of Philosophy* 60, no. 11: 295-296.

Fodor, J. A. 1965. "Explanation in Psychology." In M. Black, ed., *Philosophy in America.* Ithaca: Cornell University Press.

―――― 1968. *Psychological Explanation.* New York: Random House.

Geach, P. 1957. *Reference and Generality.* Ithaca: Cornell University Press.

Goldstein, A. 1977. "Meaning Reference and Theory-Change." Ph.D. dissertation, University of Michigan.

Haldane, J. S. 1914. *Mechanism, Life and Personality.* New York: Dutton.

Kretzmann, N. 1968. "The Main Thesis of Locke's Semantic Theory." *Philosophical Review* 77:175-196.

Kripke, S. 1972. "Naming and Necessity." In D. Davidson, ed., *Semantics of Natural Language.* New York: Humanities Press.

Kuhn, T. S. 1962. *The Structure of Scientific Revolutions.* Chicago: University of Chicago Press.

Locke, J. 1690. *An Essay Concerning Human Understanding.* New York: Dover, 1959.

Nagel, T. 1965. "Physicalism." *Philosophical Review* 74, no. 3:339-356.

―――― 1971. "Physicalism," with "Postscript." In D. Rosenthal, ed., *Materialism and the Mind-Body Problem.* Englewood Cliffs, N.J.: Prentice-Hall.

Place, U. T. 1970. "Is Consciousness a Brain Process?" In C. V. Borst, ed., *The Mind/Brain Identity Theory.* London: Macmillan.

Putnam, H. 1960. "Minds and Machines." In S. Hook, ed., *Dimensions of Mind.* New York: New York University Press.

―――― 1975a. "Brains and Behavior." In *Mind, Language, and Reality. Philosophical Papers,* vol. 2. London: Cambridge University Press.

―――― 1975b. "The Meaning of Meaning." In *Mind, Language, and Reality. Philosophical Papers,* vol. 2. London: Cambridge University Press.

―――― 1975c. "The Mental Life of Some Machines." In *Mind, Language, and Reality. Philosophical Papers,* vol. 2. London: Cambridge University Press.

―――― 1975d. "The Nature of Mental States." In *Mind, Language, and Reality. Philosophical Papers,* vol. 2. London: Cambridge University Press.

―――― 1975e. "Philosophy and Our Mental Life." In *Mind, Language, and Reality. Philosophical Papers,* vol. 2. London: Cambridge University Press.

Rorty, R. 1965. "Mind-Body Identity, Privacy and Categories." *Review of Metaphysics* 19 (September):24-54.

Schlick, M. 1959. "Positivism and Realism." In A. J. Ayer, ed., *Logical Positivism.* Glencoe, Ill.: Free Press.

Shaffer, J. 1961. "Could Mental States Be Brain Processes?" *Journal of Philosophy* 58 (December 21):813-822.

Shoemaker, S. 1975. "Functionalism and Qualia." *Philosophical Studies* 27 (May):291-315.

Smart, J. J. C. 1970. "Sensations and Brain Processes." In C. V. Borst, ed., *The Mind/Brain Identity Theory.* London: Macmillan.

Mental Events

Donald Davidson

Mental events such as perceivings, rememberings, decisions, and actions resist capture in the nomological net of physical theory.[1] How can this fact be reconciled with the causal role of mental events in the physical world? Reconciling freedom with causal determinism is a special case of the problem if we suppose that causal determinism entails capture in, and freedom requires escape from, the nomological net. But the broader issue can remain alive even for someone who believes a correct analysis of free action reveals no conflict with determinism. *Autonomy* (freedom, self-rule) may or may not clash with determinism; *anomaly* (failure to fall under a law) is, it would seem, another matter.

I start from the assumption that both the causal dependence, and the anomalousness, of mental events are undeniable facts. My aim is therefore to explain, in the face of apparent difficulties, how this can be. I am in sympathy with Kant when he says,

From Lawrence Foster and J. W. Swanson, eds., *Experience and Theory* (Amherst: University of Massachusetts Press, 1970), pp. 79-101. Copyright © 1970 by the University of Massachusetts Press. Reprinted by permission of the publisher.

it is as impossible for the subtlest philosophy as for the commonest reasoning to argue freedom away. Philosophy must therefore assume that no true contradiction will be found between freedom and natural necessity in the same human actions, for it cannot give up the idea of nature any more than that of freedom. Hence even if we should never be able to conceive how freedom is possible, at least this apparent contradiction must be convincingly eradicated. For if the thought of freedom contradicts itself or nature . . . it would have to be surrendered in competition with natural necessity.[2]

Generalize human actions to mental events, substitute anomaly for freedom, and this is a description of my problem. And of course the connection is closer, since Kant believed freedom entails anomaly.

Now let me try to formulate a little more carefully the "apparent contradiction" about mental events that I want to discuss and finally dissipate. It may be seen as stemming from three principles.

The first principle asserts that at least some mental events interact causally with physical events. (We could call this the Principle of Causal Interaction.) Thus for example if someone sank the *Bismarck*, then various mental events such as perceivings, notings, calculations, judgments, decisions, intentional actions and changes of belief played a causal role in the sinking of the *Bismarck*. In particular, I would urge that the fact that someone sank the *Bismarck* entails that he moved his body in a way that was caused by mental events of certain sorts, and that this bodily movement in turn caused the *Bismarck* to sink.[3] Perception illustrates how causality may run from the physical to the mental: if a man perceives that a ship is approaching, then a ship approaching must have caused him to come to believe that a ship is approaching. (Nothing depends on accepting these as examples of causal interaction.)

Though perception and action provide the most obvious cases where mental and physical events interact causally, I think reasons could be given for the view that all mental events ultimately, perhaps through causal relations with other mental events, have causal intercourse with physical events. But if there are mental events that have no physical events as causes or effects, the argument will not touch them.

The second principle is that where there is causality, there must be a law: events related as cause and effect fall under strict deterministic laws. (We may term this the Principle of the Nomological Character of Causality.) This principle, like the first, will be treated here as an assumption, though I shall say something by way of interpretation.[4]

The third principle is that there are no strict deterministic laws on the basis of which mental events can be predicted and explained (the Anomalism of the Mental).

The paradox I wish to discuss arises for someone who is inclined to accept these three assumptions or principles, and who thinks they are inconsistent with one another. The inconsistency is not, of course, formal unless more premises are added. Nevertheless it is natural to reason

that the first two principles, that of causal interaction, and that of the nomological character of causality, together imply that at least some mental events can be predicted and explained on the basis of laws, while the principle of the anomalism of the mental denies this. Many philosophers have accepted, with or without argument, the view that the three principles do lead to a contradiction. It seems to me, however, that all three principles are true, so that what must be done is to explain away the appearance of contradiction; essentially the Kantian line.

The rest of this paper falls into three parts. The first part describes a version of the identity theory of the mental and the physical that shows how the three principles may be reconciled. The second part argues that there cannot be strict psychophysical laws; this is not quite the principle of the anomalism of the mental, but on reasonable assumptions entails it. The last part tries to show that from the fact that there can be no strict psychophysical laws, and our other two principles, we can infer the truth of a version of the identity theory, that is, a theory that identifies at least some mental events with physical events. It is clear that this "proof" of the identity theory will be at best conditional, since two of its premises are unsupported, and the argument for the third may be found less than conclusive. But even someone unpersuaded of the truth of the premises may be interested to learn how they may be reconciled and that they serve to establish a version of the identity theory of the mental. Finally, if the argument is a good one, it should lay to rest the view, common to many friends and some foes of identity theories, that support for such theories can come only from the discovery of psychophysical laws.

I

The three principles will be shown consistent with one another by describing a view of the mental and the physical that contains no inner contradiction and that entails the three principles. According to this view, mental events are identical with physical events. Events are taken to be unrepeatable, dated individuals such as the particular eruption of a volcano, the (first) birth or death of a person, the playing of the 1968 World Series, or the historic utterance of the words, "You may fire when ready, Gridley." We can easily frame identity statements about individual events; examples (true or false) might be:

> The death of Scott = the death of the author of *Waverley*;
> The assassination of the Archduke Ferdinand = the event that started the First World War;
> The eruption of Vesuvius in A.D. 79 = the cause of the destruction of Pompeii.

The theory under discussion is silent about processes, states, and attributes if these differ from individual events.

What does it mean to say that an event is mental or physical? One natural answer is that an event is physical if it is describable in a purely physical vocabulary, mental if describable in mental terms. But if this is taken to suggest that an event is physical, say, if some physical predicate is true of it, then there is the following difficulty. Assume that the predicate 'x took place at Noosa Heads' belongs to the physical vocabulary; then so also must the predicate 'x did not take place at Noosa Heads' belong to the physical vocabulary. But the predicate 'x did or did not take place at Noosa Heads' is true of every event, whether mental or physical.[5] We might rule out predicates that are tautologically true of every event, but this will not help since every event is truly describable either by 'x took place at Noosa Heads' or by 'x did not take place at Noosa Heads.' A different approach is needed.[6]

We may call those verbs mental that express propositional attitudes like believing, intending, desiring, hoping, knowing, perceiving, noticing, remembering, and so on. Such verbs are characterized by the fact that they sometimes feature in sentences with subjects that refer to persons, and are completed by embedded sentences in which the usual rules of substitution appear to break down. This criterion is not precise, since I do not want to include these verbs when they occur in contexts that are fully extensional ('He knows Paris,' 'He perceives the moon' may be cases), nor exclude them whenever they are not followed by embedded sentences. An alternative characterization of the desired class of mental verbs might be that they are psychological verbs as used when they create apparently nonextensional contexts.

Let us call a description of the form 'the event that is M' or an open sentence of the form 'event x is M' a *mental description* or a *mental open sentence* if and only if the expression that replaces 'M' contains at least one mental verb essentially. (Essentially, so as to rule out cases where the description or open sentence is logically equivalent to one not containing mental vocabulary.) Now we may say that an event is mental if and only if it has a mental description, or (the description operator not being primitive) if there is a mental open sentence true of that event alone. Physical events are those picked out by descriptions or open sentences that contain only the physical vocabulary essentially. It is less important to characterize a physical vocabulary because relative to the mental it is, so to speak, recessive in determining whether a description is mental or physical. (There will be some comments presently on the nature of a physical vocabulary, but these comments will fall far short of providing a criterion.)

On the proposed test of the mental, the distinguishing feature of the mental is not that it is private, subjective, or immaterial, but that it exhibits what Brentano called intentionality. Thus intentional actions are clearly included in the realm of the mental along with thoughts, hopes, and regrets (or the events tied to these). What may seem doubtful is whether the criterion will include events that have often been considered paradigmatic of the mental. Is it obvious, for example, that feeling a pain or seeing an afterimage will count as mental? Sentences that report such events seem free from taint of non-extensionality, and the same should be true of reports of raw feels, sense data, and other uninterpreted sensations, if there are any.

However, the criterion actually covers not only the havings of pains and afterimages, but much more besides. Take some event one would intuitively accept as physical, let's say the collision of two stars in distant space. There must be a purely physical predicate 'Px' true of this collision, and of others, but true of only this one at the time it occurred. This particular time, though, may be pinpointed as the same time that Jones notices that a pencil starts to roll across his desk. The distant stellar collision is thus *the* event x such that Px and x is simultaneous with Jones' noticing that a pencil starts to roll across his desk. The collision has now been picked out by a mental description and must be counted as a mental event.

This strategy will probably work to show every event to be mental; we have obviously failed to capture the intuitive concept of the mental. It would be instructive to try to mend this trouble, but it is not necessary for present purposes. We can afford Spinozistic extravagance with the mental since accidental inclusions can only strengthen the hypothesis that all mental events are identical with physical events. What would matter would be failure to include bona fide mental events, but of this there seems to be no danger.

I want to describe, and presently to argue for, a version of the identity theory that denies that there can be strict laws

connecting the mental and the physical. The very possibility of such a theory is easily obscured by the way in which identity theories are commonly defended and attacked. Charles Taylor, for example, agrees with protagonists of identity theories that the sole "ground" for accepting such theories is the supposition that correlations or laws can be established linking events described as mental with events described as physical. He says, "It is easy to see why this is so: unless a given mental event is invariably accompanied by a given, say, brain process, there is no ground for even mooting a general identity between the two."[7] Taylor goes on (correctly, I think) to allow that there may be identity without correlating laws, but my present interest is in noticing the invitation to confusion in the statement just quoted. What can "a given mental event" mean here? Not a particular, dated, event, for it would not make sense to speak of an individual event being "invariably accompanied" by another. Taylor is evidently thinking of events of a given *kind*. But if the only identities are of kinds of events, the identity theory presupposes correlating laws.

One finds the same tendency to build laws into the statement of the identity theory in these typical remarks:

When I say that a sensation is a brain process or that lightning is an electrical discharge, I am using 'is' in the sense of strict identity . . . there are not two things: a flash of lightning and an electrical discharge. There is one thing, a flash of lightning, which is described scientifically as an electrical discharge to the earth from a cloud of ionized water molecules.[8]

The last sentence of this quotation is perhaps to be understood as saying that for every lightning flash there exists an electrical discharge to the earth from a cloud of ionized water molecules with which it is identical. Here we have an honest ontology of individual events and can make literal sense of identity. We can also see how there could be identities without correlating laws. It is possible, however, to have an ontology of events with the conditions of individuation specified in such a way that any identity implies a correlating law. Kim, for example, suggests that Fa and Gb "describe or refer to the same event" if and only if $a = b$ and the property of being F = the property of being G. The identity of the properties in turn entails that $(x)(Fx \longleftrightarrow Gx)$.[9] [Editor's note: In this anthology, "$\longleftrightarrow$" is used instead of the triple bar and the double arrow as the material biconditional ("if and only if").] No wonder Kim says:

> If pain is identical with brain state B, there must be a concomitance between occurrences of pain and occurrences of brain state B. . . . Thus, a necessary condition of the pain-brain state B identity is that the two expressions 'being in pain' and 'being in brain state B' have the same extension. . . . There is no conceivable observation that would confirm or refute the identity but not the associated correlation.[10]

It may make the situation clearer to give a fourfold classification of theories of the relation between mental and physical events that emphasizes the independence of claims about laws and claims of identity. On the one hand there are those who assert, and those who deny, the existence of psychophysical laws; on the other hand there are those who say mental events are identical with physical and those who deny this. Theories are thus divided into four sorts: *Nomological monism*, which affirms that there are correlating laws and that the events correlated are one (materialists belong in this category); *nomological dualism*, which comprises various forms of parallelism, interactionism, and epiphenomenalism; *anomalous dualism*, which combines ontological dualism with the general failure of laws correlating the mental and the physical (Cartesianism). And finally there is *anomalous monism*,

which classifies the position I wish to occupy.[11]

Anomalous monism resembles materialism in its claim that all events are physical, but rejects the thesis, usually considered essential to materialism, that mental phenomena can be given purely physical explanations. Anomalous monism shows an ontological bias only in that it allows the possibility that not all events are mental, while insisting that all events are physical. Such a bland monism, unbuttressed by correlating laws or conceptual economies, does not seem to merit the term "reductionism"; in any case it is not apt to inspire the nothing-but reflex ("Conceiving the *Art of the Fugue* was nothing but a complex neural event," and so forth).

Although the position I describe denies there are psychophysical laws, it is consistent with the view that mental characteristics are in some sense dependent, or supervenient, on physical characteristics. Such supervenience might be taken to mean that there cannot be two events alike in all physical respects but differing in some mental respect, or that an object cannot alter in some mental respect without altering in some physical respect. Dependence or supervenience of this kind does not entail reducibility through law or definition: if it did, we could reduce moral properties to descriptive, and this there is good reason to *believe* cannot be done; and we might be able to reduce truth in a formal system to syntactical properties, and this we *know* cannot in general be done.

This last example is in useful analogy with the sort of lawless monism under consideration. Think of the physical vocabulary as the entire vocabulary of some language L with resources adequate to express a certain amount of mathematics, and its own syntax. L' is L augmented with the truth predicate 'true-in-L,' which is "mental." In L (and hence L') it is possible to pick out, with a definite description or

open sentence, each sentence in the extension of the truth predicate, but if L is consistent there exists no predicate of syntax
(of the "physical" vocabulary), no matter
how complex, that applies to all and only
the true sentences of L. There can be no
"psychophysical law" in the form of a biconditional, '(x) (x is true-in-L if and only
if x is F)' where 'F' is replaced by a "physical" predicate (a predicate of L). Similarly,
we can pick out each mental event using
the physical vocabulary alone, but no
purely physical predicate, no matter how
complex, has, as a matter of law, the same
extension as a mental predicate.

It should now be evident how anomalous monism reconciles the three original
principles. Causality and identity are relations between individual events no matter how described. But laws are linguistic;
and so events can instantiate laws, and
hence be explained or predicted in the
light of laws, only as those events are described in one or another way. The principle of causal interaction deals with
events in extension and is therefore blind
to the mental-physical dichotomy. The
principle of the anomalism of the mental
concerns events described as mental, for
events are mental only as described. The
principle of the nomological character of
causality must be read carefully: it says
that when events are related as cause and
effect, they have descriptions that instantiate a law. It does not say that every true
singular statement of causality instan-
tiates a law.[12]

II

The analogy just bruited, between
the place of the mental amid the physical,
and the place of the semantical in a world
of syntax, should not be strained. Tarski
proved that a consistent language cannot
(under some natural assumptions) contain
an open sentence 'Fx' true of all and only
the true sentences of that language. If our
analogy were pressed, then we would expect a proof that there can be no physical
open sentence 'Px' true of all and only the

events having some mental property. In
fact, however, nothing I can say about the
irreducibility of the mental deserves to be
called a proof; and the kind of irreducibility is different. For if anomalous monism
is correct, not only can every mental event
be uniquely singled out using only physical concepts, but since the number of
events that falls under each mental predicate may, for all we know, be finite, there
may well exist a physical open sentence
coextensive with each mental predicate,
though to construct it might involve the
tedium of a lengthy and uninstructive al-
ternation. Indeed, even if finitude is not
assumed, there seems no compelling reason to deny that there could be coextensive predicates, one mental and one physical.

The thesis is rather that the mental is
nomologically irreducible: there may be
true general statements relating the mental
and the physical, statements that have the
logical form of a law; but they are not
lawlike (in a strong sense to be described).
If by absurdly remote chance we were to
stumble on a nonstochastic true psychophysical generalization, we would have
no reason to believe it more than roughly
true.

Do we, by declaring that there are no
(strict) psychophysical laws, poach on the
empirical preserves of science—a form of
hubris against which philosophers are
often warned? Of course, to judge a statement lawlike or illegal is not to decide its
truth outright; relative to the acceptance
of a general statement on the basis of instances, ruling it lawlike must be a priori.
But such relative apriorism does not in itself justify philosophy, for in general the
grounds for deciding to trust a statement
on the basis of its instances will in turn be
governed by theoretical and empirical
concerns not to be distinguished from
those of science. If the case of supposed
laws linking the mental and the physical is
different, it can only be because to allow
the possibility of such laws would amount
to changing the subject. By changing the

subject I mean here: deciding not to accept the criterion of the mental in terms of the vocabulary of the propositional attitudes. This short answer cannot prevent further ramifications of the problem, however, for there is no clear line between changing the subject and changing what one says on an old subject, which is to admit, in the present context at least, that there is no clear line between philosophy and science. Where there are no fixed boundaries only the timid never risk trespass.

It will sharpen our appreciation of the anomological character of mental-physical generalizations to consider a related matter, the failure of definitional behaviorism. Why are we willing (as I assume we are) to abandon the attempt to give explicit definitions of mental concepts in terms of behavioral ones? Not, surely, just because all actual tries are conspicuously inadequate. Rather it is because we are persuaded, as we are in the case of so many other forms of definitional reductionism (naturalism in ethics, instrumentalism and operationalism in the sciences, the causal theory of meaning, phenomenalism, and so on—the catalogue of philosophy's defeats), that there is system in the failures. Suppose we try to say, not using any mental concepts, what it is for a man to believe there is life on Mars. One line we could take is this: when a certain sound is produced in the man's presence ("Is there life on Mars?") he produces another ("Yes"). But of course this shows he believes there is life on Mars only if he understands English, his production of the sound was intentional, and was a response to the sounds as meaning something in English; and so on. For each discovered deficiency, we add a new proviso. Yet no matter how we patch and fit the non-mental conditions, we always find the need for an additional condition (provided he *notices, understands*, etc.) that is mental in character.[13]

A striking feature of attempts at definitional reduction is how little seems to hinge on the question of synonymy between definiens and definiendum. Of course, by imagining counterexamples we do discredit claims of synonymy. But the pattern of failure prompts a stronger conclusion: if we were to find an open sentence couched in behavioral terms and exactly coextensive with some mental predicate, nothing could reasonably persuade us that we had found it. We know too much about thought and behavior to trust exact and universal statements linking them. Beliefs and desires issue in behavior only as modified and mediated by further beliefs and desires, attitudes and attendings, without limit. Clearly this holism of the mental realm is a clue both to the autonomy and to the anomalous character of the mental.

These remarks apropos definitional behaviorism provide at best hints of why we should not expect nomological connections between the mental and the physical. The central case invites further consideration.

Lawlike statements are general statements that support counterfactual and subjunctive claims, and are supported by their instances. There is (in my view) no nonquestion-begging criterion of the lawlike, which is not to say there are no reasons in particular cases for a judgment. Lawlikeness is a matter of degree, which is not to deny that there may be cases beyond debate. And within limits set by the conditions of communication, there is room for much variation between individuals in the pattern of statements to which various degrees of nomologicality are assigned. In all these respects, nomologicality is much like analyticity, as one might expect since both are linked to meaning.

'All emeralds are green' is lawlike in that its instances confirm it, but 'all emeralds are grue' is not, for 'grue' means 'observed before time *t* and green, otherwise blue,' and if our observations were all made before *t* and uniformly revealed green emeralds, this would not be a reason to expect other emeralds to be blue. Nelson Goodman has suggested that this shows that some predicates, 'grue' for example, are unsuited to laws (and thus a criterion of suitable predicates could lead to a criterion of the lawlike). But it seems to me the anomalous character of 'All emeralds are grue' shows only that the predicates 'is an emerald' and 'is grue' are not suited to one another: grueness is not an inductive property of emeralds. Grueness *is* however an inductive property of entities of other sorts, for instance of emerires. (Something is an emerire if it is examined before *t* and is an emerald, and otherwise is a sapphire.) Not only is 'All emerires are grue' entailed by the conjunction of the lawlike statements 'All emeralds are green' and 'All sapphires are blue,' but there is no reason, as far as I can see, to reject the deliverance of intuition, that it is itself lawlike.[14] Nomological statements bring together predicates that we know a priori are made for each other— know, that is, independently of knowing whether the evidence supports a connection between them. 'Blue,' 'red,' and 'green' are made for emeralds, sapphires, and roses; 'grue,' 'bleen,' and 'gred' are made for sapphalds, emerires, and emeroses.

The direction in which the discussion seems headed is this: mental and physical predicates are not made for one another. In point of lawlikeness, psychophysical statements are more like 'All emeralds are grue' than like 'All emeralds are green.'

Before this claim is plausible, it must be seriously modified. The fact that emeralds examined before *t* are grue not only is no reason to believe all emeralds are grue; it is not even a reason (if we know the time) to believe *any* unobserved emeralds are grue. But if an event of a certain mental sort has usually been accompanied by an event of a certain physical sort, this often is a good reason to expect other cases to follow suit roughly in proportion. The generalizations that embody such

practical wisdom are assumed to be only roughly true, or they are explicitly stated in probabilistic terms, or they are insulated from counterexample by generous escape clauses. Their importance lies mainly in the support they lend singular causal claims and related explanations of particular events. The support derives from the fact that such a generalization, however crude and vague, may provide good reason to believe that underlying the particular case there is a regularity that could be formulated sharply and without caveat.

In our daily traffic with events and actions that must be foreseen or understood, we perforce make use of the sketchy summary generalization, for we do not know a more accurate law, or if we do, we lack a description of the particular events in which we are interested that would show the relevance of the law. But there is an important distinction to be made within the category of the rude rule of thumb. On the one hand, there are generalizations whose positive instances give us reason to believe the generalization itself could be improved by adding further provisos and conditions stated in the same general vocabulary as the original generalization. Such a generalization points to the form and vocabulary of the finished law: we may say that it is a *homonomic* generalization. On the other hand there are generalizations which when instantiated may give us reason to believe there is a precise law at work, but one that can be stated only by shifting to a different vocabulary. We may call such generalizations *heteronomic*.

I suppose most of our practical lore (and science) is heteronomic. This is because a law can hope to be precise, explicit, and as exceptionless as possible only if it draws its concepts from a comprehensive closed theory. This ideal theory may or may not be deterministic, but it is if any true theory is. Within the physical sciences we do find homonomic generalizations, generalizations such that if the evidence supports them, we then have reason to believe they may be sharpened indefinitely by drawing upon further physical concepts: there is a theoretical asymptote of perfect coherence with all the evidence, perfect predictability (under the terms of the system), total explanation (again under the terms of the system). Or perhaps the ultimate theory is probabilistic, and the asymptote is less than perfection; but in that case there will be no better to be had.

Confidence that a statement is homonomic, correctible within its own conceptual domain, demands that it draw its concepts from a theory with strong constitutive elements. Here is the simplest possible illustration; if the lesson carries, it will be obvious that the simplification could be mended.

The measurement of length, weight, temperature, or time depends (among many other things, of course) on the existence in each case of a two-place relation that is transitive and asymmetric: warmer than, later than, heavier than, and so forth. Let us take the relation *longer than* as our example. The law or postulate of transitivity is this:

(L) $L(x,y)$ and $L(y,z) \longrightarrow L(x,z)$

[*Editor's note*: In this anthology, "$\longrightarrow$" is used instead of the horseshoe and the arrow as the material conditional ("if . . . then").] Unless this law (or some sophisticated variant) holds, we cannot easily make sense of the concept of length. There will be no way of assigning numbers to register even so much as ranking in length, let alone the more powerful demands of measurement on a ratio scale. And this remark goes not only for any three items directly involved in an intransitivity: it is easy to show (given a few more assumptions essential to measurement of length) that there is no consistent assignment of a ranking to any item unless (L) holds in full generality.

Clearly (L) alone cannot exhaust the import of 'longer than'—otherwise it would not differ from 'warmer than' or 'later than.' We must suppose there is some empirical content, however difficult to formulate in the available vocabulary, that distinguishes 'longer than' from the other two-place transitive predicates of measurement and on the basis of which we may assert that one thing is longer than another. Imagine this empirical content to be partly given by the predicate '$o(x,y)$'. So we have this "meaning postulate":

(M) $o(x,y) \longrightarrow L(x,y)$

that partly interprets (L). But now (L) and (M) together yield an empirical theory of great strength, for together they entail that there do not exist three objects a, b, and c such that $o(a,b)$, $o(b,c)$, and $o(c,a)$. Yet what is to prevent this happening if '$o(x,y)$' is a predicate we can ever, with confidence, apply? Suppose we *think* we observe an intransitive triad; what do we say? We could count (L) false, but then we would have no application for the concept of length. We could say (M) gives a wrong test for length; but then it is unclear what we thought was the *content* of the idea of one thing being longer than another. Or we could say that the objects under observation are not, as the theory requires, *rigid* objects. It is a mistake to think we are forced to accept some one of these answers. Concepts such as that of length are sustained in equilibrium by a number of conceptual pressures, and theories of fundamental measurement are distorted if we force the decision, among such principles as (L) and (M): analytic or synthetic. It is better to say the whole set of axioms, laws, or postulates for the measurement of length is partly constitutive of the idea of a system of macroscopic, rigid, physical objects. I suggest that the existence of lawlike statements in physical science depends upon the existence of constitutive (or synthetic a priori) laws like those of the measurement of length within the same conceptual domain.

Just as we cannot intelligibly assign a length to any object unless a comprehensive theory holds of objects of that sort, we cannot intelligibly attribute any propositional attitude to an agent except within the framework of a viable theory of his beliefs, desires, intentions, and decisions.

There is no assigning beliefs to a person one by one on the basis of his verbal behavior, his choices, or other local signs no matter how plain and evident, for we make sense of particular beliefs only as they cohere with other beliefs, with preferences, with intentions, hopes, fears, expectations, and the rest. It is not merely, as with the measurement of length, that each case tests a theory and depends upon it, but that the content of a propositional attitude derives from its place in the pattern.

Crediting people with a large degree of consistency cannot be counted mere charity: it is unavoidable if we are to be in a position to accuse them meaningfully of error and some degree of irrationality. Global confusion, like universal mistake, is unthinkable, not because imagination boggles, but because too much confusion leaves nothing to be confused about and massive error erodes the background of true belief against which alone failure can be construed. To appreciate the limits to the kind and amount of blunder and bad thinking we can intelligibly pin on others is to see once more the inseparability of the question what concepts a person commands and the question what he does with those concepts in the way of belief, desire, and intention. To the extent that we fail to discover a coherent and plausible pattern in the attitudes and actions of others we simply forego the chance of treating them as persons.

The problem is not bypassed but given center stage by appeal to explicit speech behavior. For we could not begin to decode a man's sayings if we could not make out his attitudes towards his sentences, such as holding, wishing, or wanting them to be true. Beginning from these attitudes, we must work out a theory of what he means, thus simultaneously giving content to his attitudes and to his words. In our need to make him make sense, we will try for a theory that finds him consistent, a believer of truths, and a lover of the good (all by our own lights, it goes without saying). Life being what it is, there will be no simple theory that fully meets these demands. Many theories will effect a more or less acceptable compromise, and between these theories there may be no objective grounds for choice.

The heteronomic character of general statements linking the mental and the physical traces back to this central role of translation in the description of all propositional attitudes, and to the indeterminacy of translation.[15] There are no strict psychophysical laws because of the disparate commitments of the mental and physical schemes. It is a feature of physical reality that physical change can be explained by laws that connect it with other changes and conditions physically described. It is a feature of the mental that the attribution of mental phenomena must be responsible to the background of reasons, beliefs, and intentions of the individual. There cannot be tight connections between the realms if each is to retain allegiance to its proper source of evidence. The nomological irreducibility of the mental does not derive merely from the seamless nature of the world of thought, preference and intention, for such interdependence is common to physical theory, and is compatible with there being a single right way of interpreting a man's attitudes without relativization to a scheme of translation. Nor is the irreducibility due simply to the possibility of many equally eligible schemes, for this is compatible with an arbitrary choice of one scheme relative to which assignments of mental traits are made. The point is rather that when we use the concepts of belief, desire and the rest, we must stand prepared, as the evidence accumulates, to adjust our theory in the light of considerations of overall cogency: the constitutive ideal of rationality partly controls each phase in the evolution of what must be an evolving theory. An arbitrary choice of translation scheme would preclude such opportunistic tempering of theory; put differently, a right arbitrary choice of a translation manual would be of a manual acceptable in the light of all possible evidence, and this is a choice we cannot make. We must conclude, I think, that nomological slack between the mental and the physical is essential as long as we conceive of man as a rational animal.

III

The gist of the foregoing discussion, as well as its conclusion, will be familiar. That there is a categorial difference between the mental and the physical is a commonplace. It may seem odd that I say nothing of the supposed privacy of the mental, or the special authority an agent has with respect to his own propositional attitudes, but this appearance of novelty would fade if we were to investigate in more detail the grounds for accepting a scheme of translation. The step from the categorial difference between the mental and the physical to the impossibility of strict laws relating them is less common, but certainly not new. If there is a surprise, then, it will be to find the lawlessness of the mental serving to help establish the identity of the mental with that paradigm of the lawlike, the physical.

The reasoning is this. We are assuming, under the Principle of the Causal Dependence of the Mental, that some mental events at least are causes or effects of physical events; the argument applies only to these. A second Principle (of the Nomological Character of Causality) says that each true singular causal statement is backed by a strict law connecting events

of kinds to which the events mentioned as cause and effect belong. Where there are rough, but homonomic, laws, there are laws drawing on concepts from the same conceptual domain and upon which there is no improving in point of precision and comprehensiveness. We urged in the last section that such laws occur in the physical sciences. Physical theory promises to provide a comprehensive closed system guaranteed to yield a standardized, unique description of every physical event couched in a vocabulary amenable to law.

It is not plausible that mental concepts alone can provide such a framework, simply because the mental does not, by our first principle, constitute a closed system. Too much happens to affect the mental that is not itself a systematic part of the mental. But if we combine this observation with the conclusion that no psychophysical statement is, or can be built into, a strict law, we have the Principle of the Anomalism of the Mental: there are no strict laws at all on the basis of which we can predict and explain mental phenomena.

The demonstration of identity follows easily. Suppose m, a mental event, caused p, a physical event; then under some description m and p instantiate a strict law. This law can only be physical, according to the previous paragraph. But if m falls under a physical law, it has a physical description; which is to say it is a physical event. An analogous argument works when a physical event causes a mental event. So every mental event that is causally related to a physical event is a physical event. In order to establish anomalous monism in full generality it would be sufficient to show that every mental event is cause or effect of some physical event; I shall not attempt this.

If one event causes another, there is a strict law which those events instantiate when properly described. But it is possible (and typical) to know of the singular causal relation without knowing the law or the relevant descriptions. Knowledge requires reasons, but these are available in the form of rough heteronomic generalizations, which are lawlike in that instances make it reasonable to expect other instances to follow suit without being lawlike in the sense of being indefinitely refinable. Applying these facts to knowledge of identities, we see that it is possible to know that a mental event is identical with some physical event without knowing which one (in the sense of being able to give it a unique physical description that brings it under a relevant law). Even if someone knew the entire physical history of the world, and every mental event were identical with a physical, it would not follow that he could predict or explain a single mental event (so described, of course).

Two features of mental events in their relation to the physical—causal dependence and nomological independence—combine, then, to dissolve what has often seemed a paradox, the efficacy of thought and purpose in the material world, and their freedom from law. When we portray events as perceivings, rememberings, decisions and actions, we necessarily locate them amid physical happenings through the relation of cause and effect; but that same mode of portrayal insulates mental events, as long as we do not change the idiom, from the strict laws that can in principle be called upon to explain and predict physical phenomena.

Mental events as a class cannot be explained by physical science; particular mental events can when we know particular identities. But the explanations of mental events in which we are typically interested relate them to other mental events and conditions. We explain a man's free actions, for example, by appeal to his desires, habits, knowledge and perceptions. Such accounts of intentional behavior operate in a conceptual framework removed from the direct reach of physical law by describing both cause and effect,

reason and action, as aspects of a portrait of a human agent. The anomalism of the mental is thus a necessary condition for viewing action as autonomous. I conclude with a second passage from Kant:

> It is an indispensable problem of speculative philosophy to show that its illusion respecting the contradiction rests on this, that we think of man in a different sense and relation when we call him free, and when we regard him as subject to the laws of nature. . . . It must therefore show that not only can both of these very well co-exist, but that both must be thought *as necessarily united* in the same subject. . . .[16]

Notes

1. I was helped and influenced by Daniel Bennett, Sue Larson, and Richard Rorty, who are not responsible for the result. My research was supported by the National Science Foundation and the Center for Advanced Study in the Behavioral Sciences.

2. *Fundamental Principles of the Metaphysics of Morals*, trans. T. K. Abbott (London, 1909), pp. 75-76.

3. These claims are defended in my "Actions, Reasons and Causes," *The Journal of Philosophy*, 60 (1963), pp. 685-700 and in "Agency," a paper forthcoming in the proceedings of the November, 1968, colloquium on Agent, Action, and Reason at the University of Western Ontario, London, Canada.

4. In "Causal Relations," *The Journal of Philosophy*, 64 (1967), pp. 691-703, I elaborate on the view of causality assumed here. The stipulation that the laws be deterministic is stronger than required by the reasoning, and will be relaxed.

5. The point depends on assuming that mental events may intelligibly be said to have a location; but it is an assumption that must be true if an identity theory is, and here I am not trying to prove the theory but to formulate it.

6. I am indebted to Lee Bowie for emphasizing this difficulty.

7. Charles Taylor, "Mind-Body Identity, a Side Issue?" *The Philosophical Review*, 76 (1967), p. 202.

8. J. J. C. Smart, "Sensations and Brain Processes," *The Philosophical Review*, 68

(1959), pp. 141-56. The quoted passages are on pp. 163-165 of the reprinted version in *The Philosophy of Mind*, ed. V. C. Chappell (Englewood Cliffs, N. J., 1962). For another example, see David K. Lewis, "An Argument for the Identity Theory," *The Journal of Philosophy*, 63 (1966), pp. 17-25. Here the assumption is made explicit when Lewis takes events as universals (p. 17, footnotes 1 and 2). I do not suggest that Smart and Lewis are confused, only that their way of stating the identity theory tends to obscure the distinction between particular events and kinds of events on which the formulation of my theory depends.

9. Jaegwon Kim, "On the Psycho-Physical Identity Theory," *American Philosophical Quarterly*, 3 (1966), p. 231.

10. Ibid., pp. 227-28. Richard Brandt and Jaegwon Kim propose roughly the same criterion in "The Logic of the Identity Theory," *The Journal of Philosophy* 54 (1967), pp. 515-537. They remark that on their conception of event identity, the identity theory "makes a stronger claim than merely that there is a pervasive phenomenal-physical correlation" (p. 518). I do not discuss the stronger claim.

11. Anomalous monism is more or less explicitly recognized as a possible position by Herbert Feigl, "The 'Mental' and the 'Physical,' " in *Concepts, Theories and the Mind-Body Problem*, vol. 2, *Minnesota Studies in the Philosophy of Science* (Minneapolis, 1958); Sydney Shoemaker, "Ziff's Other Minds," *The Journal of Philosophy*, 62 (1965), p. 589; David Randall Luce, "Mind-Body Identity and Psycho-Physical Correlation," *Philosophical Studies*, 17 (1966), pp. 1-7; Charles Taylor, op. cit., p. 207. Something like my position is tentatively accepted by Thomas Nagel, "Physicalism," *The Philosophical Review*, 74 (1965),

pp. 339-356, and briefly endorsed by P. F. Strawson in *Freedom and the Will*, ed. D. F. Pears (London, 1963), pp. 63-67.

12. The point that substitutivity of identity fails in the context of explanation is made in connection with the present subject by Norman Malcolm, "Scientific Materialism and the Identity Theory," *Dialogue*, 3 (1964-65), pp. 123-124. See also my "Actions, Reasons and Causes," *The Journal of Philosophy*, 60 (1963), pp. 696-699 and "The Individuation of Events" in *Essays in Honor of Carl G. Hempel*, ed. N. Rescher, et al. (Dordrecht, 1969).

13. The theme is developed in Roderick Chisholm, *Perceiving* (Ithaca, New York, 1957), chap. 11.

14. This view is accepted by Richard C. Jeffrey, "Goodman's Query," *The Journal of Philosophy*, 62 (1966), p. 286 ff., John R. Wallace, "Goodman, Logic, Induction," same journal and issue, p. 318, and John M. Vickers, "Characteristics of Projectible Predicates," *The Journal of Philosophy*, 64 (1967), p. 285. On pp. 328-329 and 286-287 of these journal issues respectively Goodman disputes the lawlikeness of statements like "All emerires are grue." I cannot see, however, that he meets the point of my "Emeroses by Other Names," *The Journal of Philosophy*, 63 (1966), pp. 778-780.

15. The influence of W. V. Quine's doctrine of the indeterminacy of translation, as in chap. 2 of *Word and Object* (Cambridge, Mass., 1960), is, I hope, obvious. In section 45 Quine develops the connection between translation and the propositional attitudes, and remarks that "Brentano's thesis of the irreducibility of intentional idioms is of a piece with the thesis of indeterminacy of translation" (p. 221).

16. Op. cit, p. 76.

Special Sciences, or The Disunity of Science as a Working Hypothesis

Jerry A. Fodor

A typical thesis of positivistic philosophy of science is that all true theories in the special sciences should reduce to physical theories 'in the long run'. This is intended to be an empirical thesis, and part of the evidence which supports it is provided by such scientific successes as the molecular theory of heat and the physical explanation of the chemical bond. But the philosophical popularity of the reductionist program cannot be explained by reference to these achievements alone. The development of science has witnessed the proliferation of specialized disciplines at least as often as it has witnessed their elimination, so the widespread enthusiasm for the view that there will eventually be only physics can hardly be a mere induction over past reductionist successes.

I think that many philosophers who accept reductionism do so primarily because they wish to endorse the generality of physics vis-à-vis the special sciences: roughly, the view that all events which fall under the laws of any science are

From *The Language of Thought* (New York: Crowell, 1975), pp. 9-25. Originally published in *Synthese* 28 (1974): 97-115. Reprinted by permission of D. Reidel Publishing Company. Notes have been renumbered for this edition.

physical events and hence fall under the laws of physics.[1] For such philosophers, saying that physics is basic science and saying that theories in the special sciences must reduce to physical theories have seemed to be two ways of saying the same thing, so that the latter doctrine has come to be a standard construal of the former.

In what follows, I shall argue that this is a considerable confusion. What has traditionally been called 'the unity of science' is a much stronger, and much less plausible, thesis than the generality of physics. If this is true it is important. Though reductionism is an empirical doctrine, it is intended to play a regulative role in scientific practice. Reducibility to physics is taken to be a *constraint* upon the acceptability of theories in the special sciences, with the curious consequence that the more the special sciences succeed, the more they ought to disappear. Methodological problems about psychology, in particular, arise in just this way: The assumption that the subject matter of psychology is part of the subject matter of physics is taken to imply that psychological theories must reduce to physical theories, and it is this latter principle that makes the trouble. I want to avoid the trouble by challenging the inference.

Reductionism is the view that all the special sciences reduce to physics. The sense of 'reduce to' is, however, proprietary. It can be characterized as follows.[2]

Let formula (1) be a law of the special science S.

(1) $\qquad S_1x \overset{\circ}{\longrightarrow} S_2y$

Formula (1) is intended to be read as something like 'all events which consist of x's being S_1 bring about events which consist of y's being S_2'. I assume that a science is individuated largely by reference to its typical predicates, hence that if S is a special science 'S_1' and 'S_2' are not predicates of basic physics. (I also assume that the 'all' which quantifies laws of the special sciences needs to be taken with a grain of salt. Such laws are typically *not* exceptionless. This is a point to which I shall return at length.) A necessary and sufficient condition for the reduction of formula (1) to a law of physics is that the formulae (2) and (3) should be laws, and a necessary and sufficient condition for the reduction

(2a) $\qquad S_1x \overset{\circ\!-\!\circ}{} P_1x$
(2b) $\qquad S_2y \overset{\circ\!-\!\circ}{} P_2y$
(3) $\qquad P_1x \overset{\circ}{\longrightarrow} P_2y$

of S to physics is that all its laws should be so reduced.[3]

'P_1' and 'P_2' are supposed to be predicates of physics, and formula (3) is supposed to be a physical law. Formulae like (2) are often called 'bridge' laws. Their characteristic feature is that they contain predicates of both the reduced and the reducing science. Bridge laws like formula (2) are thus contrasted with 'proper' laws like formulae (1) and (3). The upshot of the remarks so far is that the reduction of a science requires that any formula which appears as the antecedent or consequent of one of its proper laws must appear as the reduced formula in some bridge law or other.[4]

Several points about the connective '$\overset{\circ}{\longrightarrow}$' are now in order. First, whatever properties that connective may have, it is

universally agreed that it must be transitive. This is important because it is usually assumed that the reduction of some of the special sciences proceeds via bridge laws which connect their predicates with those of intermediate reducing theories. Thus, psychology is presumed to reduce to physics via, say, neurology, biochemistry, and other local stops. The present point is that this makes no difference to the logic of the situation so long as the transitivity of '$\overset{\circ}{\longrightarrow}$' is assumed. Bridge laws which connect the predicates of S to those of S* will satisfy the constraints upon the reduction of S to physics so long as there are other bridge laws which, directly or indirectly, connect the predicates of S* to physical predicates.

There are, however, quite serious open questions about the interpretation of '$\overset{\circ}{\longrightarrow}$' in bridge laws. What turns on these questions is the extent to which reductionism is taken to be a physicalist thesis.

To begin with, if we read '$\overset{\circ}{\longrightarrow}$' as 'brings about' or 'causes' in proper laws, we will have to have some other connective for bridge laws, since bringing about and causing are presumably *a*symmetric, while bridge laws express symmetric relations. Moreover, unless bridge laws hold by virtue of the *identity* of the events which satisfy their antecedents with those that satisfy their consequents, reductionism will guarantee only a weak version of physicalism, and this would fail to express the underlying ontological bias of the reductionist program.

If bridge laws are not identity statements, then formulae like (2) claim at most that, by law, x's satisfaction of a P predicate and x's satisfaction of an S predicate are causally correlated. It follows from this that it is nomologically necessary that S and P predicates apply to the same things (i.e., that S predicates apply to a subset of the things that P predicates apply to). But, of course, this is compatible with a nonphysicalist ontology since it is compatible with the possibility that

x's satisfying S should not itself be a physical event. On this interpretation, the truth of reductionism does *not* guarantee the generality of physics vis-à-vis the special sciences since there are some events (satisfactions of S predicates) which fall in the domains of a special science (S) but not in the domain of physics. (One could imagine, for example, a doctrine according to which physical and psychological predicates are both held to apply to organisms, but where it is denied that the event which consists of an organism's satisfying a psychological predicate is, in any sense, a physical event. The upshot would be a kind of psychophysical dualism of a non-Cartesian variety; a dualism of events and/or properties rather than substances.)

Given these sorts of considerations, many philosophers have held that bridge laws like formula (2) ought to be taken to express contingent event identities, so that one would read formula (2a) in some such fashion as 'every event which consists of an x's satisfying S_1 is identical to some event which consists of that x's satisfying P_1 and vice versa'. On this reading, the truth of reductionism would entail that every event that falls under any scientific law is a physical event, thereby simultaneously expressing the ontological bias of reductionism and guaranteeing the generality of physics vis-à-vis the special sciences.

If the bridge laws express event identities, and if every event that falls under the proper laws of a special science falls under a bridge law, we get classical reductionism, a doctrine that entails the truth of what I shall call 'token physicalism'. Token physicalism is simply the claim that all the events that the sciences talk about are physical events. There are three things to notice about token physicalism.

First, it is weaker than what is usually called 'materialism'. Materialism claims *both* that token physicalism is true *and* that every event falls under the laws of some science or other. One could therefore be a token physicalist without being a

materialist, though I don't see why anyone would bother.

Second, token physicalism is weaker than what might be called 'type physicalism', the doctrine, roughly, that every *property* mentioned in the laws of any science is a physical property. Token physicalism does not entail type physicalism, if only because the contingent identity of a pair of events presumably does not guarantee the identity of the properties whose instantiation constitutes the events; not even when the event identity is nomologically necessary. On the other hand, if an event is simply the instantiation of a property, then type physicalism does entail token physicalism; two events will be identical when they consist of the instantiation of the same property by the same individual at the same time.

Third, token physicalism is weaker than reductionism. Since this point is, in a certain sense, the burden of the argument to follow, I shan't labor it here. But, as a first approximation, reductionism is the conjunction of token physicalism with the assumption that there are natural kind predicates in an ideally completed physics which correspond to each natural kind predicate in any ideally completed special science. It will be one of my morals that reductionism cannot be inferred from the assumption that token physicalism is true. Reductionism is a sufficient, but not a necessary, condition for token physicalism.

To summarize: I shall be reading reductionism as entailing token physicalism since, if bridge laws state nomologically necessary contingent event identities, a reduction of psychology to neurology would require that any event which consists of the instantiation of a psychological property is identical with some event which consists of the instantiation of a neurological property. Both reductionism and token physicalism entail the generality of physics, since both hold that any event which falls within the universe of discourse of a special science will also fall within the universe of discourse of physics. Moreover, it is a consequence of both doctrines that any prediction which follows from the laws of a special science (and a statement of initial conditions) will follow equally from a theory which consists only of physics and the bridge laws (together with the statement of initial conditions). Finally, it is assumed by both reductionism and token physicalism that physics is the *only* basic science; *viz.*, that it is the only science that is general in the senses just specified.

I now want to argue that reductionism is too strong a constraint upon the unity of science, but that, for any reasonable purposes, the weaker doctrine will do.

Every science implies a taxonomy of the events in its universe of discourse. In particular, every science employs a descriptive vocabulary of theoretical and observation predicates, such that events fall under the laws of the science by virtue of satisfying those predicates. Patently, not every true description of an event is a description in such a vocabulary. For example, there are a large number of events which consist of things having been transported to a distance of less than three miles from the Eiffel Tower. I take it, however, that there is no science which contains 'is transported to a distance of less than three miles from the Eiffel Tower' as part of its descriptive vocabulary. Equivalently, I take it that there is no natural law which applies to events in virtue of their instantiating the property *is transported to a distance of less than three miles from the Eiffel Tower* (though I suppose it is just conceivable that there is some law that applies to events in virtue of their instantiating some distinct but coextensive property). By way of abbreviating these facts, I shall say that the property *is transported* . . . does not determine a (*natural*) *kind,* and that predicates which express that property are not (natural) kind predicates.

If I knew what a law is, and if I believed that scientific theories consist just of bodies of laws, then I could say that 'P' is a kind predicate relative to S iff S contains proper laws of the form '$P_x \multimap \ldots y$' or '$\ldots y \multimap P_x$': roughly, the kind predicates of a science are the ones whose terms are the bound variables in its proper laws. I am inclined to say this even in my present state of ignorance, accepting the consequence that it makes the murky notion of a kind viciously dependent on the equally murky notions of *law* and *theory.* There is no firm footing here. If we disagree about what a kind is, we will probably also disagree about what a law is, and for the same reasons. I don't know how to break out of this circle, but I think that there are some interesting things to say about which circle we are in.

For example, we can now characterize the respect in which reductionism is too strong a construal of the doctrine of the unity of science. If reductionism is true, then *every* kind is, or is coextensive with, a physical kind. (Every kind *is* a physical kind if bridge statements express nomologically necessary property identities, and every kind is coextensive with a physical kind if bridge statements express nomologically necessary event identities.) This follows immediately from the reductionist premise that every predicate which appears as the antecedent or consequent of a law of a special science must appear as one of the reduced predicates in some bridge law, together with the assumption that the kind predicates are the ones whose terms are the bound variables in proper laws. If, in short, some physical law is related to each law of a special science in the way that formula (3) is related to formula (1), then every kind predicate of a special science is related to a kind predicate of physics in the way that formula (2) relates 'S_1' and 'S_2' to 'P_1' and 'P_2' respectively.

I now want to suggest some reasons for believing that this consequence is intolerable. These are not supposed to be knock-down reasons; they couldn't be, given that the question of whether reductionism is too strong is finally an *empirical* question. (The world could turn out to be such that every kind corresponds to a physical kind, just as it could turn out to be such that the property *is transported to a distance of less than three miles from the Eiffel Tower* determines a kind in, say, hydrodynamics. It's just that, as things stand, it seems very unlikely that the world *will* turn out to be either of these ways.)

The reason it is unlikely that every kind corresponds to a physical kind is just that (a) interesting generalizations (e.g., counterfactual supporting generalizations) can often be made about events whose physical descriptions have nothing in common; (b) it is often the case that *whether* the physical descriptions of the events subsumed by such generalizations have anything in common is, in an obvious sense, entirely irrelevant to the truth of the generalizations, or to their interestingness, or to their degree of confirmation, or, indeed, to any of their epistemologically important properties; and (c) the special sciences are very much in the business of formulating generalizations of this kind.

I take it that these remarks are obvious to the point of self-certification; they leap to the eye as soon as one makes the (apparently radical) move of taking the existence of the special sciences at all seriously. Suppose, for example, that Gresham's 'law' really is true. (If one doesn't like Gresham's law, then any true and counterfactual supporting generalization of any conceivable future economics will probably do as well.) Gresham's law says something about what will happen in monetary exchanges under certain conditions. I am willing to believe that physics is general *in the sense that it implies that any event which consists of a monetary exchange* (hence any event which falls under Gresham's law) *has a true descrip-*

tion in the vocabulary of physics and in virtue of which it falls under the laws of physics. But banal considerations suggest that a physical description which covers all such events must be wildly disjunctive. Some monetary exchanges involve strings of wampum. Some involve dollar bills. And some involve signing one's name to a check. What are the chances that a disjunction of physical predicates which covers all these events (i.e., a disjunctive predicate which can form the right hand side of a bridge law of the form '*x* is a monetary exchange ∘—∘ . . .') expresses a physical kind? In particular, what are the chances that such a predicate forms the antecedent or consequent of some proper law of physics? The point is that monetary exchanges have interesting things in common; Gresham's law, if true, says what one of these interesting things is. But what is interesting about monetary exchanges is surely not their commonalities under *physical* description. A kind like a monetary exchange *could* turn out to be coextensive with a physical kind; but if it did, that would be an accident on a cosmic scale.

In fact, the situation for reductionism is still worse than the discussion thus far suggests. For reductionism claims not only that all kinds are coextensive with physical kinds, but that the coextensions are nomologically necessary: bridge laws are *laws*. So, if Gresham's law is true, it follows that there is a (bridge) law of nature such that '*x* is a monetary exchange ∘—∘ *x* is *P*' is true for every value of *x*, and such that *P* is a term for a physical kind. But, surely, there is no such law. If there were, then *P* would have to cover not only all the systems of monetary exchange that there *are*, but also all the systems of monetary exchange that there *could be*; a law must succeed with the counterfactuals. What physical predicate is a candidate for *P* in '*x* is a nomologically possible monetary exchange iff *Px*'?

To summarize: An immortal econophysicist might, when the whole show is over, find a predicate in physics that was, in brute fact, coextensive with 'is a monetary exchange'. If physics is general—if the ontological biases of reductionism are true—then there must *be* such a predicate. But (a) to paraphrase a remark Professor Donald Davidson made in a slightly different context, nothing but brute enumeration could convince us of this brute coextensivity, and (b) there would seem to be no chance at all that the physical predicate employed in stating the coextensivity would be a physical kind term, and (c) there is still less chance that the coextension would be lawful (i.e., that it would hold not only for the nomologically possible world that turned out to be real, but for any nomologically possible world at all).[5]

I take it that the preceding discussion strongly suggests that economics is not reducible to physics in the special sense of reduction involved in claims for the unity of science. There is, I suspect, nothing peculiar about economics in this respect; the reasons why economics is unlikely to reduce to physics are paralleled by those which suggest that psychology is unlikely to reduce to neurology.

If psychology is reducible to neurology, then for every psychological kind predicate there is a coextensive neurological kind predicate, and the generalization which states this coextension is a law. Clearly, many psychologists believe something of the sort. There are departments of psychobiology or psychology and brain science in universities throughout the world whose very existence is an institutionalized gamble that such lawful coextensions can be found. Yet, as has been frequently remarked in recent discussions of materialism, there are good grounds for hedging these bets. There are no firm data for any but the grossest correspondence between types of psychological states and types of neurological states, and it is entirely possible that the nervous system of higher organisms characteristically achieves a given psychological end by a wide variety of neurological means. It is also possible that given neurological structures subserve many different psychological functions at different times, depending upon the character of the activities in which the organism is engaged.[6] In either event, the attempt to pair neurological structures with psychological functions could expect only limited success. Physiological psychologists of the stature of Karl Lashley have held this sort of view.

The present point is that the reductionist program in psychology is clearly *not* to be defended on ontological grounds. Even if (token) psychological events are (token) neurological events, it does not follow that the kind predicates of psychology are coextensive with the kind predicates of any other discipline (including physics). That is, the assumption that every psychological event is a physical event does not guarantee that physics (or, a fortiori, any other discipline more general than psychology) can provide an appropriate vocabulary for psychological theories. I emphasize this point because I am convinced that the make-or-break commitment of many physiological psychologists to the reductionist program stems precisely from having confused that program with (token) physicalism.

What I have been doubting is that there are neurological kinds coextensive with psychological kinds. What seems increasingly clear is that, even if there are such coextensions, they cannot be lawful. For it seems increasingly likely that there are nomologically possible systems other than organisms (viz., automata) which satisfy the kind predicates of psychology but which satisfy no neurological predicates at all. Now, as Putnam has emphasized (1960a, b), if there are any such systems, then there must be vast numbers, since equivalent automata can, in principle, be made out of practically anything.

If this observation is correct, then there can be no serious hope that the class of automata whose psychology is effectively identical to that of some organism can be described by *physical* kind predicates (though, of course, if token physicalism is true, that class can be picked out by some physical predicate or other). The upshot is that the classical formulation of the unity of science is at the mercy of progress in the field of computer simulation. This is, of course, simply to say that that formulation was too strong. The unity of science was intended to be an empirical hypothesis, defeasible by possible scientific findings. But no one had it in mind that it should be defeated by Newell, Shaw, and Simon.

I have thus far argued that psychological reductionism (the doctrine that every psychological natural kind is, or is coextensive with, a neurological natural kind) is not equivalent to, and cannot be inferred from, token physicalism (the doctrine that every psychological event is a neurological event). It may, however, be argued that one might as well take the doctrines to be equivalent since the only possible *evidence* one could have for token physicalism would also be evidence for reductionism: *viz.*, that such evidence would have to consist in the discovery of type-to-type psychophysical correlations.

A moment's consideration shows, however, that this argument is not well taken. If type-to-type psychophysical correlations would be evidence for token physicalism, so would correlations of other specifiable kinds.

We have type-to-type correlations where, for every *n*-tuple of events that are of the same psychological kind, there is a correlated *n*-tuple of events that are of the same neurological kind.[7] Imagine a world in which such correlations are *not* forthcoming. What is found, instead, is that for every *n*-tuple of type identical psychological events, there is a spatiotemporally correlated *n*-tuple of type *distinct* neuro-

logical events. That is, every psychological event is paired with some neurological event or other, but psychological events of the same kind are sometimes paired with neurological events of different kinds. My present point is that such pairings would provide as much support for token physicalism as type-to-type pairings do *so long as we are able to show that the type distinct neurological events paired with a given kind of psychological event are identical in respect of whatever properties are relevant to type identification in psychology.* Suppose, for purposes of explication, that psychological events are type identified by reference to their behavioral consequences.[8] Then what is required of all the neurological events paired with a class of type homogeneous psychological events is only that they be identical in respect of their behavioral consequences. To put it briefly, type identical events do not, of course, have *all* their properties in common, and type distinct events must nevertheless be identical in *some* of their properties. The empirical confirmation of token physicalism does not depend on showing that the neurological counterparts of type identical psychological events are themselves type identical. What needs to be shown is just that they are identical in respect of those properties which determine what kind of *psychological* event a given event is.

Could we have evidence that an otherwise heterogeneous set of neurological events has those kinds of properties in common? Of course we could. The neurological theory might itself explain why an *n*-tuple of neurologically type distinct events are identical in their behavioral consequences, or, indeed, in respect of any of indefinitely many other such relational properties. And, if the neurological theory failed to do so, some science more basic than neurology might succeed.

My point in all this is, once again, not that correlations between type homogeneous psychological states and type heterogeneous neurological states would prove that token physicalism is true. It is only that such correlations might give us as much reason to be token physicalists as type-to-type correlations would. If this is correct, then epistemological arguments from token physicalism to reductionism must be wrong.

It seems to me (to put the point quite generally) that the classical construal of the unity of science has really badly misconstrued the *goal* of scientific reduction. The point of reduction is *not* primarily to find some natural kind predicate of physics coextensive with each kind predicate of a special science. It is, rather, to explicate the physical mechanisms whereby events conform to the laws of the special sciences. I have been arguing that there is no logical or epistemological reason why success in the second of these projects should require success in the first, and that the two are likely to come apart *in fact* wherever the physical mechanisms whereby events conform to a law of the special sciences are heterogeneous.

I take it that the discussion thus far shows that reductionism is probably too strong a construal of the unity of science; on the one hand, it is incompatible with probable results in the special sciences, and, on the other, it is more than we need to assume if what we primarily want, from an ontological point of view, is just to be good token physicalists. In what follows, I shall try to sketch a liberalized version of the relation between physics and the special sciences which seems to me to be just strong enough in these respects. I shall then give a couple of independent reasons for supposing that the revised doctrine may be the right one.

The problem all along has been that there is an open empirical possibility that what corresponds to the kind predicates of a reduced science may be a heterogeneous and unsystematic disjunction of predicates in the reducing science. We do

not want the unity of science to be prejudiced by this possibility. Suppose, then, that we allow that bridge statements may be of this form,

(4) $Sx \mathrel{\circ\!\!-\!\!\circ} P_1x \vee P_2x \vee \ldots \vee P_nx$

where '$P_1 \vee P_2 \vee \ldots \vee P_n$' is *not* a kind predicate in the reducing science. I take it that this is tantamount to allowing that at least some 'bridge laws' may, in fact, not turn out to be laws, since I take it that a necessary condition on a universal generalization being lawlike is that the predicates which constitute its antecedent and consequent should be kind predicates. I am thus assuming that it is enough, for purposes of the unity of science, that every law of the special sciences should be reducible to physics by bridge statements which express true empirical generalizations. Bearing in mind that bridge statements are to be construed as species of identity statements, formula (4) will be read as something like 'every event which consists of x's satisfying S is identical with some event which consists of x's satisfying some or other predicate belonging to the disjunction $P_1 \vee P_2 \vee \ldots \vee P_n$'.

Now, in cases of reduction where what corresponds to formula (2) is not a law, what corresponds to formula (3) will not be either, and for the same reason: *viz.*, the predicates appearing in the antecedent and consequent will, by hypothesis, not be kind predicates. Rather, what we will have is something that looks like Figure 6-1. That is, the antecedent and consequent of the reduced law will each be connected with a disjunction of predicates in the reducing science. Suppose, for the moment, that the reduced law is exceptionless, *viz.*, that no S_1 events satisfy P'. Then there will be laws of the reducing science which connect the satisfaction of *each* member of the disjunction associated with the antecedent of the reduced law with the satisfaction of some member of the disjunction associated with the consequent of the reduced law. That is, if S_1x

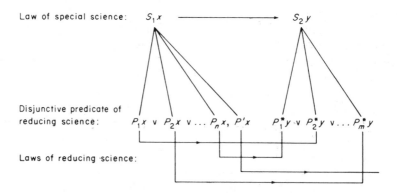

Figure 6-1. Schematic representation of the proposed relation between the reduced and the reducing science on a revised account of the unity of science. If any S₁ events are of the type P', they will be exceptions to the law S₁x —° S₂y.

—° S_2y is exceptionless, then there must be some proper law of the reducing science which either states or entails that P_1x —° P^* for some P^*, and similarly for P_2x through P_nx. Since there must be such laws, and since each of them is a 'proper' law in the sense in which we have been using that term, it follows that each disjunct of P_1 v P_2 v . . . v P_n is a kind predicate, as is each disjunct of P^*_1 v P^*_2 v . . . v P^*_n.

This, however, is where push comes to shove. For it might be argued that if each disjunct of the P disjunction is lawfully connected to some disjunct of the P^* disjunction, then it follows that formula (5) is itself a law.

(5) P_1x v P_2x v . . . v P_nx —° P^*_1y v P^*_2y
           v . . . v P^*_ny

The point would be that the schema in Figure 6-1 implies P_1x —° P^*_2y, P_2x —° P^*_my, etc., and the argument from a premise of the form $(P + R)$ *and* $(Q + S)$ to a conclusion of the form $(P$ v $Q) +$ $(R$ v $S)$ is valid. [*Editor's note:* In this anthology, "+" is used instead of the horseshoe and the arrow as the material conditional ("if . . . then").]

What I am inclined to say about this

is that it just shows that 'it's a law that ——' defines a nontruth functional context (or, equivalently for these purposes, that not all truth functions of kind predicates are themselves kind predicates); in particular, that one may not argue from: 'it's a law that P brings about R' and 'it's a law that Q brings about S' to 'it's a law that P or Q brings about R or S'. (Though, of course, the argument from those premises to 'P or Q brings about R or S' *simpliciter* is fine.) I think, for example, that it is a law that the irradiation of green plants by sunlight causes carbohydrate synthesis, and I think that it is a law that friction causes heat, but I do not think that it is a law that (either the irradiation of green plants by sunlight or friction) causes (either carbohydrate synthesis or heat). Correspondingly, I doubt that 'is either carbohydrate synthesis or heat' is plausibly taken to be a kind predicate.

It is not strictly mandatory that one should agree with all this, but one denies it at a price. In particular, if one allows the full range of truth-functional arguments inside the context 'it's a law that ——', then one gives up the possibility of identifying the kind predicates of a science with the ones which constitute the antecedents or consequents of its proper laws.

(Thus formula (5) would be a proper law of physics which fails to satisfy that condition.) One thus inherits the need for an alternative construal of the notion of a kind, and I don't know what that alternative would be like.

The upshot seems to be this. If we do not require that bridge statements must be laws, then either some of the generalizations to which the laws of special sciences reduce are not themselves lawlike, or some laws are not formulable in terms of kinds. Whichever way one takes formula (5) the important point is that the relation between sciences proposed by Figure 6-1 is weaker than what standard reductionism requires. In particular, it does not imply a correspondence between the kind predicates of the reduced and the reducing science. Yet it does imply physicalism given the same assumption that makes standard reductionism physicalistic: viz., that bridge statements express token event identities. But these are precisely the properties that we wanted a revised account of the unity of science to exhibit.

I now want to give two further reasons for thinking that this construal of the unity of science is right. First, it allows us to see how the laws of the special sciences could reasonably have exceptions, and, second, it allows us to see why there are special sciences at all. These points in turn.

Consider, again, the model of reduction implicit in formulae (2) and (3). I assume that the laws of basic science are strictly exceptionless, and I assume that it is common knowledge that the laws of the special sciences are not. But now we have a dilemma to face. Since '$—°$' expresses a relation (or relations) which must be transitive, formula (1) can have exceptions only if the bridge laws do. But if the bridge laws have exceptions, reductionism loses its ontological bite, since we can no longer say that every event which consists of the satisfaction of an S-predicate consists of the satisfaction of a P-predicate. In short,

given the reductionist model, we cannot consistently assume that the bridge laws and the basic laws are exceptionless while assuming that the special laws are not. But we cannot accept the violation of the bridge laws unless we are willing to vitiate the ontological claim that is the main point of the reductionist program.

We can get out of this (*salve* the reductionist model) in one of two ways. We can give up the claim that the special laws have exceptions or we can give up the claim that the basic laws are exceptionless. I suggest that both alternatives are undesirable—the first because it flies in the face of fact. There is just no chance at all that the true, counterfactual supporting generalizations of, say, psychology, will turn out to hold in strictly each and every condition where their antecedents are satisfied. Even when the spirit is willing the flesh is often weak. There are always going to be behavioral lapses which are physiologically explicable but which are uninteresting from the point of view of psychological theory. But the second alternative is not much better. It may, after all, turn out that the laws of basic science have exceptions. But the question arises whether one wants the unity of science to depend on the assumption that they do.

On the account summarized in Figure 6-1, however, everything works out satisfactorily. A nomologically sufficient condition for an exception to $S_1x \:—°\: S_2y$ is that the bridge statements should identify some occurrence of the satisfaction of S_1 with an occurrence of the satisfaction of a P-predicate which is not itself lawfully connected to the satisfaction of any P^*-predicate (i.e., suppose S_1 is connected to P' such that there is no law which connects P' to any predicate which bridge statements associate with S_2. Then any instantiation of S_1 which is contingently identical to an instantiation of P' will be an event which constitutes an exception to $S_1x \:—°\: S_2y$). Notice that, in this case, we need assume no exceptions to the laws of the *reducing* science since, by hypothesis, formula (5) is not a law.

In fact, strictly speaking, formula (5) has no status in the reduction at all. It is simply what one gets when one universally quantifies a formula whose antecedent is the physical disjunction corresponding to S_1 and whose consequent is the physical disjunction corresponding to S_2. As such, it will be true when $S_1x \longrightarrow^\circ S_2y$ is exceptionless and false otherwise. What does the work of expressing the physical mechanisms whereby n-tuples of events conform, or fail to conform, to $S_1x \longrightarrow^\circ S_2y$ is not formula (5) but the laws which severally relate elements of the disjunction $P_1 \vee P_2 \vee \ldots \vee P_n$ to elements of the disjunction $P^*_1 \vee P^*_2 \vee \ldots \vee P^*_m$. Where there is a law which relates an event that satisfies one of the P disjuncts to an event which satisfies one of the P^* disjuncts, the pair of events so related conforms to $S_1x \longrightarrow^\circ S_2y$. When an event which satisfies a P-predicate is not related by law to an event which satisfies a P^*-predicate, that event will constitute an exception to $S_1x \longrightarrow^\circ S_2y$. The point is that none of the laws which effect these several connections need themselves have exceptions in order that $S_1x \longrightarrow^\circ S_2y$ should do so.

To put this discussion less technically: We could, if we liked, *require* the taxonomies of the special sciences to correspond to the taxonomy of physics by insisting upon distinctions between the kinds postulated by the former whenever they turn out to correspond to distinct kinds in the latter. This would *make* the laws of the special sciences exceptionless if the laws of basic science are. But it would also likely lose us precisely the generalizations which we want the special sciences to express. (If economics were to posit as many *kinds* of monetary systems as there are physical realizations of monetary systems, then the generalizations of economics *would* be exceptionless. But, presumably, only vacuously so, since there would be

no generalizations left for economists to state. Gresham's law, for example, would have to be formulated as a vast, open disjunction about what happens in monetary system$_1$ or monetary system$_n$ under conditions which would themselves defy uniform characterization. We would not be able to say what happens in monetary systems *tout court* since, by hypothesis, 'is a monetary system' corresponds to no kind predicate of physics.)

In fact, what we do is precisely the reverse. We allow the generalizations of the special sciences to *have* exceptions, thus preserving the kinds to which the generalizations apply. But since we know that the *physical* descriptions of the members of these kinds may be quite heterogeneous, and since we know that the physical mechanisms which connect the satisfaction of the antecedents of such generalizations to the satisfaction of their consequents may be equally diverse, we expect both that there will be exceptions to the generalizations and that these will be 'explained away' at the level of the reducing science. This is one of the respects in which physics really is assumed to be bedrock science; exceptions to *its* generalizations (if there are any) had better be random, because there is nowhere 'further down' to go in explaining the mechanism whereby the exceptions occur.

This brings us to why there are special sciences at all. Reductionism, as we remarked at the outset, flies in the face of the facts about the scientific institution: the existence of a vast and interleaved conglomerate of special scientific disciplines which often appear to proceed with only the most casual acknowledgment of the constraint that their theories must turn out to be physics 'in the long run'. I mean that the acceptance of this constraint often plays little or no role in the practical validation of theories. Why is this so? Presumably, the reductionist answer must be *entirely* epistemological. If only physical particles weren't so small (if only brains were on the *outside*, where one can get a look at them), *then* we would do physics instead of paleontology (neurology instead of psychology, psychology instead of economics, and so on down). There is an epistemological reply: viz., that even if brains were out where they could be looked *at*, we wouldn't, as things now stand, know what to look *for*. We lack the appropriate theoretical apparatus for the psychological taxonomy of neurological events.

If it turns out that the functional decomposition of the nervous system corresponds precisely to its neurological (anatomical, biochemical, physical) decomposition, then there are only epistemological reasons for studying the former instead of the latter. But suppose that there is no such correspondence? Suppose the functional organization of the nervous system cross-cuts its neurological organization. Then the existence of psychology depends not on the fact that neurons are so depressingly small, but rather on the fact that neurology does not posit the kinds that psychology requires.

I am suggesting, roughly, that there are special sciences not because of the nature of our epistemic relation to the world, but because of the way the world is put together: not all the kinds (not all the classes of things and events about which there are important, counterfactual supporting generalizations to make) are, or correspond to, physical kinds. A way of stating the classical reductionist view is that things which belong to different physical kinds ipso facto can have none of their projectable descriptions in common[9]: that if *x* and *y* differ in those descriptions by virtue of which they fall under the proper laws of physics, they must differ in those descriptions by virtue of which they fall under any laws at all. But why should we believe that this is so? Any pair of entities, however different their physical structure, must nevertheless converge in indefinitely many of their

properties. Why should there not be, among those convergent properties, some whose lawful interrelations support the generalizations of the special sciences? Why, in short, should not the kind predicates of the special sciences *cross-classify* the physical natural kinds?[10]

Physics develops the taxonomy of its subject matter which best suits its purposes: the formulation of exceptionless laws which are basic in the several senses discussed above. But this is not the only taxonomy which may be required if the purposes of science in general are to be served: e.g., if we are to state such true, counterfactual supporting generalizations as there are to state. So there are special sciences, with their specialized taxonomies, in the business of stating some of these generalizations. If science is to be unified, then all such taxonomies must apply *to the same things*. If physics is to be basic science, then each of these things had better be a physical thing. But it is not further required that the taxonomies which the special sciences employ must themselves reduce to the taxonomy of physics. It is not required, and it is probably not true.

Notes

1. For expository convenience, I shall usually assume that sciences are about events in at least the sense that it is the occurrence of events that makes the laws of a science true. Nothing, however, hangs on this assumption.

2. The version of reductionism I shall be concerned with is a stronger one than many philosophers of science hold, a point worth emphasizing since my argument will be precisely that it is too strong to get away with. Still, I think that what I shall be attacking is what many people have in mind when they refer to the unity of science, and I suspect (though I shan't try to prove it) that many of the liberalized versions of reductionism suffer from the same basic defect as what I shall take to be the classical form of the doctrine.

3. There is an implicit assumption that a science simply *is* a formulation of a set of laws.

I think that this assumption is implausible, but it is usually made when the unity of science is discussed, and it is neutral so far as the main argument of this chapter is concerned.

4. I shall sometimes refer to 'the predicate which constitutes the antecedent or consequent of a law'. This is shorthand for 'the predicate such that the antecedent or consequent of a law consists of that predicate, together with its bound variables and the quantifiers which bind them'. (Truth functions of elementary predicates are, of course, themselves predicates in this usage.)

5. Oppenheim and Putnam (1958) argue that the social sciences probably *can* be reduced to physics assuming that the reduction proceeds via (individual) psychology. Thus, they remark, "in economics, if very weak assumptions are satisfied, it is possible to represent the way in which an individual orders his choices by means of an individual preference function. In terms of these functions, the economist attempts to explain group phenomena, such as the market, to account for collective consumer behavior, to solve the problems of welfare economics, etc." (p. 17). They seem not to have noticed, however, that even if such explanations can be carried through, they would not yield the kind of *predicate-by-predicate* reduction of economics to psychology that Oppenheim and Putnam's own account of the unity of science requires.

Suppose that the laws of economics hold because people have the attitudes, motives, goals, needs, strategies, etc., that they do. Then the fact that economics is the way it is can be explained by reference to the fact that people are the way that they are. But it doesn't begin to follow that the typical predicates of economics can be reduced to the typical predicates of psychology. Since bridge laws entail biconditionals, P_1 reduces to P_2 only if P_1 and P_2 are at least coextensive. But while the typical predicates of economics subsume (e.g.) monetary systems, cash flows, commodities, labor pools, amounts of capital invested, etc., the typical predicates of psychology subsume stimuli, responses, and mental states. Given the proprietary sense of 'reduction' at issue, to reduce economics to psychology would therefore involve a very great deal more than showing that the economic behavior of groups is determined by the psychology of the individuals that constitute them. In particular, it

would involve showing that such notions as *commodity*, *labor pool*, etc., can be reconstructed in the vocabulary of stimuli, responses and mental states and that, moreover, the predicates which affect the reconstruction express psychological kinds (viz., occur in the proper laws of psychology). I think it's fair to say that there is no reason at all to suppose that such reconstructions can be provided; prima facie there is every reason to think that they cannot.

6. This would be the case if higher organisms really are interestingly analogous to general purpose computers. Such machines exhibit no detailed structure-to-function correspondence over time; rather, the function subserved by a given structure may change from instant to instant depending upon the character of the program and of the computation being performed.

7. To rule out degenerate cases, we assume that n is large enough to yield correlations that are significant in the statistical sense.

8. I don't think there is any chance at all that this is true. What is more likely is that type identification for psychological states can be carried out in terms of the 'total states' of an abstract automaton which models the organism whose states they are. For discussion, see Block and Fodor (1972).

9. For the notion of projectability, see Goodman (1965). All projectable predicates are kind predicates, though not, presumably, vice versa.

10. As, by the way, the predicates of natural languages quite certainly do. (For discussion, see Chomsky, 1965.) To assert that the taxonomies employed by the special sciences cross-classify physical kinds is to deny that the special sciences, together with physics, constitute a hierarchy. To deny that the sciences constitute a hierarchy is to deny precisely what I take the classical doctrine of the unity of science to assert insofar as it asserts anything more than token physicalism.

References

Block, N. J. and Fodor, J. (1972). What psychological states are not. *Philosophical Review*, 81, 159-181.

Chomsky, N. (1965). "Aspects of the Theory of Syntax." MIT Press, Cambridge, Massachusetts.

Goodman, N. (1965). "Fact, Fiction and Forecast," Bobbs-Merrill, Indianapolis, Indiana.

Oppenheim, P. and Putnam, H. (1958). Unity of science as a working hypothesis. In "Minnesota Studies in the Philosophy of Science, Vol. II" (H. Feigl, M. Scriven and G. Mazwell, eds.), Univ. of Minnesota Press, Minneapolis, Minnesota.

Putnam, H. (1960a). Dreaming and depth grammar. In "Analytic Philosophy," (R. J. Butler, ed.), Barnes and Noble, New York.

Putnam, H. (1960b). Minds and machines. In "Dimensions of Mind" (S. Hook, ed.), N.Y. Univ. Press, New York.

Philosophy and Our Mental Life

Hilary Putnam

The question which troubles laymen, and which has long troubled philosophers, even if it is somewhat disguised by today's analytic style of writing philosophy, is this: are we made of matter or soul-stuff?[1] To put it as bluntly as possible, are we just material beings, or are we 'something more'? In this paper, I will argue as strongly as possible that this whole question rests on false assumptions. My purpose is not to dismiss the question, however, so much as to speak to the real concern which is behind the question. The real concern is, I believe, with the autonomy of our mental life.

People are worried that we may be debunked, that our behavior may be exposed as really explained by something mechanical. Not, to be sure, mechanical in the old sense of cogs and pulleys, but in the newer sense of electricity and magnetism and quantum chemistry and so forth. In this paper, part of what I want to do is to argue that this can't happen. Mentality

is a real and autonomous feature of our world.

But even more important, at least in my feeling, is the fact that this whole question has nothing to do with our substance. Strange as it may seem to common sense and to sophisticated intuition alike, the question of the autonomy of our mental life does not hinge on and has nothing to do with that all too popular, all too old question about matter or soul-stuff. We could be made of Swiss cheese and it wouldn't matter.

Failure to see this, stubborn insistence on formulating the question as *matter or soul*, utterly prevents progress on these questions. Conversely, once we see that our substance is not the issue, I do not see how we can help but make progress.

The concept which is key to unravelling the mysteries in the philosophy of mind, I think, is the concept of *functional isomorphism*. Two systems are functionally isomorphic if *there is a correspondence between the states of one and the states of the other that preserves functional relations*. To start with computing machine examples, if the functional relations are just sequence relations, e.g. *state* A *is always followed by state* B, then, for F to

From *Mind, Language, and Reality*, Philosophical Papers, vol. 2 (London: Cambridge University Press, 1975), pp. 291-303. Reprinted by permission of Cambridge University Press and the author. Notes have been numbered for this edition.

be a functional isomorphism, it must be the case that state A is followed by state B in system 1 if and only if state $F(A)$ is followed by state $F(B)$ in system 2. If the functional relations are, say, data or print-out relations, e.g. *when symbol S is scanned on the tape, system 1 goes into state A*, these must be preserved. *When symbol S is scanned on the tape, system 2 goes into state F(A)*, if F is a functional isomorphism between system 1 and system 2. More generally, if T is a correct theory of the functioning of system 1, at the functional or psychological level, then an isomorphism between system 1 and system 2 must map each property and relation defined in system 2 in such a way that T comes out true when all references to system 1 are replaced by references to system 2, and all property and relation symbols in T are reinterpreted according to the mapping.

The difficulty with the notion of functional isomorphism is that it *presupposes the notion of a thing's being a functional or psychological description.* It is for this reason that, in various papers on this subject, I introduced and explained the notion in terms of Turing machines. And I felt constrained, therefore, to defend the thesis that *we* are Turing machines. Turing machines come, so to speak, with a normal form for their functional description, the so-called machine table—a standard style of program. But it does not seem fatally sloppy to me, although it is sloppy, if we apply the notion of functional isomorphism to systems for which we have no detailed idea at present what the normal form description would look like—systems like ourselves. The point is that even if we don't have any idea what a comprehensive psychological theory would look like, I claim that we know enough (and here analogies from computing machines, economic systems, games and so forth are helpful) to point out illuminating differences between any possible psychological theory of a human being, or even a func-

tional description of a computing machine or an economic system, and a physical or chemical description. Indeed, Dennett and Fodor have done a great deal along these lines in recent books.

This brings me back to the question of *copper, cheese, or soul.* One point we can make immediately as soon as we have the basic concept of functional isomorphism is this: two systems can have quite different constitutions and be functionally isomorphic. For example, a computer made of electrical components can be isomorphic to one made of cogs and wheels. In other words, for each state in the first computer there is a corresponding state in the other, and, as we said before, the sequential relations are the same—if state S is followed by state B in the case of the electronic computer, state A would be followed by state B in the case of the computer made of cogs and wheels, and it doesn't matter at all that the *physical realizations* of those states are totally different. So a computer made of electrical components can be isomorphic to one made of cogs and wheels or to human clerks using paper and pencil. A computer made of one sort of wire, say copper wire, or one sort of relay, etc. will be in a different physical and chemical state when it computes than a computer made of a different sort of wire and relay. But the functional description may be the same.

We can extend this point still further. Assume that one thesis of materialism (I shall call it the 'first thesis') is correct, and we are, as wholes, just material systems obeying physical laws. Then the second thesis of classical materialism cannot be correct—namely, our mental states, e.g. *thinking about next summer's vacation,* cannot be *identical* with any physical or chemical states. For it is clear from what we already know about computers etc., that whatever the program of the brain may be, it must be physically possible, though not necessarily feasible, to produce something with that same program but quite a different physical and chemical constitution. Then to identify the state in question with its physical or chemical realization would be quite absurd, given that that realization is in a sense quite accidental, from the point of view of psychology, anyway (which is the relevant science).[2] It is as if we met Martians and discovered that they were in all functional respects isomorphic to us, but we refused to admit that they could feel pain because their C fibers were different.

Now, imagine two possible universes, perhaps 'parallel worlds', in the science fiction sense, in one of which people have good old fashioned souls, operating through pineal glands, perhaps, and in the other of which they have complicated brains. And suppose that the souls in the soul world are functionally isomorphic to the brains in the brain world. Is there any more sense to attaching importance to this difference than to the difference between copper wires and some other wires in the computer? Does it matter that the soul people have, so to speak, immaterial brains, and that the brain people have material souls? What matters is the common structure, the theory T of which we are, alas, in deep ignorance, and not the hardware, be it ever so ethereal.

One may raise various objections to what I have said. I shall try to reply to some of them.

One might, for example, say that if the souls of the soul people are isomorphic to the brains of the brain people, then their souls must be automata-like, and that's not the sort of soul we are interested in. 'All your argument really shows is that there is no need to distinguish between a brain and an automaton-like soul.' But what precisely does that objection come to?

I think there are two ways of understanding it. It might come to the claim that the notion of functional organization or functional isomorphism only makes sense for automata. But that is totally false. Sloppy as our notions are at present, we at least know this much, as Jerry Fodor has emphasized: we know that the notion of functional organization applies to anything to which the notion of a psychological theory applies. I explained the most general notion of functional isomorphism by saying that two systems are functionally isomorphic if there is an isomorphism that makes both of them models for the same psychological theory. (That is stronger than just saying that they are both models for the same psychological theory—they are isomorphic realizations of the same abstract structure.) To say that real old fashioned souls would not be in the domain of definition of the concept of functional organization or of the concept of functional isomorphisms would be to take the position that whatever we mean by the soul, it is something for which there can be no theory. That seems pure obscurantism. I will assume, henceforth, that it is not built into the notion of mind or soul or whatever that it is unintelligible or that there couldn't be a theory of it.

Secondly, someone might say more seriously that even if there is a theory of the soul or mind, the soul, at least in the full, rich old fashioned sense, is supposed to have powers that no mechanical system could have. In the latter part of this chapter I shall consider this claim.

If it is built into one's notions of the soul that the soul can do things that violate the laws of physics, then I admit I am stumped. There cannot be a soul which is isomorphic to a brain, if the soul can read the future clairvoyantly, in a way that is not in any way explainable by physical law. On the other hand, if one is interested in more modest forms of magic like telepathy, it seems to me that there is no reason in principle why we couldn't construct a device which would project subvocalized thoughts from one brain to another. As to reincarnation, if we are, as I am urging, a certain kind of functional structure (my identity is, as it were, my functional structure), there seems to be in principle no reason why that could not be reproduced after a thousand years or a million years or a billion years. Resurrection: as you know, Christians believe in resurrection in the flesh, which completely bypasses the need for an immaterial vehicle. So even if one is interested in those questions (and they are not my concern in this paper, although I am concerned to speak to people who have those concerns), even then one doesn't need an immaterial brain or soul-stuff.

So if I am right, and the question of matter or soul-stuff is really irrelevant to any question of philosophical or religious significance, why so much attention to it, why so much heat? The crux of the matter seems to be that both the Diderots of this world and the Descartes of this world have agreed that if we are matter, then there is a physical explanation for how we behave, disappointing or exciting. I think the traditional dualist says *'wouldn't it be terrible if we turned out to be just matter, for then there is a physical explanation for everything we do'.* And the traditional materialist says *'if we are just matter, then there is a physical explanation for everything we do. Isn't that exciting!'* (It is like the distinction between the optimist and the pessimist: an optimist is a person who says 'this is the best of all possible worlds'; and a pessimist is a person who says 'you're right'.)[3]

I think they are both wrong. I think Diderot and Descartes were both wrong in assuming that if we are matter, or our souls are material, then there is a physical explanation for our behavior.

Let me try to illustrate what I mean by a very simple analogy. Suppose we have a very simple physical system—a board in which there are two holes, a circle one inch in diameter and a square one inch high, and a cubical peg one-sixteenth of an inch less than one inch high. We have the following very simple fact to explain: *the peg passes through the square hole, and it does not pass through the round hole.*

In explanation of this, one might attempt the following. One might say that the peg is, after all, a cloud or, better, a rigid lattice of atoms. One might even attempt to give a description of that lattice, compute its electrical potential energy, worry about why it does not collapse, produce some quantum mechanics to explain why it is stable, etc. The board is also a lattice of atoms. I will call the peg 'system A', and the holes 'region 1' and 'region 2'. One could compute all possible trajectories of system A (there are, by the way, very serious questions about these computations, their effectiveness, feasibility, and so on, but let us assume this), and perhaps one could deduce from just the laws of particle mechanics or quantum electrodynamics that system A never passes through region 1, but that there is at least one trajectory which enables it to pass through region 2. Is this an explanation of the fact that the peg passes through the square hole and not the round hole?

Very often we are told that if something is made of matter, its behavior must have a physical explanation. And the argument is that if it is made of matter (and we make a lot of assumptions), then there should be a deduction of its behavior from its material structure. *What makes you call this deduction an explanation?*

On the other hand, if you are not 'hipped' on the idea that *the* explanation must be at the level of the ultimate constituents, and that in fact the explanation might have the property that *the ultimate constituents don't matter, that only the higher level structure matters,* then there is a very simple explanation here. The explanation is that the board is rigid, the peg is rigid, and as a matter of geometrical fact, the round hole is smaller than the peg, the square hole is bigger than the cross-section of the peg. The peg passes through the hole that is large enough to take its cross-section, and does not pass through the hole that is too small to take its cross-section. That is a correct explanation whether the peg consists of molecules, or continuous rigid substance, or whatever. (If one wanted to amplify the explanation, one might point out the geometrical fact that a square one inch high is bigger than a circle one inch across.)

Now, one can say that in this explanation certain *relevant structural features of the situation* are brought out. The geometrical features are brought out. It is *relevant* that a square one inch high is bigger than a circle one inch around. And the relationship between the size and shape of the peg and the size and shape of the holes is *relevant*. It is *relevant* that both the board and the peg are *rigid* under transportation. And nothing else is relevant. The same explanation will go in any world (whatever the microstructure) in which those *higher level structural features* are present. In that sense *this explanation is autonomous.*

People have argued that I am wrong to say that the microstructural deduction is not an explanation. I think that in terms of the *purposes for which we use the notion of explanation*, it is not an explanation. If you want to, let us say that the deduction *is* an explanation, it is just a terrible explanation, and why look for terrible explanations when good ones are available?

Goodness is not a subjective matter. Even if one agrees with the positivists who saddled us with the notion of explanation as deduction from laws, one of the things we do in science is to look for laws. Explanation is superior not just subjectively, but *methodologically*, in terms of facilitating the aims of scientific inquiry, if it brings out relevant laws. An explanation is superior if it is more general.

Just taking those two features, and there are many many more one could

think of, compare the explanation at the higher level of this phenomenon with the atomic explanation. The explanation at the higher level brings out the relevant geometrical relationships. The lower level explanation conceals those laws. Also notice that the higher level explanation applies to a much more interesting class of systems (of course that has to do with what we are interested in).

The fact is that we are much more interested in generalizing to other structures which are rigid and have various geometrical relations, than we are in generalizing to *the next peg that has exactly this molecular structure*, for the very good reason that there is not going to *be* a next peg that has exactly this molecular structure. So in terms of real life disciplines, real life ways of slicing up scientific problems, the higher level explanation is far more general, which is why it is *explanatory.*

We were only able to deduce a statement which is lawful at the *higher* level, that the peg goes through the hole which is larger than the cross-section of the peg. When we try to deduce the possible trajectories of 'system A' from statements about the individual atoms, we use premises which are totally accidental—this atom is here, this carbon atom is there, and so forth. And that is one reason that it is very misleading to talk about a reduction of a science like economics to the level of the elementary particles making up the players of the economic game. In fact, their motions—buying this, selling that, arriving at an equilibrium price—these motions cannot be deduced from just the equations of motion. Otherwise they would be *physically necessitated*, not *economically necessitated*, to arrive at an equilibrium price. They play that game because they are particular systems with particular boundary conditions which are totally accidental from the point of view of physics. This means that the derivation of the laws of economics from *just* the laws of physics is *in principle* impossible. The derivation of the laws of economics from the laws of physics and *accidental statements about which particles were where when* by a Laplacian supermind might be in principle possible, but why want it? A few chapters of, e.g. von Neumann, will tell one far more about regularities at the level of economic structure than such a deduction ever could.

The conclusion I want to draw from this is that we do have the kind of autonomy that we are looking for in the mental realm. Whatever our mental functioning may be, there seems to be no serious reason to believe that it is *explainable* by our physics and chemistry. And what we are interested in is not: given that we consist of such and such particles, could someone have predicted that we would have this mental functioning? because such a prediction is not *explanatory*, however great a feat it may be. What we are interested in is: can we say at this autonomous level that since we have this sort of structure, this sort of program, it follows that we will be able to learn this, we will tend to like that, and so on? These are the problems of mental life—the description of this autonomous level of mental functioning —and that is what is to be discovered.

In previous papers, I have argued for the hypothesis that (1) a whole human being is a Turing machine, and (2) that psychological states of a human being are Turing machine states or disjunctions of Turing machine states. In this section I want to argue that this point of view was essentially wrong, and that I was too much in the grip of the reductionist outlook.

Let me begin with a technical difficulty. A *state* of a Turing machine is described in such a way that a Turing machine can be in exactly one state at a time. Moreover, memory and learning are not represented in the Turing machine model

as acquisition of new states, but as acquisition of new information printed on the machine's tape. Thus, if human beings have any states at all which resemble Turing machine states, those states must (1) be states the human can be in at any time, independently of learning and memory; and (2) be *total* instantaneous states of the human being—states which determine, together with learning and memory, what the next state will be, as well as totally specifying the present condition of the human being ('totally' from the standpoint of psychological theory, that means).

These characteristics establish that *no* psychological state in any customary sense can be a Turing machine state. Take a particular kind of pain to be a 'psychological state'. If I *am* a Turing machine, then my present 'state' must determine not only whether or not I am having that particular kind of pain, but also whether or not I am about to say 'three', whether or not I am hearing a shrill whine, etc. So the psychological state in question (the pain) is not the same as my 'state' in the sense of *machine state*, although it is possible (so far) that my machine state *determines* my psychological state. Moreover, *no* psychological theory would pretend that having a pain of a particular kind, being about to say 'three', or hearing a shrill whine, etc., all belong to *one* psychological state, although there could well be a machine state characterized by the fact that I was in it only when simultaneously having that pain, being about to say 'three', hearing a shrill whine, etc. So, even if I am a Turing machine, my machine states are *not* the same as my psychological states. My description *qua* Turing machine (machine table) and my description *qua* human being (*via* a psychological theory) are descriptions at two totally different levels of organization.

So far it is still possible that a psychological state is a large disjunction (practically speaking, an almost infinite disjunction) of machine states, although no *single* machine state is a psychological state. But this is very unlikely when we move away from states like 'pain' (which are almost *biological*) to states like 'jealousy' or 'love' or 'competitiveness'. Being jealous is certainly not an *instantaneous* state, and it depends on a great deal of information and on many learned facts and habits. But Turing machine states are instantaneous and are independent of learning and memory. That is, learning and memory may cause a Turing machine to go into a state, but the identity of the state does not depend on learning and memory, whereas, no matter what state I am in, identifying that state as 'being jealous of X's regard for Y' involves specifying that I have learned that X and Y are persons and a good deal about social relations among persons. Thus jealousy can neither be a machine state nor a disjunction of machine states.

One might attempt to modify the theory by saying that being jealous = either being in State A and having tape c_1 *or* being in State A and having tape c_2 *or* . . . being in State B and having tape d_1 *or* being in State B and having tape d_2 . . . *or* being in State Z and having tape y_1 . . . *or* being in State Z and having tape y_n—i.e. define a psychological state as a disjunction, the individual disjuncts being not Turing machine states, as before, but conjunctions of a machine state and a tape (i.e. a total description of the content of the memory bank). Besides the fact that such a description would be literally infinite, the theory is now without content, for the original purpose was to use the machine table as a model of a psychological theory, whereas it is now clear that the machine table description, although different from the description at the elementary particle level, is as removed from the description *via* a psychological theory as the physico-chemical description is.

What is the importance of machines in the philosophy of mind? I think that machines have both a positive and a negative importance. The positive importance of machines was that it was in connection with machines, computing machines in particular, that the notion of functional organization first appeared. Machines forced us to distinguish between an abstract structure and its concrete realization. Not that that distinction came into the world for the first time with machines. But in the case of computing machines, we could not avoid rubbing our noses against the fact that what we had to count as to all intents and purposes the same structure could be realized in a bewildering variety of different ways; that the important properties were not physical-chemical. That the machines made us catch on to the idea of functional organization is extremely important. The negative importance of machines, however, is that they tempt us to oversimplification. The notion of functional organization became clear to us through systems with a very restricted, very specific functional organization. So the temptation is present to assume that we must have that restricted and specific kind of functional organization.

Now I want to consider an example—an example which may seem remote from what we have been talking about, but which may help. This is not an example from the philosophy of mind at all. Consider the following fact. The earth does not go around the sun in a circle, as was once believed, it goes around the sun in an ellipse, with the sun at one of the foci, not in the center of the ellipse. Yet one statement which would hold true if the orbit was a circle and the sun was at the centre still holds true, surprisingly. That is the following statement: the radius vector from the sun to the earth sweeps out equal areas in equal times. If the orbit were a circle, and the earth were moving with a constant velocity, that would be trivial. But the orbit is not a circle. Also the velocity is not constant—when the earth is farthest away from the sun, it is going most slowly, when it is closest to the sun, it is going fastest. The earth is speeding up and slowing down. But the earth's radius vector sweeps out equal areas in equal times.[4] Newton deduced that law in his *Principia*, and his deduction shows that the only thing on which that law depends is that the force acting on the earth is in the direction of the sun. That is absolutely the only fact one needs to deduce that law. Mathematically it is equivalent to that law.[5] That is all well and good when the gravitational law is that every body attracts every other body according to an inverse square law, because then there is always a force on the earth in the direction of the sun. If we assume that we can neglect all the other bodies, that their influence is slight, then that is all we need, and we can use Newton's proof, or a more modern, simpler proof.

But today we have very complicated laws of gravitation. First of all, we say what is really going is that the world lines of freely falling bodies in space-time are geodesics. And the geometry is determined by the mass-energy tensor, and the ankle bone is connected to the leg bone, etc. So, one might ask, how would a modern relativity theorist explain Kepler's law? He would explain it very simply. *Kepler's laws are true because Newton's laws are approximately true.* And, in fact, an attempt to replace that argument by a deduction of Kepler's laws from the field equations would be regarded as almost as ridiculous (but not quite) as trying to deduce that the peg will go through one hole and not the other from the positions and velocities of the individual atoms.

I want to draw the philosophical conclusion that Newton's laws *have a kind of reality in our world* even though they are not *true*. The point is that it will be necessary to appeal to Newton's laws in order to explain Kepler's laws. Methodologically, I can make that claim at least plausible. One remark—due to Alan Garfinkel —is that *a good explanation is invariant under small perturbations of the assumptions.* One problem with deducing Kepler's laws from the gravitational field equations is that if we do it, tomorrow the gravitational field equations are likely to be different. Whereas the explanation which consists in showing that whichever equation we have implies Newton's equation to a first approximation is invariant under even moderate perturbations, quite big perturbations, of the assumptions. One might say that every explanation of Kepler's laws 'passes through' Newton's laws.

Let me come back to the philosophy of mind, now. If we assume a thorough atomic structure of matter, quantization and so forth, then, at first blush, it looks as if *continuities* cannot be relevant to our brain functioning. Mustn't it all be discrete? Physics says that the deepest level is discrete.

There are two problems with this argument. One is that there are continuities even in quantum mechanics, as well as discontinuities. But ignore that, suppose quantum mechanics were a thoroughly discrete theory.

The other problem is that if that were a good argument, it would be an argument against the utilizability of the model of air as a continuous liquid, which is the model on which aeroplane wings are constructed, at least if they are to fly at anything less than supersonic speeds. There are two points: one is that a discontinuous structure, a discrete structure, can approximate a continuous structure. The discontinuities may be irrelevant, just as in the case of the peg and the board. The fact that the peg and the board are not continuous solids is irrelevant. One can say that the peg and the board only approximate perfectly rigid continuous solids. But if the error in the approximation is irrelevant to the level of description, so what? It is not just that discrete systems can approximate continuous systems; the fact is that the system may behave in the way it does *because* a continuous system would behave in such and such a way, and the system approximates a continuous system.

This is not a Newtonian world. Tough. Kepler's law comes out true because the sun-earth system approximates a Newtonian system. And the error in the approximation is quite irrelevant at that level.

This analogy is not perfect because physicists are interested in laws to which the error in the approximation is relevant. It seems to me that in the psychological case the analogy is even better, that continuous models (for example, Hull's model for rote learning which used a continuous potential) could perfectly well be correct, whatever the ultimate structure of the brain is. We cannot deduce that a digital model has to be the correct model from the fact that ultimately there are neurons. The brain may work the way it does because it approximates some system whose laws are best conceptualized in terms of continuous mathematics. What is more, the errors in that approximation may be irrelevant at the level of psychology.

What I have said about *continuity* goes as well for many other things. Let us come back to the question of the soul people and the brain people, and the isomorphism between the souls in one world and the brains in the other. One objection was, if there is a functional isomorphism between souls and brains, wouldn't the souls have to be rather simple? The answer is no. Because brains can be essentially infinitely complex. A system with as many degrees of freedom as the brain can imitate to within the accuracy relevant to psychological theory any structure one can hope to describe. It might be, so to speak, that the ultimate physics of the soul will be quite different from the ultimate physics of the brain, but that at the level we are interested in, the level of functional organization, the same description might go for both. And also that that description might be formally incompatible

with the actual physics of the brain, in the way that the description of the air flowing around an aeroplane wing as a continuous incompressible liquid is *formally incompatible with the actual structure of the air.*

Let me close by saying that these examples support the idea that our substance, what we are made of, places almost no first order restrictions on our form. And that what we are really interested in, as Aristotle saw,[6] is form and not matter. *What is our intellectual form?* is the question, not what the matter is. And whatever our substance may be, soul-stuff, or matter or Swiss cheese, it is not going to place any interesting first order restrictions on the answer to this question. It may, of course, place interesting higher order restrictions. Small effects may have to be explained in terms of the actual physics of the brain. But when we are not even at the level of an *idealized* description of the functional organization of the brain, to talk about the importance of small perturbations seems decidedly premature. My conclusion is that we have what we always wanted—an autonomous mental life. And we need no mysteries, no ghostly agents, no *élan vital* to have it.

Notes

1. This paper was presented as a part of a Foerster symposium on 'Computers and the Mind' at the University of California (Berkeley) in October, 1973. I am indebted to Alan Garfinkel for comments on earlier versions of this paper.

2. Even if it were not physically possible to realize human psychology in a creature made of anything but the usual protoplasm, DNA, etc., it would still not be correct to say that psychological states are identical with their physical realizations. For, as will be argued below, such an identification has no *explanatory* value *in psychology*. On this point, compare Fodor, 1968.

3. Joke Credit: Joseph Weizenbaum.

4. This is one of Kepler's laws.

5. Provided that the two bodies—the sun and the earth—are the whole universe. If

there are other forces, then, of course, Kepler's law cannot be *exactly* correct.

6. E.g. Aristotle says: '. . . we can wholly dismiss as unnecessary the question whether the soul and the body are one: it is as meaningless to ask whether the wax and the shape given to it by the stamp are one, or generally the matter of a thing and that of which it is the matter.' (See *De Anima*, 412 a6-b9.)

Excerpt from "Identity and Necessity"

Saul A. Kripke

[handwritten marginalia]
Correlational thesis too weak:
If thinking, I (as the mind/exist) can't draw
If perceiving, I (as the body) exist ? together
Mind correlates w/ body

To state the view succinctly: we use both the terms 'heat' and 'the motion of molecules' as rigid designators for a certain external phenomenon. Since heat is in fact the motion of molecules, and the designators are rigid, by the argument I have given here, it is going to be *necessary* that heat is the motion of molecules. What gives us the illusion of contingency is the fact we have identified the heat by the contingent fact that there happen to be creatures on this planet—(namely, ourselves) who are sensitive to it in a certain way, that is, who are sensitive to the motion of molecules or to heat—these are one and the same thing. And this is contingent. So we use the description, 'that which causes such and such sensations, or that which we sense in such and such a way', to identify heat. But in using this fact we use a contingent property of heat, just as we use the contingent property of Cicero as having written such and such works to identify him. We then use the terms

From "Identity and Necessity," in Milton Munitz, ed., *Identity and Individuation* (New York: New York University Press, 1971), pp. 160-164. Copyright © 1971 by New York University. Reprinted by permission of New York University Press. Notes have been renumbered for this edition.

'heat' in the one case and 'Cicero' in the other *rigidly* to designate the objects for which they stand. And of course the term 'the motion of molecules' is rigid; it always stands for the motion of molecules, never for any other phenomenon. So, as Bishop Butler said, "everything is what it is and not another thing." Therefore, "Heat is the motion of molecules" will be necessary, not contingent, and one only has the *illusion* of contingency in the way one could have the illusion of contingency in thinking that this table might have been made of ice. We might think one could imagine it, but if we try, we can see on reflection that what we are really imagining is just there being another lectern in this very position here which was in fact made of ice. The fact that we may identify this lectern by being the object we see and touch in such and such a position is something else.

Now how does this relate to the problem of mind and body? It is usually held that this is a contingent identity statement just like "Heat is the motion of molecules." That cannot be. It cannot be a contingent identity statement just like "Heat is the motion of molecules" because, if I am right, "Heat is the motion of molecules" is not a contingent identity statement. Let us look at this statement. For example, "My being in pain at such and such a time is my being in such and such a brain state at such and such a time," or, "Pain in general is such and such a neural (brain) state."

This is held to be contingent on the following grounds. First, we can imagine the brain state existing though there is no pain at all. It is only a scientific fact that whenever we are in a certain brain state we have a pain. Second, one might imagine a creature being in pain, but not being in any specified brain state at all, maybe not having a brain at all. People even think, at least prima facie, though they may be wrong, that they can imagine totally disembodied creatures, at any rate certainly not creatures with bodies anything like our own. So it seems that we can imagine definite circumstances under which this relationship would have been false. Now, if these circumstances are circumstances, notice that we cannot deal with them simply by saying that this is just an illusion, something we can apparently imagine, but in fact cannot in the way we thought erroneously that we could imagine a situation in which heat was not the motion of molecules. Because although we can say that we pick out heat contingently by the contingent property that it affects us in such and such a way, we cannot similarly say that we pick out pain contingently by the fact that it affects us in such and such a way. On such a picture there would be the brain state, and we pick it out by the contingent fact that it affects us as pain. Now that might be true of the brain state, but it cannot be true of the pain. The experience itself has to be *this experience*, and I cannot say that it is a contingent property of the pain I now have that it is a pain.[1] In fact, it would seem that both the terms, 'my pain' and 'my being in such and such a brain state' are, first of all, both rigid designators. That is, whenever anything is such and such a pain, it is essentially that very object, namely, such and such a pain, and

wherever anything is such and such a brain state, it is essentially that very object, namely, such and such a brain state. So both of these are rigid designators. One cannot say this pain might have been something else, some other state. These are both rigid designators.

Second, the way we would think of picking them out—namely, the pain by its being an experience of a certain sort, and the brain state by its being the state of a certain material object, being of such and such molecular configuration—both of these pick out their objects essentially and not accidentally, that is, they pick them out by essential properties. Whenever the molecules *are* in this configuration, we *do* have such and such a brain state. Whenever you feel *this*, you do have a pain. So it seems that the identity theorist is in some trouble, for, since we have two rigid designators, the identity statement in question is necessary. Because they pick out their objects essentially, we cannot say the case where you seem to imagine the identity statement false is really an illusion like the illusion one gets in the case of heat and molecular motion, because that illusion depended on the fact that we pick out heat by a certain contingent property. So there is very little room to maneuver; perhaps none.[2] The identity theorist, who holds that pain is the brain state, also has to hold that it necessarily is the brain state. He therefore cannot concede, but has to deny, that there would have been situations under which one would have had pain but not the corresponding brain state. Now usually in arguments on the identity theory, this is very far from being denied. In fact, it is conceded from the outset by the materialist as well as by his opponent. He says, "Of course, it *could* have been the case that we had pains without the brain states. It is a contingent identity." But that cannot be. He has to hold that we are under some illusion in thinking that we can imagine that there could have been pains without brain states. And the only model I can think of for what the illusion might be, or at least the model given by the analogy the materialists themselves suggest, namely, heat and molecular motion, simply does not work in this case. So the materialist is up against a very stiff challenge. He has to show that these things we think we can see to be possible are in fact not possible. He has to show that these things which we can imagine are not in fact things we can imagine. And that requires some very different philosophical argument from the sort which has been given in the case of heat and molecular motion. And it would have to be a deeper and subtler argument than I can fathom and subtler than has ever appeared in any materialist literature that I have read. So the conclusion of this investigation would be that the analytical tools we are using go against the identity thesis and so go against the general thesis that mental states are just physical states.[3]

The next topic would be my own solution to the mind-body problem, but that I do not have.

Notes

1. The most popular identity theories advocated today explicitly fail to satisfy this simple requirement. For these theories usually hold that a mental state is a brain state, and that what makes the brain state into a mental state is its 'causal role', the fact that it tends to produce certain behavior (as intentions produce actions, or pain, pain behavior) and to be produced by certain stimuli (e.g. pain, by pinpricks). If the relations between the brain state and its causes and effects are regarded as contingent, then *being such-and-such-a-mental state* is a contingent property of the brain state. Let X be a pain. The causal-role identity theorist holds (1) that X is a brain state, (2) that the fact that X is a pain is to be analyzed (roughly) as the fact that X is produced by certain stimuli and produces certain behavior. The fact mentioned in (2) is, of course, regarded as contingent; the brain state X might well exist and not tend to produce the appropriate behavior in the absence of other conditions. Thus (1) and

(2) assert that a certain pain X might have existed, yet not have been a pain. This seems to me self-evidently absurd. Imagine any pain: is it possible that *it itself* could have existed, yet not have been a pain?

If X = Y, then X and Y share all properties, including modal properties. If X is a pain and Y the corresponding brain state, then *being a pain* is an essential property of X, and *being a brain state* is an essential property of Y. If the correspondence relation is, in fact, identity, then it must be *necessary* of Y that it corresponds to a pain, and *necessary* of X that it correspond to a brain state, indeed to this particular brain state, Y. Both assertions seem false; it *seems* clearly possible that X should have existed without the corresponding brain state; or that the brain state should have existed without being felt as pain. Identity theorists cannot, contrary to their almost universal present practice, accept these intuitions; they must deny them, and explain them away. This is none too easy a thing to do.

2. A brief restatement of the argument may be helpful here. If "pain" and "C-fiber stimulation" are rigid designators of phenomena, one who identifies them must regard the identity as necessary. How can this necessity be reconciled with the apparent fact that C-fiber stimulation might have turned out not to be correlated with pain at all? We might try to reply by analogy to the case of heat and molecular motion: the latter identity, too, is necessary, yet someone may believe that, before scientific investigation showed otherwise, molecular motion might have turned out not to be heat. The reply is, of course, that what really is possible is that people (or some rational sentient beings) could have been in the *same epistemic situation* as we actually are, and identify *a phenomenon* in the same way we identify heat, namely, by feeling it by the sensation we call "the sensation of heat," without the phenomenon being molecular motion. Further, the beings might not have been sensitive to molecular motion (i.e., to heat) by any neural mechanism whatsoever. It is impossible to explain the apparent possibility of C-fiber stimulations not having been pain in the same way. Here, too, we would have to suppose that we could have been in the same epistemological situation, and identify something in the same way we identify pain, without its corresponding to C-fiber stimulation. But the way

behavior is a complicated system —
Pain produces a tendency
toward certain behavior

we identify pain is by feeling it, and if a C-fiber stimulation could have occurred without our feeling any pain, then the C-fiber stimulation would have occurred without there *being* any pain, contrary to the necessity of the identity. The trouble is that although 'heat' is a rigid designator, heat is picked out by the contingent property of its being felt in a certain way; pain, on the other hand, is picked out by an essential (indeed necessary and sufficient) property. For a sensation to be *felt* as pain is for it to *be* pain.

3. All arguments against the identity theory which rely on the necessity of identity, or on the notion of essential property, are, of course, inspired by Descartes' argument for his dualism. The earlier arguments which superficially were rebutted by the analogies of heat and molecular motion, and the bifocals inventor who was also Postmaster General, had such an inspiration; and so does my argument here. R. Albritton and M. Slote have informed me that they independently have attempted to give essentialist arguments against the identity theory, and probably others have done so as well.

The simplest Cartesian argument can perhaps be restated as follows: Let 'A' be a *name* (rigid designator) of Descartes' body. Then Descartes argues that since he could exist even if A did not, P $-$(Descartes $= A$), hence $-$(Descartes $= A$). [*Editor's note:* In this anthology, "P" is used as the possibility operator.] Those who have accused him of a modal fallacy have forgotten that 'A' is rigid. His argument is valid, and his conclusion is correct, provided its (perhaps dubitable) premise is accepted. On the other hand, provided that Descartes is regarded as having ceased to exist upon his death, "$-$(Descartes $= A$)" can be established without the use of a modal argument; for if so, no doubt A survived Descartes when A was a corpse. Thus A had a property (existing at a certain time) which Descartes did not. The same argument can establish that a statue is not the hunk of stone, or the congery of molecules, of which it is composed. Mere non-identity, then, may be a weak conclusion. (See D. Wiggins, *Philosophical Review*, Vol. 77 (1968), pp. 90 ff.) The Cartesian modal argument, however, surely can be deployed to maintain relevant stronger conclusions as well.

Experience of heat != exp. of pain.
heat can be absence of cold, painful, uncomfortable
hence a subjective measure (temperature)
yet a rigid concept

Identity, Necessity, and Events

Fred Feldman

In "Kripke on the Identity Theory," I discussed Saul Kripke's arguments against several different forms of the identity theory.[1] I want to focus here on one version of the identity theory, and Kripke's argument against it. By doing this, I hope to clarify the reasoning behind some claims I made in the paper concerning Kripke's argument. The claims in question apparently strike some readers as being very implausible.

Following Kripke, we can distinguish three different families of contingent psychophysical identity theory. The first contains all those versions of the contingent identity theory that are theories about the identity of mental and physical substances, things, or "continuants." The second contains theories about the identity of particular mental and physical events, happenings, or "occurrents." The third contains theories about the identity of more abstract entities, such as "types," "phenomena," and properties.

I shall concentrate here on the second family of identity theories. So, for the most part, I shall be talking about contin-

Delivered at the meeting of the American Philosophical Association, Eastern Division, December 1974.

gent psychophysical *event* identity theories. My plan is as follows. First, I shall try to distinguish among three main views about the nature of events; I shall try to explain why the event identity theory ought to be thought of as a theory about events construed according to the third of these three views. Then I shall make a few comments about the theory, thus construed. Next, I shall try to explain why I think Kripke's argument fails to refute the theory, if taken as a theory about events of this third kind. But I shall also try to explain why it might be thought to refute the theory, if it were taken as a theory about events of either of the first two kinds. My suggestion, then, is this: perhaps some of those who are impressed by Kripke's argument are impressed in part because they think of the contingent psychophysical event identity theory as a theory about events of the first or second kind. Some of those who are less impressed by Kripke's argument may be less impressed by it, in part, because they think of the theory as a theory about events of the third kind. Hence reflections on the nature of events may serve to explain why Kripke's argument impresses some and fails to impress others.

The first task, then, is to say something about these three views about events.

I

According to the first view, which we can call the "propositional view",[2] events have several important features. First, they are capable of serving as the objects of the so-called propositional attitudes. Thus, if you hope that Jones is amused, then the object of your hope, Jones's being amused, is an event. Second, events need not occur in order to exist. So even if Jones is never amused, there is such an event as Jones's being amused; it just fails to occur. Third, a given event may occur, stop occurring, and then occur again. If some humorous incident amuses the ordinarily moody and depressed Jones, and then he returns to his more normal state, and then another humorous incident amuses him, we should say that Jones's being amused occurred, then did not occur for a while, and then occurred again. The very same event recurred.

The heart of this view about events is its criterion of event identity. Most simply stated, it is this: an event e is identical to an event e' if and only if it is necessary that, for any person S and propositional attitude A, S has A to e if and only if S has A to e'. In other words, if Jones's being amused is the same event as Jones's being lightheartedly entertained, then it would follow that it is necessary that we believe Jones is amused if and only if we believe Jones is lightheartedly entertained; we hope Jones is amused if and only if we hope Jones is lightheartedly entertained; and so on for the other attitudes.

It seems to me that it will be virtually impossible to formulate a coherent version of the contingent psychophysical event identity theory if we presuppose that it is a theory about events understood according to the propositional view. The explanation of this is simple. Suppose extensive research leads to the conclusion that a person is amused if and only if his A-fibers are stimulated. An identity theorist might wish to say, then, that the event of Jones's being amused is identical to the event of Jones's having stimulated A-fibers. But, given the criterion of event identity associated with the propositional view, it would follow from this claim that it is necessary that we believe Jones is amused if and only if we believe Jones has stimulated A-fibers; that we hope Jones is amused if and only if we hope Jones has stimulated A-fibers; and so on. These results are quite obviously unacceptable. Hence, some other view about events seems to be required, if we are going to formulate a plausible version of the contingent psychophysical event identity theory. Perhaps Roderick M. Chisholm had something like this in mind when he said that if the events in the theory are taken to be "states of affairs" (what I call "propositional events") "then, of course, the theory would be obviously false."[3]

According to a second view, which we can call the "structural view," events are complex, structured entities the main constituents of which are properties, individuals, and times. For any suitable property, individual, and time, if the individual has the property at the time, then there is such a thing as the event of that individual's having that property at that time. So if Jones is amused now, there is an event whose constituents are the property of being amused, the individual, Jones, and the time, now. This event is not to be confused with the ordered set of that property, individual, and time, for the set exists whether or not the individual has the property at the time. The event, in this view, exists only if Jones is amused now.

If events are complex structures of property, individual, and time, it would seem natural to say that events are identical if and only if they are structures containing the same property, individual, and time. In other words, if a's being F at t is an event, and b's being G at t' is an event, then a's being F at t is the same event as b's being G at t' if and only if the individual a is identical to the individual b; the property of being F is identical to the property of being G; and the time t is identical to the time t'. This criterion of event identity is the heart of the second, or structural, view about events, which has been developed and ably defended by Jaegwon Kim.[4]

It seems to me that this view about events does not fit naturally with the contingent psychophysical event identity theory, for several reasons. For example, the proposition that someone is amused if and only if he has stimulated A-fibers is supposed to be a contingent, scientific hypothesis. But it is hard to see how it could be so, if we adopt the structural view of events. The problem is as follows. Suppose Jones's being amused now is the same event as Jones's having stimulated A-fibers now. According to the structural view, it follows that the property of being amused is the same property as the property of having stimulated A-fibers. Assuming that the predicate 'is amused' expresses the former, the predicate 'has stimulated A-fibers' expresses the latter, and that predicates that express the same property are synonymous or at least necessarily equivalent, we get the odd result that the predicate 'is amused' is synonymous with, or at least necessarily equivalent to, the predicate 'has stimulated A-fibers'. In light of this result, one wonders how it could be a contingent, scientific hypothesis that someone is amused if and only if he has stimulated A-fibers.

Not everyone is impressed by this line of reasoning. I realize that it depends upon some controversial views about language. I rest my case here on a simpler point. We would like the contingent psychophysical *event* identity theory to be logically weaker than the contingent psychophysical *property* identity theory. That is, identity theories in family two are not supposed to entail corresponding theories in family three. Otherwise, the

intuitive distinctions among the families seem to go down the drain. If, however, we adopt the structural view of events, then the event identity theory entails the identity of the psychological and the physical properties. Hence, in this context, we should not adopt the structural view concerning events.

The third view about events, or the "concrete events view," is somewhat harder to state than either of the others.[5] Roughly, the idea is that events are "concrete" entities, more "coarsely individuated" than they are according to the other views. Jones's being amused now is the same event as Jones's being amused now about what happened to the chickens, even though the property of being amused is diverse from the property of being amused about what happened to the chickens, and even though we can believe that Jones is amused without believing that he is amused about what happened to the chickens.

According to the concrete events view, a given event may be associated with any number of logically unrelated, nonsynonymous sentences. Events, like concrete individuals of other kinds, can be described in a variety of nonequivalent ways. For example, consider these sentences:

(a) Jones is very amused.
(b) Jones is amused about what happened to the chickens.

Neither sentence entails the other. Yet it is possible that the event that makes (a) true is the same event as the one that makes (b) true. In other words, Jones's being very amused might be the same event as Jones's being amused about what happened to the chickens. This apparently could not happen according to either of the earlier views.

Some have suggested that, if we adopt the concrete events view, we should take causal indiscernibility to be our criterion of event identity. Thus we should say that an event *e* is identical to an event *e'* if and only if something is a cause of *e* if and only if it is a cause of *e'*; something is an effect of *e* if and only if it is an effect of *e'*. It seems to me that this criterion of event identity is not very helpful. In the first place, it is covertly circular—it presupposes some concept of event identity, for until we have a criterion of event identity, we cannot tell whether the effects of *e* are the same as, or diverse from, the effects of *e'*. After all, effects are events, too. Second, the criterion appeals to the notions of cause and effect, which seem to me to be too obscure to do much to clarify the concept of event.

In spite of this problem, which I acknowledge to be very serious, I want to proceed as if we had some clear idea of what a coarse-grained, concrete event is supposed to be. It seems to me that the concept may be clear enough to permit at least some useful communication. I propose, then, that it is most reasonable to construe the target of Kripke's attack as a contingent, psychophysical event identity theory, in which the events are assumed to be concrete. Construed in any other way, it is hard to see how the theory can get off the ground. Now that we have a somewhat clearer idea of the view of events most naturally associated with the contingent psychophysical event identity theory, we can turn to a consideration of some interesting features of the theory itself.

II

In the first place, as I understand it, the theory does not entail that any distinction between psychological and physical properties can be drawn. But, assuming that such a distinction can be drawn, the theory does not entail that psychological properties are identical to, or reducible to, or eliminable in favor of, physical properties. Thus the theory may fail to be a form of materialism. If materialism is taken to be the doctrine that everything that happens can be completely described in a purely physicalist language, then the contingent psychophysical event identity theory does not entail materialism. If materialism is taken to be the weaker view that every event is physical, then perhaps this version of the identity theory is naturally associated with materialism. Of course, by itself it does not imply that every event is physical; it only implies that every *psychological* event is physical.

A third point about the target of Kripke's attack is that it is supposed to be a "contingent identity" theory. Using one interpretation, this view can be expressed by saying that it is contingently true that every psychological event is a physical event, or

(A) $(e)(Me \longrightarrow Pe) \ \& \ -N(e)(Me \longrightarrow Pe)$.

[*Editor's note:* In this anthology, "$\longrightarrow$" is used instead of the horseshoe and the arrow as the material conditional ("if . . . then"). "N" is used as the necessity operator and "P" as the possibility operator.] The idea behind putting the view in this way is clear enough. In our world, every psychological event is a physical event. In other possible worlds, however, there are psychological events that are not physical events. This leaves open the possibility that in some other possible world, some blithe spirit is amused but has no body. Some of those who have emphasized the contingency of the contingent psychophysical event identity theory may have wanted to affirm something like this.

We may interpret the thesis about contingency in another, somewhat more interesting way. Some materialists may have believed in this more interesting view, although it is hard to tell from what they wrote. The idea may be stated, somewhat misleadingly in my opinion, in terms of contingent identity. We can say that every psychological event is identical to some physical event, but each physical event that is identical to a psychological event is such that it is only a contingent matter of fact that it is identical to a psychological event at all. That very event, in fact identical to a psychological event, could have occurred without being identical to a psychological event. This can be stated as follows:

(B) $(e)(Me \longrightarrow (Ee')(Pe'\ \&\ e=e'$
            $\&\ -N(Ee'')(Me''\ \&\ e=e')))$

A much more straightforward way of putting this would be to say that each psychological event is a physical event and not necessarily a psychological event:

(C) $(e)(Me \longrightarrow Pe\ \&\ -NMe)$

(B) and (C) are logically equivalent, although (C) certainly appears far less confusing.

I think there is some evidence that some early identity theorists may have held something like (C). One place in which I think it is suggested is in the discussion of the first objection in J. J. C. Smart's "Sensations and Brain Processes."[6] Whether they have held it or not, it strikes me as something suggested by their work, and something that may very well be true.

My main point here, however, is that if we interpret the contingent psychophysical event identity theory in either of the ways I have suggested, it is not equivalent to, and does not imply, any such doctrine as this:

(D) $(e)(Me \longrightarrow (Ee')(Pe'\ \&\ e=e'$
            $\&\ -Ne=e'))$

(D) strikes me as being at the very best extremely implausible. What it says is that every psychological event e is such that there is some physical event e' such that e and e' are the very same event, and yet there is some possible world in which this very event e (or e', call it what you like) is diverse from itself. I find this rather hard to understand.

III

Now, having done a little to bring out the main features of a few rough, but I hope not utterly implausible, versions of the doctrine Kripke set out to refute, we can turn to a consideration of what I take to be the most interesting of his arguments against it. Let us use the letter 'a' as a rigid designator for the event of Jones's being amused and the letter 'b' as a rigid designator for the event of Jones's having stimulated A-fibers. Let us assume that some proponent of the contingent psychophysical event identity theory wants to maintain that a is identical to b. Kripke's argument, with some slight alterations, is this:[7]

Argument G

(1) 'a' and 'b' are rigid designators.
(2) 'P $-(a=b)$' is true.
(3) If A is rigid, and B is rigid, and #P$- (A=B)$# is true, then #$-(A=B)$# is true.
(4) '$-(a=b)$' is true.

[*Editor's note:* In this anthology, "#" is used instead of the corner quote.] The most important question to be raised about Argument G is "What is the justification for (2), the premise that says, in effect, that it is possible that a is diverse from b?"

Someone might hold that the contingent psychophysical event identity theory itself entails (2), since it is the view that every psychological event is contingently identical to whatever physical event it happens to be identical to. It must be admitted, I believe, that some defenders of the identity theory have written in such a way as to suggest something like this. In my opinion, any such version of the theory verges on incoherence. Kripke's argument refutes it. Yet neither of the versions of the theory that I have presented—(A) and (C)—entails (2). The contingent psychophysical event identity theory surely does not *have* to be understood in such a way as to imply that each mental event is contingently identical to itself. So we need to find some other defense for premise (2) of Argument G.

Kripke's main argument for this controversial premise, modified to fit our example, can be put as follows. Prima facie it would seem that it is at least logically possible that b should have occurred (Jones's brain could have been in exactly that state at the time in question) without Jones's being amused at all, and thus without the presence of a.[8] Kripke's first point is entirely correct. We surely can grant that there is a possible world in which b, Jones's having stimulated A-fibers, occurs but in which Jones is not amused. We can even grant, if we like, that there is a world in which b occurs but in which Jones is utterly unconscious. But it does not follow from this alone that it is possible for b to occur without a. Hence, we have no proof of (2) yet.

Some people find this an odd claim. How, they ask, can a, which is Jones's being amused, occur in a world if Jones is not amused there? It seems impossible. The answer to this question is straightforward. Being a case of someone's being amused may not be an essential property of that event. It may be a property that the event has in this world, but lacks in other worlds. This case is like the more familiar case of Benjamin Franklin and his inventiveness. We might just as sensibly ask how Franklin, the inventor of bifocals, can exist in a world in which there are no inventors. Well, assuming he is only accidentally an inventor, he can do it easily; he just has to stick to politics and publishing and keep out of the laboratory. Similarly, if the event a is only accidentally a case of someone's being amused, it can just as easily exist in a world in which no one is amused.

Kripke was aware of this when he presented his argument in "Naming and Necessity." His answer, modified again to fit our example, is this: Can any case of essence be more obvious than the fact that being a case of someone's being amused is a necessary property of each event which in fact is a case of someone's being amused? Consider some particular occasion on which you were amused. Do you find it at all plausible to suppose that that very event could have occurred without being a case of someone's being amused, in the way a certain inventor (Franklin) could have existed without being an inventor?[9] Kripke apparently assumes that we all find it very implausible to suppose that a could have occurred without being a case of someone's being amused.

If Kripke is right about this, and a, Jones's being amused, cannot occur without being a case of someone's being amused, then a and b are possibly diverse, for there surely is a possible world in which b occurs without anyone's being amused. In that world, if Kripke is right, a cannot occur. Hence, there is a possible world in which b occurs without a. From this it follows that, in that world, it is not the case that b is identical to a. So premise (2) of Argument G would be established.

Obviously, Kripke's argument depends upon his claim that a, Jones's being amused, cannot occur without being a case of someone's being amused. What reason is there to accept this claim? It seems to me that it is here that our reflections on the nature of events may begin to bear fruit. If a is a propositional event, then I think Kripke is right, for it surely makes little sense to suppose that the proposition that Jones is amused could have failed to be the proposition that Jones is amused. Can there be a possible world in which the proposition that Jones is amused is true, but in which Jones is not amused? I cannot imagine how that could be the case. Thus it seems to me that Jones's being amused, if it is a propositional event, just has to be a case of someone's being amused. For this reason, it seems to me that if a is a propositional event, then a cannot fail to be a case of someone's being amused. So if Kripke assumes that a is a propositional event, he has good reason to believe that a is essentially a case of someone's being amused.

As I attempted to show earlier, however, it looks as if it is going to be very difficult to formulate a coherent version of the contingent psychophysical event identity theory if we assume that the events in question are propositional. The problems arise at the outset. If Jones's being amused is the same event as Jones's having stimulated A-fibers, and this is a propositional event, then it is necessary that we believe that Jones is amused if and only if we believe that Jones has stimulated A-fibers. It is obvious that this is not the case, so we should not assume that the events of the contingent psychophysical event identity theory are propositional events.

If *a* and *b* are structural events, then a plausible argument for Kripke's point can be presented. According to the structural view, events are structures of property, individual, and time. They are individuated by reference to their components. We have the same event if and only if we have the same property, individual, and time. From this it seems to follow that having the property, individual, and time it in fact has is essential to each event. Hence, *a*, Jones's being amused now, could not occur without having the property of being amused as its first component. It follows that being a case of someone's being amused is an essential property of *a*.

In fact, I do not believe that this argument is perfectly watertight, but I can sense its appeal. I can see why someone who understood events according to the structural view might be moved by such an argument to believe that Jones's being amused is essentially a case of someone's being amused. So if Kripke was assuming that *a* is a structural event, he may have had good reason to say what he did. Once again, however, as I tried to show earlier, it is difficult to formulate a coherent event identity theory with structural events. The problems here also arise at the outset. If Jones's being amused is the same event as Jones's having stimulated A-fibers, and

this is a structural event, then the property of being amused is the same property as the property of having stimulated A-fibers. Yet these are supposed to be two different properties, of course. Thus the identity theory should not be construed as a theory about structural events.

If *a* and *b* are concrete events, then, so far as I can see, Kripke's point cannot be established. Event *a* is a case of someone's being amused, but why should it be essentially so? It is as concrete an individual as Jones himself. Surely no one would say that Jones is essentially someone who is amused. Just as being amused is a contingent property of Jones, so being a case of someone's being amused may be a contingent property of *a*.

If we are to have a coherent version of the contingent psychophysical event identity theory, then it seems most reasonable to assume that the events in question are concrete events. And if we do this, then Kripke's argument loses its foothold. He has no way to show that *a* is essentially a case of someone's being amused. For all we know, that very event could have occurred without anyone's being amused. Hence the fact that we can imagine *b* occurring without anyone's being amused does not substantiate the claim that we can imagine *b* occurring without *a*. There is no proof for premise (2) of Argument G.

Furthermore, the contingent psychophysical event identity theory may be designed to *entail* that *a* is not essentially a case of someone's being amused. If the contingency of the theory is to be explained in the more interesting of the two ways I mentioned earlier, this can be shown. For suppose the view is this:

(C) $(e)(Me \rightarrow Pe \ \& \ -NMe)$

If the identity theory is (C), the thesis that every psychological event is a physical event, and each such physical event is such that it is only accidentally a psychological event, then the identity theory entails that Jones's being amused is only accidentally a psychological event. From this we can infer that it is only accidentally a case of someone's being amused. Hence, the contingent psychophysical event identity theory, if construed in this way, entails the denial of Kripke's assertion. Kripke's argument thus appears to turn on an undefended, controversial premise, and the premise may be one that his philosophical opponents have intended to reject from the very start.

IV

I have tried to explain, in an admittedly rough way, how the contingent psychophysical event identity theory should be understood. My central point has been that it seems best to frame the view in terms of concrete events. I have attempted to show that, if we understand the theory in this way and are careful to state the thesis about contingency correctly, then there is no good reason to be moved by Kripke's main argument against it.

Notes

1. Fred Feldman, "Kripke on the Identity Theory," *Journal of Philosophy* 71, no. 18 (October 24, 1974): 665-676. See also my "Kripke's Argument against Materialism," *Philosophical Studies* 24, no. 6 (November 1973): 416-419.

2. Roderick M. Chisholm has presented and defended what I here call the "propositional view" in several places. See his "Events and Propositions," *Nous* 4, no. 1 (February 1970): 15-24; "States of Affairs Again," *Nous* 5, no. 2 (May 1971): 179-189; "Language, Logic and State of Affairs," in Sidney Hook, ed., *Language and Philosophy* (New York: New York University Press, 1969), pp. 241-248.

3. Idem, *Person and Object* (LaSalle, Ill.: Open Court, 1976), p. 219, n.32.

4. See Jaegwon Kim, "On the Psycho-Physical Identity Theory," *American Philosophical Quarterly* 3 (1966): 231-32; "Events and Their Descriptions: Some Considerations," in Nicholas Rescher et al., eds., *Essays in Honor of Carl G. Hempel* (Dordrecht: Reidel,

1969); "Causation, Nomic Subsumption, and The Concept of Event," mimeographed (1972?). A similar view is presented by Alvin Goldman in *A Theory of Human Action* (Englewood Cliffs, N.J.: Prentice-Hall, 1970).

5. Donald Davidson is apparently a leading proponent of this view. See his "Events as Particulars," *Nous* 4, no. 1 (February 1970): 25-32; "The Individuation of Events," in Nicholas Rescher et al., eds., *Essays in Honor of Carl G. Hempel.* "On Events and Event Descriptions," in Joseph Margolis, ed., *Fact and Existence* (Oxford: Blackwell, 1969); "Eternal vs. Ephemeral Events," *Nous* 5, no. 4 (November 1971):335-349.

6. J. J. C. Smart, "Sensations and Brain Processes," *Philosophical Review* 68 (1959): 141-156.

7. See Saul Kripke, "Naming and Necessity," in Donald Davidson and Gilbert Harman, eds., *Semantics of Natural Language* (Dordrecht: Reidel, 1972), pp. 253-355.

8. Ibid., p. 335.

9. Ibid.

Anomalous Monism and Kripke's Cartesian Intuitions

Colin McGinn

I am going to argue that Davidson's anomalous monism[1] is not imperilled by Kripke's animadversions on the identity theory.[2] The argument will turn crucially upon a sharp distinction between type-type and token-token identity theories.

Suppose someone claims that pain is identical with C-fibre stimulation. Then, according to Kripke, he is committed to the necessity of that identity; there couldn't be pain without C-fibre stimulation, and *vice versa*. But, Kripke insists, there is a strong intuition, not to be lightly dismissed, that there is an 'element of contingency' in this relationship: for it seems imaginable, and hence possible, that the mental state should exist without the physical, and *vice versa*. Certainly it seems that it could have *turned out* that pain was "associated with" some other brain state. If the identity theorist is to sustain his thesis, he is under an obligation to account for this intuition compatibly with the mooted identity. Kripke throws him the following line: the case of pain and C-fibre stimulation is analogous to the case of heat and molecular motion; for here too there abided a stubborn intui-

From *Analysis* 37, no. 2 (1977):78-80. Reprinted by permission of the author.

tion that, since matters could have turned out otherwise, they could have *been* otherwise. But, Kripke claims, the natural explanation of the intuition of contingency in this case is not available to the mind-brain identity theorist. The following schematic reconstruction of Kripke's reasoning here will help us see why.

Take it that we have accepted the essentialist thesis:

(1)   NQ*a*;

but suppose also that, despite conviction of (1), we are strongly disposed to believe:

(2)   It could have turned out that [−Q*a*].

[*Editor's note:* In this anthology, "N" is used as the necessity operator and "P" as the possibility operator.] Now, Kripke says, (1) and (2) are, as they stand, inconsistent, because of the principle that if it could have turned out that *p* it could have been that *p*.[3] His way out of the antinomy is to reconstrue the thought behind (2) along these lines:

(3)   P(E*x*) (*x* is an *epistemic counterpart* of *a* & −Q*x*).

[*Editor's note:* In this anthology, the ordinary "E" is used instead of the backward "E" as the existential quantifier.] That is, what we really conceive in conceiving (mendaciously) that $[-Qa]$ is our being confronted with some entity *distinct* from *a* which is such that it puts us in qualitatively the same epistemic state as *a* does in the actual world but which yet lacks Q; and *this* possibility in no wise tells against the necessity of Qa. Thus, e.g., some phenomenon distinct from heat (= molecular motion) might produce qualitatively the same sensation in us as is actually produced by heat; and again, although *this* table is necessarily not made of ice, it is possible that there should be *a* table, with all the appearance of this one, which is made of ice. In each case, it is possibilities of this sort that account for the 'illusion of contingency'.

Now Kripke's central contention here is that we cannot get a true instance of (3) in the case of pain and C-fibre stimulation. The reason is this: *any epistemic counterpart of pain must itself be pain.* This is simply because being presented with a counterpart of an entity of a certain sort in a (metaphysically) possible world is precisely being in a mental state indistinguishable from that in which one is when presented with that counterpart's prototype in the actual world. Hence, all epistemic counterparts of (phenomenologically identified) mental states of a given type are themselves states of that type. But then, if pain just *is* C-fibre stimulation, all counterparts of pain, since they are themselves pain, must *ex hypothesi* be C-fibre stimulation. So we have not succeeded in conceiving a world in which the mental and physical states in question come apart, and have therefore failed to explain away the stubborn Cartesian intuition.

I agree that this point is powerful against the type-type theorist who accepts Kripke's conditions on an adequate reply to the Cartesian. But I want to insist, against Kripke, that his favoured style of

explanation of the impression of contingency *is* available to the token-token theorist. Here is why. Let '*a*' in the schemata (1)-(3) be instantiated, not by the name of a mental type, e.g. 'pain', but by the name of a mental token, e.g. 'my feeling pain at noon 17.7.76'; and let Q be the property of being identical with the token brain state named by 'my C-fibres firing at noon 17.7.76'. Now, is it possible, according to anomalous monism, that there should exist a token mental state qualitatively indistinguishable from *a* which yet lacks Q? It is not only possible, it is actual; indeed, it is possible (and probable) that there be a token pain distinct from *a* which isn't even of the same physical type, *viz.* the C-fibre firing type, as that token brain state with which *a* is identical. And these possibilities compromise neither the necessity of the token-token identity in question nor the status of *a* as necessarily a C-fibre stimulation (which is what Leibniz's law requires if that modal property holds of the brain state token with which *a* is identical).[4] In this respect, token mental states are like particular tables: they can be (and be essentially) of a type such that other tokens of that type fail to have properties which they, *qua* tokens, necessarily have. And there is nothing especially puzzling about this.

That shows, I think, that token-token theories can meet the requirements on an adequate rebuttal of the Cartesian challenge that Kripke lays down. Moreover, such theories are actually strengthened by Kripkean considerations. For these considerations help warrant the rejection of type-type theories in favour of token-token theories; and this is especially significant where, as with Davidson's anomalous monism, it is a *premiss* of the argument to the identity of particular mental and physical events and states that there is no (nomologically) correlating mental and physical types.[5]

What Is It Like to Be a Bat?

Thomas Nagel

Consciousness is what makes the mind-body problem really intractable. Perhaps that is why current discussions of the problem give it little attention or get it obviously wrong. The recent wave of reductionist euphoria has produced several analyses of mental phenomena and mental concepts designed to explain the possibility of some variety of materialism, psychophysical identification, or reduction.[1] But the problems dealt with are those common to this type of reduction and other types, and what makes the mind-body problem unique, and unlike the water-H_2O problem or the Turing machine-IBM machine problem or the lightning-electrical discharge problem or the gene-DNA problem or the oak tree-hydrocarbon problem, is ignored.

Every reductionist has his favorite analogy from modern science. It is most unlikely that any of these unrelated examples of successful reduction will shed light on the relation of mind to brain. But philosophers share the general human weakness for explanations of what is incomprehensible in terms suited for what is familiar and well understood, though entirely different. This has led to the acceptance of implausible accounts of the mental largely because they would permit familiar kinds of reduction. I shall try to explain why the usual examples do not help us to understand the relation between mind and body—why, indeed, we have at present no conception of what an explanation of the physical nature of a mental phenomenon would be. Without consciousness the mind-body problem would be much less interesting. With consciousness it seems hopeless. The most important and characteristic feature of conscious mental phenomena is very poorly understood. Most reductionist theories do not even try to explain it. And careful examination will show that no currently available concept of reduction is applicable to it. Perhaps a new theoretical form can be devised for the purpose, but such a solution, if it exists, lies in the distant intellectual future.

Conscious experience is a widespread phenomenon. It occurs at many levels of animal life, though we cannot be sure of its presence in the simpler organisms, and it is very difficult to say in general what provides evidence of it. (Some extremists have been prepared to deny it even of

From *Philosophical Review* 83 (1974):435-450. Reprinted by permission of *Philosophical Review* and the author.

mammals other than man.) No doubt it occurs in countless forms totally unimaginable to us, on other planets in other solar systems throughout the universe. But no matter how the form may vary, the fact that an organism has conscious experience *at all* means, basically, that there is something it is like to *be* that organism. There may be further implications about the form of the experience; there may even (though I doubt it) be implications about the behavior of the organism. But fundamentally an organism has conscious mental states if and only if there is something that it is like to *be* that organism—something it is like *for* the organism.

We may call this the subjective character of experience. It is not captured by any of the familiar, recently devised reductive analyses of the mental, for all of them are logically compatible with its absence. It is not analyzable in terms of any explanatory system of functional states, or intentional states, since these could be ascribed to robots or automata that behaved like people though they experienced nothing.[2] It is not analyzable in terms of the causal role of experiences in relation to typical human behavior—for similar reasons.[3] I do not deny that conscious mental states and events cause behavior, nor that they may be given functional characterizations. I deny only that this kind of thing exhausts their analysis. Any reductionist program has to to be based on an analysis of what is to be reduced. If the analysis leaves something out, the problem will be falsely posed. It is useless to base the defense of materialism on any analysis of mental phenomena that fails to deal explicitly with their subjective character. For there is no reason to suppose that a reduction which seems plausible when no attempt is made to account for consciousness can be extended to include consciousness. Without some idea, therefore, of what the subjective character of experience is, we cannot know what is required of a physicalist theory.

While an account of the physical basis of mind must explain many things, this appears to be the most difficult. It is impossible to exclude the phenomenological features of experience from a reduction in the same way that one excludes the phenomenal features of an ordinary substance from a physical or chemical reduction of it—namely, by explaining them as effects on the minds of human observers.[4] If physicalism is to be defended, the phenomenological features must themselves be given a physical account. But when we examine their subjective character it seems that such a result is impossible. The reason is that every subjective phenomenon is essentially connected with a single point of view, and it seems inevitable that an objective, physical theory will abandon that point of view.

Let me first try to state the issue somewhat more fully than by referring to the relation between the subjective and the objective, or between the *pour-soi* and the *en-soi*. This is far from easy. Facts about what it is like to be an X are very peculiar, so peculiar that some may be inclined to doubt their reality, or the significance of claims about them. To illustrate the connection between subjectivity and a point of view, and to make evident the importance of subjective features, it will help to explore the matter in relation to an example that brings out clearly the divergence between the two types of conception, subjective and objective.

I assume we all believe that bats have experience. After all, they are mammals, and there is no more doubt that they have experience than that mice or pigeons or whales have experience. I have chosen bats instead of wasps or flounders because if one travels too far down the phylogenetic tree, people gradually shed their faith that there is experience there at all. Bats, although more closely related to us than those other species, nevertheless present a range of activity and a sensory apparatus so different from ours that the problem I want to pose is exceptionally vivid (though it certainly could be raised with other species). Even without the benefit of philosophical reflection, anyone who has spent some time in an enclosed space with an excited bat knows what it is to encounter a fundamentally *alien* form of life.

I have said that the essence of the belief that bats have experience is that there is something that it is like to be a bat. Now we know that most bats (the microchiroptera, to be precise) perceive the external world primarily by sonar, or echolocation, detecting the reflections, from objects within range, of their own rapid, subtly modulated, high-frequency shrieks. Their brains are designed to correlate the outgoing impulses with the subsequent echoes, and the information thus acquired enables bats to make precise discriminations of distance, size, shape, motion, and texture comparable to those we make by vision. But bat sonar, though clearly a form of perception, is not similar in its operation to any sense that we possess, and there is no reason to suppose that it is subjectively like anything we can experience or imagine. This appears to create difficulties for the notion of what it is like to be a bat. We must consider whether any method will permit us to extrapolate to the inner life of the bat from our own case,[5] and if not, what alternative methods there may be for understanding the notion.

Our own experience provides the basic material for our imagination, whose range is therefore limited. It will not help to try to imagine that one has webbing on one's arms, which enables one to fly around at dusk and dawn catching insects in one's mouth; that one has very poor vision, and perceives the surrounding world by a system of reflected high-frequency sound signals; and that one spends the day hanging upside down by one's feet in an attic. In so far as I can imagine this (which is not very far), it tells me only what it would be like for *me* to behave as a bat behaves. But that is not the question.

I want to know what it is like for a *bat* to be a bat. Yet if I try to imagine this, I am restricted to the resources of my own mind, and those resources are inadequate to the task. I cannot perform it either by imagining additions to my present experience, or by imagining segments gradually subtracted from it, or by imagining some combination of additions, subtractions, and modifications.

To the extent that I could look and behave like a wasp or a bat without changing my fundamental structure, my experiences would not be anything like the experiences of those animals. On the other hand, it is doubtful that any meaning can be attached to the supposition that I should possess the internal neurophysiological constitution of a bat. Even if I could by gradual degrees be transformed into a bat, nothing in my present constitution enables me to imagine what the experiences of such a future stage of myself thus metamorphosed would be like. The best evidence would come from the experiences of bats, if we only knew what they were like.

So if extrapolation from our own case is involved in the idea of what it is like to be a bat, the extrapolation must be incompletable. We cannot form more than a schematic conception of what it *is* like. For example, we may ascribe general *types* of experience on the basis of the animal's structure and behavior. Thus we describe bat sonar as a form of three-dimensional forward perception; we believe that bats feel some versions of pain, fear, hunger, and lust, and that they have other, more familiar types of perception besides sonar. But we believe that these experiences also have in each case a specific subjective character, which it is beyond our ability to conceive. And if there is conscious life elsewhere in the universe, it is likely that some of it will not be describable even in the most general experiential terms available to us.[6] (The problem is not confined to exotic cases, however, for it exists between one person and another. The subjective character of the experience of a person deaf and blind from birth is not accessible to me, for example, nor presumably is mine to him. This does not prevent us each from believing that the other's experience has such a subjective character.)

If anyone is inclined to deny that we can believe in the existence of facts like this whose exact nature we cannot possibly conceive, he should reflect that in contemplating the bats we are in much the same position that intelligent bats or Martians[7] would occupy if they tried to form a conception of what it was like to be us. The structure of their own minds might make it impossible for them to succeed, but we know they would be wrong to conclude that there is not anything precise that it is like to be us: that only certain general types of mental state could be ascribed to us (perhaps perception and appetite would be concepts common to us both; perhaps not). We know they would be wrong to draw such a skeptical conclusion because we know what it is like to be us. And we know that while it includes an enormous amount of variation and complexity, and while we do not possess the vocabulary to describe it adequately, its subjective character is highly specific, and in some respects describable in terms that can be understood only by creatures like us. The fact that we cannot expect ever to accommodate in our language a detailed description of Martian or bat phenomenology should not lead us to dismiss as meaningless the claim that bats and Martians have experiences fully comparable in richness of detail to our own. It would be fine if someone were to develop concepts and a theory that enabled us to think about those things; but such an understanding may be permanently denied to us by the limits of our nature. And to deny the reality or logical significance of what we can never describe or understand is the crudest form of cognitive dissonance.

This brings us to the edge of a topic that requires much more discussion than I can give it here: namely, the relation between facts on the one hand and conceptual schemes or systems of representation on the other. My realism about the subjective domain in all its forms implies a belief in the existence of facts beyond the reach of human concepts. Certainly it is possible for a human being to believe that there are facts which humans never *will* possess the requisite concepts to represent or comprehend. Indeed, it would be foolish to doubt this, given the finiteness of humanity's expectations. After all, there would have been transfinite numbers even if everyone had been wiped out by the Black Death before Cantor discovered them. But one might also believe that there are facts which *could* not ever be represented or comprehended by human beings, even if the species lasted forever—simply because our structure does not permit us to operate with concepts of the requisite type. This impossibility might even be observed by other beings, but it is not clear that the existence of such beings, or the possibility of their existence, is a precondition of the significance of the hypothesis that there are humanly inaccessible facts. (After all, the nature of beings with access to humanly inaccessible facts is presumably itself a humanly inaccessible fact.) Reflection on what it is like to be a bat seems to lead us, therefore, to the conclusion that there are facts that do not consist in the truth of propositions expressible in a human language. We can be compelled to recognize the existence of such facts without being able to state or comprehend them.

I shall not pursue this subject, however. Its bearing on the topic before us (namely, the mind-body problem) is that it enables us to make a general observation about the subjective character of experience. Whatever may be the status of facts about what it is like to be a human being, or a bat, or a Martian, these appear to be facts that embody a particular point of view.

I am not adverting here to the alleged privacy of experience to its possessor. The point of view in question is not one accessible only to a single individual. Rather it is a *type*. It is often possible to take up a point of view other than one's own, so the comprehension of such facts is not limited to one's own case. There is a sense in which phenomenological facts are perfectly objective: one person can know or say of another what the quality of the other's experience is. They are subjective, however, in the sense that even this objective ascription of experience is possible only for someone sufficiently similar to the object of ascription to be able to adopt his point of view—to understand the ascription in the first person as well as in the third, so to speak. The more different from oneself the other experiencer is, the less success one can expect with this enterprise. In our own case we occupy the relevant point of view, but we will have as much difficulty understanding our own experience properly if we approach it from another point of view as we would if we tried to understand the experience of another species without taking up *its* point of view.[8]

This bears directly on the mind-body problem. For if the facts of experience—facts about what it is like *for* the experiencing organism—are accessible only from one point of view, then it is a mystery how the true character of experiences could be revealed in the physical operation of that organism. The latter is a domain of objective facts *par excellence*—the kind that can be observed and understood from many points of view and by individuals with differing perceptual systems. There are no comparable imaginative obstacles to the acquisition of knowledge about bat neurophysiology by human scientists, and intelligent bats or

Martians might learn more about the human brain than we ever will.

This is not by itself an argument against reduction. A Martian scientist with no understanding of visual perception could understand the rainbow, or lightning, or clouds as physical phenomena, though he would never be able to understand the human concepts of rainbow, lightning, or cloud, or the place these things occupy in our phenomenal world. The objective nature of the things picked out by these concepts could be apprehended by him because, although the concepts themselves are connected with a particular point of view and a particular visual phenomenology, the things apprehended from that point of view are not: they are observable from the point of view but external to it; hence they can be comprehended from other points of view also, either by the same organisms or by others. Lightning has an objective character that is not exhausted by its visual appearance, and this can be investigated by a Martian without vision. To be precise, it has a *more* objective character than is revealed in its visual appearance. In speaking of the move from subjective to objective characterization, I wish to remain noncommittal about the existence of an end point, the completely objective intrinsic nature of the thing, which one might or might not be able to reach. It may be more accurate to think of objectivity as a direction in which the understanding can travel. And in understanding a phenomenon like lightning, it is legitimate to go as far away as one can from a strictly human viewpoint.[9]

In the case of experience, on the other hand, the connection with a particular point of view seems much closer. It is difficult to understand what could be meant by the *objective* character of an experience, apart from the particular point of view from which its subject apprehends it. After all, what would be left of what it was like to be a bat if one removed the viewpoint of the bat? But if experience does not have, in addition to its subjective character, an objective nature that can be apprehended from many different points of view, then how can it be supposed that a Martian investigating my brain might be observing physical processes which were my mental processes (as he might observe physical processes which were bolts of lightning), only from a different point of view? How, for that matter, could a human physiologist observe them from another point of view?[10]

We appear to be faced with a general difficulty about psychophysical reduction. In other areas the process of reduction is a move in the direction of greater objectivity, toward a more accurate view of the real nature of things. This is accomplished by reducing our dependence on individual or species-specific points of view toward the object of investigation. We describe it not in terms of the impressions it makes on our senses, but in terms of its more general effects and of properties detectable by means other than the human senses. The less it depends on a specifically human viewpoint, the more objective is our description. It is possible to follow this path because although the concepts and ideas we employ in thinking about the external world are initially applied from a point of view that involves our perceptual apparatus, they are used by us to refer to things beyond themselves—toward which we *have* the phenomenal point of view. Therefore we can abandon it in favor of another, and still be thinking about the same things.

Experience itself, however, does not seem to fit the pattern. The idea of moving from appearance to reality seems to make no sense here. What is the analogue in this case to pursuing a more objective understanding of the same phenomena by abandoning the initial subjective viewpoint toward them in favor of another that is more objective but concerns the same thing? Certainly it *appears* unlikely that we will get closer to the real nature of human experience by leaving behind the particularity of our human point of view and striving for a description in terms accessible to beings that could not imagine what it was like to be us. If the subjective character of experience is fully comprehensible only from one point of view, then any shift to greater objectivity—that is, less attachment to a specific viewpoint —does not take us nearer to the real nature of the phenomenon: it takes us farther away from it.

In a sense, the seeds of this objection to the reducibility of experience are already detectable in successful cases of reduction; for in discovering sound to be, in reality, a wave phenomenon in air or other media, we leave behind one viewpoint to take up another, and the auditory, human or animal viewpoint that we leave behind remains unreduced. Members of radically different species may both understand the same physical events in objective terms, and this does not require that they understand the phenomenal forms in which those events appear to the senses of members of the other species. Thus it is a condition of their referring to a common reality that their more particular viewpoints are not part of the common reality that they both apprehend. The reduction can succeed only if the species-specific viewpoint is omitted from what is to be reduced.

But while we are right to leave this point of view aside in seeking a fuller understanding of the external world, we cannot ignore it permanently, since it is the essence of the internal world, and not merely a point of view on it. Most of the neobehaviorism of recent philosophical psychology results from the effort to substitute an objective concept of mind for the real thing, in order to have nothing left over which cannot be reduced. If we acknowledge that a physical theory of mind must account for the subjective character of experience, we must admit that no presently available conception gives us a clue how this could be done. The problem is unique. If mental processes are indeed physical processes, then there is something it is like, intrinsically,[11] to undergo certain physical processes. What it is for such a thing to be the case remains a mystery.

What moral should be drawn from these reflections, and what should be done next? It would be a mistake to conclude that physicalism must be false. Nothing is proved by the inadequacy of physicalist hypotheses that assume a faulty objective analysis of mind. It would be truer to say that physicalism is a position we cannot understand because we do not at present have any conception of how it might be true. Perhaps it will be thought unreasonable to require such a conception as a condition of understanding. After all, it might be said, the meaning of physicalism is clear enough: mental states are states of the body; mental events are physical events. We do not know *which* physical states and events they are, but that should not prevent us from understanding the hypothesis. What could be clearer than the words "is" and "are"?

But I believe it is precisely this apparent clarity of the word "is" that is deceptive. Usually, when we are told that X is Y we know *how* it is supposed to be true, but that depends on a conceptual or theoretical background and is not conveyed by the "is" alone. We know how both "X" and "Y" refer, and the kinds of things to which they refer, and we have a rough idea how the two referential paths might converge on a single thing, be it an object, a person, a process, an event, or whatever. But when the two terms of the identification are very disparate it may not be so clear how it could be true. We may not have even a rough idea of how the two

referential paths could converge, or what kind of things they might converge on, and a theoretical framework may have to be supplied to enable us to understand this. Without the framework, an air of mysticism surrounds the identification.

This explains the magical flavor of popular presentations of fundamental scientific discoveries, given out as propositions to which one must subscribe without really understanding them. For example, people are now told at an early age that all matter is really energy. But despite the fact that they know what "is" means, most of them never form a conception of what makes this claim true, because they lack the theoretical background.

At the present time the status of physicalism is similar to that which the hypothesis that matter is energy would have had if uttered by a pre-Socratic philosopher. We do not have the beginnings of a conception of how it might be true. In order to understand the hypothesis that a mental event is a physical event, we require more than an understanding of the word "is." The idea of how a mental and a physical term might refer to the same thing is lacking, and the usual analogies with theoretical identification in other fields fail to supply it. They fail because if we construe the reference of mental terms to physical events on the usual model, we either get a reappearance of separate subjective events as the effects through which mental reference to physical events is secured, or else we get a false account of how mental terms refer (for example, a causal behaviorist one).

Strangely enough, we may have evidence for the truth of something we cannot really understand. Suppose a caterpillar is locked in a sterile safe by someone unfamiliar with insect metamorphosis, and weeks later the safe is reopened, revealing a butterfly. If the person knows that the safe has been shut the whole time, he has reason to believe that the butterfly

[margin note: X is Y when X + Y are very different]

is or was once the caterpillar, without having any idea in what sense this might be so. (One possibility is that the caterpillar contained a tiny winged parasite that devoured it and grew into the butterfly.)

It is conceivable that we are in such a position with regard to physicalism. Donald Davidson has argued that if mental events have physical causes and effects, they must have physical descriptions. He holds that we have reason to believe this even though we do not—and in fact *could* not—have a general psychophysical theory.[12] His argument applies to intentional mental events, but I think we also have some reason to believe that sensations are physical processes, without being in a position to understand how. Davidson's position is that certain physical events have irreducibly mental properties, and perhaps some view describable in this way is correct. But nothing of which we can now form a conception corresponds to it; nor have we any idea what a theory would be like that enabled us to conceive of it.[13]

Very little work has been done on the basic question (from which mention of the brain can be entirely omitted) whether any sense can be made of experiences' having an objective character at all. Does it make sense, in other words, to ask what my experiences are *really* like, as opposed to how they appear to me? We cannot genuinely understand the hypothesis that their nature is captured in a physical description unless we understand the more fundamental idea that they *have* an objective nature (or that objective processes can have a subjective nature).[14]

I should like to close with a speculative proposal. It may be possible to approach the gap between subjective and objective from another direction. Setting aside temporarily the relation between the mind and the brain, we can pursue a more objective understanding of the mental in its own right. At present we are completely unequipped to think about the subjective character of experience without relying on the imagination—without taking up the point of view of the experiential subject. This should be regarded as a challenge to form new concepts and devise a new method—an objective phenomenology not dependent on empathy or the imagination. Though presumably it would not capture everything, its goal would be to describe, at least in part, the subjective character of experiences in a form comprehensible to beings incapable of having those experiences.

We would have to develop such a phenomenology to describe the sonar experiences of bats; but it would also be possible to begin with humans. One might try, for example, to develop concepts that could be used to explain to a person blind from birth what it was like to see. One would reach a blank wall eventually, but it should be possible to devise a method of expressing in objective terms much more than we can at present, and with much greater precision. The loose intermodal analogies—for example, "Red is like the sound of a trumpet"—which crop up in discussions of this subject are of little use. That should be clear to anyone who has both heard a trumpet and seen red. But structural features of perception might be more accessible to objective description, even though something would be left out. And concepts alternative to those we learn in the first person may enable us to arrive at a kind of understanding even of our own experience which is denied us by the very ease of description and lack of distance that subjective concepts afford.

Apart from its own interest, a phenomenology that is in this sense objective may permit questions about the physical[15] basis of experience to assume a more intelligible form. Aspects of subjective experience that admitted this kind of objective description might be better candidates for objective explanations of a more familiar sort. But whether or not this guess is correct, it seems unlikely that any physical theory of mind can be contemplated until more thought has been given to the general problem of subjective and objective. Otherwise we cannot even pose the mind-body problem without sidestepping it.[16]

Notes

1. Examples are J. J. C. Smart, *Philosophy and Scientific Realism* (London, 1963); David K. Lewis, "An Argument for the Identity Theory," *Journal of Philosophy*, 63 (1966), reprinted with addenda in David M. Rosenthal, *Materialism and the Mind-Body Problem* (Englewood Cliffs, N.J., 1971); Hilary Putnam, "Psychological Predicates" in Capitan and Merrill, *Art, Mind, and Religion* (Pittsburgh, 1967), reprinted in Rosenthal, *op. cit.*, as "The Nature of Mental States"; D. M. Armstrong, *A Materialist Theory of the Mind* (London, 1968); D. C. Dennett, *Content and Consciousness* (London, 1969). I have expressed earlier doubts in "Armstrong on the Mind," *Philosophical Review*, 79 (1970), 394-403; "Brain Bisection and the Unity of Consciousness," *Synthese*, 22 (1971); and a review of Dennett, *Journal of Philosophy*, 69 (1972). See also Saul Kripke, "Naming and Necessity" in Davidson and Harman, *Semantics of Natural Language* (Dordrecht, 1972), esp. pp. 334-342; and M. T. Thornton, "Ostensive Terms and Materialism," *The Monist*, 56 (1972).

2. Perhaps there could not actually be such robots. Perhaps anything complex enough to behave like a person would have experiences. But that, if true, is a fact which cannot be discovered merely by analyzing the concept of experience.

3. It is not equivalent to that about which we are incorrigible, both because we are not incorrigible about experience and because experience is present in animals lacking language and thought, who have no beliefs at all about their experiences.

4. Cf. Richard Rorty, "Mind-Body Identity, Privacy, and Categories," *The Review of Metaphysics*, 19 (1965), esp. 37-38.

5. By "our own case" I do not mean just "my own case," but rather the mentalistic ideas that we apply unproblematically to ourselves and other human beings.

6. Therefore the analogical form of the English expression "what it is *like*" is misleading. It does not mean "what (in our experience) it *resembles*," but rather "how it is for the subject himself."

7. Any intelligent extraterrestrial beings totally different from us.

8. It may be easier than I suppose to transcend inter-species barriers with the aid of the imagination. For example, blind people are able to detect objects near them by a form of sonar, using vocal clicks or taps of a cane. Perhaps if one knew what that was like, one could by extension imagine roughly what it was like to possess the much more refined sonar of a bat. The distance between oneself and other persons and other species can fall anywhere on a continuum. Even for other persons the understanding of what it is like to be them is only partial, and when one moves to species very different from oneself, a lesser degree of partial understanding may still be available. The imagination is remarkably flexible. My point, however, is not that we cannot *know* what it is like to be a bat. I am not raising that epistemological problem. My point is rather that even to form a *conception* of what it is like to be a bat (and a fortiori to know what it is like to be a bat) one must take up the bat's point of view. If one can take it up roughly, or partially, then one's conception will also be rough or partial. Or so it seems in our present state of understanding.

9. The problem I am going to raise can therefore be posed even if the distinction between more subjective and more objective descriptions or viewpoints can itself be made only within a larger human point of view. I do not accept this kind of conceptual relativism, but it need not be refuted to make the point that psychophysical reduction cannot be accommodated by the subjective-to-objective model familiar from other cases.

10. The problem is not just that when I look at the "Mona Lisa," my visual experience has a certain quality, no trace of which is to be found by someone looking into my brain. For even if he did observe there a tiny image of the "Mona Lisa," he would have no reason to identify it with the experience.

11. The relation would therefore not be a contingent one, like that of a cause and its distinct effect. It would be necessarily true that a certain physical state felt a certain way. Saul Kripke (*op. cit.*) argues that causal behaviorist

and related analyses of the mental fail because they construe, e.g., "pain" as a merely contingent name of pains. The subjective character of an experience ("its immediate phenomenological quality" Kripke calls it [p. 340]) is the essential property left out by such analyses, and the one in virtue of which it is, necessarily, the experience it is. My view is closely related to his. Like Kripke, I find the hypothesis that a certain brain state should *necessarily* have a certain subjective character incomprehensible without further explanation. No such explanation emerges from theories which view the mind-brain relation as contingent, but perhaps there are other alternatives, not yet discovered.

A theory that explained how the mind-brain relation was necessary would still leave us with Kripke's problem of explaining why it nevertheless appears contingent. That difficulty seems to me surmountable, in the following way. We may imagine something by representing it to ourselves either perceptually, sympathetically, or symbolically. I shall not try to say how symbolic imagination works, but part of what happens in the other two cases is this. To imagine something perceptually, we put ourselves in a conscious state resembling the state we would be in if we perceived it. To imagine something sympathetically, we put ourselves in a conscious state resembling the thing itself. (This method can be used only to imagine mental events and states—our own or another's.) When we try to imagine a mental state occurring without its associated brain state, we first sympathetically imagine the occurrence of the mental state: that is, we put ourselves into a state that resembles it mentally. At the same time, we attempt to perceptually imagine the non-occurrence of the associated physical state, by putting ourselves into another state unconnected with the first: one resembling that which we would be in if we perceived the non-occurrence of the physical state. Where the imagination of physical features is perceptual and the imagination of mental features is sympathetic, it appears to us that we can imagine any experience occurring without its associated brain state, and vice versa. The relation between them will appear contingent even if it is necessary, because of the independence of the disparate types of imagination.

(Solipsism, incidentally, results if one misinterprets sympathetic imagination as if it worked like perceptual imagination: it then seems impossible to imagine any experience that is not one's own.)

12. See "Mental Events" in Foster and Swanson, *Experience and Theory* (Amherst, 1970); though I don't understand the argument against psychophysical laws.

13. Similar remarks apply to my paper "Physicalism," *Philosophical Review* 74 (1965), 339-356, reprinted with postscript in John O'Connor, *Modern Materialism* (New York, 1969).

14. This question also lies at the heart of the problem of other minds, whose close connection with the mind-body problem is often overlooked. If one understood how subjective experience could have an objective nature, one would understand the existence of subjects other than oneself.

15. I have not defined the term "physical." Obviously it does not apply just to what can be described by the concepts of contemporary physics, since we expect further developments. Some may think there is nothing to prevent mental phenomena from eventually being recognized as physical in their own right. But whatever else may be said of the physical, it has to be objective. So if our idea of the physical ever expands to include mental phenomena, it will have to assign them an objective character—whether or not this is done by analyzing them in terms of other phenomena already regarded as physical. It seems to me more likely, however, that mental-physical relations will eventually be expressed in a theory whose fundamental terms cannot be placed clearly in either category.

16. I have read versions of this paper to a number of audiences, and am indebted to many people for their comments.

Part Three
Functionalism

Introduction: What Is Functionalism?

Ned Block

IT IS DOUBTFUL whether doctrines known as "functionalism" in fields as disparate as anthropology, literary criticism, psychology, and philosophy of psychology have anything in common but the name. Even in philosophy of psychology, the term is used in a number of distinct senses. The functionalisms of philosophy of psychology are, however, a closely knit group; indeed, they appear to have a common origin in the works of Aristotle (see Hartman, 1977, especially chap. 4).

Three functionalisms have been enormously influential in philosophy of mind and psychology:

Functional analysis. In this sense of the term, functionalism is a type of explanation and, derivatively, a research strategy, the research strategy of looking for explanations of that type. A functional explanation is one that relies on a decomposition of a system into its component parts; it explains the working of the system in terms of the capacities of the parts and the way the parts are integrated with one another. For example, we can explain how a factory can produce refrigerators by appealing to the capacities of the various assembly lines, their workers and machines, and the organization of these components. The article by Robert Cummins (chapter 12) describes functionalism in this sense. (See also Fodor, 1965, 1968a, 1968b; Dennett, 1975.)

Computation-representation functionalism. In this sense of the term, "functionalism" applies to an important special case of functional explanation as defined above, namely, to psychological explanation seen as akin to providing a computer program for the mind. Whatever mystery our mental life may initially seem to have is dissolved by functional analysis of mental processes to the point where they are seen to be composed of computations as mechanical as the primitive operations of a digital computer—processes so stupid that appealing to them in psychological explanations involves no hint of question-begging. The key notions of functionalism in this sense are representation and computation. Psychological states are seen as systematically representing the world via a language of thought, and psychological processes are seen as computations involving these representations. Functionalism in this sense of the term is not explored here but is discussed in volume 2, part one, "Mental Representation."

Metaphysical functionalism. The last functionalism, the one that this part is mainly about, is a theory of *the nature of the mind*, rather than a theory of psychological explanation. Metaphysical functionalists are concerned not with how mental states account for behavior, but rather with what they *are*. The functionalist answer to "What are mental states?" is simply that mental states are functional states. Thus theses of metaphysical functionalism are sometimes described as functional state identity theses. The main concern of metaphysical functionalism is the same as that of behaviorism (see part one, "Behaviorism") and physicalism (see part two, "Reductionism and Physicalism"). All three doctrines address themselves to such questions as "What is pain?"—or at least to "What is there in common to all pains in virtue of which they are pains?"

It is important to note that metaphysical functionalism is concerned (in the first instance) with mental state *types*, not tokens—with *pain*, for instance, and not with particular *pains*. (For further explanation of this distinction see Boyd, introduction to part two; Davidson, chapter 5; Fodor, chapter 6.) Most functionalists are willing to allow that each *particular* pain is a physical state or event, and indeed that for each type of pain-feeling organism, there is (perhaps) a single type of physical state that realizes pain in that type of organism. Where functionalists differ with physicalists, however, is with respect to the question of what is common to all pains in virtue of which they are pains. The functionalist says the something in common is functional, while the physicalist says it is physical (and the behaviorist says it is behavioral).[1] Thus, in one respect, the disagreement between functionalists and physicalists (and behaviorists) is *metaphysical without being ontological*. Functionalists can be physicalists in allowing that all the entities (things, states, events, and so on) that exist are physical entities, denying only

that what binds certain types of things together is a physical property.

Metaphysical functionalists characterize mental states in terms of their causal roles, particularly, in terms of their causal relations to sensory stimulations, behavioral outputs, and other mental states. Thus, for example, a metaphysical functionalist theory of pain might characterize pain in part in terms of its tendency to be caused by tissue damage, by its tendency to cause the desire to be rid of it, and by its tendency to produce action designed to separate the damaged part of the body from what is thought to cause the damage.

What I have said about metaphysical functionalism so far is rather vague, but, as will become clear, disagreements among metaphysical functionalists preclude easy characterization of the doctrine. Before going on to describe metaphysical functionalism in more detail, I shall briefly sketch some of the connections among the functionalist doctrines just enumerated. One connection is that functionalism in all the senses described has something to do with the notion of a Turing machine (described in the next section). Metaphysical functionalism often identifies mental states with Turing machine "table states" (also described in the next section). Computation-representation functionalism sees psychological explanation as something like providing a computer program for the mind. Its aim is to give a functional analysis of mental capacities broken down into their component mechanical processes. If these mechanical processes are *algorithmic*, as is sometimes assumed (without much justification, in my view) then they will be Turing-computable as well (as the Church-Turing thesis assures us).[2] Functional analysis, however, is concerned with the notion of a Turing machine mainly in that providing something like a computer program for the mind is a special case of functional analysis.

Another similarity among the functionalisms mentioned is their relation to physical characterizations. The causal structures with which metaphysical functionalism identifies mental states are realizable by a vast variety of physical systems. Similarly, the information processing mechanisms postulated by a particular computation-representation functionalist theory could be realized hydraulically, electrically, or even mechanically. Finally, functional analysis would normally characterize a manufacturing process abstractly enough to allow a wide variety of types of machines (wood or metal, steam-driven or electrical), workers (human or robot or animal), and physical setups (a given number of assembly lines or half as many dual-purpose assembly lines). A third similarity is that each type of functionalism described legitimates at least one notion of functional equivalence. For example, for functional analysis, one sense of functional equivalence would be: has capacities that contribute in similar ways to the capacities of a whole.

In what follows, I shall try to give the reader a clearer picture of metaphysical functionalism. ("Functionalism" will be used to mean metaphysical functionalism in what follows.)

Machine Versions of Functionalism

Some versions of functionalism are couched in terms of the notion of a Turing machine, while others are not. A Turing machine is specified by two functions: one from inputs and states to outputs, and one from inputs and states to states. A Turing machine has a finite number of states, inputs, and outputs, and the two functions specify a set of conditionals, one for each combination of state and input. The conditionals are of this form: if the machine is in state S and receives input I, it will then emit output O and go into next state S'. This set of conditionals is often expressed in the form of a machine table (see below). Any system that has a set of inputs, outputs, and states related in the way speci-

fied by the machine table is *described* by the machine table and is a *realization* of the abstract automaton specified by the machine table. (This definition actually characterizes a finite automaton, which is just one kind of Turing machine.)

One very simple version of machine functionalism states that each system that has mental states is described by at least one Turing machine table of a certain specifiable sort; it also states that each type of mental state of the system is identical to one of the machine table states specified in the machine table (see Putnam, chapter 17; Block and Fodor, chapter 20). Consider, for example, the Turing machine described in the following "Coke machine" machine table (compare Nelson, 1975):

	S_1	S_2
nickel input	Emit no output Go to S_2	Emit a Coke Go to S_1
dime input	Emit a Coke Stay in S_1	Emit a Coke and a nickel Go to S_1

One can get a crude picture of the simple version of machine functionalism described above by considering the claim that S_1 = dime-desire, and S_2 = nickel-desire. Of course, no functionalist would claim that a Coke machine desires anything. Rather, the simple version of machine functionalism described above makes an analogous claim with respect to a much more complex machine table.

Machine versions of functionalism are useful for many purposes, but they do not provide the most general characterization of functionalism. One can achieve more generality by characterizing functionalism as the view that what makes a pain a pain (and, generally, what makes any mental state the mental state it is) is its having a certain causal role.[3] But this formulation buys generality at the price of vagueness. A more precise formulation can be introduced as follows.[4] Let T be a psychological theory (of either common sense or scientific psychology) that tells us (among other things) the relations among pain, other mental states, sensory inputs, and behavioral outputs. Reformulate T so that it is a single conjunctive sentence with all mental state terms as singular terms; for example, 'is angry' becomes 'has anger'. Let T so reformulated be written as

$$T(s_1 \ldots s_n)$$

where $s_1 \ldots s_n$ are terms that designate mental states. Replace each mental state term with a variable and prefix existential quantifiers to form the Ramsey sentence of the theory

$$Ex_1 \ldots x_n T(x_1 \ldots x_n).$$

[In this anthology, the ordinary "E" is used instead of the backward "E" as the existential quantifier.] Now, if x_i is the variable that replaced 'pain', we can define 'pain' as follows:

y has pain if and only if
$$Ex_1 \ldots x_n[T(x_1 \ldots x_n) \ \& \ y \text{ has } x_i].$$

That is, one has pain just in case he has a state that has certain relations to other states that have certain relations to one another (and to inputs and outputs; I have omitted reference to inputs and outputs for the sake of simplicity). It will be convenient to think of pain as the property expressed by the predicate 'x has pain', that is, to think of pain as the property ascribed to someone in saying that he has pain.[5] Then, relative to theory T, pain can be identified with the property expressed by the predicate

$$Ex_1 \ldots x_n[T(x_1 \ldots x_n) \ \& \ y \text{ has } x_i].$$

For example, take T to be the ridiculously simple theory that pain is caused by pin pricks and causes worry and the emission of loud noises, and worry, in turn, causes brow wrinkling. The Ramsey sentence of T is

$Ex_1Ex_2(x_1$ is caused by pin pricks and causes x_2 and emission of loud noises & x_2 causes brow wrinkling).

Relative to T, pain is the property expressed by the predicate obtained by adding a conjunct as follows:

$Ex_1Ex_2[(x_1$ is caused by pin pricks and causes x_2 and emission of loud noises & x_2 causes brow wrinkling) & y has $x_1]$.

That is, pain is the property that one has when one has a state that is caused by pin pricks, and causes emission of loud noises, and also causes something else, that, in turn, causes brow wrinkling.

We can make this somewhat less cumbersome by letting an expression of the form '%xFx' be a singular term meaning the same as an expression of the form 'the property of being an x such that x is F', that is, 'being F'. So %$x(x$ is bigger than a mouse & x is smaller than an elephant) = being bigger than a mouse and smaller than an elephant. Using this notation, we can say

pain = %$yEx_1Ex_2[(x_1$ is caused by pin pricks and causes x_2 and emission of loud noises & x_2 causes brow wrinkling) & y has $x_1]$,

rather than saying that pain is the property expressed by the predicate

$Ex_1Ex_2[(x_1$ is caused by pin pricks and causes x_2 and emission of loud noises & x_2 causes brow wrinkling) & y has $x_1]$.

It may be useful to consider a non-mental example. It is sometimes supposed that automotive terms like 'valve-lifter' or 'carburetor' are functional terms. Anything that lifts valves in an engine with a certain organizational structure is a valve-lifter. ('Camshaft', on the other hand, is a "structural" term, at least relative to 'valve-lifter'; a camshaft is *one* kind of device for lifting valves.)

Consider the "theory" that says: "The carburetor mixes gasoline and air and sends the mixture to the ignition chamber, which, in turn . . ." Let us consider 'gasoline' and 'air' to be input terms, and let x_1 replace 'carburetor', and x_2 replace 'ignition chamber'. Then the property of being a carburetor would be

%y Ex$_1$ . . . x_n[(The x_1 mixes gasoline and air and sends the mixture to the x_2, which, in turn . . .) & y is an x_1] .

That is, being a carburetor $=$ being what mixes gasoline and air and sends the mixture to something else, which, in turn . . .

This identification, and the identification of pain with the property one has when one is in a state that is caused by pin pricks and causes loud noises and also causes something else that causes brow wrinkling, would look less silly if the theories of pain (and carburetion) were more complex. But the essential idea of functionalism, as well as its major weakness, can be seen clearly in the example, albeit rather starkly. Pain is identified with an abstract causal property tied to the real world only via its relations, direct and indirect, to inputs and outputs. The weakness is that it seems so clearly conceivable that something could have that causal property, yet *not be* a pain. This point is discussed in detail in "Troubles with Functionalism" (Block, chapter 22; see Shoemaker, chapter 21, and Lycan, forthcoming, for critiques of such arguments).

Functionalism and Behaviorism

Many functionalists (such as David Lewis, D. M. Armstrong, and J. J. C. Smart) consider themselves descendants of behaviorists, who attempted to define a mental state in terms of what behaviors would tend to be emitted in the presence of specified stimuli. E.g., the desire for an ice-cream cone might be identified with a set of dispositions, including the disposition to reach out and grasp an ice-cream cone if one is proffered, other things being equal. But, as functionalist critics have emphasized, the phrase "other things being equal" is behavioristically illicit, because it can only be filled in with references to *other mental states* (see Putnam, chapter 2; the point dates back at least to Chisholm, 1957, chap. 11; and Geach, 1957, p. 8). One who desires an ice-cream cone will be disposed to reach for it only if he *knows* it is an ice-cream cone (and not, in general, if he believes it to be a tube of axle-grease), and only if he does not *think* that taking an ice-cream cone would conflict with *other desires* of more importance to him (such as the desire to lose weight, avoid obligations, or avoid cholesterol). The final nail in the behaviorist coffin was provided by the well-known "perfect actor" family of counterexamples. As Putnam argued in convincing detail (see chapter 2), it is possible to imagine a community of perfect actors who, by virtue of lawlike regularities, have exactly the behavioral dispositions envisioned by the behaviorists to be associated with absence of pain, even though they do in fact have pain. This shows that no behavioral disposition is a necessary condition of pain, and an exactly analogous example of perfect pain-pretenders shows that no behavioral disposition is a sufficient condition of pain, either.

Functionalism in all its forms differs from behaviorism in two major respects. First, while behaviorists defined mental states in terms of stimuli and responses, they did not think mental states were *themselves* causes of the responses and effects of the stimuli. Behaviorists took mental states to be "pure dispositions." Gilbert Ryle, for example, emphasized that "to possess a dispositional property is not to be in a particular state, or to undergo a particular change" (1949, p. 43). Brittleness, according to Ryle, is not a *cause* of breaking, but merely the fact of breaking easily. Similarly, to attribute pain to someone is not to attribute a cause or effect of anything, but simply to say what he would do in certain circumstances. Behaviorists are fictionalists about the mental, hence they cannot allow that mental states have causal powers. Functionalists, by contrast, claim it to be an advantage of their account that it "allows experiences to be something real, and so to be the effects of their occasions, and the causes of their manifestations (Lewis, 1966, p. 166). Armstrong says that "[when I think] it is not simply that I would speak or act if some conditions that are unfulfilled were to be fulfilled. Something is currently going on. Rylean behaviorism denies this, and so it is unsatisfactory" (chapter 13).

The second difference between functionalism and behaviorism is that functionalists emphasize not just the connections between pain and its stimuli and responses, but also its connections to other mental states. Notice, for example, that any full characterization of S_1 in the machine table above would have to refer to S_2 in one way or another, since it is one of the defining characteristics of S_1 that anything in S_1 goes into S_2 when it receives a nickel input. Another example, recall that the Ramsey sentence formulation identifies pain with

$$\% \, y\text{E}x_1 \ldots x_n[T(x_1 \ldots x_n) \, \& \, y \text{ has } x_i]$$

where the variable x_i replaced 'pain', and the rest of $x_1 \ldots x_n$ replaced the other mental state terms in T. So the functionalist expression that designates pain includes a specification of the relations between pain and all the other mental states related to it, and to inputs and outputs as well. (The role of inputs and outputs would have been better indicated had I written T as

$$T(s_1 \ldots s_n, o_1 \ldots o_m, i_1 \ldots i_k),$$

explicitly including terms for inputs and outputs.)

Behaviorism is a vague doctrine, and one that is sometimes defined in a way that would make functionalism a version of behaviorism. Even functionalists have offered definitions of 'behaviorism' that would make functionalists behaviorists. For example, if we defined 'behaviorism' as the doctrine that mental states (such as pain) can be characterized in nonmental terms, versions of functionalism along the lines of the Ramsey sentence version sketched above (held by Lewis, Armstrong, Smart, and Sydney Shoemaker) would qualify as versions of behaviorism (since all of the original mental state terms are replaced by variables in the Ramsey sentence). Many other definitions of 'behaviorism' count functionalism as a type of behaviorism. But it would be ludicrously literal-minded to take such definitions very seriously. Clear and general formulations of functionalism were not available until recently, so standard definitions of behaviorism could hardly be expected to draw the boundaries between behaviorism and functionalism with perfect accuracy. Furthermore, given an explicit definition of behaviorism, logical ingenuity can often disguise a functionalist account so as to fit the definition (see Bealer, 1978; Thomas, 1978, for accomplishments of this rather dubious variety). Definitions of behaviorism that count functionalism as behaviorist are misguided precisely *because* they blur the distinctions between functionalism and behaviorism just sketched. A characterization of pain can hardly be counted as behaviorist if it allows that a system could behave (and be disposed to behave) exactly as if it were in pain in all possible circumstances, yet not be in pain.[6]

Is Functionalism Reductionist?

Functionalists sometimes formulate their claim by saying that mental states can only be characterized in terms of other mental states. For instance, a person desires such and such if he would do so and so if he believed doing so and so will get him such and such, and if he believed doing so and so would not conflict with other desires. This much functionalism brings in no reductionism, but functionalists have rarely stopped there. Most regard mental terms as eliminable *all at once.* Armstrong says, for example, "The logical dependence of purpose on perception and belief, and of perception and belief upon purpose is not circularity in definition. What it shows is that the corresponding concepts must be introduced *together or not at all"* (1977, p. 88). Shoemaker says, "On one construal of it, functionalism in the philosophy of mind is the doctrine that mental or psychological terms are in principle eliminable in a certain way" (chapter 21). Lewis is more explicit, using a formulation much like the Ramsey sentence formulation given above, which designates mental states by expressions that do not contain any mental terminology (see chapter 15 for details).

The same sort of point applies to machine functionalism. Putnam says, "The S_i, to repeat, are specified only *implicitly* by the description" (chapter 17). In the Coke machine automaton described above, the only antecedently understood terms (other than 'emit', 'go to', and so on) are the input and output terms, 'nickel', 'dime', and 'Coke'. The state terms 'S_1' and 'S_2' in the Coke machine automaton—as in every Turing machine—are given their content entirely in terms of input and output terms (+ logical terms).

Thus functionalism could be said to reduce mentality to input-output structures (note that S_1 and S_2 can have any natures at all, so long as these natures connect them to one another and to the acceptance of nickels and dimes and disbursement of nickels and Cokes as described in the machine table). But functionalism gives us reduction without elimination. Functionalism is not fictionalist about mentality, for each of the functionalist ways of characterizing mental states in terms of inputs and outputs commits

itself to the existence of mental states by the use of quantification over mental states, or some equivalent device.[7]

The Varieties of Functionalism

Thus far, I have characterized functionalism without adverting to any of the confusing disagreements among functionalists. I believe that my characterization is correct, but its application to the writings of some functionalists is not immediately apparent. Indeed, the functionalist literature (or, rather, what is generally, and I think correctly, regarded as the functionalist literature) exhibits some bizarre disagreements, the most surprising of which has to do with the relation between functionalism and physicalism. Some philosophers (Armstrong, 1968, 1977, chapter 13; Lewis, 1966, chapters 15, 18; Smart, 1971) take functionalism as showing that physicalism is probably *true,* while others (Fodor, 1965; Putnam, 1966; Block and Fodor, chapter 20) take functionalism as showing that physicalism is probably *false.* This is the most noticeable difference among functionalist writings. I shall argue that the Lewis-Armstrong-Smart camp is mistaken in holding that functionalism supports an interesting version of physicalism, and furthermore, that the functionalist insight that they share with the Putnam-Fodor-Harman camp *does* have the consequence that physicalism is probably false. I shall begin with a brief historical sketch.

While functionalism dates back to Aristotle, in its current form it has two main contemporary sources. (A third source, Sellars's and, later, Harman's views on meaning as conceptual role, has also been influential.)

Source I

Putnam (1960) compared the mental states of a person with the machine table states of a Turing machine. He then rejected any identification of mental states with machine table states, but in a series of articles over the years he moved closer to such an identification, a pattern culminating in "Psychological Predicates" (1967, reprinted as chapter 17, this volume). In this article, Putnam came close to advocating a view—which he defended in his philosophy of mind lectures in the late 1960s—that mental states can be identified with machine table states, or rather disjunctions of machine table states. (See Thomas, 1978, for a defence of roughly this view; see Block and Fodor, chapter 20, and Putnam, chapter 7, for a critique of such views.)

Fodor (1965, 1968a) developed a similar view (though it was not couched in terms of Turing machines) in the context of a functional-analysis view of psychological explanation (see Cummins, chapter 12). Putnam's and Fodor's positions were characterized in part by their opposition to physicalism, the view that each *type* of mental state is a physical state.[8] Their argument is at its clearest with regard to the simple version of Turing machine functionalism described above, the view that pain, for instance, is a machine table state. What physical state could be common to all and only realizations of S_1 of the Coke machine automaton described above? The Coke machine could be made of an enormous variety of materials, and it could operate via an enormous variety of mechanisms; it could even be a "scattered object," with parts all over the world, communicating by radio. If someone suggests a putative physical state common to all and only realizations of S_1, it is a simple matter to dream up a nomologically possible machine that satisfies the machine table but does not have the designated physical state. Of course, it is one thing to *say* this and another thing to prove it, but the claim has such overwhelming prima facie plausibility that the burden of proof is on the critic to come up with reason for thinking otherwise. Published critiques (Kalke, 1969; Gendron, 1971; Kim, 1972; Nelson, 1976; Causey,

1977) have in my view failed to meet this challenge.

If we could formulate a machine table for a human, it would be absurd to identify any of the machine table states with a type of *brain* state, since presumably all manner of brainless machines could be described by that table as well. So if pain is a machine table state, it is not a brain state. It should be mentioned, however, that it is possible to *specify* a sense in which a functional state F can be said to be physical. For example, F might be said to be physical if every system that in fact has F is a physical object, or, alternatively, if every realization of F (that is, every state that plays the causal role specified by F) is a physical state. Of course, the doctrines of "physicalism" engendered by such stipulations should not be confused with the version of physicalism that functionalists have argued against (see note 8).

Jaegwon Kim objects that "the less the physical basis of the nervous system of some organisms resembles ours, the less temptation there will be for ascribing to them sensations or other phenomenal events" (chapter 19). But his examples depend crucially on considering creatures whose functional organization is much more primitive than ours. He also points out that "the mere fact that the physical bases of two nervous systems are different in material composition or physical organization with respect to a certain scheme of classification does not entail that they cannot be in the same physical state with respect to a different scheme." Yet the functionalist does not (or, better, should not) claim that functionalism *entails* the falsity of physicalism, but only that the burden of proof is on the physicalist. Kim (chapter 19) and Lewis (chapter 18; see also Causey, 1977, p. 149) propose species-specific identities: pain is one brain state in dogs and another in people. As should be clear from this introduction, however, this move sidesteps the main metaphysical question: "What is common to the pains of dogs and people (and all other pains) in virtue of which they are pains?"

Source II

The second major strand in current functionalism descends from Smart's early article on mind-body identity (1959). Smart worried about the following objection to mind-body identity: So what if pain is a physical state? It can still have a variety of phenomenal *properties*, such as sharpness, and these phenomenal properties may be irreducibly mental. Then Smart and other identity theorists would be stuck with a "double aspect" theory: pain is a physical state, but it has both physical and irreducibly mental properties. He attempted to dispel this worry by analyzing mental concepts in a way that did not carry with it any commitment to the mental or physical status of the concepts.[9] These "topic-neutral analyses," as he called them, specified mental states in terms of the stimuli that caused them (and the behavior that they caused, although Smart was less explicit about this). His analysis of first-person sensation avowals were of the form "There is something going on in me which is like what goes on when . . . ," where the dots are filled in by descriptions of typical stimulus situations. In these analyses, Smart broke decisively with behaviorism in insisting that mental states were real things with causal efficacy; Armstrong, Lewis, and others later improved his analyses, making explicit the behavioral effects clauses, and including mental causes and effects. Lewis's formulation, especially, is now very widely accepted among Smart's and Armstrong's adherents (Smart, 1971, also accepts it). In a recent review in the *Australasian Journal of Philosophy*, Alan Reeves declares, "I think that there is some consensus among Australian materialists that Lewis has provided an exact statement of their viewpoint" (1978).

Smart used his topic-neutral analyses only to defeat an a priori objection to the identity theory. As far as an argument *for* the identity theory went, he relied on considerations of simplicity. It was absurd, he thought, to suppose that there should be a perfect correlation between mental states and brain states and yet that the states could be nonidentical. (See Kim, 1966; Brandt and Kim, 1967, for an argument against Smart; but see also Block, 1971, 1979; and Causey, 1972, 1977, for arguments against Kim and Brandt.) But Lewis and Smart's Australian allies (notably D. M. Armstrong) went beyond Smart, arguing that something like topic-neutral analyses could be used to argue *for* mind-brain identity. In its most persuasive version (Lewis's), the argument for physicalism is that pain can be seen (by conceptual analysis) to be the occupant of causal role R; a certain neural state will be found to be the occupant of causal role R; thus it follows that pain = that neural state. Functionalism comes in by way of showing that the meaning of 'pain' is the same as a certain definite description that spells out causal role R.

Lewis and Armstrong argue from functionalism to the truth of physicalism because they have a "functional specification" version of functionalism. Pain is a functionally specified state, perhaps a functionally specified brain state, according to them. Putnam and Fodor argue from functionalism to the falsity of physicalism because they say there are functional states (or functional properties), and that mental states (or properties) are identical to these functional states. No functional state is likely to be a physical state.

The difference between a functional state identity claim and a functional specification claim can be made clearer as follows. Recall that the functional state identity claim can be put thus:

$$\text{pain} = \%y \text{Ex}_1 \ldots \text{Ex}_n [T(x_1 \ldots x_n) \ \& \ y \text{ has } x_1];$$

where x_1 is the variable that replaced

'pain'. A functional specification view could be stated as follows:[10]

$$\text{pain} = \text{the } x_1 \text{Ex}_2 \ldots \text{Ex}_n T(x_1 \ldots x_n).$$

In terms of the example mentioned earlier, the functional state identity theorist would identify pain with the property one has when one is in a state that is caused by pin pricks and causes loud noises and also something else that causes brow wrinkling. The functional specifier would define pain as *the thing* that is caused by pin pricks and causes loud noises and also something else that causes brow wrinkling.

According to the functional specifier, the thing that has causal role R (for example, the thing that is caused by pin pricks and causes something else and so forth) might be a state of one physical type in one case and a state of another physical type in another case. The functional state identity theorist is free to accept this claim as well, but what he insists on is that *pain* is not identical to a physical state. What pains have in common in virtue of which they are pains is causal role R, not any physical property.

In terms of the carburetor example, functional state identity theorists say that being a carburetor = being what mixes gas and air and sends the mixture to something else, which, in turn . . . Functional specifiers say that the carburetor is *the thing* that mixes gas and air and sends the mixture to something else, which, in turn . . . What the difference comes to is that the functional specifier says that the carburetor is a type of physical object, though perhaps one type of physical object in a Mercedes and another type of physical object in a Ford. The functional state identity theorist can agree with this, but he insists that *what it is to be a carburetor* is to have a certain functional role, not a certain physical structure.

At this point, it may seem to the reader that the odd disagreement about whether functionalism justifies physicalism or the negation of physicalism owes simply to ambiguities in 'functionalism' and 'physicalism'. In particular, it may seem that the functional specification view justifies *token* physicalism (the doctrine that every particular pain is a physical state token), while the functional state identity view justifies the negation of *type* physicalism (the doctrine that *pain* is a type of physical state).

This response oversimplifies matters greatly, however. First, it is textually mistaken, since those functional specifiers who see the distinction between type and token materialism clearly have type materialism in mind. For example, Lewis says, "A dozen years or so ago, D. M. Armstrong and I (independently) proposed a materialist theory of mind that joins claims of *type-type* psychophysical identity with a behaviorist or functionalist way of characterizing mental states such as pain" (chapter 16; emphasis added). More important, the functional specification doctrine *commits* its proponents to a functional state identity claim. Since the latter doctrine counts against type physicalism, so does the former. It is easy to see that the functional specification view commits its proponents to a functional state identity claim. According to functional specifiers, it is a conceptual truth that pain is the state with causal role R. But then *what it is to be a pain* is to have causal role R. Thus the functional specifiers are committed to the view that what pains have in common by virtue of which they are pains is their causal role, rather than their physical nature. (Again, Lewis is fairly clear about this: "Our view is that the concept of pain . . . is the concept of a state that occupies a certain causal role.")

I suspect that what has gone wrong in the case of *many* functional specifiers is simply failure to appreciate the distinction between type and token for mental states. If pain in Martians is one physical state, pain in humans another, and so on for pain in every pain-feeling organism, then each particular pain is a token of some physical type. This is token physicalism. Perhaps functional specifiers ought to be *construed* as arguing for token physicalism (even though Lewis and others explicitly say they are arguing for type physicalism). I shall give three arguments against such a construal. First, as functional state identity theorists have often pointed out, a *nonphysical* state could conceivably have a causal role typical of a mental state. In functional specification terms, there might be a creature in which pain is a functionally specified *soul* state. So functionalism opens up the possibility that even if *our* pains are physical, other pains might not be. In the light of this point, it seems that the support that functionalism gives even to token physicalism is equivocal. Second, the *major* arguments for token physicalism involve no functionalism at all (see Davidson, chapter 5, and Fodor, chapter 6). Third, token physicalism is a much weaker doctrine than physicalists have typically wanted.

In sum, functional specifiers *say* that functionalism supports physicalism, but they are committed to a functionalist answer, not a physicalist answer, to the question of what all pains have in common in virtue of which they are pains. And if what all pains have in common in virtue of which they are pains is a functional property, it is very unlikely that pain is coextensive with any physical state. If, on the contrary, functional specifiers have *token* physicalism in mind, functionalism provides at best equivocal support for the doctrine; better support is available elsewhere; and the doctrine is a rather weak form of physicalism to boot.

Lewis's views deserve separate treatment. He insists that pain is a brain state only because he takes 'pain' to be a non-rigid designator meaning 'the state with such and such causal role'.[11] Thus, in Lewis's view, to say that pain is a brain state should not be seen as saying what all pains have in common in virtue of which

they are pains, just as saying that the winning number is 37 does not suggest that 37 is what all winning numbers have in common. Many of Lewis's opponents disagree about the rigidity of 'pain', but the dispute is irrelevant to our purposes, since Lewis does take 'having pain' to be rigid, and so he does accept (he tells me) a functional property identity view: having pain = having a state with such and such a typical causal role. I think that most functional state identity theorists would be as willing to rest on the thesis that having pain is a functional property as on the thesis that pain is a functional state.

In conclusion, while there is considerable disagreement among the philosophers whom I have classified as metaphysical functionalists, there is a single insight about the nature of the mind to which they are all committed.

Notes

1. Discussions of functional state identity theses have sometimes concentrated on one or another weaker thesis in order to avoid issues about identity conditions on entities such as states or properties (see, for example, Block and Fodor, chapter 20). Consider the following theses:

(1) Pain = functional state S.
(2) Something is a pain just in case it is a (token of) S.
(3) The conditions under which x and y are both pains are the same as the conditions under which x and y are both tokens of S.

(1) is a full-blooded functional state identity thesis that entails (2) and (3). Theses of the form of (2) and (3) can be used to state what it is that all pains have in common in virtue of which they are pains.

2. Dennett (1975) and Rey (1979) make this appeal to the Church-Turing thesis. But if the mechanical processes involved analog rather than digital computation, then the processes could fail to be algorithmic in the sense required by the Church-Turing thesis. The experiments discussed in volume 2, part two, "Imagery" suggest that mental images are (at

least partially) analog representations, and that the computations that operate on images are (at least partially) analog operations.

3. Strictly speaking, even the causal role formulation is insufficiently general, as can be seen by noting that Turing machine functionalism is not a special case of causal role functionalism. Strictly speaking, none of the states of a Turing machine need cause any of the other states. All that is required for a physical system to satisfy a machine table is that the counterfactuals specified by the table are true of it. This can be accomplished by some causal agent outside the machine. Of course, one can always choose to speak of a *different* system, one that includes the causal agent as part of the machine, but that is irrelevant to my point.

4. Formulations of roughly this sort were first advanced by Lewis, 1966, 1970, 1972; Martin, 1966. (See also Harman, 1973; Grice, 1975; Field, 1978; Block, chapter 22.)

5. See Field, 1978, for an alternative convention.

6. Characterizations of mental states along the lines of the Ramsey sentence formulation presented above wear their incompatibility with behaviorism on their sleeves in that they involve explicit quantification over mental states. Both Thomas and Bealer provide ways of transforming functionalist definitions or identifications so as to disguise such transparent incompatibility.

7. The machine table states of a finite automaton can be defined explicitly in terms of inputs and outputs by a Ramsey sentence method, or by the method described in Thomas (1978). Both of these methods involve one or another sort of commitment to the existence of the machine table states.

8. 'Physical state' could be spelled out for these purposes as the state of something's having a first-order property that is expressible by a predicate of a true physical theory. Of course, this analysis requires some means of characterizing physical theory. A first-order property is one whose definition does not require quantification over properties. A second-order property is one whose definition requires quantification over first-order properties (but not other properties). The physicalist doctrine that functionalists argue against is the doctrine that mental properties are *first-order* physical properties. Functionalists need not deny that mental properties are second-order physical properties (in various senses of that phrase).

9. As Kim has pointed out (1972), Smart did not need these analyses to avoid "double aspect" theories. Rather, a device Smart introduces elsewhere in the same paper will serve the purpose. Smart raises the objection that if afterimages are brain states, then since an afterimage can be orange, the identity theorist would have to conclude that a brain state can be orange. He replies by saying that the identity theorist need only identify the *experience of having an orange afterimage* with a brain state; this state is not orange, and so no orange brain states need exist. Images, says Smart, are not really mental entities; it is experiences of images that are the real mental entities. In a similar manner, Kim notes, the identity theorist can "bring" the phenomenal properties into the mental states themselves; for example, the identity theorist can concern himself with states such as John's having a sharp pain; this state is not sharp, and so the identity theorist is not committed to sharp brain states. This technique does the trick, although of course it commits its perpetrators to the unfortunate doctrine that pains do not exist, or at least that they are not mental entities; rather, it is the havings of sharp pains and the like that are the real mental entities.

10. The functional specification view I give here is a much simplified version of Lewis's formulation (see chapter 15).

11. A rigid designator is a singular term that names the same thing in each possible world. 'The color of the sky' is nonrigid, since it names blue in worlds where the sky is blue, and red in worlds where the sky is red. 'Blue' is rigid, since it names blue in all possible worlds, even in worlds where the sky is red.

References

Armstrong, D. M. 1968. *A Materialist Theory of Mind*. London: Routledge & Kegan Paul.

—— 1970. *The Nature of Mind*. In C. V. Borst, ed., *The Mind/Brain Identity Theory*. London: Macmillan. Reprinted as chapter 13, this volume.

—— 1977. "The Causal Theory of the Mind." In *Neue Heft für Philosophie*, no. 11, pp. 82-95. Vendenhoek and Ruprecht.

Bealer, G. 1978. "An Inconsistency in Functionalism." *Synthese* 38:333-372.

Block, N. 1971. "Physicalism and Theoretical Identity." Ph.D. dissertation, Harvard University.

——— 1978. "Troubles with Functionalism." In C. W. Savage, ed., *Minnesota Studies in Philosophy of Science.* Vol. 9. Minneapolis: University of Minnesota Press. Reprinted as chapter 22, this volume.

——— 1979. "Reductionism." In *Encyclopedia of Bioethics.* New York: Macmillan.

Block, N., and J. A. Fodor. 1972. "What Psychological States Are Not." *Philosophical Review* 81, no. 2:159-182. Reprinted as chapter 20, this volume.

Brandt, R., and J. Kim. 1967. "The Logic of the Identity Theory." *Journal of Philosophy* 64, no. 17:515-537.

Causey, R. 1972. "Attribute Identities in Micro-reductions." *Journal of Philosophy* 69, no. 14:407-422.

——— 1977. *Unity of Science.* Dordrecht: Reidel.

Chisholm, R. M. 1957. *Perceiving.* Ithaca: Cornell University Press.

Cummins, R. 1975. "Functional Analysis." *Journal of Philosophy* 72, no. 20:741-764. Reprinted in part as chapter 12, this volume.

Dennett, D. 1975. "Why the Law of Effect Won't Go Away." *Journal for the Theory of Social Behavior* 5:169-187.

Field, H. 1978. "Mental Representation." *Erkenntniss* 13:9-61.

Fodor, J. A. 1965. "Explanations in Psychology." In M. Black, ed., *Philosophy in America.* London: Routledge & Kegan Paul.

——— 1968a. "The Appeal to Tacit Knowledge in Psychological Explanation." *Journal of Philosophy* 65:627-640.

——— 1968b. *Psychological Explanation.* New York: Random House.

Geach, P. 1957. *Mental Acts.* London: Routledge & Kegan Paul.

Gendron, B. 1971. "On the Relation of Neurological and Psychological Theories: A Critique of the Hardware Thesis." In R. C. Buck and R. S. Cohen, eds., *Boston Studies in the Philosophy of Science.* Vol. 8. Dordrecht: Reidel.

Grice, H. P. 1975. "Method in Philosophical Psychology (from the Banal to the Bizarre)." *Proceedings and Addresses of the American Philosophical Association.* Newark, Del.: American Philosophical Association.

Harman, G. 1973. *Thought.* Princeton: Princeton University Press.

Hartman, E. 1977. *Substance, Body and Soul.* Princeton: Princeton University Press.

Kalke, W. 1969. "What Is Wrong with Fodor and Putnam's Functionalism?" *Nous* 3: 83-93.

Kim, J. 1966. "On the Psycho-physical Identity Theory." *American Philosophical Quarterly* 3, no. 3:227-235.

——— 1972. "Phenomenal Properties, Psychophysical Law, and the Identity Theory." *Monist* 56, no. 2:177-192.

Lewis, D. 1966. "An Argument for the Identity Theory." Reprinted in D. Rosenthal, ed., *Materialism and the Mind-Body Problem.* Englewood Cliffs, N.J.: Prentice-Hall, 1971.

——— 1969. "Review of *Art, Mind and Religion.*" *Journal of Philosophy* 66, no. 1:23-35. Reprinted in part as chapter 18, this volume.

——— 1970. "How to Define Theoretical Terms." *Journal of Philosophy* 67, no. 13: 427-444.

——— 1972. "Psychophysical and Theoretical Identification." *Australasian Journal of Philosophy* 50, no. 3:249-258. Reprinted as chapter 15, this volume.

Lycan, W. In press. "A New Lilliputian Argument against Machine Functionalism." *Philosophical Studies.*

Martin, R. M. 1966. "On Theoretical Constants and Ramsey Constants." *Philosophy of Science* 31:1-13.

Nagel, T. 1970. "Armstrong on the Mind." *Philosophical Review* 79:394-403. Reprinted as chapter 14, this volume.

Nelson, R. J. 1975. "Behaviorism, Finite Automata and Stimulus Response Theory." *Theory and Decision* 6:249-267.

——— 1976. "Mechanism, Functionalism and the Identity Theory." *Journal of Philosophy* 73, no. 13:365-386.

Putnam, H. 1960. "Minds and Machines." In S. Hook, ed., *Dimensions of Mind.* New York: New York University Press.

——— 1963. "Brains and Behavior." Reprinted in *Mind, Language, and Reality: Philosophical Papers.* Vol. 2. London: Cambridge University Press, 1975.

——— 1966. "The Mental Life of Some Machines." Reprinted in *Mind, Language and Reality: Philosophical Papers.* Vol. 2. London: Cambridge University Press, 1975.

————— 1967. "The Nature of Mental States" (originally published as "Psychological Predicates"). In W. H. Capitan and D. D. Merrill, eds., *Art, Mind, and Religion.* Pittsburgh: University of Pittsburgh Press. Reprinted as chapter 17, this volume.

————— 1970. "On Properties." In *Mathematics, Matter and Method: Philosophical Papers.* Vol. 1. London: Cambridge University Press.

————— 1975. "Philosophy and Our Mental Life." In *Mind, Language and Reality: Philosophical Papers.* Vol. 2. London: Cambridge University Press. Reprinted as chapter 7, this volume.

Reeves, A. 1978. "Review of W. Matson, *Sentience." Australasian Journal of Philosophy* 56, no. 2 (August):189-192.

Rey, G. 1979. "Functionalism and the Emotions." In A. Rorty, ed., *Explaining Emotions.* Berkeley and Los Angeles: University of California Press.

Ryle, G. 1949. *The Concept of Mind.* London: Hutchinson.

Sellars, W. 1968. *Science and Metaphysics.* London: Routledge & Kegan Paul, chap. 6.

Shoemaker, S. 1975. "Functionalism and Qualia." *Philosophical Studies* 27:271-315. Reprinted as chapter 21, this volume.

Smart, J. J. C. 1959. "Sensations and Brain Processes." *Philosophical Review* 68:141-156.

————— 1971. "Reports of Immediate Experience." *Synthese* 22:346-359.

Thomas, S. 1978. *The Formal Mechanics of Mind.* Ithaca: Cornell University Press.

12

Functional Analysis

Robert Cummins

I will sketch briefly an account of functional explanation which takes seriously the intuition that it is a genuinely distinctive style of explanation. Previous work on the problem has relied on the assumptions (A) that the point of functional characterization in science is to explain the presence of the item that is functionally characterized and (B) that for something to perform its function is for it to have certain effects on a containing system, which effects help sustain some activity or condition of the containing system. These assumptions form the core of approaches that seek to minimize the differences between functional explanations and explanations not formulated in functional terms. Such approaches have not given much attention to the characterization of the special explanatory strategy science employs in using functional language, for the problem as it was conceived in such approaches was to show that functional explanation is not really different in essentials from other kinds of scientific

explanation. Once the problem is conceived in this way, one is almost certain to miss the distinctive features of functional explanation, and hence to miss the point of functional description. The account of this section reverses this tendency by placing primary emphasis on the kind of problem that is solved by appeal to functions.

1. Functions and Dispositions

Something may be capable of pumping even though it does not function as a pump (ever) and even though pumping is not its function. On the other hand, if something functions as a pump in a system s or if the function of something in a system s is to pump, then it must be capable of pumping in s.[1] Thus, function-ascribing statements imply disposition statements; to attribute a function to something is, in part, to attribute a disposition to it. If the function of x in s is to F, then x has a disposition to F in s. For instance, if the function of the contractile vacuole in fresh-water protozoans is to eliminate excess water from the organism, then there must be circumstances under which the contractile vacuole would actually manifest a disposition to eliminate excess water from the protozoan that incorporates it.

From *Journal of Philosophy* 72, no. 20 (November 20, 1975), section III. Reprinted, with revisions by the author, by permission of *Journal of Philosophy* and the author. Notes have been renumbered for this edition.

To attribute a disposition d to an object a is to assert that the behavior of a is subject to (exhibits or would exhibit) a certain lawlike regularity: to say a has d is to say that a would manifest d (shatter, dissolve) were any of a certain range of events to occur (a is put in water, a is struck sharply). The regularity associated with a disposition—call it the *dispositional regularity*—is a regularity that is special to the behavior of a certain kind of object and obtains in virtue of some special fact(s) about that kind of object. Not everything is water-soluble: such things behave in a special way in virtue of certain (structural) features special to water-soluble things. Thus it is that dispositions require explanation: if x has d, then x is subject to a regularity in behavior special to things having d, and such a fact needs to be explained.

To explain a dispositional regularity is to explain how manifestations of the disposition are brought about given the requisite precipitating conditions. In what follows, I will describe two distinct strategies for accomplishing this. It is my contention that the appropriateness of function-ascribing statements corresponds to the appropriateness of the second of these two strategies. This, I think, explains the intuition that functional explanation is a special *kind* of explanation.

2. Two Explanatory Strategies

(i) The Subsumption Strategy. Suppose a has a disposition d. The associated dispositional regularity consists in the fact that certain kinds of events would cause a to manifest d. One way to explain this fact would be to discover some feature of a which allowed us to represent the connection between precipitating events and manifestations as instances of one or more *general* laws, i.e., laws governing the behavior of things generally, not just things having d. Brian O'Shaughnessy has provided an example which allows a particularly simple illustration of this strategy.[2]

Consider the disposition he calls *elevancy:* the tendency of an object to rise in water of its own accord. To explain elevancy, we must explain why freeing a submerged elevant object causes it to rise.[3] This we may do as follows. In every case, the ratio of an elevant object's mass to its nonpermeable volume is less than the density (mass per unit volume) of water. Archimedes' principle tells us that water exerts an upward force on a submerged object equal to the weight of the water displaced. In the case of an elevant object, this force evidently exceeds the weight of the object by some amount f. Freeing the object changes the net force on it from zero to a net force of magnitude f in the direction of the surface, and the object rises accordingly. Here, we subsume the connection between freeings and risings under a general law connecting changes in net force with changes in motion by citing a feature of elevant objects which allows us (via Archimedes' principle) to represent freeing them under water as an instance of introducing a net force in the direction of the surface.

(ii) The Analytical Strategy. Rather than subsume a dispositional regularity under a law not special to the disposed objects, the analytical strategy proceeds by analyzing a disposition d of a into a number of other dispositions $d_1 \ldots d_n$ had by a or components of a such that programmed manifestation of the d_i results in or amounts to a manifestation of d.[4] The two strategies will fit together into a unified account if the analyzing dispositions (the d_i) can be made to yield to the subsumption strategy.

When the analytical strategy is in the offing, one is apt to speak of capacities (or abilities) rather than of dispositions. This shift in terminology will put a more familiar face on the analytical strategy,[5] for we often explain capacities by analyzing them. Assembly-line production provides a transparent example of what I mean. Production is broken down into a number of distinct tasks. Each point on the line is responsible for a certain task, and it is the function of the workers/machines at that point to complete that task. If the line has the capacity to produce the product, it has it in virtue of the fact that the workers/machines have the capacities to perform their designated tasks, and in virtue of the fact that when these tasks are performed in a certain organized way—according to a certain program—the finished product results. Here we can explain the line's capacity to produce the product—i.e., explain how it is able to produce the product—by appeal to certain capacities of the workers/machines and their organization into an assembly line. Against this background, we may pick out a certain capacity of an individual exercise of which is his function on the line. Of the many things he does and can do, his function on the line is doing whatever it is that we appeal to in explaining the capacity of the line as a whole. If the line produces several products, i.e., if it has several capacities, then, although a certain capacity c of a worker is irrelevant to one capacity of the line, exercise of c by that worker may be his function with respect to another capacity of the line as a whole.

Schematic diagrams in electronics provide another obvious illustration. Since each symbol represents any physical object whatever having a certain capacity, a schematic diagram of a complex device constitutes an analysis of the electronic capacities of the device as a whole into the capacities of its components. Such an analysis allows us to explain how the device as a whole exercises the analyzed capacity, for it allows us to see exercises of the analyzed capacity as programmed exercise of the analyzing capacities. In this case, the "program" is given by the lines indicating how the components are hooked up. (Of course, the lines are themselves function symbols.)

Functional analysis in biology is essentially similar. The biologically significant capacities of an entire organism are explained by analyzing the organism into a number of "systems"—the circulatory system, the digestive system, the nervous system, etc.—each of which has its characteristic capacities.[6] These capacities are in turn analyzed into capacities of component organs and structures. Ideally, this strategy is pressed until pure physiology takes over, i.e., until the analyzing capacities are amenable to the subsumption strategy. We can easily imagine biologists expressing their analyses in a form analogous to the schematic diagrams of electrical engineering, with special symbols for pumps, pipes, filters, and so on. Indeed, analyses of even simple cognitive capacities are typically expressed in flow charts or programs, forms designed specifically to represent analyses of information processing capacities generally.

Perhaps the most extensive use of the analytical strategy in science occurs in psychology, for a large part of the psychologist's job is to explain how the complex behavioral capacities of organisms are acquired and how they are exercised. Both goals are greatly facilitated by analysis of the capacities in question, for then acquisition of the analyzed capacity resolves itself into acquisition of the analyzing capacities and the requisite organization, and the problem of performance resolves itself into the problem of how the analyzing capacities are exercised. This sort of strategy has dominated psychology ever since Watson attempted to explain such complex capacities as the ability to run a maze by analyzing the performance into a series of conditioned responses, the stimulus for each response being the previous response or something encountered as the result of the previous response.[7] Acquisition of the complex capacity is resolved into a number of distinct cases of simple conditioning, i.e., the ability to learn the maze is resolved into the capacity for stimulus substitution, and the capacity to run the maze is resolved into abilities to respond in certain simple ways to certain simple stimuli. Watson's analysis proved to be of limited value, but the analytic strategy remains the dominant mode of explanation in behavioral psychology.[8]

3. Functions and Functional Analysis

In the context of an application of the analytical strategy, exercise of an analyzing capacity emerges as a function: it will be appropriate to say that x functions as a F in s, or that the function of x in s is F-ing, when we are speaking against the background of an analytical explanation of some capacity of s which appeals to the fact that x has a capacity to F in s. It is appropriate to say that the heart functions as a pump against the background of an analysis of the circulatory system's capacity to transport food, oxygen, wastes, and so on, which appeals to the fact that the heart is capable of pumping. Since this is the usual background, it goes without saying, and this accounts for the fact that "The heart functions as a pump" sounds right, and "The heart functions as a noise-maker" sounds wrong, in some context-free sense. This effect is strengthened by the absence of any actual application of the analytical strategy which makes use of the fact that the heart makes noise.[9]

We can capture this implicit dependence on an analytical context by entering an explicit relativization in our regimented reconstruction of function-ascribing statements:

(9) x functions as a F in s (or: the function of x in s is to F) relative to an analytical account A of s's capacity to G just in case x is capable of F-ing in s and A appropriately and adequately accounts for s's capacity to G by, in part, appealing to the capacity of x to F in s.

Sometimes we explain a capacity of s by analyzing it into other capacities of s, as when we explain how someone ignorant of cookery is able to bake cakes by pointing out that he followed a recipe each instruction of which requires no special capacities for its execution. Here, we don't speak of, e.g., stirring as a function of the cook, but rather of the function of stirring. Since stirring has different functions in different recipes and at different points in the same recipe, a statement like 'The function of stirring the mixture is to keep it from sticking to the bottom of the pot' is implicitly relativized to a certain (perhaps somewhat vague) recipe. To take account of this sort of case, we need a slightly different schema: where e is an activity or behavior of a system s (as a whole), the function of e in s is to F relative to an analytical account A of s's capacity to G just in case A appropriately and adequately accounts for s's capacity to G by, in part, appealing to s's capacity to engage in e.

4. Function-Analytical Explanation

If the account I have been sketching is to draw any distinctions, the availability and appropriateness of analytical explanations must be a nontrivial matter.[10] So let us examine an obviously trivial application of the analytical strategy with an eye to determining whether it can be dismissed on principled grounds.

(10) Each part of the mammalian circulatory system makes its own distinctive sound, and makes it continuously. These combine to form the "circulatory noise" characteristic of all mammals. The mammalian circulatory system is capable of producing this sound at various volumes and various tempos. The heartbeat is responsible for the throbbing character of the sound, and it is the capacity of the heart to beat at various rates that explains the capacity of the circulatory system to produce a variously tempoed sound.

Everything in (10) is, presumably, true. The question is whether it allows us to say that the function of the heart is to produce a variously tempoed throbbing sound.[11] To answer this question we must, I think, get clear about the motivation for applying the analytical strategy. For my contention will be that the analytical strategy is most significantly applied in cases very unlike that envisaged in (10).

The explanatory interest of an analytical account is roughly proportional to (i) the extent to which the analyzing capacities are less sophisticated than the analyzed capacities, (ii) the extent to which the analyzing capacities are different in type from the analyzed capacities, and (iii) the relative sophistication of the program appealed to, i.e., the relative complexity of the organization of component parts/processes that is attributed to the system. (iii) is correlative with (i) and (ii): the greater the gap in sophistication and type between analyzing capacities and analyzed capacities, the more sophisticated the program must be to close the gap.

It is precisely the width of these gaps which, for instance, makes automata theory so interesting in its application to psychology. Automata theory supplies us with extremely powerful techniques for constructing diverse analyses of very sophisticated tasks into very unsophisticated tasks. This allows us to see how, in principle, a mechanism such as the brain, consisting of physiologically unsophisticated components (relatively speaking), can acquire very sophisticated capacities. It is the prospect of promoting the capacity to store ones and zeros into the capacity to solve logic problems and recognize patterns that makes the analytical strategy so appealing in cognitive psychology.

As the program absorbs more and more of the explanatory burden, the physical facts underlying the analyzing capacities become less and less special to the analyzed system. This is why it is plausible to suppose that the capacity of a person and of a machine to solve a certain problem might have substantially the same explanation, although it is not plausible to suppose that the capacities of a synthesizer and of a bell to make similar sounds have substantially similar explanations. There is no work to be done by a sophisticated hypothesis about the organization of various capacities in the case of the bell. Conversely, the less weight borne by the program, the less point to analysis. At this end of the scale we have cases like (10) in which the analyzed and analyzing capacities differ little if at all in type and sophistication. Here we could apply the subsumption strategy without significant loss, and thus talk of functions is comparatively strained and pointless. It must be admitted, however, that there is no black-white distinction here, but a case of more-or-less. As the role of organization becomes less and less significant, the analytical strategy becomes less and less appropriate, and talk of functions makes less and less sense. This may be philosophically disappointing, but there is no help for it.

Notes

1. Throughout this section I am discounting appeals to the intentions of designers or users. x may be intended to prevent accidents without actually being capable of doing so. With reference to this intention it *would* be proper in certain contexts to say, "x's function is to prevent accidents, though it is not actually capable of doing so."

There can be no doubt that a thing's function is often identified with what it is typically or "standardly" used to do, or with what it was designed to do. But the sorts of things for which it is an important scientific problem to provide functional analyses—brains, organisms, societies, social institutions—either do not have designers or standard or regular uses at all, or it would be inappropriate to appeal to these in constructing and defining a scientific theory because the designer or use is not known—brains, devices dug up by archaeologists—or because there is some likelihood that real and intended function diverge—social institutions, complex computers. Functional talk may have originated in contexts in which reference to intentions and purposes loomed large, but reference to intentions and purposes does not figure at all in the sort of functional analysis favored by contemporary natural scientists.

2. "The Powerlessness of Dispositions," *Analysis*, 31.1, 139 (October 1970):1-15. See also my discussion of this example in "Dispositions, States and Causes," *ibid.*, 34.6, 162 (June 1974):194-204.

3. Also, we must explain why submerging a free elevant object causes it to rise, and why a free submerged object's becoming elevant causes it to rise. One of the convenient features of elevancy is that the same considerations dispose of all these cases. This does not hold generally: gentle rubbing, a sharp blow, or a sudden change in temperature may each cause a glass to manifest a disposition to shatter, but the explanations in these cases are significantly different.

4. By "programmed" I simply mean organized in a way that could be specified in a program or flow chart: each instruction (box) specifies manifestation of one of the d_i such that, if the program is executed (the chart followed), a manifests d.

5. Some might want to distinguish between dispositions and capacities, and argue that to ascribe a function to x is in part to ascribe a *capacity* to x, not a disposition as I have claimed. Certainly (1) is strained in a way (2) is not.

(1) Hearts are disposed to pump.
    Hearts have a disposition to pump.
    Sugar is capable of dissolving.
    Sugar has a capacity to dissolve.
(2) Hearts are capable of pumping.
    Hearts have a capacity to pump.
    Sugar is disposed to dissolve.
    Sugar has a disposition to dissolve.

6. Indeed, what makes something part of, e.g., the nervous system is that its capacities figure in an analysis of the capacity to respond to external stimuli, coordinate movement, etc. Thus, there is no question that the glial cells are part of the brain, but there is some question as to whether they are part of the nervous system or merely auxiliary to it.

7. John B. Watson, *Behaviorism* (New York: Norton, 1930) chs. 9 and 11.

8. Writers on the philosophy of psychology, especially Jerry Fodor, have grasped the connection between functional characterization and the analytical strategy in psychological theorizing, but have not applied the lesson to the problem of functional explanation generally. The clearest statement occurs in J. A. Fodor, "The Appeal to Tacit Knowledge in Psychological Explanation," *Journal of Philosophy*, 65, 24 (December 19, 1968): 627-640.

9. It is sometimes suggested that heart-sounds do have a psychological function. In the context of an analysis of a psychological disposition appealing to the heart's noise-making capacity, "The heart functions as a noise-maker" (e.g., as a producer of regular thumps), would not even *sound* odd.

10. Of course, it might be that there are none but arbitrary distinctions to be drawn. Perhaps (9) describes usage, and usage is arbitrary, but I am unable to take this possibility seriously.

11. The issue is not whether (10) forces us, via (9), to say something false. Relative to *some* analytical explanation, it may be true that the function of the heart is to produce a variously tempoed throbbing. But the availability of (10) should not support such a claim.

The Nature of Mind

D. M. Armstrong

Men have minds, that is to say, they perceive, they have sensations, emotions, beliefs, thoughts, purposes, and desires.[1] What is it to have a mind? What is it to perceive, to feel emotion, to hold a belief, or to have a purpose? In common with many other modern philosophers, I think that the best clue we have to the nature of mind is furnished by the discoveries and hypotheses of modern science concerning the nature of man.

What does modern science have to say about the nature of man? There are, of course, all sorts of disagreements and divergencies in the views of individual scientists. But I think it is true to say that one view is steadily gaining ground, so that it bids fair to become established scientific doctrine. This is the view that we can give a complete account of man *in purely physico-chemical terms.* This view has received a tremendous impetus in the last decade from the new subject of molecular biology, a subject which promises to unravel the physical and chemical mechanisms which lie at the basis of life. Before

From *The Nature of Mind* by David Armstrong (Brisbane: University of Queensland Press, 1980). Originally published in C. V. Borst, ed., *The Mind/Brain Identity Theory* (London: Macmillan, 1970), pp. 67-79. Reprinted by permission.

that time, it received great encouragement from pioneering work in neurophysiology pointing to the likelihood of a purely electro-chemical account of the working of the brain. I think it is fair to say that those scientists who still reject the physico-chemical account of man do so primarily for philosophical, or moral, or religious reasons, and only secondarily, and half-heartedly, for reasons of scientific detail. This is not to say that in the future new evidence and new problems may not come to light which will force science to reconsider the physico-chemical view of man. But at present the drift of scientific thought is clearly set towards the physico-chemical hypothesis. And we have nothing better to go on than the present.

For me, then, and for many philosophers who think like me, the moral is clear. We must try to work out an account of the nature of mind which is compatible with the view that man is nothing but a physico-chemical mechanism.

And in this paper I shall be concerned to do just this: to sketch (in barest outline) what may be called a Materialist or Physicalist account of the mind.

But before doing this I should like to go back and consider a criticism of my position which must inevitably occur to some. What reason have I, it may be asked, for taking my stand on science? Even granting that I am right about what is the currently dominant scientific view of man, why should we concede science a special authority to decide questions about the nature of man? What of the authority of philosophy, of religion, of morality, or even of literature and art? Why do I set the authority of science above all these? Why this 'scientism'?

It seems to me that the answer to this question is very simple. If we consider the search for truth, in all its fields, we find that it is only in science that men versed in their subject can, after investigation that is more or less prolonged, and which may in some cases extend beyond a single human lifetime, reach substantial agreement about what is the case. It is only as a result of scientific investigation that we ever seem to reach an intellectual consensus about controversial matters.

In the Epistle Dedicatory to his *De Corpore* Hobbes wrote of William Harvey, the discoverer of the circulation of the blood, that he was 'the only man I know, that conquering envy, hath established a new doctrine in his life-time'.

Before Copernicus, Galileo and Harvey, Hobbes remarks, 'there was nothing certain in natural philosophy.' And, we might add, with the exception of mathematics, there was nothing certain in any other learned discipline.

These remarks of Hobbes are incredibly revealing. They show us what a watershed in the intellectual history of the human race the seventeenth century was. Before that time inquiry proceeded, as it were, in the dark. Men could not hope to see their doctrine *established*, that is to say, accepted by the vast majority of those properly versed in the subject under discussion. There was no intellectual consensus. Since that time, it has become a commonplace to see new doctrines, sometimes of the most far-reaching kind, established to the satisfaction of the learned,

often within the lifetime of their first proponents. Science has provided us with a method of deciding disputed questions. This is not to say, of course, that the consensus of those who are learned and competent in a subject cannot be mistaken. Of course such a consensus can be mistaken. Sometimes it has been mistaken. But, granting fallibility, what better authority have we than such a consensus?

Now this is of the utmost importance. For in philosophy, in religion, in such disciplines as literary criticism, in moral questions in so far as they are thought to be matters of truth and falsity, there has been a notable failure to achieve an intellectual consensus about disputed questions among the learned. Must we not then attach a peculiar authority to the discipline that can achieve a consensus? And if it presents us with a certain vision of the nature of man, is this not a powerful reason for accepting that vision?

I will not take up here the deeper question *why* it is that the methods of science have enabled us to achieve an intellectual consensus about so many disputed matters. That question, I think, could receive no brief or uncontroversial answer. I am resting my argument on the simple and uncontroversial fact that, as a result of scientific investigation, such a consensus has been achieved.

It may be replied—it often is replied —that while science is all very well in its own sphere—the sphere of the physical, perhaps—there are matters of fact on which it is not competent to pronounce. And among such matters, it may be claimed, is the question what is the whole nature of man. But I cannot see that this reply has much force. Science has provided us with an island of truths, or, perhaps one should say, a raft of truths, to bear us up on the sea of our disputatious ignorance. There may have to be revisions and refinements, new results may set old findings in a new perspective, but what science has given us will not be altogether superseded. Must we not therefore appeal to these relative certainties for guidance when we come to consider uncertainties elsewhere? Perhaps science cannot help us to decide whether or not there is a God, whether or not human beings have immortal souls, or whether or not the will is free. But if science cannot assist us, what can? I conclude that it is the scientific vision of man, and not the philosophical or religious or artistic or moral vision of man, that is the best clue we have to the nature of man. And it is rational to argue from the best evidence we have.

Having in this way attempted to justify my procedure, I turn back to my subject: the attempt to work out an account of mind, or, if you prefer, of mental process, within the framework of the physico-chemical, or, as we may call it, the Materialist view of man.

Now there is one account of mental process that is at once attractive to any philosopher sympathetic to a Materialist view of man: this is Behaviourism. Formulated originally by a psychologist, J. B. Watson, it attracted widespread interest and considerable support from scientifically oriented philosophers. Traditional philosophy had tended to think of the mind as a rather mysterious inward arena that lay behind, and was responsible for, the outward or physical behaviour of our bodies. Descartes thought of this inner arena as a *spiritual substance,* and it was this conception of the mind as spiritual object that Gilbert Ryle attacked, apparently in the interest of Behaviourism, in his important book *The Concept of Mind.* He ridiculed the Cartesian view as the dogma of 'the ghost in the machine'. The mind was not something behind the behaviour of the body, it was simply part of that physical behaviour. My anger with you is not some modification of a spiritual substance which somehow brings about aggressive behaviour; rather it is the aggressive behaviour itself; my addressing

strong words to you, striking you, turning my back on you, and so on. Thought is not an inner process that lies behind, and brings about, the words I speak and write: it is my speaking and writing. The mind is not an inner arena, it is outward act.

It is clear that such a view of mind fits in very well with a completely Materialistic or Physicalist view of man. If there is no need to draw a distinction between mental processes and their expression in physical behaviour, but if instead the mental processes are identified with their so-called 'expressions', then the existence of mind stands in no conflict with the view that man is nothing but a physico-chemical mechanism.

However, the version of Behaviourism that I have just sketched is a very crude version, and its crudity lays it open to obvious objections. One obvious difficulty is that it is our common experience that there can be mental processes going on although there is no behaviour occurring that could possibly be treated as expressions of these processes. A man may be angry, but give no bodily sign; he may think, but say or do nothing at all.

In my view, the most plausible attempt to refine Behaviourism with a view to meeting this objection was made by introducing the notion of *a disposition to behave.* (Dispositions to behave play a particularly important part in Ryle's account of the mind.) Let us consider the general notion of disposition first. Brittleness is a disposition, a disposition possessed by materials like glass. Brittle materials are those which, when subjected to relatively small forces, break or shatter easily. But breaking and shattering easily is not brittleness, rather it is the *manifestation* of brittleness. Brittleness itself is the tendency or liability of the material to break or shatter easily. A piece of glass may never shatter or break throughout its whole history, but it is still the case that it is brittle: it is liable to shatter or break if dropped quite a small way or hit quite lightly. Now a disposition to *behave* is simply a tendency or liability of a person to behave in a certain way under certain circumstances. The brittleness of glass is a disposition that the glass retains throughout its history, but clearly there could also be dispositions that come and go. The dispositions to behave that are of interest to the Behaviourist are, for the most part, of this temporary character.

Now how did Ryle and others use the notion of a disposition to behave to meet the obvious objection to Behaviourism that there can be mental processes going on although the subject is engaging in no relevant behaviour? Their strategy was to argue that in such cases, although the subject was not behaving in any relevant way, he or she was *disposed* to behave in some relevant way. The glass does not shatter, but it is still brittle. The man does not behave, but he does have a disposition to behave. We can say he thinks although he does not speak or act because at that time he was disposed to speak or act in a certain way. *If* he had been asked, perhaps, he would have spoken or acted. We can say he is angry although he does not behave angrily, because he is disposed so to behave. *If* only one more word had been addressed to him, he would have burst out. And so on. In this way it was hoped that Behaviourism could be squared with the obvious facts.

It is very important to see just how these thinkers conceived of dispositions. I quote from Ryle

> To possess a dispositional property *is not to be in a particular state, or to undergo a particular change;* it is to be bound or liable to be in a particular state, or to undergo a particular change, when a particular condition is realised. (*The Concept of Mind*, p. 43, my italics.)

So to explain the breaking of a lightly struck glass on a particular occasion by saying it was brittle is, on this view of dis-

positions, simply to say that the glass broke because it is the sort of thing that regularly breaks when quite lightly struck. The breaking was the normal behaviour, or not abnormal behaviour, of such a thing. The brittleness is not to be conceived of as a *cause* for the breakage, or even, more vaguely, a *factor* in bringing about the breaking. Brittleness is just the fact that things of that sort break easily.

But although in this way the Behaviourists did something to deal with the objection that mental processes can occur in the absence of behaviour, it seems clear, now that the shouting and the dust have died, that they did not do enough. When I think, but my thoughts do not issue in any action, it seems as obvious as anything is obvious that there is something actually going on in me which constitutes my thought. It is not simply that I would speak or act if some conditions that are unfulfilled were to be fulfilled. Something is currently going on, in the strongest and most literal sense of 'going on', and this something is my thought. Rylean Behaviourism denies this, and so it is unsatisfactory as a theory of mind. Yet I know of no version of Behaviourism that is more satisfactory. The moral for those of us who wish to take a purely physicalistic view of man is that we must look for some other account of the nature of mind and of mental processes.

But perhaps we need not grieve too deeply about the failure of Behaviourism to produce a satisfactory theory of mind. Behaviourism is a profoundly unnatural account of mental processes. If somebody speaks and acts in certain ways it is natural to speak of this speech and action as the *expression* of his thought. It is not at all natural to speak of his speech and action as identical with his thought. We naturally think of the thought as something quite distinct from the speech and action which, under suitable circumstances, brings the speech and action about. Thoughts are not to be identified with behaviour, we think, they lie behind behaviour. A man's behaviour constitutes the *reason* we have for attributing certain mental processes to him, but the behaviour cannot be identified with the mental processes.

This suggests a very interesting line of thought about the mind. Behaviourism is certainly wrong, but perhaps it is not altogether wrong. Perhaps the Behaviourists are wrong in identifying the mind and mental occurrences with behaviour, but perhaps they are right in thinking that our notion of a mind and of individual mental states is *logically tied to behaviour*. For perhaps what we mean by a mental state is some state of the person which, under suitable circumstances, *brings about* a certain range of behaviour. Perhaps mind can be defined not as behaviour, but rather as the inner *cause* of certain behaviour. Thought is not speech under suitable circumstances, rather it is something within the person which, in suitable circumstances, brings about speech. And, in fact, I believe that this is the true account, or, at any rate, a true first account, of what we mean by a mental state.

How does this line of thought link up with a purely physicalist view of man? The position is, I think, that while it does not make such a physicalist view inevitable, it does make it *possible*. It does not entail, but it is compatible with, a purely physicalist view of man. For if our notion of the mind and mental states is nothing but that of a cause within the person of certain ranges of behaviour, then it becomes a scientific question, and not a question of logical analysis, what in fact the intrinsic nature of that cause is. The cause might be, as Descartes thought it was, a spiritual substance working through the pineal gland to produce the complex bodily behaviour of which men are capable. It might be breath, or specially smooth and mobile atoms dispersed throughout the body; it might be many other things. But in fact the verdict of

modern science seems to be that the sole cause of mind-betokening behaviour in man and the higher animals is the physico-chemical workings of the central nervous system. And so, assuming we have correctly characterised our concept of a mental state as nothing but the cause of certain sorts of behaviour, then we can identify these mental states with purely physical states of the central nervous system.

At this point we may stop and go back to the Behaviourists' dispositions. We saw that, according to them, the brittleness of glass or, to take another example, the elasticity of rubber, is not a state of the glass or the rubber, but is simply the fact that things of that sort behave in the way they do. But now let us consider how a scientist would think about brittleness or elasticity. Faced with the phenomenon of breakage under relatively small impacts, or the phenomenon of stretching when a force is applied followed by contraction when the force is removed, he will assume that there is some current *state* of the glass or the rubber which is responsible for the characteristic behaviour of samples of these two materials. At the beginning he will not know what this state is, but he will endeavour to find out, and he may succeed in finding out. And when he has found out he will very likely make remarks of this sort: 'We have discovered that the brittleness of glass is in fact a certain sort of pattern in the molecules of the glass.' That is to say, he will *identify* brittleness with the state of the glass that is responsible for the liability of the glass to break. For him, a disposition of an object is a state of the object. What makes the state a state of brittleness is the fact that it gives rise to the characteristic manifestations of brittleness. But the disposition itself is distinct from its manifestations: it is the state of the glass that gives rise to these manifestations in suitable circumstances.

You will see that this way of looking at dispositions is very different from that of Ryle and the Behaviourists. The great difference is this: If we treat dispositions as actual states, as I have suggested that scientists do, even if states whose intrinsic nature may yet have to be discovered, then we can say that dispositions are actual *causes*, or causal factors, which, in suitable circumstances, actually bring about those happenings which are the manifestations of the disposition. A certain molecular constitution of glass which constitutes its brittleness is actually *responsible* for the fact that, when the glass is struck, it breaks.

Now I shall not argue the matter here, because the detail of the argument is technical and difficult,[2] but I believe that the view of dispositions as states, which is the view that is natural to science, is the correct one. I believe it can be shown quite strictly that, to the extent that we admit the notion of dispositions at all, we are committed to the view that they are actual *states* of the object that has the disposition. I may add that I think that the same holds for the closely connected notions of capacities and powers. Here I will simply assume this step in my argument.

But perhaps it can be seen that the rejection of the idea that mind is simply a certain range of man's behaviour in favour of the view that mind is rather the inner *cause* of that range of man's behaviour is bound up with the rejection of the Rylean view of dispositions in favour of one that treats disposition as states of objects and so as having actual causal power. The Behaviourists were wrong to identify the mind with behaviour. They were not so far off the mark when they tried to deal with cases where mental happenings occur in the absence of behaviour by saying that these are dispositions to behave. But in order to reach a correct view, I am suggesting, they would have to conceive of these dispositions as actual *states* of the person who has the disposition, states that have actual power to bring about behaviour in suitable circumstances. But to do

this is to abandon the central inspiration of Behaviourism: that in talking about the mind we do not have to go behind outward behaviour to inner states.

And so two separate but interlocking lines of thought have pushed me in the same direction. The first line of thought is that it goes profoundly against the grain to think of the mind as behaviour. The mind is, rather, that which stands behind and brings about our complex behaviour. The second line of thought is that the Behaviourists' dispositions, properly conceived, are really states that underlie behaviour, and, under suitable circumstances, bring about behaviour. Putting these two together, we reach the conception of a mental state as *a state of the person apt for producing certain ranges of behaviour*. This formula: a mental state is a state of the person apt for producing certain ranges of behaviour, I believe to be a very illuminating way of looking at the concept of a mental state. I have found it very fruitful in the search for detailed logical analyses of the individual mental concepts.

Now, I do not think that Hegel's dialectic has much to tell us about the nature of reality. But I think that human thought often moves in a dialectical way, from thesis to antithesis and then to the synthesis. Perhaps thought about the mind is a case in point. I have already said that classical philosophy tended to think of the mind as an inner arena of some sort. This we may call the Thesis. Behaviourism moved to the opposite extreme: the mind was seen as outward behaviour. This is the Antithesis. My proposed Synthesis is that the mind is properly conceived as an inner principle, but a principle that is identified in terms of the outward behaviour it is apt for bringing about. This way of looking at the mind and mental states does not itself entail a Materialist or Physicalist view of man, for nothing is said in this analysis about the intrinsic nature of these mental states. But if we have, as I have asserted that we do have, general scientific grounds for thinking that man is nothing but a physical mechanism, we can go on to argue that the mental states are in fact nothing but physical states of the central nervous system.

Along these lines, then, I would look for an account of the mind that is compatible with a purely Materialist theory of man. I have tried to carry out this programme in detail in *A Materialist Theory of the Mind*. There are, as may be imagined, all sorts of powerful objections that can be made to this view. But in the rest of this paper I propose to do only one thing. I will develop one very important objection to my view of the mind—an objection felt by many philosophers—and then try to show how the objection should be met.

The view that our notion of mind is nothing but that of an inner principle apt for bringing about certain sorts of behaviour may be thought to share a certain weakness with Behaviourism. Modern philosophers have put the point about Behaviourism by saying that although Behaviourism may be a satisfactory account of the mind from an *other-person point of view*, it will not do as a *first-person* account. To explain. In our encounters with other people, all we ever observe is their behaviour: their actions, their speech, and so on. And so, if we simply consider other people, Behaviourism might seem to do full justice to the facts. But the trouble about Behaviourism is that it seems so unsatisfactory as applied to our *own* case. In our own case, we seem to be aware of so much more than mere behaviour.

Suppose that now we conceive of the mind as an inner principle apt for bringing about certain sorts of behaviour. This again fits the other-person cases very well. Bodily behaviour of a very sophisticated sort is observed, quite different from the behaviour that ordinary physical objects display. It is inferred that this behaviour must spring from a very special sort of inner cause in the object that exhibits this behaviour. This inner cause is christened 'the mind', and those who take a physicalist view of man argue that it is simply the central nervous system of the body observed. Compare this with the case of glass. Certain characteristic behaviour is observed: the breaking and shattering of the material when acted upon by relatively small forces. A special inner state of the glass is postulated to explain this behaviour. Those who take a purely physicalist view of glass then argue that this state is a *natural* state of the glass. It is, perhaps, an arrangement of its molecules, and not, say, the peculiarly malevolent disposition of the demons that dwell in glass.

But when we turn to our own case, the position may seem less plausible. We are conscious, we have experiences. Now can we say that to be conscious, to have experiences, is simply for something to go on within us apt for the causing of certain sorts of behaviour? Such an account does not seem to do any justice to the phenomena. And so it seems that our account of the mind, like Behaviourism, will fail to do justice to the first-person case.

In order to understand the objection better it may be helpful to consider a particular case. If you have driven for a very long distance without a break, you may have had experience of a curious state of automatism, which can occur in these conditions. One can suddenly 'come to' and realise that one has driven for long distances without being aware of what one was doing, or, indeed, without being aware of anything. One has kept the car on the road, used the brake and the clutch perhaps, yet all without any awareness of what one was doing.

Now, if we consider this case it is obvious that *in some sense* mental processes are still going on when one is in such an automatic state. Unless one's will was still operating in some way, and unless one was still perceiving in some way, the car would not still be on the road. Yet, of course, *something* mental is lacking. Now, I think, when it is alleged that an account of mind as an inner principle apt for the production of certain sorts of behaviour leaves out consciousness or experience, what is alleged to have been left out is just whatever is missing in the automatic driving case. It is conceded that an account of mental processes as states of the person apt for the production of certain sorts of behaviour may very possibly be adequate to deal with such cases as that of automatic driving. It may be adequate to deal with most of the mental processes of animals, who perhaps spend a good deal of their lives in this state of automatism. But, it is contended, it cannot deal with the consciousness that we normally enjoy.

I will now try to sketch an answer to this important and powerful objection. Let us begin in an apparently unlikely place, and consider the way that an account of mental processes of the sort I am giving would deal with *sense-perception.*

Now psychologists, in particular, have long realised that there is a very close logical tie between sense-perception and *selective behaviour.* Suppose we want to decide whether an animal can perceive the difference between red and green. We might give the animal a choice between two pathways, over one of which a red light shines and over the other of which a green light shines. If the animal happens by chance to choose the green pathway we reward it; if it happens to choose the other pathway we do not reward it. If, after some trials, the animal systematically takes the green-lighted pathway, and if we become assured that the only relevant differences in the two pathways are the differences in the colour of the lights, we are entitled to say that the animal can see this colour difference. Using its eyes, it selects between red-lighted and green-lighted pathways. So we say it can

see the difference between red and green.

Now a Behaviourist would be tempted to say that the animal's regularly selecting the green-lighted pathway *was* its perception of the colour difference. But this is unsatisfactory, because we all want to say that perception is something that goes on within the person or animal—within its mind—although, of course, this mental event is normally *caused* by the operation of the environment upon the organism. Suppose, however, that we speak instead of *capacities* for selective behaviour towards the current environment, and suppose we think of these capacities, like dispositions, as actual inner states of the organism. We can then think of the animal's perception as a state within the animal apt, if the animal is so impelled, for selective behaviour between the red- and green-lighted pathways.

In general, we can think of perceptions as inner states or events apt for the production of certain sorts of selective behaviour towards our environment. To perceive is like acquiring a key to a door. You do not have to use the key: you can put it in your pocket and never bother about the door. But if you do want to open the door the key may be essential. The blind man is a man who does not acquire certain keys, and, as a result, is not able to operate in his environment in the way that somebody who has his sight can operate. It seems, then, a very promising view to take of perceptions that they are inner states defined by the sorts of selective behaviour that they enable the perceiver to exhibit, if so impelled.

Now how is this discussion of perception related to the question of consciousness or experience, the sort of thing that the driver who is in a state of automatism has not got, but which we normally do have? Simply this. My proposal is that consciousness, in this sense of the word, is nothing but *perception or awareness of the state of our own mind.* The driver in a state of automatism perceives, or is aware of, the road. If he did not, the car would be in a ditch. But he is not currently aware of his awareness of the road. He perceives the road, but he does not perceive his perceiving, or anything else that is going on in his mind. He is not, as we normally are, conscious of what is going on in his mind.

And so I conceive of consciousness or experience, in this sense of the words, in the way that Locke and Kant conceived it, as like perception. Kant, in a striking phrase, spoke of 'inner sense'. We cannot directly observe the minds of others, but each of us has the power to observe directly our own minds, and 'perceive' what is going on there. The driver in the automatic state is one whose 'inner eye' is shut: who is not currently aware of what is going on in his own mind.

Now if this account is along the right lines, why should we not give an account of this inner observation along the same lines as we have already given of perception? Why should we not conceive of it as an inner state, a state in this case directed towards other inner states and not to the environment, which enables us, if we are so impelled, to behave in a selective way *towards our own states of mind?* One who is aware, or conscious, of his thoughts or his emotions is one who has the capacity to make discriminations between his different mental states. His capacity might be exhibited in words. He might say that he was in an angry state of mind when, and only when, he *was* in an angry state of mind. But such verbal behaviour would be the mere *expression* or *result* of the awareness. The awareness itself would be an inner state: the sort of inner state that gave the man a capacity for such behavioural expressions.

So I have argued that consciousness of our own mental state may be assimilated to *perception* of our own mental state, and that, like other perceptions, it may then be conceived of as an inner state or event giving a capacity for selective behaviour, in this case selective behaviour

towards our own mental state. All this is meant to be simply a logical analysis of consciousness, and none of it entails, although it does not rule out, a purely physicalist account of what these inner states are. But if we are convinced, on general scientific grounds, that a purely physical account of man is likely to be the true one, then there seems to be no bar to our identifying these inner states with purely physical states of the central nervous system. And so consciousness of our own mental state becomes simply the scanning of one part of our central nervous system by another. Consciousness is a self-scanning mechanism in the central nervous system.

As I have emphasised before, I have done no more than sketch a programme for a philosophy of mind. There are all sorts of expansions and elucidations to be made, and all sorts of doubts and difficulties to be stated and overcome. But I hope I have done enough to show that a purely physicalist theory of the mind is an exciting and plausible intellectual option.

Notes

1. Inaugural lecture of the Challis Professor of Philosophy at the University of Sydney (1965); slightly amended (1968).

2. It is presented in my book *A Materialist Theory of the Mind* (1968) ch. 6, sec. VI.

14

Armstrong on the Mind

Thomas Nagel

I

Much of the recent materialist literature has defended a materialism of common sense: the view that identification of the mental and the physical requires no adjustment or alteration of our plain psychological concepts. It is held that materialism is not paradoxical and does not require us to abandon the ordinary conception of man. Armstrong's weighty, lucid, and readable book carries the defense of this position considerably farther than it has been taken before.[1] It does this partly by improving and clarifying arguments which have already appeared elsewhere; partly by a number of original moves, some of them extremely penetrating; and partly by sheer bulk. I believe that the resulting philosophy of mind has certain defects inherent in the attempt to portray materialism as an undisturbing doctrine. But let me outline the position before embarking on criticism.

Armstrong's task is set for him in the following way:

From *Philosophical Review* 79 (1970):394-403. Reprinted by permission of *Philosophical Review* and the author.

The object that we call a "brain" is called a brain in virtue of certain physical characteristics: it is a certain sort of physical object found inside people's skulls. Yet if we say that this object is also the mind, then, since the word "mind" does not mean the same as the word "brain," it seems that the brain can only be the mind in virtue of some *further* characteristic that the brain has [p. 78].

He concludes that this further characteristic, or set of characteristics, must also be physical, if materialism is true. The solution is to provide a causal analysis of the mental concepts, according to which they pick out "states of the person apt for bringing about a certain sort of behavior." (To avoid circularity this must be purely "physical behavior" rather than "behavior proper.") Secondarily, some mental states are also states of the person apt for being brought about by a certain sort of stimulus. The word "apt" is meant to cover a multitude of relations.

An essential feature of this analysis is that it tells us nothing about the intrinsic nature of mental states. They fall under the concept of mind because of their role as intermediaries in the causal chain between stimulus and response, but beyond that the mental concepts tell us nothing about them: those concepts are topic-neutral. Therefore if the causal analysis can be carried forward purely in terms of physical stimuli and physical behavior, the way will be clear for an identification of the states, processes, and events so specified with states, processes, and events in the central nervous system. And no additional, nonphysical attributes will have been presupposed by the application of mental concepts. The resulting identification will be similar in many ways to the identification of the gene with the DNA molecule.

The truth of materialism can be established only by neurophysiology, to which Armstrong defers frequently in the course of the book. But the possibility of materialism requires that a reductionist analysis of mental concepts be correct. A complete reduction to physical terms, such as behaviorism, is unacceptable because it does not preserve the logical possibility of disembodied minds, something which Armstrong feels must be allowed by a correct theory. His causal analysis admits this possibility while preserving the connection between mind and behavior, for the analysis does not entail that the causes of behavior are physical: hence it leaves open the possibility that they should be phenomena of a sort which could exist apart from the body. To be precise (though Armstrong does not put it quite this way), the topic-neutral analysis leaves it logically possible that what falls under a mental concept should be something whose disembodied existence is possible. But of course it is also logically possible that mental states should turn out, as Armstrong maintains, to be phenomena whose disembodied existence is not possible.

The first third of the book raises difficulties for various alternative theories of mind and outlines the case for central-state materialism. It includes a lengthy attack on incorrigibility, which Armstrong believes would be fatal to his position. Al-

most all of the remainder is taken up by Part Two, *The Concept of Mind*, which is described as the intellectual center of the book. There Armstrong provides causal analyses of an enormous number of mental concepts. Many of them are causal reworkings of behaviorist or dispositional analyses. Indeed, he says:

> We can be very sanguine in advance about the success of our programme, because we shall inherit all the astonishing progress made by Analytical Behaviourism in unfolding the nature of mental concepts, without having to accept the doctrine that proved the downfall of Behaviourism: the denial of inner mental states [p. 118].

Much of the resulting theory is impressive, although I am inclined to think that the attempt at comprehensiveness is a mistake. (In the section on emotions, for example, embarrassment gets six lines, disgust five, and despair three.)

One notion to which Armstrong devotes a good deal of attention is that of purpose. It is fundamental not only to his account of the will, but also to his account of perception. The model for purposive behavior is the feedback control of a homing rocket, with the important qualification that the feedback cause must be information supplied by perception or some other form of awareness. Perception in turn is analyzed in terms of the capacity for discriminatory behavior. Armstrong maintains that perceptions are not the *basis* of perceptual judgments, but are simply the acquirings of those judgments themselves. Their causal analysis depends on their providing a necessary precondition for appropriate discriminatory behavior, should the organism want to do something which requires this. But then the threat of circularity arises, for on the one hand, the discriminatory behavior referred to in the analysis of perception must be purposive, and on the other hand, purposive behavior is distinguished from a merely mechanical adjustment (like alteration of body temperature) by the former's dependence on perception as a feedback cause. Armstrong's suggestion for dealing with this problem is that the two concepts of perception and purpose cannot be independently applied—that both become applicable only when the feedback mechanism is enormously complex, and that the quantity, subtlety, and temporal scope of the information responded to in genuine purposive behavior, as well as the complexity of the resulting behavioral modifications, provide a sufficient distinction between this and the simpler feedback mechanisms that we do not characterize in the same terms.

Chapter 11, in which he develops this view, is described by Armstrong as the central chapter of the whole book. But I believe that its most important and original philosophical contribution appears in the succeeding chapter, on secondary qualities. He describes his position as a realistic reductionism, and it is much more persuasive than the behavioristic reductionism developed by J. J. C. Smart to accommodate these same recalcitrant concepts to a materialist view. Armstrong simply employs the same device in the analysis of secondary qualities that he has already employed in the analysis of mental states: he analyzes them as states possessing certain external, causal properties, but whose intrinsic nature is left unspecified by this identification. Redness, for example, is a property common to various familiar objects and substances, which normal observers can detect by means of their eyes. In addition, it is one of the determinates falling under a single determinable, in a familiar order with other colors. But this analysis of the concept carries no implications about what that property or that determinable is—just as the causal analysis of a mental state implies nothing about the intrinsic nature of that state. And just as the mental state can therefore be contingently identical with a physical state of the central nervous sys-

tem, so the color or other secondary quality can be contingently identified with a physical property of objects or their surfaces, if we discover what is responsible for our ability to make the relevant discriminations and classifications just by looking.[2] Armstrong later applies the same method of analysis to bodily sensations. Pain, for example, is described as the perception of a bodily disturbance of a type which characteristically evokes a desire that the perception should cease: but nothing more about the intrinsic nature of the disturbance is implied by this, so it can be "contingently" identified with the stimulation of pain-receptors.

In view of his analysis of secondary qualities, I do not understand Armstrong's remarks about the possibility of inverted spectra, a possibility which he wants to defend. He says that half of the population might have one inner state when they looked at red objects and another when they looked at green objects, while the other half had the reverse. And he claims (p. 258) that even if their behavior did not differ, at least one of the groups would have false beliefs about the world. But what false beliefs could they be? On Armstrong's analysis, the content of ordinary perceptual judgments would remain unaffected if both groups were affected in their different ways by a common property of red objects. The judgment "This is red" would have the same analysis for both. If that is true, how can one group be right and the other wrong? Moreover, if Armstrong is correct in maintaining that perceptions are merely the acquiring of perceptual judgments, the two groups will not have different perceptions, although the same perception will be a different physical state in each group.

It is not possible to discuss here most of the analyses which Armstrong offers. Mental states are accounted for in terms of many different relations to behavior, including direct cause, necessary condition, and mere resemblance to other mental states that stand in causal relations to behavior. He analyzes introspection as the inner perception of one's mental states. Like outer perception, its behavioral manifestations involve the capacity to discriminate, control, and take into account the circumstances of which it is a perception, these being themselves states of the person apt for the production of certain behavior.

The book contains a discussion of knowledge based on (a) a causal theory of inferring and (b) a definition of noninferential knowledge which employs the notion of a belief being *empirically sufficient* for its own truth. Except for adding the qualification *"in this particular situation,"* Armstrong leaves the notion of empirical sufficiency unexplained, and I find it opaque. Does it imply anything, for example, about the causal relation (in either direction) between the belief and the circumstance which makes it true? And how is "this particular situation" defined? Since the situation as it is includes the truth of the belief, some interpretation is necessary. Despite the book's length, its effort to cover so much ground sometimes results in skimpy treatment of large issues.

II

I now wish to raise some general questions about the type of materialism whose possibility Armstrong defends, and about the causal analysis of mental concepts. My first problem is this: why should a materialist theory of the operation of human beings correspond closely enough to any mentalist picture to permit identification of items from the two theories? Even if some form of materialism is true, it will not automatically be expressible in the framework of common-sense psychology. Currently available data about the central nervous system do not seem to me to encourage such a hope; and some of them positively discourage it: for example, the fundamental left-right bifurcation of cerebral function, to which nothing in the common-sense psychology of perception and action corresponds.

There is an important respect in which Armstrong's analogy between materialism and the equation of the gene and the DNA molecule fails. Pre-molecular genetics was an exact scientific theory: the concept of the gene was introduced in the service of scientific explanation, and subsequent work in molecular biology which makes the equation plausible has had the same aim. But the psychology of common sense, embodied in the ordinary concepts of belief, desire, sensation, perception, emotion, and so forth is not a scientific theory. The mental states for which Armstrong offers causal analyses are picked out by a system which has evolved naturally, and whose form may depend significantly on its extra-scientific functions. Our dealings with and declarations to one another require a specialized vocabulary, and although it serves us moderately well in ordinary life, its narrowness and inadequacy as a psychological theory become evident when we attempt to apply it in the formulation of general descriptions of human behavior or in the explanation of abnormal mental conditions.

The crude and incomplete causal theory embodied in common-sense psychology should not be expected to survive the next hundred years of central nervous system studies intact. It would be surprising if concepts like belief and desire found correspondents in a neurophysiological theory, considering how limited their explanatory and predictive power is, even for gross behavior. The physical behavior which, on Armstrong's analysis, a given intention is apt to cause, may be the product of causes whose complexity cannot be brought into even rough correspondence with the simple elements of a present-day psychological explanation.

If that is so, then a physicalist theory of human functioning will not take the form of identifications between old-style psychological states and microscopically described physical states of the central nervous system. It will be couched instead in the concepts of a more advanced theory of human higher functioning. Moreover, it cannot be assumed that these concepts will be drawn from among those now available for the description of the brain. Neurophysiology may uncover phenomena with which we are not familiar and which do not simply reduce to multiple occurrences of phenomena with which we are familiar. (Armstrong recognizes this possibility, and even the possibility that the materialism which turns out to be correct will not be a physico-chemical materialism.) I therefore doubt that the terms for expressing the two sides of a physicalist identity are at present available; and the development of physiological psychology could leave us with terms so tied to a common theory that any true identities we tried to formulate would be tautological. None of this is an objection to materialism, but it suggests that the formulation of that doctrine needs to progress beyond the terms of the traditional identity theory.

I want to ask next what the exact status of Armstrong's causal analyses is, and whether they are successful in what they set out to accomplish. On pages 84-85, he says he is not attempting to provide *translations* of mental statements, but only to *do justice* to the nature of mental states by means of purely physical or neutral concepts. But on page 90 he refers to the enterprise as a logical analysis of the mental concepts, and as a conceptual thesis. I take it that he regards his analyses as partial—as rough indications of the kinds of physical phenomena to which our mental concepts are tied. In fact, he relies largely on our ordinary nonverbal knowledge of the behavior characteristic of conscious beings, and does not provide much detailed physical analysis at all. But there is no need, for his purposes, to provide any analysis in physical terms *independent* of the psychological vocabulary. If the men-

tal concepts are applied to conditions causally related to certain behavior, it is unlikely that we possess the vocabulary for an independent description of precisely that behavior, without reference to the kind of mental state which it typically manifests. It cannot in general be assumed that a physical feature to which we respond uniformly, and whose name we can therefore learn, will be analyzable in terms of component physical features for which we also happen to possess (or could come to acquire) a vocabulary. Most of our nonartificial concepts may be in this sense logically primitive.

But if that is so, there is no need to seek *analyses* of the mental concepts in other terms. Armstrong's causal theory can state truths about our mental states, even if it does not provide adequate analyses of the mental concepts. A materialism of the type Armstrong favors would require that mental states *do in fact* enter into the causation of behavior. But as regards the *analysis* of mind, it need impose only a negative requirement: that mental concepts not entail the involvement of any nonphysical substance or attribute.

Even Armstrong's defense of this negative thesis, however, raises serious difficulties. It leads him to the unusual claim that the intrinsic nature of our mental states plays no part in our mental concepts, and indeed will not be known to us until it is discovered what the causes of our behavior are. It is a striking feature of Armstrong's book that he does not regard this as a claim which one might find it difficult to accept. He never takes seriously the natural objection that we must know the intrinsic nature of our *own* mental states, since we experience them directly.[3]

Consider, for example, how he accounts for the conceivability of disembodied existence. Armstrong believes that this is taken care of by the topic-neutral element in his causal analysis, which allows for the possibility that the causes of our behavior may be nonphysical. But note that this is not the same as allowing the possibility of disembodied existence: it is only allowing the possibility of that possibility. This is not a trivial distinction. Armstrong is content to maintain that we do not know that the disembodied existence of the mind is inconceivable. But some philosophers would maintain that we know that the disembodied existence of the mind *is* conceivable. The latter, stronger thesis is the basis of Descartes's proof that the mind and the body are distinct. He did not hold merely that the mind might, for all we know, be something distinct from the body and therefore in principle capable of independent existence. Rather he held that we can without difficulty conceive of its independent existence, and therefore it must be something distinct from the body.

This is a powerful argument. To oppose it one must maintain, as Armstrong does, that in being subject to his own mental states Descartes is not aware of their intrinsic nature, so he has no grounds for claiming that he can conceive, for example, *this set of sensations* occurring even though his body does not exist. Clearly it would not content Descartes to be told that he cannot be certain that the disembodied occurrence of those sensations is *in*conceivable; for he is certain that it *is* conceivable, having conceived it.

Descartes's argument also has the following turned-around version, which to my knowledge he never employed. The existence of the body without the mind is just as conceivable as the existence of the mind without the body. That is, I can conceive of my body doing precisely what it is doing now, inside and out, with complete physical causation of its behavior (including typically self-conscious behavior), but without any of the mental states which I am now experiencing, or any others, for that matter. If that is really conceivable, then the mental states must be distinct from the body's physical states,

and Armstrong's causal analysis of mental concepts cannot be correct, for on that analysis the presence of appropriately complex physical causes of appropriately complex behavior would *entail* the existence of conscious mental states.

The conceptual exercises on which these arguments depend are very convincing. If Armstrong is right, they are illusory. But then what am I doing when I conceive of my mind without my body, or vice versa? I am certainly not just imagining that the causes of my bodily behavior are states of a nonphysical substance, which can therefore be conceived separated from that body. The type of possibility involved here has nothing to do with analyticity. What is being claimed is not that under a certain description (namely, a mental one), there is no contradiction in supposing that my mental states should exist apart from my body. Rather it is being claimed that in virtue of what they *are*, their separability is conceivable.[4] The real issue is whether one can know that one has conceived such a thing, and whether one's immediate acquaintance with the contents of one's own mind puts one in a better position to do this than to conceive of the Morning Star persisting and the Evening Star being destroyed. (That is not conceivable, since they are the same. And its conceivability cannot be proved by arguing that it is not a contradiction, for that only shows that those descriptions do not *entail* that it is inconceivable.) What must be shown, to defeat the Cartesian argument, is that when we try to conceive of our minds without our bodies, or vice versa, we do not succeed in doing that, but instead do something else, which we mistake for it. We may, for example, conceive of other beings psychologically similar to ourselves, but having a different psychophysical constitution; this would not be to conceive of our own mental states proceeding without bodies of the sort we now have. Either Descartes is mistaken in thinking that we can conceive of their separate existence, or else some kind of dualism is correct.

One sign of something seriously wrong is that Armstrong regards it as a *virtue* of his theory that it makes short work of the problem of other minds. He says:

> Suppose a human body exhibits the right sort of behaviour. Given our analysis of the nature of mental states we need only three premises to infer the existence of a mind that this behaviour is an expression of. (*i*) The behaviour has *some* cause; (*ii*) the cause lies in the behaving person; (*iii*) the cause is an "adequate" cause—it has a complexity that corresponds to the complexity of the behaviour. Given only these quite modest assumptions, the existence of another mind is necessary [pp. 124-125].

But this "solution" to the problem leaves it a complete mystery why it has ever bothered anyone. The problem arises precisely at the point where Armstrong's three premises are satisfied, and we discover that the existence of a mind can still be doubted. A theory of mind which overrules this doubt without accounting for its source has left some serious philosophical work undone.

I suspect that these are not difficulties for materialism per se, but rather stem from features of the first-person application of mental concepts which have not been revealed by Armstrong's straightforward causal analysis. This may bear on the usefulness of Armstrong's theory as a formulation of materialism. But there is also a question whether our ordinary mental concepts, however analyzed, will prove to have any exact connection with a true physical theory of the operation of those organisms that we describe as human. If not, the assumption that we are persons may have to be re-examined.[5]

Notes

1. *A Materialist Theory of the Mind.* By D. M. Armstrong. (London, Routledge and Kegan Paul; New York, Humanities Press, 1968. Pp. xii, 372.)

2. At one point (p. 275) Armstrong suggests that the analysis of the concept of redness provides us only with *contingent* truths about redness. Although he does not put it quite this way, one might add that what is necessarily true of redness, its intrinsic nature, can be discovered only by empirical investigation. This suggests the possibility of a more general attack on the traditional association of necessity with analyticity and a priori knowledge. Such a program has in fact been carried out by Saul Kripke, but his results are not published. They also suggest, however, that we should not regard central-state materialism simply as a contingent thesis, but should say instead that if Armstrong's version of materialism is true, it is necessarily true of the mental states that they are physical states, but only contingently true of them that they are mental states, since that depends on their effects rather than on their intrinsic nature. What is analytically true of something under a certain description may not be necessarily true of it, since that description may fit the thing only contingently. On the other hand, a nonanalytic statement about it may be necessarily true; if, for example, it says what the thing is.

3. Though his attack on incorrigibility presupposes a rejection of the idea of direct acquaintance with our own mental states: he contends, as it were, that we know them only by description.

4. Here again I have been led by Kripke's work on possibility and necessity to see that there is more to the Cartesian argument than a mere confusion between synonymy and identity. It is based on the recognition that if a mental event *is* a physical event, then it is not possible for the former to occur without the latter.

5. My research was supported in part by the National Science Foundation.

Psychophysical and Theoretical Identifications

David Lewis

Psychophysical identity theorists often say that the identifications they anticipate between mental and neural states are essentially like various uncontroversial theoretical identifications: the identification of water with H_2O, of light with electromagnetic radiation, and so on. Such theoretical identifications are usually described as pieces of voluntary theorizing, as follows. Theoretical advances make it possible to simplify total science by positing bridge laws identifying some of the entities discussed in one theory with entities discussed in another theory. In the name of parsimony, we posit those bridge laws forthwith. Identifications are made, not found.

In 'An Argument for the Identity Theory',[1] I claimed that this was a bad picture of psychophysical identification, since a suitable physiological theory could *imply* psychophysical identities—not merely make it reasonable to posit them for the sake of parsimony. The implication was as follows:

Mental state M = the occupant of causal role R (by definition of M).

Neural state N = the occupant of causal role R (by the physiological theory).

Therefore, mental state M = neural state N (by transitivity of =).

If the meanings of the names of mental states were really such as to provide the first premise, and if the advance of physiology were such as to provide the second premise, then the conclusion would follow. Physiology and the meanings of words would leave us no choice but to make the psychophysical identification.

In this sequel, I shall uphold the view that psychophysical identifications thus described would be like theoretical identifications, though they would not fit the usual account thereof. For the usual account, I claim, is wrong; theoretical identifications *in general* are implied by the theories that make them possible—not posited independently. This follows from a general hypothesis about the meanings of theoretical terms: that they are definable functionally, by reference to causal roles.[2] Applied to common-sense psychology—folk science rather than professional science, but a theory nonetheless—we get the hypothesis of my previous paper[3] that a mental state M (say, an experience) is

From *Australasian Journal of Philosophy* 50 (1972): 249-258. Reprinted by permission of *Australasian Journal of Philosophy* and the author.

definable as the occupant of a certain causal role *R*—that is, as the state, of whatever sort, that is causally connected in specified ways to sensory stimuli, motor responses, and other mental states.

First, I consider an example of theoretical identification chosen to be remote from past philosophizing; then I give my general account of the meanings of theoretical terms and the nature of theoretical identifications; finally I return to the case of psychophysical identity.

I

We are assembled in the drawing room of the country house; the detective reconstructs the crime. That is, he proposes a *theory* designed to be the best explanation of phenomena we have observed: the death of Mr. Body, the blood on the wallpaper, the silence of the dog in the night, the clock seventeen minutes fast, and so on. He launches into his story:

> *X, Y* and *Z* conspired to murder Mr. Body. Seventeen years ago, in the gold fields of Uganda, *X* was Body's partner . . . Last week, *Y* and *Z* conferred in a bar in Reading . . . Tuesday night at 11:17, *Y* went to the attic and set a time bomb . . . Seventeen minutes later, *X* met *Z* in the billiard room and gave him the lead pipe . . . Just when the bomb went off in the attic, *X* fired three shots into the study through the French windows . . .

And so it goes: a long story. Let us pretend that it is a single long conjunctive sentence.

The story contains the three names '*X*', '*Y*' and '*Z*'. The detective uses these new terms without explanation, as though we knew what they meant. But we do not. We never used them before, at least not in the senses they bear in the present context. All we know about their meanings is what we gradually gather from the story itself. Call these *theoretical terms* (*T-terms* for short) because they are introduced by a theory. Call the rest of the terms in the

story *O-terms*. These are all the *other* terms except the T-terms; they are all the *old, original* terms we understood before the theory was proposed. We could call them our 'pre-theoretical' terms. But 'O' does *not* stand for 'observational'. Not all the O-terms are observational terms, whatever those may be. They are just any old terms. If part of the story was mathematical—if it included a calculation of the trajectory that took the second bullet to the chandelier without breaking the vase —then some of the O-terms will be mathematical. If the story says that something happened because of something else, then the O-terms will include the intensional connective 'because', or the operator 'it is a law that', or something of the sort.

Nor do the theoretical terms name some sort of peculiar theoretical, unobservable, semi-fictitious entities. The story makes plain that they name *people*. Not theoretical people, different somehow from ordinary, observational people —just people!

On my account, the detective plunged right into his story, using '*X*', '*Y*' and '*Z*' as if they were names with understood denotation. It would have made little difference if he had started, instead, with initial existential quantifiers: 'There exist *X, Y* and *Z* such that . . .' and then told the story. In that case, the terms '*X*', '*Y*' and '*Z*' would have been bound variables rather than T-terms. But the story would have had the same explanatory power. The second version of the story, with the T-terms turned into variables bound by existential quantifiers, is the Ramsey sentence of the first. Bear in mind, as evidence for what is to come, how little difference the initial quantifiers seem to make to the detective's assertion.

Suppose that after we have heard the detective's story, we learn that it is true of a certain three people: Plum, Peacock and Mustard. If we put the name 'Plum' in place of '*X*', 'Peacock' in place of '*Y*', and

'Mustard' in place of 'Z' throughout, we get a true story about the doings of those three people. We will say that Plum, Peacock and Mustard together *realize* (or are a *realization* of) the detective's theory.

We may also find out that the story is not true of any other triple.[4] Put in any three names that do not name Plum, Peacock and Mustard (in that order) and the story we get is false. We will say that Plum, Peacock and Mustard *uniquely realize* (are the *unique realization* of) the theory.

We might learn both of these facts. (The detective might have known them all along, but held them back to spring his trap; or he, like us, might learn them only after his story had been told.) And if we did, we would surely conclude that X, Y and Z in the story were Plum, Peacock and Mustard. I maintain that we would be compelled so to conclude, given the senses borne by the terms 'X', 'Y' and 'Z' in virtue of the way the detective introduced them in his theorizing, and given our information about Plum, Peacock and Mustard.

In telling his story, the detective set forth three roles and said that they were occupied by X, Y and Z. He must have specified the meanings of the three T-terms 'X', 'Y' and 'Z' thereby; for they had meanings afterwards, they had none before, and nothing else was done to give them meanings. They were introduced by an implicit functional definition, being reserved to name the occupants of the three roles. When we find out who are the occupants of the three roles, we find out who are X, Y and Z. Here is our theoretical identification.

In saying that the roles were occupied by X, Y and Z, the detective implied that they were occupied. That is, his theory implied its Ramsey sentence. That seems right; if we learnt that no triple realized the story, or even came close, we would have to conclude that the story was false. We would also have to deny that the

names 'X', 'Y' and 'Z' named anything; for they were introduced as names for the occupants of roles that turned out to be unoccupied.

I also claim that the detective implied that the roles were uniquely occupied, when he reserved names for their occupants and proceeded as if those names had been given definite referents. Suppose we learnt that two different triples realized the theory: Plum, Peacock, Mustard; and Green, White, Scarlet. (Or the two different triples might overlap: Plum, Peacock, Mustard; and Green, Peacock, Scarlet.) I think we would be most inclined to say that the story was false, and that the names 'X', 'Y' and 'Z' did not name anything. They were introduced as names for the occupants of certain roles; but there is no such thing as *the* occupant of a doubly occupied role, so there is nothing suitable for them to name.

If, as I claim, the T-terms are definable as naming the first, second, and third components of the unique triple that realizes the story, then the T-terms can be treated like definite descriptions. If the story is uniquely realized, they name what they ought to name; if the story is unrealized or multiply realized, they are like improper descriptions. If too many triples realize the story, 'X' is like 'the moon of Mars'; if too few triples—none—realize the story, 'X' is like 'the moon of Venus'. Improper descriptions are not meaningless. Hilary Putnam has objected that on this sort of account of theoretical terms, the theoretical terms of a falsified theory come out meaningless.[5] But they do not, if theoretical terms of unrealized theories are like improper descriptions. 'The moon of Mars' and 'the moon of Venus' do not (in any normal way) name anything here in our actual world; but they are not meaningless, because we know very well what they name in certain alternative possible worlds. Similarly, we know what 'X' names in any world where the detective's

210   David Lewis

theory is true, whether or not our actual world is such a world.

A complication: what if the theorizing detective has made one little mistake? He should have said that Y went to the attic at 11:37, not 11:17. The story as told is unrealized, true of no one. But another story is realized, indeed uniquely realized: the story we get by deleting or correcting the little mistake. We can say that the story as told is *nearly realized*, has a unique *near-realization*. (The notion of a near-realization is hard to analyze, but easy to understand.) In this case the T-terms ought to name the components of the near-realization. More generally: they should name the components of the nearest realization of the theory, provided there is a unique nearest realization and it is near enough. Only if the story comes nowhere near to being realized, or if there are two equally near nearest realizations, should we resort to treating the T-terms like improper descriptions. But let us set aside this complication for the sake of simplicity, though we know well that scientific theories are often nearly realized but rarely realized, and that theoretical reduction is usually blended with revision of the reduced theory.

This completes our example. It may seem atypical: the T-terms are names, not predicates or functors. But that is of no importance. It is a popular exercise to recast a language so that its nonlogical vocabulary consists entirely of predicates; but it is just as easy to recast a language so that its nonlogical vocabulary consists entirely of names (provided that the logical vocabulary includes a copula). These names, of course, may purport to name individuals, sets, attributes, species, states, functions, relations, magnitudes, phenomena or what have you; but they are still names. Assume this done, so that we may replace all T-terms by variables of the same sort.

II

We now proceed to a general account of the functional definability of T-terms and the nature of theoretical identification. Suppose we have a new theory, T, introducing the new terms $t_1 \ldots t_n$. These are our T-terms. (Let them be names.) Every other term in our vocabulary, therefore, is an O-term. The theory T is presented in a sentence called the *postulate* of T. Assume this is a single sentence, perhaps a long conjunction. It says of the entities—states, magnitudes, species, or whatever—named by the T-terms that they occupy certain *causal roles*; that they stand in specified causal (and other) relations to entities named by O-terms, and to one another. We write the postulate thus:[6]

$$T[t].$$

Replacing the T-terms uniformly by free variables $x_1 \ldots x_n$, we get a formula in which only O-terms appear:

$$T[x].$$

Any n-tuple of entities which satisfies this formula is a realization of the theory t. Prefixing existential quantifiers, we get the *Ramsey sentence* of T, which says that T has at least one realization:

$$Ex\ T[x].$$

[*Editor's note:* In this anthology, the ordinary "E" is used instead of the backward "E" as the existential quantifier.] We can also write a *modified Ramsey sentence* which says that T has a unique realization:[7]

$$E_1x\ T[x].$$

The Ramsey sentence has exactly the same O-content as the postulate of T; any sentence free of T-terms follows logically from one if and only if it follows from the other.[8] The modified Ramsey sentence has slightly more O-content. I claim that this surplus O-content does belong to the theory T—there are more theorems of T than follow logically from the postulate alone. For in presenting the postulate as if the T-terms have been well-defined thereby, the theorist has implicitly asserted that T is uniquely realized.

We can write the *Carnap sentence* of T: the conditional of the Ramsey sentence and the postulate, which says that if T is realized, then the T-terms name the components of some realization of T:

$$\text{If } \text{Ex } T[x] \text{ then } T[t].$$

Carnap has suggested this sentence as a meaning postulate for T;[9] but if we want T-terms of unrealized or multiply realized theories to have the status of improper descriptions, our meaning postulates should instead be a *modified Carnap sentence*, this conditional with our modified Ramsey sentence as antecedent:

$$\text{If } E_1x \, T[x] \text{ then } T[t],$$

together with another conditional to cover the remaining cases:[10]

$$\text{If } -E_1x \, T[x] \text{ then } t = * \, .$$

This pair of meaning postulates is logically equivalent[11] to a sentence which explicitly defines the T-terms by means of O-terms:

$$t = \text{the x } T[x].$$

This is what I have called functional definition. The T-terms have been defined as the occupants of the causal roles specified by the theory T; as *the* entities, whatever those may be, that bear certain causal relations to one another and to the referents of the O-terms.

If I am right, T-terms are eliminable —we can always replace them by their definientia. Of course, this is not to say that theories are fictions, or that theories are uninterpreted formal abacuses, or that theoretical entities are unreal. Quite the

opposite! Because we understand the O-terms, and we can define the T-terms from them, theories are fully meaningful; we have reason to think a good theory true; and if a theory is true, then whatever exists according to the theory really *does* exist.

I said that there are more theorems of T than follow logically from the postulate alone. More precisely: the theorems of T are just those sentences which follow from the postulate together with the corresponding functional definition of the T-terms. For that definition, I claim, is given implicitly when the postulate is presented as bestowing meanings on the T-terms introduced in it.

It may happen, after the introduction of the T-terms, that we come to believe of a certain n-tuple of entities, specified otherwise than as the entities that realize T, that they do realize T. That is, we may come to accept a sentence

$$T[r]$$

where $r_1 \ldots r_n$ are either O-terms or theoretical terms of some other theory, introduced into our language independently of $t_1 \ldots t_n$. This sentence, which we may call a *weak reduction premise* for T, is free of T-terms. Our acceptance of it might have nothing to do with our previous acceptance of T. We might accept it as part of some new theory; or we might believe it as part of our miscellaneous, unsystematized general knowledge. Yet having accepted it, for whatever reason, we are logically compelled to make theoretical identifications. The reduction premise, together with the functional definition of the T-terms and the postulate of T, logically implies the identity:

$$t = r.$$

In other words, the postulate and the weak reduction premise definitionally imply the identities $t_i = r_i$.

Or we might somehow come to believe of a certain n-tuple of entities that they *uniquely* realize T; that is, to accept a sentence

$$(x)(T[x] \text{ iff } x = r)$$

where $r_1 \ldots r_n$ are as above. We may call this a *strong reduction premise* for T, since it definitionally implies the theoretical identifications by itself, without the aid of the postulate of T. The strong reduction premise logically implies the identity

$$r = \text{the } xT[x]$$

which, together with the functional definition of the T-terms, implies the identities $t_i = r_i$ by transitivity of identity.

These theoretical identifications are not voluntary posits, made in the name of parsimony; they are deductive inferences. According to their definitions, the T-terms name the occupants of the causal roles specified by the theory T. According to the weak reduction premise and T, or the strong reduction premise by itself, the occupants of those causal roles turn out to be the referents of $r_1 \ldots r_n$. Therefore, those are the entities named by the T-terms. That is how we inferred that X, Y and Z were Plum, Peacock and Mustard; and that, I suggest, is how we make theoretical identifications in general.

III

And that is how, someday, we will infer that[12] the mental states M_1, M_2, . . . are the neural states N_1, N_2, ...

Think of commonsense psychology as a term-introducing scientific theory, though one invented long before there was any such institution as professional science. Collect all the platitudes you can think of regarding the causal relations of mental states, sensory stimuli, and motor responses. Perhaps we can think of them as having the form:

When someone is in so-and-so combination of mental states and receives sensory stimu-

li of so-and-so kind, he tends with so-and-so probability to be caused thereby to go into so-and-so mental states and produce so-and-so motor responses.

Add also all the platitudes to the effect that one mental state falls under another —'toothache is a kind of pain', and the like. Perhaps there are platitudes of other forms as well. Include only platitudes which are common knowledge among us —everyone knows them, everyone knows that everyone else knows them, and so on. For the meanings of our words are common knowledge, and I am going to claim that names of mental states derive their meaning from these platitudes.

Form the conjunction of these platitudes; or better, form a cluster of them— a disjunction of all conjunctions of *most* of them. (That way it will not matter if a few are wrong.) This is the postulate of our term-introducing theory. The names of mental states are the T-terms.[13] The O-terms used to introduce them must be sufficient for speaking of stimuli and responses, and for speaking of causal relations among these and states of unspecified nature.

From the postulate, form the definition of the T-terms; it defines the mental states by reference to their causal relations to stimuli, responses, and each other. When we learn what sort of states occupy those causal roles definitive of the mental states, we will learn what states the mental states are—exactly as we found out who X was when we found out that Plum was the man who occupied a certain role, and exactly as we found out what light was when we found that electromagnetic radiation was the phenomenon that occupied a certain role.

Imagine our ancestors first speaking only of external things, stimuli, and responses—and perhaps producing what we, but not they, may call *Aüsserungen* of mental states—until some genius invented the theory of mental states, with its newly introduced T-terms, to explain the regularities among stimuli and responses. But that did not happen. Our commonsense psychology was never a newly invented term-introducing scientific theory—not even of prehistoric folk-science. The story that mental terms were introduced as theoretical terms is a myth.

It is, in fact, Sellars' myth of our Rylean ancestors.[14] And though it is a myth, it may be a good myth or a bad one. It is a good myth if our names of mental states do in fact mean just what they would mean if the myth were true.[15] I adopt the working hypothesis that it is a good myth. This hypothesis can be tested, in principle, in whatever way any hypothesis about the conventional meanings of our words can be tested. I have not tested it; but I offer one item of evidence. Many philosophers have found Rylean behaviorism at least plausible; more have found watered down, 'criteriological' behaviorism plausible. There is a strong odor of analyticity about the platitudes of common-sense psychology. The myth explains the odor of analyticity and the plausibility of behaviorism. If the names of mental states are like theoretical terms, they name nothing unless the theory (the cluster of platitudes) is more or less true. Hence it is analytic that *either* pain, etc., do not exist *or* most of our platitudes about them are true. If this *seems* analytic to you, you should accept the myth, and be prepared for psychophysical identifications.

The hypothesis that names of mental states are like functionally defined theoretical terms solves a familiar problem about mental explanations. How can my behavior be explained by an explanans consisting of nothing but particular-fact premises about my present state of mind? Where are the covering laws? The solution is that the requisite covering laws are implied by the particular-fact premises. Ascriptions to me of various particular beliefs and desires, say, cannot be true if there are no such states as belief and desire; cannot be true, that is, unless the causal roles definitive of belief and desire are occupied. But these roles can only be occupied by states causally related in the proper lawful way to behavior.

Formally, suppose we have a mental explanation of behavior as follows.

$$\frac{C_1[t], \; C_2[t], \ldots}{E}$$

Here E describes the behavior to be explained; $C_1[t]$, $C_2[t]$, . . . are particular-fact premises describing the agent's state of mind at the time. Various of the mental terms $t_1 \ldots t_n$ appear in these premises, in such a way that the premises would be false if the terms named nothing. Now let $L_1[t]$, $L_2[t]$, . . . be the platitudinous purported causal laws whereby—according to the myth—the mental terms were introduced. Ignoring clustering for simplicity, we may take the term-introducing postulate to be the conjunction of these. Then our explanation may be rewritten:

$$\frac{E_1x \, (L_1[x] \; \& \; L_2[x] \; \& \ldots \& \; C_1[x] \; \& \; C_2[x] \; \& \ldots)}{E}$$

The new explanans is a definitional consequence of the original one. In the expanded version, however, laws appear explicitly alongside the particular-fact premises. We have, so to speak, an existential generalization of an ordinary covering-law explanation.[16]

The causal definability of mental terms has been thought to contradict the necessary infallibility of introspection.[17] Pain is one state; belief that one is in pain is another. (Confusingly, either of the two may be called 'awareness of pain'.) Why cannot I believe that I am in pain without being in pain—that is, without being in whatever state it is that occupies so-and-so causal role? Doubtless I am so built that this normally does not happen; but what makes it impossible?

I do not know whether introspection

is (in some or all cases) infallible. But if it is, that is no difficulty for me. Here it is important that, on my version of causal definability, the mental terms stand or fall together. If common-sense psychology fails, all of them are alike denotationless.

Suppose that among the platitudes are some to the effect that introspection is reliable: 'belief that one is in pain never occurs unless pain occurs' or the like. Suppose further that these platitudes enter the term-introducing postulate as conjuncts, not as cluster members; and suppose that they are so important that an n-tuple that fails to satisfy them perfectly is not even a near-realization of common-sense psychology. (I neither endorse nor repudiate these suppositions.) Then the necessary infallibility of introspection is assured. Two states cannot be pain and belief that one is in pain, respectively (in the case of a given individual or species) if the second *ever* occurs without the first. The state that *usually* occupies the role of belief that one is in pain may, of course, occur without the state that *usually* occupies the role of pain; but in that case (under the suppositions above) the former no longer is the state of belief that one is in pain, and the latter no longer is pain. Indeed, the victim no longer is in any mental state whatever, since his states no longer realize (or nearly realize) common-sense psychology. Therefore it is impossible to believe that one is in pain and not be in pain.[18]

Notes

1. *Journal of Philosophy*, 63 (1966): 17-25.

2. See my 'How to Define Theoretical Terms', *Journal of Philosophy*, 67 (1970): 427-446.

3. Since advocated also by D. M. Armstrong, in *A Materialist Theory of the Mind* (New York: Humanities Press, 1968). He expresses it thus: 'The concept of a mental state is primarily the concept of a state of the person apt for bringing about a certain sort of behaviour [and secondarily also, in some cases] apt for being brought about by a certain sort of stimulus', p. 82.

4. The story itself might imply this. If, for instance, the story said 'X saw Y give Z the candlestick while the three of them were alone in the billiard room at 9:17', then the story could not possibly be true of more than one triple.

5. 'What Theories Are Not', in Nagel, Suppes and Tarski, eds., *Logic, Methodology and Philosophy of Science* (Stanford University Press, 1962): 247.

6. Notation: boldface names and variables denote n-tuples; the corresponding subscripted names and variables denote components of n-tuples. For instance, $\mathbf{t}$ is the n-tuple whose first member is t_1 and whose last member is t_n. This notation is easily dispensable, and hence carries no ontic commitment to n-tuples.

7. That is, $(Ey)(x)(T[x] \text{ iff } y = x)$. Note that $E_1 x_1 \ldots E_1 x_n T[x]$ does not imply $E_1 \mathbf{x} T[\mathbf{x}]$, and does not say that T is uniquely realized.

8. On the assumptions—reasonable for the postulate of a scientific theory—that the T-terms occur purely referentially in the postulate, and in such a way that the postulate is false if any of them are denotationless. We shall make these assumptions henceforth.

9. Most recently in *Philosophical Foundations of Physics* (New York: Basic Books, 1966): 265-274. Carnap, of course, has in mind the case in which the O-terms belong to an observation language.

10. $\mathbf{t} = *$ means that each t_i is denotationless. Let $\star$ be some chosen necessarily denotationless name; then $*$ is the n-tuple each of whose members is $\star$ and $\mathbf{t} = *$ is equivalent to the conjunction of all the identities $t_i = \star$.

11. Given a theory of descriptions which makes an identity true whenever both its terms have the status of improper descriptions, false whenever one term has that status and the other does not. This might best be the theory of descriptions in Dana Scott, 'Existence and Description in Formal Logic', in R. Schoenman, ed., *Bertrand Russell: Philosopher of the Century* (London: Allen & Unwin, 1967).

12. In general, or in the case of a given species, or in the case of a given person. It might turn out that the causal roles definitive of mental states are occupied by different neu-

ral (or other) states in different organisms. See my discussion of Hilary Putnam 'Psychological Predicates' in *Journal of Philosophy*, 66 (1969): 23-25. [*Editor's note:* Putnam's paper is reprinted as "The Nature of Mental States," chap. 17, this volume. Lewis's discussion is reprinted as chap. 18, this volume.]

13. It may be objected that the number of mental states is infinite, or at least enormous; for instance, there are as many states of belief as there are propositions to be believed. But it would be better to say that there is one state of belief, and it is a relational state, relating people to propositions. (Similarly, centigrade temperature is a relational state, relating objects to numbers.) The platitudes involving belief would, of course, contain universally quantified proposition-variables. Likewise for other mental states with intentional objects.

14. Wilfrid Sellars, 'Empiricism and the Philosophy of Mind', in Feigl and Scriven, eds., *Minnesota Studies in the Philosophy of Science*, 1 (University of Minnesota Press, 1956): 309-320.

15. Two myths which cannot both be true together can nevertheless both be good together. Part of my myth says that names of color-sensations were T-terms, introduced using names of colors as O-terms. If this is a good myth, we should be able to define 'sensation of red' roughly as 'that state apt for being brought about by the presence of something red (before one's open eyes, in good light,

etc.)'. A second myth says that names of colors were T-terms introduced using names of color-sensations as O-terms. If this second myth is good, we should be able to define 'red' roughly as 'that property of things apt for bringing about the sensation of red'. The two myths could not both be true, for which came first: names of color-sensations or of colors? But they could both be good. We could have a circle in which colors are correctly defined in terms of sensations and sensations are correctly defined in terms of colors. We could not discover the meanings *both* of names of colors and of names of color-sensations just by looking at the circle of correct definitions, but so what?

16. See 'How to Define Theoretical Terms': 440-441.

17. By Armstrong, in *A Materialist Theory of the Mind*, pp. 100-113. He finds independent grounds for denying the infallibility of introspection.

18. Previous versions of this paper were presented at a conference on Philosophical Problems of Psychology held at Honolulu in March, 1968; at the annual meeting of the Australasian Association of Philosophy held at Brisbane in August, 1971; and at various university colloquia. This paper also appears in Chung-ying Cheng, ed., *Philosophical Aspects of the Mind-Body Problem* (University Press of Hawaii, 1975).

16
Mad Pain and Martian Pain

David Lewis

I

There might be a strange man who sometimes feels pain, just as we do, but whose pain differs greatly from ours in its causes and effects. Our pain is typically caused by cuts, burns, pressure, and the like; his is caused by moderate exercise on an empty stomach. Our pain is generally distracting; his turns his mind to mathematics, facilitating concentration on that but distracting him from anything else. Intense pain has no tendency whatever to cause him to groan or writhe, but does cause him to cross his legs and snap his fingers. He is not in the least motivated to prevent pain or to get rid of it. In short, he feels pain but his pain does not at all occupy the typical causal role of pain. He would doubtless seem to us to be some sort of madman, and that is what I shall call him, though of course the sort of madness I have imagined may bear little resemblance to the real thing.

I said there might be such a madman. I don't know how to prove that something

This paper was presented at a conference on mind-body identity held at Rice University in April 1978. I am grateful to many friends, and especially to Patricia Kitcher, for valuable discussions of the topic.

is possible, but my opinion that this is a possible case seems pretty firm. If I want a credible theory of mind, I need a theory that does not deny the possibility of mad pain. I needn't mind conceding that perhaps the madman is not in pain in *quite* the same sense that the rest of us are, but there had better be some straightforward sense in which he and we are both in pain.

Also, there might be a Martian who sometimes feels pain, just as we do, but whose pain differs greatly from ours in its physical realization. His hydraulic mind contains nothing like our neurons. Rather, there are varying amounts of fluid in many inflatable cavities, and the inflation of any one of these cavities opens some valves and closes others. His mental plumbing pervades most of his body—in fact, all but the heat exchanger inside his head. When you pinch his skin you cause no firing of C-fibers—he has none—but, rather, you cause the inflation of many smallish cavities in his feet. When these cavities are inflated, he is in pain. And the effects of his pain are fitting: his thought and activity are disrupted, he groans and writhes, he is strongly motivated to stop you from pinching him and to see to it that you never do again. In short, he feels pain but lacks the bodily states that either are pain or else accompany it in us.

There might be such a Martian; this opinion too seems pretty firm. A credible theory of mind had better not deny the possibility of Martian pain. I needn't mind conceding that perhaps the Martian is not in pain in *quite* the same sense that we Earthlings are, but there had better be some straightforward sense in which he and we are both in pain.

II

A credible theory of mind needs to make a place both for mad pain and for Martian pain. Prima facie, it seems hard for a materialist theory to pass this two-fold test. As philosophers, we would like to characterize pain a priori. (We might settle for less, but let's start by asking for all we want.) As materialists, we want to characterize pain as a physical phenomenon. We can speak of the place of pain in the causal network from stimuli to inner states to behavior. And we can speak of the physical processes that go on when there is pain and that take their place in that causal network. We seem to have no other resources but these. But the lesson of mad pain is that pain is associated only contingently with its causal role, while the lesson of Martian pain is that pain is connected only contingently with its physical realization. How can we characterize pain a priori in terms of causal role and physical realization, and yet respect both kinds of contingency?

A simple identity theory straightforwardly solves the problem of mad pain. It goes just as straightforwardly wrong about Martian pain. A simple behaviorism or functionalism goes the other way: right about the Martian, wrong about the madman. The theories that fail our two-fold test so decisively are altogether too simple. (Perhaps they are too simple ever to have had adherents.) It seems that a theory that can pass our test will have to be a mixed theory. It will have to be able to tell us that the madman and the Martian are both in pain, but for different reasons: the madman because he is in the right physical state, the Martian because he is in a state rightly situated in the causal network.

Certainly we can cook up a mixed theory. Here's an easy recipe: First, find a theory to take care of the common man and the madman, disregarding the Martian—presumably an identity theory. Second, find a theory to take care of the common man and the Martian, disregarding the madman—presumably some sort of behaviorism or functionalism. Then disjoin the two: say that to be in pain is to be in pain either according to the first theory or according to the second. Alternatively, claim ambiguity: say that to be in pain in one sense is to be in pain according to the first theory, to be in pain in another sense is to be in pain according to the second theory.

This strategy seems desperate. One wonders why we should have a disjunctive or ambiguous concept of pain, if common men who suffer pain are always in pain according to both disjuncts or both disambiguations. It detracts from the credibility of a theory that it posits a useless complexity in our concept of pain —useless in application to the common man, at least, and therefore useless almost always.

I don't object to the strategy of claiming ambiguity. As you'll see, I shall defend a version of it. But it's not plausible to cook up an ambiguity *ad hoc* to account for the compossibility of mad pain and Martian pain. It would be better to find a widespread sort of ambiguity, a sort we would believe in no matter what we thought about pain, and show that it will solve our problem. That is my plan.

III

A dozen years or so ago, D. M. Armstrong and I (independently) proposed a materialist theory of mind that joins claims of type-type psychophysical identity with a behaviorist or functionalist way of characterizing mental states such as pain.[1] I believe our theory passes the twofold test. Positing no ambiguity without independent reason, it provides natural senses in which both madman and Martian are in pain. It wriggles through between Scylla and Charybdis.

Our view is that the concept of pain, or indeed of any other experience or mental state, is the concept of a state that occupies a certain causal role, a state with certain typical causes and effects. It is the concept of a state apt for being caused by certain stimuli and apt for causing certain behavior. Or, better, of a state apt for being caused in certain ways by stimuli plus other mental states and apt for combining with certain other mental states to jointly cause certain behavior. It is the concept of a member of a system of states that together more or less realize the pattern of causal generalizations set forth in commonsense psychology. (That system may be characterized as a whole and its members characterized afterward by reference to their place in it.)

If the concept of pain is the concept of a state that occupies a certain causal role, then whatever state does occupy that role is pain. If the state of having neurons hooked up in a certain way and firing in a certain pattern is the state properly apt for causing and being caused, as we materialists think, then that neural state is pain. But the concept of pain is not the concept of that neural state. ("The concept of . . ." is an intensional functor.) The concept of pain, unlike the concept of that neural state which in fact is pain, would have applied to some different state if the relevant causal relations had been different. Pain might have not been pain. The occupant of the role might have not occupied it. Some other state might have occupied it instead. Something that is not pain might have been pain.

This is not to say, of course, that it might have been that pain was not pain and nonpain was pain; that is, that it might have been that the occupant of the role did not occupy it and some nonoccupant did. Compare: "The winner might have lost" (true) versus "It might have been that the winner lost" (false). No wording is entirely unambiguous, but I trust my meaning is clear.

In short, the concept of pain as Armstrong and I understand it is a *nonrigid* concept. Likewise the word "pain" is a nonrigid designator. It is a contingent matter what state the concept and the word apply to. It depends on what causes what. The same goes for the rest of our concepts and ordinary names of mental states.

Some need hear no more. The notion that mental concepts and names are nonrigid, wherefore what *is* pain might not have been, seems to them just self-evidently false.[2] I cannot tell why they think so. Bracketing my own theoretical commitments, I think I would have no opinion one way or the other. It's not that I don't care about shaping theory to respect naive opinion as well as can be, but in this case I have no naive opinion to respect. If I am not speaking to your condition, so be it.

If pain is identical to a certain neural state, the identity is contingent. Whether it holds is one of the things that varies from one possible world to another. But take care. I do not say that here we have two states, pain and some neural state, that are contingently identical, identical at this world but different at another. Since I'm serious about the identity, we have not two states but one. This one state, this neural state which is pain, is not contingently identical to itself. It does not differ from itself at any world. Nothing does.[3] What's true is, rather, that the concept and name of pain contingently apply to some neural state at this world, but do not apply to it at another. Similarly, it is a contingent truth that Bruce is our cat, but it's wrong to say that Bruce and our cat are contingently identical. Our cat Bruce is necessarily self-identical. What is contingent is that the nonrigid concept of being our cat applies to Bruce rather than to some other cat, or none.

IV

Nonrigidity might begin at home. All

actualities are possibilities, so the variety of possibilities includes the variety of actualities. Though some possibilities are thoroughly otherworldly, others may be found on planets within range of our telescopes. One such planet is Mars.

If a nonrigid concept or name applies to different states in different possible cases, it should be no surprise if it also applies to different states in different actual cases. Nonrigidity is to logical space as other relativities are to ordinary space. If the word "pain" designates one state at our actual world and another at a possible world where our counterparts have a different internal structure, then also it may designate one state on Earth and another on Mars. Or, better, since Martians may come here and we may go to Mars, it may designate one state for Earthlings and another for Martians.

We may say that some state *occupies a causal role for a population.* We may say this whether the population is situated entirely at our actual world, or partly at our actual world and partly at other worlds, or entirely at other worlds. If the concept of pain is the concept of a state that occupies that role, then we may say that a state *is pain for a population.* Then we may say that a certain pattern of firing of neurons is pain for the population of actual Earthlings and some but not all of our otherworldly counterparts, whereas the inflation of certain cavities in the feet is pain for the population of actual Martians and some of their otherworldly counterparts. Human pain is the state that occupies the role of pain for humans. Martian pain is the state that occupies the same role for Martians.

A state occupies a causal role for a population, and the concept of occupant of that role applies to it, if and only if, with few exceptions, whenever a member of that population is in that state, his being in that state has the sort of causes and effects given by the role.

The thing to say about Martian pain is that the Martian is in pain because he is in a state that occupies the causal role of pain for Martians, whereas we are in pain because we are in a state that occupies the role of pain for us.

V

Now, what of the madman? He is in pain, but he is not in a state that occupies the causal role of pain for him. He is in a state that occupies that role for most of us, but he is an exception. The causal role of a pattern of firing of neurons depends on one's circuit diagram, and he is hooked up wrong.

His state does not occupy the role of pain for a population comprising himself and his fellow madmen. But it does occupy that role for a more salient population—mankind at large. He is a man, albeit an exceptional one, and a member of that larger population.

We have allowed for exceptions. I spoke of the definitive syndrome of *typical* causes and effects. Armstrong spoke of a state *apt for* having certain causes and effects; that does not mean that it has them invariably. Again, I spoke of a system of states that *comes near to* realizing commonsense psychology. A state may therefore occupy a role for mankind even if it does not at all occupy that role for some mad minority of mankind.

The thing to say about mad pain is that the madman is in pain because he is in the state that occupies the causal role of pain for the population comprising all mankind. He is an exceptional member of that population. The state that occupies the role for the population does not occupy it for him.

VI

We may say that X is in pain *simpliciter* if and only if X is in the state that occupies the causal role of pain for the *appropriate* population. But what is the appropriate population? Perhaps (1) it should be *us;* after all, it's our concept and our word. On the other hand, if it's X we're talking about, perhaps (2) it should be a population that X himself belongs to, and (3) it should preferably be one in which X is not exceptional. Either way, (4) an appropriate population should be a natural kind—a species, perhaps.

If X is you or I—human and unexceptional—all four considerations pull together. The appropriate population consists of mankind as it actually is, extending into other worlds only to an extent that does not make the actual majority exceptional.

Since the four criteria agree in the case of the common man, which is the case we usually have in mind, there is no reason why we should have made up our minds about their relative importance in cases of conflict. It should be no surprise if ambiguity and uncertainty arise in such cases. Still, some cases do seem reasonably clear.

If X is our Martian, we are inclined to say that he is in pain when the cavities in his feet are inflated; and so says the theory, provided that criterion (1) is outweighed by the other three, so that the appropriate population is taken to be the species of Martians to which X belongs.

If X is our madman, we are inclined to say that he is in pain when he is in the state that occupies the role of pain for the rest of us; and so says the theory, provided that criterion (3) is outweighed by the other three, so that the appropriate population is taken to be mankind.

We might also consider the case of a mad Martian, related to other Martians as the madman is to the rest of us. If X is a mad Martian, I would be inclined to say that he is in pain when the cavities in his feet are inflated; and so says our theory, provided that criteria (2) and (4) together outweigh either (1) or (3) by itself.

Other cases are less clear-cut. Since the balance is less definitely in favor of one population or another, we may perceive the relativity to population by feeling genuinely undecided. Suppose the state that plays the role of pain for us plays instead the role of thirst for a certain small subpopulation of mankind, and vice versa. When one of them has the state that is pain for us and thirst for him, there may be genuine and irresolvable indecision about whether to call him pained or thirsty—that is, whether to think of him as a madman or as a Martian. Criterion (1) suggests calling his state pain and regarding him as an exception; criteria (2) and (3) suggest shifting to a subpopulation and calling his state thirst. Criterion (4) could go either way, since mankind and the exceptional subpopulation may both be natural kinds. (Perhaps it is relevant to ask whether membership in the subpopulation is hereditary.)

The interchange of pain and thirst parallels the traditional problem of inverted spectra. I have suggested that there is no determinate fact of the matter about whether the victim of interchange undergoes pain or thirst. I think this conclusion accords well with the fact that there seems to be no persuasive solution one way or the other to the old problem of inverted spectra. I would say that there is a good sense in which the alleged victim of inverted spectra sees red when he looks at grass: he is in a state that occupies the role of seeing red for mankind in general. And there is an equally good sense in which he sees green: he is in a state that occupies the role of seeing green for him, and for a small subpopulation of which he is an unexceptional member and which has some claim to be regarded as a natural kind. You are right to say either, though not in the same breath. Need more be said?

To sum up. Armstrong and I claim to give a schema that, if filled in, would characterize pain and other states a priori. If the causal facts are right, then also we characterize pain as a physical phenomenon. By allowing for exceptional members of a population, we associate pain only contingently with its causal role. Therefore we do not deny the possibility of mad pain, provided there is not too much of it. By allowing for variation from one population to another (actual or merely possible) we associate pain only contingently with its physical realization. Therefore we do not deny the possibility of Martian pain. If different ways of filling in the relativity to population may be said to yield different senses of the word "pain," then we plead ambiguity. The madman is in pain in one sense, or relative to one population. The Martian is in pain in another sense, or relative to another population. (So is the mad Martian.)

But we do not posit ambiguity *ad hoc*. The requisite flexibility is explained simply by supposing that we have not bothered to make up our minds about semantic niceties that would make no difference to any commonplace case. The ambiguity that arises in cases of inverted spectra and the like is simply one instance of a commonplace kind of ambiguity—a kind that may arise whenever we have tacit relativity and criteria of selection that sometimes fail to choose a definite *relatum*. It is the same kind of ambiguity that arises if someone speaks of relevant studies without making clear whether he means relevance to current affairs, to spiritual well-being, to understanding, or what.

VII

We have a place for commonplace pain, mad pain, Martian pain, and even mad Martian pain. But one case remains problematic. What about pain in a being who is mad, alien, and unique? Have we made a place for that? It seems not. Since he is mad, we may suppose that his alleged state of pain does not occupy the proper causal role for him. Since he is alien, we may also suppose that it does not occupy the proper role for us. And since he is unique, it does not occupy the proper role for others of his species. What is left?

(One thing that might be left is the population consisting of him and his un-actualized counterparts at other worlds. If he went mad as a result of some improbable accident, perhaps we can say that he is in pain because he is in the state that occupies the role for most of his alternative possible selves; the state that would have occupied the role for him if he had developed in a more probable way. To make the problem as hard as possible, I must suppose that this solution is unavailable. He did *not* narrowly escape being so constituted that his present state would have occupied the role of pain.)

I think we cannot and need not solve this problem. Our only recourse is to deny that the case is possible. To stipulate that the being in this example is in pain was illegitimate. That seems credible enough. Admittedly, I might have thought offhand that the case was possible. No wonder; it merely combines elements of other cases that are possible. But I am willing to change my mind. Unlike my opinions about the possibility of mad pain and Martian pain, my naive opinions about this case are not firm enough to carry much weight.

VIII

Finally, I would like to try to preempt an objection. I can hear it said that I have been strangely silent about the very center of my topic. *What is it like* to be the madman, the Martian, the mad Martian, the victim of interchange of pain and thirst, or the being who is mad, alien, and unique? What is the *phenomenal character* of his state? If it *feels* to him like pain, then it *is* pain, whatever its causal role or physical nature. If not, it isn't. It's that simple!

Yes. It would indeed be a mistake to consider whether a state is pain while ignoring what it is like to have it. Fortunately, I have not made that mistake. Indeed, it is an impossible mistake to make. It is like the impossible mistake of considering whether a number is composite while ignoring the question of what factors it has.

Pain is a feeling.[4] Surely that is uncontroversial. To have pain and to feel pain are one and the same. For a state to be pain and for it to feel painful are likewise one and the same. A theory of what it is for a state to be pain is inescapably a theory of what it is like to be in that state, of how that state feels, of the phenomenal character of that state. Far from ignoring questions of how states feel in the odd cases we have been considering, I have been discussing nothing else! Only if you believe on independent grounds that considerations of causal role and physical realization have no bearing on whether a state is pain should you say that they have no bearing on how that state feels.

Notes

1. D. M. Armstrong, *A Materialist Theory of the Mind* (London: Routledge, 1968); "The Nature of Mind," in C. V. Borst, ed., *The Mind/Brain Identity Theory* (London: Macmillan, 1970), pp. 67-97; "The Causal Theory of the Mind," *Neue Heft für Philosophie*, no. 11 (Vendenhoek & Ruprecht, 1977), pp. 82-95. David Lewis, "An Argument for the Identity Theory," *Journal of Philosophy* 63 (1966): 17-25, reprinted with additions in David M. Rosenthal, ed., *Materialism and the Mind-Body Problem* (Englewood Cliffs, N.J.: Prentice-Hall, 1971), pp. 162-171; "Review of *Art, Mind, and Religion*," *Journal of Philosophy* 66 (1969): 22-27, particularly pp. 23-25; "Psychophysical and Theoretical Identifications," *Australasian Journal of Philosophy* 50 (1972): 249-258; "Radical Interpretation," *Synthese* 23 (1974): 331-344.

2. For instance, see Saul A. Kripke, "Naming and Necessity," in Gilbert Harman and Donald Davidson, eds., *Semantics of Natural Language* (Dordrecht: Reidel, 1972), pp. 253-355, 763-769, particularly pp. 335-336. Note that the sort of identity theory that Kripke opposes by argument, rather than by appeal to self-evidence, is not the sort that Armstrong and I propose.

3. The closest we can come is to have something at one world with twin counterparts at another. See my "Counterpart Theory and Quantified Modal Logic," *Journal of Philosophy* 65 (1968): 113-126. That possibility is irrelevant to the present case.

4. Occurrent pain, that is. Maybe a disposition that sometimes but not always causes occurrent pain might also be called "pain."

The Nature of Mental States

Hilary Putnam

The typical concerns of the Philosopher of Mind might be represented by three questions: (1) How do we know that other people have pains? (2) Are pains brain states? (3) What is the analysis of the concept *pain?* I do not wish to discuss questions (1) and (3) in this paper. I shall say something about question (2).[1]

I. Identity Questions

"Is pain a brain state?" (Or, "Is the property of having a pain at time *t* a brain state?")[2] It is impossible to discuss this question sensibly without saying something about the peculiar rules which have grown up in the course of the development of "analytical philosophy"—rules which, far from leading to an end to all conceptual confusions, themselves represent considerable conceptual confusion. These rules—which are, of course, implicit rather than explicit in the practice of most analytical philosophers—are (1) that

From W. H. Capitan and D. D. Merrill, eds., *Art, Mind, and Religion* (Pittsburgh: University of Pittsburgh Press, 1967), pp. 37-48. Copyright © 1967 by the University of Pittsburgh Press. Reprinted by permission of the publisher and the author. Originally published as "Psychological Predicates"; the title has been changed at the request of the author.

a statement of the form "being *A* is being *B*" (e.g., "being in pain is being in a certain brain state") can be *correct* only if it follows, in some sense, from the meaning of the terms *A* and *B*; and (2) that a statement of the form "being *A* is being *B*" can be philosophically *informative* only if it is in some sense reductive (e.g. "being in pain is having a certain unpleasant sensation" is not philosophically informative, "being in pain is having a certain behavior disposition" is, if true, philosophically informative). These rules are excellent rules if we still believe that the program of reductive analysis (in the style of the 1930's) can be carried out; if we don't, then they turn analytical philosophy into a mug's game, at least so far as "is" questions are concerned.

In this paper I shall use the term 'property' as a blanket term for such things as being in pain, being in a particular brain state, having a particular behavior disposition, and also for magnitudes such as temperature, etc.—i.e., for things which can naturally be represented by one-or-more-place predicates or functors. I shall use the term 'concept' for things which can be identified with synonymy-classes of expressions. Thus the concept *temperature* can be identified (I maintain) with the synonymy-class of the word 'temperature.'[3] (This is like saying that the number 2 can be identified with the class of all pairs. This is quite a different statement from the peculiar statement that 2 *is* the class of all pairs. I do not maintain that concepts *are* synonymy-classes, whatever that might mean, but that they can be identified with synonymy-classes, for the purpose of formalization of the relevant discourse.)

The question "What is the concept *temperature?*" is a very "funny" one. One might take it to mean "What is temperature? Please take my question as a conceptual one." In that case an answer might be (pretend for a moment 'heat' and 'temperature' are synonyms) "temperature is heat," or even "the concept of temperature is the same concept as the concept of heat." Or one might take it to mean "What are *concepts*, really? For example, what is 'the concept of temperature'?" In that case heaven knows what an "answer" would be. (Perhaps it would be the statement that concepts *can be identified with* synonymy-classes.)

Of course, the question "What is the property temperature?" is also "funny." And one way of interpreting it is to take it as a question about the concept of temperature. But this is not the way a physicist would take it.

The effect of saying that the property P_1 can be identical with the property P_2 only if the terms P_1, P_2 are in some suitable sense "synonyms" is, to all intents and purposes, to collapse the two notions of "property" and "concept" into a single notion. The view that concepts (intensions) *are* the same as properties has been explicitly advocated by Carnap (e.g., in *Meaning and Necessity*). This seems an unfortunate view, since "temperature is mean molecular kinetic energy" appears to be a perfectly good example of a true statement of identity of properties, whereas "the concept of temperature is the same

concept as the concept of mean molecular kinetic energy" is simply false.

Many philosophers believe that the statement "pain is a brain state" violates some rules or norms of English. But the arguments offered are hardly convincing. For example, if the fact that I can know that I am in pain without knowing that I am in brain state S shows that pain cannot be brain state S, then, by exactly the same argument, the fact that I can know that the stove is hot without knowing that the mean molecular kinetic energy is high (or even that molecules exist) shows that it is *false* that temperature is mean molecular kinetic energy, physics to the contrary. In fact, all that immediately follows from the fact that I can know that I am in pain without knowing that I am in brain state S is that the concept of pain is not the same concept as the concept of being in brain state S. But either pain, or the state of being in pain, or some pain, or some pain state, might still be brain state S. After all, the concept of temperature is not the same concept as the concept of mean molecular kinetic energy. But temperature is mean molecular kinetic energy.

Some philosophers maintain that both 'pain is a brain state' and 'pain states are brain states' are unintelligible. The answer is to explain to these philosophers, as well as we can, given the vagueness of all scientific methodology, what sorts of considerations lead one to make an empirical reduction (i.e., to say such things as "water is H_2O," "light is electro-magnetic radiation," "temperature is mean molecular kinetic energy"). If, without giving reasons, he still maintains in the face of such examples that one cannot imagine parallel circumstances for the use of 'pains are brain states' (or, perhaps, 'pain states are brain states') one has grounds to regard him as perverse.

Some philosophers maintain that "P_1 is P_2" is something that can be true, when the 'is' involved is the 'is' of empirical reduction, only when the properties P_1 and P_2 are (a) associated with a spatio-temporal region; and (b) the region is one and the same in both cases. Thus "temperature is mean molecular kinetic energy" is an admissible empirical reduction, since the temperature and the molecular energy are associated with the same space-time region, but "having a pain in my arm is being in a brain state" is not, since the spatial regions involved are different.

This argument does not appear very strong. Surely no one is going to be deterred from saying that mirror images are light reflected from an object and then from the surface of a mirror by the fact that an image can be "located" three feet *behind* the mirror. (Moreover, one can always find *some* common property of the reductions one is willing to allow—e.g., temperature is mean molecular kinetic energy—which is not a property of some one identification one wishes to disallow. This is not very impressive unless one has an argument to show that the very purposes of such identification depend upon the common property in question.)

Again, other philosophers have contended that all the predictions that can be derived from the conjunction of neurophysiological laws with such statements as "pain states are such-and-such brain states" can equally well be derived from the conjunction of the same neurophysiological laws with "being in pain is correlated with such-and-such brain states," and hence (sic!) there can be no methodological grounds for saying that pains (or pain states) *are* brain states, as opposed to saying that they are *correlated* (invariantly) with brain states. This argument, too, would show that light is only correlated with electromagnetic radiation. The mistake is in ignoring the fact that, although the theories in question may indeed lead to the same predictions, they open and exclude different *questions*. "Light is in-

variantly correlated with electromagnetic radiation" would leave open the questions "What is the light then, if it isn't the same as the electromagnetic radiation?" and "What makes the light accompany the electromagnetic radiation?" — questions which are excluded by saying that the light *is* the electromagnetic radiation. Similarly, the purpose of saying that pains are brain states is precisely to exclude from empirical meaningfulness the questions "What is the pain, then, if it isn't the same as the brain state?" and "What makes the pain accompany the brain state?" If there are grounds to suggest that these questions represent, so to speak, the wrong way to look at the matter, then those grounds are grounds for a theoretical identification of pains with brain states.

If all arguments to the contrary are unconvincing, shall we then conclude that it is meaningful (and perhaps true) to say either that pains are brain states or that pain states are brain states?

(1) It is perfectly meaningful (violates no "rule of English," involves no "extension of usage") to say "pains are brain states."

(2) It is not meaningful (involves a "changing of meaning" or "an extension of usage," etc.) to say "pains are brain states."

My own position is not expressed by either (1) or (2). It seems to me that the notions "change of meaning" and "extension of usage" are simply so ill-defined that one cannot in fact say *either* (1) or (2). I see no reason to believe that either the linguist, or the man-on-the-street, or the philosopher possesses today a notion of "change of meaning" applicable to such cases as the one we have been discussing. The *job* for which the notion of change of meaning was developed in the history of the language was just a *much* cruder job than this one.

But, if we don't assert either (1) or (2)

—in other words, if we regard the "change of meaning" issue as a pseudo-issue in this case—then how are we to discuss the question with which we started? "Is pain a brain state?"

The answer is to allow statements of the form "pain is A," where 'pain' and 'A' are in no sense synonyms, and to see whether any such statement can be found which might be acceptable on empirical and methodological grounds. This is what we shall now proceed to do.

II. Is Pain a Brain State?

We shall discuss "Is pain a brain state?," then. And we have agreed to waive the "change of meaning" issue.

Since I am discussing not what the concept of pain comes to, but what pain is, in a sense of 'is' which requires empirical theory-construction (or, at least, empirical speculation), I shall not apologize for advancing an empirical hypothesis. Indeed, my strategy will be to argue that pain is *not* a brain state, not on *a priori* grounds, but on the grounds that another hypothesis is more plausible. The detailed development and verification of my hypothesis would be just as Utopian a task as the detailed development and verification of the brain-state hypothesis. But the putting-forward, not of detailed and scientifically "finished" hypotheses, but of schemata for hypotheses, has long been a function of philosophy. I shall, in short, argue that pain is not a brain state, in the sense of a physical-chemical state of the brain (or even the whole nervous system), but another *kind* of state entirely. I propose the hypothesis that pain, or the state of being in pain, is a functional state of a whole organism.

To explain this it is necessary to introduce some technical notions. In previous papers I have explained the notion of a Turing Machine and discussed the use of this notion as a model for an organism. The notion of a Probabilistic Automaton is defined similarly to a Turing Machine, except that the transitions between "states" are allowed to be with various probabilities rather than being "deterministic." (Of course, a Turing Machine is simply a special kind of Probabilistic Automaton, one with transition probabilities 0, 1.) I shall assume the notion of a Probabilistic Automaton has been generalized to allow for "sensory inputs" and "motor outputs"—that is, the Machine Table specifies, for every possible combination of a "state" and a complete set of "sensory inputs," an "instruction" which determines the probability of the next "state," and also the probabilities of the "motor outputs." (This replaces the idea of the Machine as printing on a tape.) I shall also assume that the physical realization of the sense organs responsible for the various inputs, and of the motor organs, is specified, but that the "states" and the "inputs" themselves are, as usual, specified only "implicitly"—i.e., by the set of transition probabilities given by the Machine Table.

Since an empirically given system can simultaneously be a "physical realization" of many different Probabilistic Automata, I introduce the notion of a *Description* of a system. A Description of S where S is a system, is any true statement to the effect that S possesses distinct states $S_1, S_2, \ldots, S_n$ which are related to one another and to the motor outputs and sensory inputs by the transition probabilities given in such-and-such a Machine Table. The Machine Table mentioned in the Description will then be called the Functional Organization of S relative to that Description, and the S_i such that S is in state S_i at a given time will be called the Total State of S (at that time) relative to that Description. It should be noted that knowing the Total State of a system relative to a Description involves knowing a good deal about how the system is likely to "behave," given various combinations of sensory inputs, but does *not* involve knowing the physical realization of the S_i as, e.g., physical-chemical states of the brain. The S_i, to repeat, are specified only *implicitly* by the Description—i.e., specified *only* by the set of transition probabilities given in the Machine Table.

The hypothesis that "being in pain is a functional state of the organism" may now be spelled out more exactly as follows:

(1) All organisms capable of feeling pain are Probabilistic Automata.

(2) Every organism capable of feeling pain possesses at least one Description of a certain kind (i.e., being capable of feeling pain *is* possessing an appropriate kind of Functional Organization).

(3) No organism capable of feeling pain possesses a decomposition into parts which separately possess Descriptions of the kind referred to in (2).

(4) For every Description of the kind referred to in (2), there exists a subset of the sensory inputs such that an organism with that Description is in pain when and only when some of its sensory inputs are in that subset.

This hypothesis is admittedly vague, though surely no vaguer than the brain-state hypothesis in its present form. For example, one would like to know more about the kind of Functional Organization that an organism must have to be capable of feeling pain, and more about the marks that distinguish the subset of the sensory inputs referred to in (4). With respect to the first question, one can probably say that the Functional Organization must include something that resembles a "preference function," or at least a preference partial ordering, and something that resembles an "inductive logic" (i.e., the Machine must be able to "learn from experience"). (The meaning of these conditions, for Automata models, is discussed in my paper "The Mental Life of Some Machines.") In addition, it seems natural to require that the Machine possess "pain sensors," i.e., sensory organs which normally signal damage to the Machine's body, or dangerous temperatures, pressures, etc., which transmit a special subset of the inputs, the subset referred to in (4). Finally, and with respect to the second question, we would want to require at least that the inputs in the distinguished subset have a high disvalue on the Machine's preference function or ordering (further conditions are discussed in "The Mental Life of Some Machines"). The purpose of condition (3) is to rule out such "organisms" (if they can count as such) as swarms of bees as single pain-feelers. The condition (1) is, obviously, redundant, and is only introduced for expository reasons. (It is, in fact, empty, since everything is a Probabilistic Automaton under *some* Description.)

I contend, in passing, that this hypothesis, in spite of its admitted vagueness, is far *less* vague than the "physical-chemical state" hypothesis is today, and far more susceptible to investigation of both a mathematical and an empirical kind. Indeed, to investigate this hypothesis is just to attempt to produce "mechanical" models of organisms—and isn't this, in a sense, just what psychology is about? The difficult step, of course, will be to pass from models of *specific* organisms to a *normal form* for the psychological description of organisms—for this is what is required to make (2) and (4) precise. But this too seems to be an inevitable part of the program of psychology.

I shall now compare the hypothesis just advanced with (a) the hypothesis that pain is a brain state, and (b) the hypothesis that pain is a behavior disposition.

III. Functional State versus Brain State

It may, perhaps, be asked if I am not somewhat unfair in taking the brain-state theorist to be talking about *physical-chemical* states of the brain. But (a) these are the only sorts of states ever mentioned by brain-state theorists. (b) The brain-state theorist usually mentions (with a certain pride, slightly reminiscent of the Village Atheist) the incompatibility of his hypothesis with all forms of dualism and mentalism. This is natural if physical-chemical states of the brain are what is at issue. However, functional states of whole systems are something quite different. In particular, the functional-state hypothesis is *not* incompatible with dualism! Although it goes without saying that the hypothesis is "mechanistic" in its inspiration, it is a slightly remarkable fact that a system consisting of a body and a "soul," if such things there be, can perfectly well be a Probabilistic Automaton. (c) One argument advanced by Smart is that the brain-state theory assumes only "physical" properties, and Smart finds "non-physical" properties unintelligible. The Total States and the "inputs" defined above are, of course, neither mental nor physical *per se*, and I cannot imagine a functionalist advancing this argument. (d) If the brain-state theorist does mean (or at least allow) states other than physical-chemical states, then his hypothesis is completely empty, at least until he specifies *what* sort of "states" he *does* mean.

Taking the brain-state hypothesis in this way, then, what reasons are there to prefer the functional-state hypothesis over the brain-state hypothesis? Consider what the brain-state theorist has to do to make good his claims. He has to specify a physical-chemical state such that *any* organism (not just a mammal) is in pain if and only if (a) it possesses a brain of a suitable physical-chemical structure; and (b) its brain is in that physical-chemical state. This means that the physical-chemical state in question must be a possible state of a mammalian brain, a reptilian brain, a mollusc's brain (octopuses are mollusca, and certainly feel pain), etc. At the same time, it must *not* be a possible (physically possible) state of the brain of any physically possible creature that cannot feel pain. Even if such a state can be found, it must be nomologically certain that it will also be a state of the brain of any extraterrestrial life that may be found that will

be capable of feeling pain before we can even entertain the supposition that it may *be* pain.

It is not altogether impossible that such a state will be found. Even though octopus and mammal are examples of parallel (rather than sequential) evolution, for example, virtually identical structures (physically speaking) have evolved in the eye of the octopus and in the eye of the mammal, notwithstanding the fact that this organ has evolved from different kinds of cells in the two cases. Thus it is at least possible that parallel evolution, all over the universe, might *always* lead to *one and the same* physical "correlate" of pain. But this is certainly an ambitious hypothesis.

Finally, the hypothesis becomes still more ambitious when we realize that the brain state theorist is not just saying that *pain* is a brain state; he is, of course, concerned to maintain that *every* psychological state is a brain state. Thus if we can find even one psychological predicate which can clearly be applied to both a mammal and an octopus (say "hungry"), but whose physical-chemical "correlate" is different in the two cases, the brain-state theory has collapsed. It seems to me overwhelmingly probable that we can do this. Granted, in such a case the brain-state theorist can save himself by *ad hoc* assumptions (e.g., defining the disjunction of two states to be a single "physical-chemical state"), but this does not have to be taken seriously.

Turning now to the considerations *for* the functional-state theory, let us begin with the fact that we identify organisms as in pain, or hungry, or angry, or in heat, etc., on the basis of their *behavior*. But it is a truism that similarities in the behavior of two systems are at least a reason to suspect similarities in the functional organization of the two systems, and a much *weaker* reason to suspect similarities in the actual physical details. Moreover, we expect the various psychological states—at least the basic ones, such as hunger, thirst, aggression, etc.—to have more or less similar "transition probabilities" (within wide and ill-defined limits, to be sure) with each other and with behavior in the case of different species, because this is an artifact of the way in which we identify these states. Thus, we would not count an animal as *thirsty* if its "unsatiated" behavior did not seem to be directed toward drinking and was not followed by "satiation for liquid." Thus any animal that we count as capable of these various states will at least *seem* to have a certain rough kind of functional organization. And, as already remarked, if the program of finding psychological laws that are not species-specific—i.e., of finding a normal form for psychological theories of different species—ever succeeds, then it will bring in its wake a delineation of the kind of functional organization that is necessary and sufficient for a given psychological state, as well as a precise definition of the notion "psychological state." In contrast, the brain-state theorist has to hope for the eventual development of neurophysiological laws that are species-independent, which seems much less reasonable than the hope that psychological laws (of a sufficiently general kind) may be species-independent, or, still weaker, that a species-independent *form* can be found in which psychological laws can be written.

IV. Functional State versus Behavior-Disposition

The theory that being in pain is neither a brain state nor a functional state but a behavior disposition has one apparent advantage: it appears to agree with the way in which we verify that organisms are in pain. We do not in practice know anything about the brain state of an animal when we say that it is in pain; and we possess little if any knowledge of its functional organization, except in a crude intuitive way. In fact, however, this "advantage" is no advantage at all: for, although statements about how we verify that x is A may have a good deal to do with what the concept of being A comes to, they have precious little to do with what the property A *is*. To argue on the ground just mentioned that pain is neither a brain state nor a functional state is like arguing that heat is not mean molecular kinetic energy from the fact that ordinary people do not (they think) ascertain the mean molecular kinetic energy of something when they verify that it is hot or cold. It is not necessary that they should; what is necessary is that the marks that they take as indications of heat should in fact be explained by the mean molecular kinetic energy. And, similarly, it is necessary to our hypothesis that the marks that are taken as behavioral indications of pain should be explained by the fact that the organism is in a functional state of the appropriate kind, but not that speakers should *know* that this is so.

The difficulties with "behavior disposition" accounts are so well known that I shall do little more than recall them here. The difficulty—it appears to be more than a "difficulty," in fact—of specifying the required behavior disposition except as "the disposition of X to behave as if X were in *pain*," is the chief one, of course. In contrast, we *can* specify the functional state with which we propose to identify pain, at least roughly, without using the notion of pain. Namely, the functional state we have in mind is the state of receiving sensory inputs which play a certain role in the Functional Organization of the organism. This role is characterized, at least partially, by the fact that the sense organs responsible for the inputs in question are organs whose function is to detect damage to the body, or dangerous extremes of temperature, pressure, etc., and by the fact that the "inputs" themselves, whatever their physical realization, represent a condition that the organism assigns a high disvalue to. As I stressed in "The Mental

Life of Some Machines," this does *not* mean that the Machine will always *avoid* being in the condition in question ("pain"); it only means that the condition will be avoided unless not avoiding it is necessary to the attainment of some more highly valued goal. Since the behavior of the Machine (in this case, an organism) will depend not merely on the sensory inputs, but also on the Total State (i.e., on other values, beliefs, etc.), it seems hopeless to make any general statement about how an organism in such a condition *must* behave; but this does not mean that we must abandon hope of characterizing the condition. Indeed, we have just characterized it.[4]

Not only does the behavior-disposition theory seem hopelessly vague; if the "behavior" referred to is peripheral behavior, and the relevant stimuli are peripheral stimuli (e.g., we do not say anything about what the organism will do if its brain is operated upon), then the theory seems clearly false. For example, two animals with all motor nerves cut will have the same actual and potential "behavior" (viz., none to speak of); but if one has cut pain fibers and the other has uncut pain fibers, then one will feel pain and the other won't. Again, if one person has cut pain fibers, and another suppresses all pain responses deliberately due to some strong compulsion, then the actual and potential peripheral behavior may be the same, but one will feel pain and the other won't. (Some philosophers maintain that this last case is conceptually impossible, but the only evidence for this appears to be that *they* can't, or don't want to, conceive of it.)[5] If, instead of pain, we take some sensation the "bodily expression" of which is easier to suppress—say, a slight coolness in one's left little finger—the case becomes even clearer.

Finally, even if there *were* some behavior disposition invariantly correlated with pain (species-independently!), and specifiable without using the term 'pain,' it would still be more plausible to identify being in pain with some state whose presence *explains* this behavior disposition— the brain state or functional state—than with the behavior disposition itself. Such considerations of plausibility may be somewhat subjective; but if other things *were* equal (of course, they aren't) why shouldn't we allow considerations of plausibility to play the deciding role?

V. Methodological Considerations

So far we have considered only what might be called the "empirical" reasons for saying that being in pain is a functional state, rather than a brain state or a behavior disposition; viz., that it seems more likely that the functional state we described is invariantly "correlated" with pain, species-independently, than that there is either a physical-chemical state of the brain (must an organism have a *brain* to feel pain? perhaps some ganglia will do) or a behavior disposition so correlated. If this is correct, then it follows that the identification we proposed is at least a candidate for consideration. What of methodological considerations?

The methodological considerations are roughly similar in all cases of reduction, so no surprises need be expected here. First, identification of psychological states with functional states means that the laws of psychology can be derived from statements of the form "such-and-such organisms have such-and-such Descriptions" together with the identification statements ("being in pain is such-and-such a functional state," etc.). Secondly, the presence of the functional state (i.e., of inputs which play the role we have described in the Functional Organization of the organism) is not merely "correlated with" but actually explains the pain behavior on the part of the organism. Thirdly, the identification serves to exclude questions which (if a naturalistic view is correct) represent an altogether wrong way of looking at the matter, e.g., "What *is* pain if it isn't either the brain state or the functional state?" and "What causes the pain to be always accompanied by this sort of functional state?" In short, the identification is to be tentatively accepted as a theory which leads to both fruitful predictions and to fruitful *questions*, and which serves to discourage fruitless and empirically senseless questions, where by 'empirically senseless' I mean "senseless" not merely from the standpoint of verification, but from the standpoint of what there in fact *is*.

Notes

1. I have discussed these and related topics in the following papers: "Minds and Machines," in *Dimensions of Mind*, ed. Sidney Hook, New York, 1960, pp. 148-179; "Brains and Behavior," in *Analytical Philosophy*, second series, ed. Ronald Butler, Oxford, 1965, pp. 1-20; and "The Mental Life of Some Machines," in *Intentionality, Minds, and Perception*, ed. Hector-Neri Castañeda, Detroit, 1967, pp. 177-200.

2. In this paper I wish to avoid the vexed question of the relation between *pains* and *pain states*. I only remark in passing that one common argument *against* identification of these two—viz., that a pain can be in one's arm but a state (of the organism) cannot be in one's arm—is easily seen to be fallacious.

3. There are some well-known remarks by Alonzo Church on this topic. Those remarks do not bear (as might at first be supposed) on the identification of concepts with synonymy-classes as such, but rather support the view that (in formal semantics) it is necessary to retain Frege's distinction between the normal and the "oblique" use of expressions. That is, even if we say that the concept of temperature *is* the synonymy-class of the word 'temperature,' we must not thereby be led into the error of supposing that 'the concept of temperature' is synonymous with 'the synonymy-class of the word "temperature" ' —for then 'the concept of temperature' and 'der Begriff der Temperatur' would not be synonymous, which they are. Rather, we must say that 'the concept of temperature' *refers to* the synonymy-class of the word 'temperature' (on this particular reconstruction); but that class is *identified* not as "the synonymy class to which such-and-such a word belongs," but in another way (e.g., as the synonymy-class whose members have such-and-such a characteristic use).

4. In "The Mental Life of Some Machines" a further, and somewhat independent, characteristic of the pain inputs is discussed in terms of Automata models—namely the spontaneity of the inclination to withdraw the injured part, etc. This raises the question, which is discussed in that paper, of giving a functional analysis of the notion of a spontaneous inclination. Of course, still further characteristics come readily to mind—for example, that feelings of pain are (or seem to be) *located* in the parts of the body.

5. Cf. the discussion of "super-spartans" in "Brains and Behavior."

Review of Putnam

David Lewis

Representing mind, there is Hilary Putnam's "Psychological Predicates," one of several papers[1] in which Putnam presents the hypothesis that mental states— pain, for example—are not brain states and not behavior dispositions, but rather *functional states* of organisms. A functional state is a state specified implicitly by its place in a *functional description* of the organism: a true statement to the effect that the organism possesses states $S_1, \ldots, S_n$ governed by a network of laws of the form:

If the organism is in state S_i and receives so-and-so sensory input, then with so-and-so probability the organism will go into state S_j and produce so-and-so motor output.

An example of a functional description (in which the transition probabilities are all 0 or 1) is given by the machine table for a Turing machine, provided we regard the tape not as part of the machine but as an external source of inputs and recipient of

From "Review of *Art, Mind, and Religion*" in *Journal of Philosophy* 66 (1969): 23-35. Reprinted by permission of *Journal of Philosophy* and the author. [*Editor's note:* Putnam's "Psychological Predicates" is reprinted as "The Nature of Mental States," chap. 17, this volume.]

outputs. I take it that a (nonphysiological) psychological theory—or better, the Ramsey sentence thereof—is a functional description, and that state-names introduced by that theory name functional states.

Putnam offers his hypothesis that pain is a functional state as a rival to the hypothesis that pain is a brain state; hence he takes it that whatever reasons count in favor of the functional-state hypothesis count also against the brain-state hypothesis. Putnam announces that his strategy "will be to argue that pain is not a brain state, not on *a priori* grounds, but on the grounds that another hypothesis is more plausible." In fact, he starts by *defending* the brain-state hypothesis against some attempted *a priori* refutations.

I do not think Putnam has shown that pain cannot be *both* a brain state and a functional state, these being identical. The concept of any functional state as such does, of course, differ from the concept of any brain state as such. But Putnam is alive to the possibility that different concepts might be concepts of the same state; this observation is part of his own defense of the brain-state hypothesis against *a priori* objections. Suppose pain is indeed a certain functional state S_{17} in an appropriate functional description;

suppose the description is realized *inter alia* by the human brain states $B_1, \ldots, B_n$, respectively. Those are the states that are lawfully related to one another, and to suitable human inputs and outputs, by the proper transition probabilities. Why not conclude that pain $= S_{17} = B_{17}$ (in the case of humans)? On this view, a functional state is better called a *functionally specified* state, and might happen to be a functionally specified brain state.

Putnam argues that the brain-state hypothesis (and with it, the functionally-specified-brain-state hypothesis) ought to be rejected as scientifically implausible. He imagines the brain-state theorist to claim that all organisms in pain—be they men, mollusks, Martians, machines, or what have you—are in some single common nondisjunctive physical-chemical brain state. Given the diversity of organisms, that claim *is* incredible. But the brain-state theorist who makes it is a straw man. A reasonable brain-state theorist would anticipate that pain might well be one brain state in the case of men, and some other brain (or nonbrain) state in the case of mollusks. It might even be one brain state in the case of Putnam, another in the case of Lewis. No mystery: that is just like saying that the winning number is 17 in the case of this week's lottery, 137 in the case of last week's. The seeming contradiction (one thing identical to two things) vanishes once we notice the tacit relativity to context in one term of the identities. Of course no one says that the *concept* of pain is different in the case of different organisms (or that the *concept* of the winning number is different in the case of different lotteries). It is the *fixed* concept expressed by 'pain' that determines how the denotation of 'pain' varies with the nature of the organism in question. Moral: the brain-state theorist cannot afford the old prejudice that a name of a necessary being (such as a state) must name it necessarily and independently of context.

Notes

1. Others are: "Minds and Machines," in *Dimensions of Mind*, ed. S. Hook (New York: N.Y.U. Press, 1960); "Brains and Behavior," in *Analytical Philosophy: Second Series*, ed. R. Butler (Oxford: Blackwell & Mott, 1965); "The Mental Life of Some Machines," in *Intentionality, Minds, and Perception*, ed. H.-N. Castañeda (Detroit: Wayne State Univ. Press, 1966); "Robots: Machines or Artificially Created Life?" *Journal of Philosophy* 61, 21 (Dec. 12, 1964): 668-691.

Physicalism and the Multiple Realizability of Mental States

Jaegwon Kim

In a series of articles Hilary Putnam has argued against the identity theory. His central contention has been that the theory makes an extremely strong empirical claim which, in Putnam's opinion, we have reason to believe to be false. And this empirical claim is just what we have called the thesis of psychophysical correspondence. According to Putnam,

> [The identity theorist] has to specify a physical-chemical state such that *any* organism (not just a mammal) is in pain if and only if (a) it possesses a brain of a suitable physical-chemical structure; and (b) its brain is in that physical-chemical state. This means that the physical-chemical state in question must be a possible state of a mammalian brain, a reptilian brain, a mollusc's brain . . . At the same time, it must *not* be a possible (physically possible) state of the brain of any physically possible creature that cannot feel pain. . . .
>
> Finally, the hypothesis becomes still more ambitious when we realize that the brain state theorist is not just saying that *pain* is a brain state; he is, of course, con-

cerned to maintain that *every* psychological state is a brain state. Thus if we can find even one psychological predicate which can clearly be applied to both a mammal and an octopus (say "hungry"), but whose physical-chemical "correlate" is different in the two cases, the brain-state theory has collapsed. It seems to me overwhelmingly probable that we can do this.[1]

Now, it is of course to be granted that a mollusc's brain is indeed very different from the human brain in its physico-chemical structure—in fact, in its biological organization. What can we infer from this? Take even a more extreme case: the very crude nervous system of the planarian. Here the overwhelming temptation is to say that because of the primitive structure of the nervous system, the creature does not, in fact cannot, have any sensations. And if a creature is found that exhibits what we would consider an appropriate pattern of avoidance behavior with respect to a certain type of "noxious stimulus" we would still not likely attribute to it the *sensation* of pain if the physicochemical organization of its "brain" were found to be radically different from ours.[2]

In any case, the fact that two brains are physico-chemically different does not entail that the two brains cannot be in the

From "Phenomenal Properties, Psychophysical Laws, and the Identity Theory," *Monist* 56, no. 2 (1972): 177-192. Reprinted by permission of the publisher and the author. Notes have been renumbered for this edition.

"same physico-chemical state." Even if we disallow the *ad hoc* creation of new states by forming arbitrary disjunctions, the remaining possibilities are indeed limitless. To argue that the human brain and the canine brain cannot be in the same brain state because of their different physico-chemical structure is like arguing that there can be no microphysical state underlying temperature because all kinds of objects with extremely diverse microphysical compositions can have the same temperature; or that water-solubility cannot have a microstructural "correlate" because both salt and sugar which differ a great deal from each other in atomic composition are soluble in water. If the human brain and the reptilian brain can be in the same "temperature state," why can they be not in the same "brain state," where this state is characterized in physico-chemical terms?

Two considerations, therefore, seem to mitigate the sting of Putnam's argument considerably. First, the less the physical basis of the nervous system of some organisms resembles ours, the less temptation there will be for ascribing to them sensations or other phenomenal events. Second, the mere fact that the physical bases of two nervous systems are different in material composition or physical organization with respect to a certain scheme of classification does not entail that they cannot be in the same physical state with respect to a different scheme. Sameness and difference of states depend on the abstract characterization of the states involved; difference in material composition with respect to the kinds of atoms involved, for example, does not imply difference in the mean kinetic energy of the molecules.

Further, there seems to be another, more direct way of handling Putnam's objection. Let us assume that the brain correlate of pain is species-dependent, so that we have generalizations like "Humans are in pain just in case they are in brain state A," "Canines are in pain just in case they are in brain state B," and so on. These species-dependent correlations do not of course warrant the species-independent blanket identification of pains with a "single" brain state (assuming that we refrain from making up "disjunctive states," although I think this is an arguable point). But they clearly do warrant—at least they are not inconsistent with—the identification of *human pains* with *human brain state A*, canine pains with *canine brain state B*, and so on. That is to say, *species-specific correlations warrant species-specific identities*.

There seems to be no reason to think that such species-specific identities are insufficient for the identity theory. If all mental events are brought under such identities, a monistic theory of the mental in which the mental is identified with the physical on the basis of empirically discovered mental-physical correlations will have been attained. And these correlations with limited scopes would be just as good as broader correlations in providing reductive explanations of specific mental phenomena in terms of physical laws; they would provide us with "bridge laws" for the mental and the physical; and if the species-independent psychophysical laws turn out to be "nomological danglers" under dualism, these species-dependent psychophysical laws would equally dangle under a dualistic interpretation. Thus, there seems to be no philosophical or methodological reason for thinking that the situation would be radically altered for the identity theory if species-specific psychophysical correlations are all we could get.

We of course should not expect to find a physical correlate for every type of mental event we commonly distinguish in daily discourse; it seems unlikely, for example, that there is some uniform neural correlate for thinking of Vienna, remembering to pay the rent, or wanting to go to the Bahamas.[3] But this situation is hardly peculiar to mental events; we do not expect to find a microphysical basis uniquely correlating with, say, tables either. But this is not to say that some tables are not physico-chemical structures or that some aspects of tables are not explicable in terms of their microphysical properties. And it is for these "aspects" of tables that we expect to find microphysical correlates: temperature, inflammability, ductility (a given table may be made of stainless steel), thermal and electrical conductivity, color, and so on. Somewhat analogously, wanting to go to the Bahamas may have different "contents" in each case of its exemplifications; I may be thinking (in the occurrent sense) of the beautiful beaches, you may be having the visual image of the green ocean, and someone else may be recalling a pictorial spread in a promotional magazine. And each of these events may have a neural correlate. Or, perhaps, they have to be analyzed into more basic phenomenal (and perhaps also dispositional) components before we can seriously look for neural correlates.

What are the "aspects" or "components" of a given occurrence of wanting to go to the Bahamas for which we would expect, or need, neural correlates? How do we distinguish these from the rest for which we do not have such expectations? And why? And what implications do answers to these questions have for the possibility of a complete reductive explanation of the mental on the basis of the neural?

I do not believe we have clear answers to these questions—not even when they are raised with respect to reductive explanations within the physical domain. In any case, the task of finding neural correlates seems a good deal more promising for sensory events, and, as earlier noted, the identity theory is most often formulated as a thesis about sensations and other phenomenal events. The important point is that we cannot at this point be definite about the range of mental properties to be comprehended by the thesis of psychophysical correspondence, that is, those mental properties for which we need to find neural correlates to make the thesis true. And there probably is no way of fixing these properties once and for all. These properties roughly correspond to what we might call "natural kinds" among mental properties, and the classification of a given property as a natural kind depends very much on the role it plays in the scientific theorizing of the time.[4] As progress is made in the relevant branches of science, the map of the mental will be redrawn many times before we obtain, if ever, a map that is roughly isomorphic to a map of the neural. But of course this kind of conceptual readjustment would be by no means a peculiar feature of the mental-physical reduction.

Notes

1. Hilary Putnam, "Psychological Predicates," in *Art, Mind and Religion*, ed. by W. H. Capitan and D. D. Merrill (Pittsburgh: University of Pittsburgh Press, 1967), pp. 44-45.

2. Especially if, as some physiological psychologists believe, the sensory aspect of pain can be distinguished physiologically from its affective and motivational aspects. See, e.g., Ronald Melzack, "The Perception of Pain," *Scientific American*, February 1961.

3. This is noted by Nagel, in "Physicalism," pp. 351-352.

4. See, e.g., Carl G. Hempel, *Fundamentals of Concept Formation in Empirical Science* (Chicago: University of Chicago Press, 1952); and W. V. Quine, "Natural Kinds" in his *Ontological Relativity and Other Essays* (New York: Columbia University Press, 1969).

What Psychological States Are Not

Ned Block and Jerry A. Fodor

I

As far as anyone knows, different organisms are often in psychological states of exactly the same type at one time or another, and a given organism is often in psychological states of exactly the same type at different times. Whenever either is the case, we shall say of the psychological states of the organism(s) in question that they are *type identical.*[1]

One thing that currently fashionable theories in the philosophy of mind often try to do is characterize the conditions for type identity of psychological states. For example, some varieties of philosophical behaviorism claim that two organisms are in type-identical psychological states if and only if certain of their behaviors or behavioral dispositions are type identical. Analogously, some (though not all) varieties of physicalism claim that organisms are in type-identical psychological states if and only if certain of their physical states are type identical.[2]

In so far as they are construed as theories about the conditions for type identity of psychological states, it seems in-

From *Philosophical Review* 81, no. 2 (April 1972): 159-181. Reprinted, with revisions by the authors, by permission of *Philosophical Review* and the authors.

creasingly unlikely that either behaviorism or physicalism is true. Since the arguments for this conclusion are widely available in the literature, we shall provide only the briefest review here.[3]

The fundamental argument against behaviorism is simply that what an organism does or is disposed to do at a given time is a very complicated function of its beliefs and desires together with its current sensory inputs and memories. It is thus enormously unlikely that it will prove possible to pair behavioral predicates with psychological predicates in the way that behaviorism requires—namely, that, for each type of psychological state, an organism is in that state if and only if a specified behavioral predicate is true of it. This suggests that behaviorism is overwhelmingly likely to be false simply in virtue of its empirical consequences and independent of its implausibility as a semantic thesis. Behaviorism cannot be true unless mind/behavior correlationism is true, and mind/behavior correlationism is not true.

The argument against physicalism rests upon the empirical likelihood that creatures of different composition and structure, which are in no interesting sense in identical physical states, can nevertheless be in identical psychological states; hence that types of psychological states are not in correspondence with types of physical states. This point has been made persuasively in Putnam's "Psychological Predicates." In essence, it rests on appeals to the following three kinds of empirical considerations.

First, the Lashleyan doctrine of neurological equipotentiality holds that any of a wide variety of psychological functions can be served by any of a wide variety of brain structures. While the generality of this doctrine may be disputed, it does seem clear that the central nervous system is highly labile and that a given type of psychological process is in fact often associated with a variety of distinct neurological structures. For example, though linguistic functions are normally represented in the left hemisphere of right-handed persons, insult to the left hemisphere can lead to the establishment of these functions in the *right* hemisphere. (Of course, this point is not *conclusive*, since there may be some relevant neurological property in common to the structures involved.) Physicalism, as we have been construing it, requires that organisms are in type-identical psychological states if and only if they are in type-identical physical states. Hence, equipotentiality (if true) provides evidence against physicalism.

The second consideration depends on the assumption that the Darwinian doctrine of convergence applies to the phylogeny of psychology as well as to the phylogeny of morphology and of behavior. It is well known that superficial morphological similarities between organisms may represent no more than parallel evolutionary solutions of the same environmental problem: in particular, that they may be the expression of quite different types of physiological structure. The analogous point about behavioral similarities across species has been widely recognized in the ethological literature: organisms of

widely differing phylogeny and morphology may nevertheless come to exhibit superficial behavioral similarities in response to convergent environmental pressures. The present point is that the same considerations may well apply to the phylogeny of the psychology of organisms. Psychological similarities across species may often reflect convergent environmental selection rather than underlying physiological similarities. For example, we have no particular reason to suppose that the physiology of pain in man must have much in common with the physiology of pain in phylogenetically remote species. But if there are organisms whose psychology is homologous to our own but whose physiology is quite different, such organisms may provide counterexamples to the psychophysical correlations physicalism requires.

Finally, if we allow the conceptual possibility that psychological predicates could apply to artifacts, then it seems likely that physicalism will prove empirically false. For it seems very likely that given any psychophysical correlation which holds for an organism, it is possible to build a machine which is similar to the organism psychologically, but physiologically sufficiently different from the organism that the psychophysical correlation does not hold for the machine.

What these arguments seem to show is that the conditions that behaviorism and physicalism seek to place upon the type identity of psychological states of organisms are, in a relevant sense, insufficiently abstract. It seems likely that organisms which differ in their behavior or behavioral dispositions can nevertheless be in type-identical psychological states, as can organisms that are in different physical states. (We shall presently discuss a "functionalist" approach to type identity which attempts to set the identity criteria at a level more abstract than physicalism or behaviorism acknowledge.)

Of course, it is *possible* that the type-to-type correspondences required by behaviorism or by physicalism should turn out to obtain. The present point is that even if behavioral or physical states *are* in one-to-one correspondence with psychological states, we have no current evidence that this is so; hence we have no warrant for adopting philosophical theories which *require* that it be so. The paradox about behaviorism and physicalism is that while most of the arguments that have surrounded these doctrines have been narrowly "conceptual," it seems increasingly likely that the decisive arguments against them are empirical.

It is often suggested that one might meet these arguments by supposing that, though neither behavioral nor physical states correspond to psychological states in a one-to-one fashion, they may nevertheless correspond many-to-one. That is, it is supposed that, for each type of psychological state, there is a distinct disjunction of types of behavioral (or physical) states, such that an organism is in the psychological state if and only if it is in one of the disjuncts.

This sort of proposal is, however, shot through with serious difficulties. First, it is less than obvious that there is, in fact, a *distinct* disjunction of behavioral (or physical) states corresponding to each psychological state. For example, there is really no reason to believe that the class of types of behaviors which, in the whole history of the universe, have (or will have) expressed rage for some organism or other, is distinct from the class of types of behaviors which have expressed, say, pain. In considering this possibility, one should bear in mind that practically any behavior might, in the appropriate circumstances, become the conventional expression of practically any psychological state and that a given organism in a given psychological state might exhibit almost any behavioral disposition depending on its beliefs and preferences. The same kind of point applies, *mutatis mutandis*, against

the assumption that there is a distinct disjunction of types of physical states corresponding to each type of psychological state, since it seems plausible that practically any type of physical state could realize practically any type of psychological state in some kind of physical system or other.

But even if there *is* a distinct disjunction of types of behavioral (or physical) states corresponding to each type of psychological state, there is no reason whatever to believe that this correspondence is lawlike; and it is not obvious what philosophical interest would inhere in the discovery of a behavioral (or physical) property which happened, accidentally, to be coextensive with a psychological predicate. Thus, as Davidson has pointed out, on the assumption that psycho-behavioral correlations are not lawlike, even "if we were to find an open sentence couched in behavioral terms and exactly coextensive with some mental predicate, nothing could reasonably persuade us that we had found it" ("Mental Events"). As Davidson has also pointed out, the same remark applies, *mutatis mutandis*, to physical predicates.

Finally, a theory which says that each psychological predicate is coextensive with a distinct disjunction of behavioral (or physical) predicates[4] is incompatible with what we have been assuming is an obvious truth: namely, that a given behavioral state may express (or a given physical state realize) different psychological states at different times. Suppose, for example, that we have a theory which says that the psychological predicate p_1 is coextensive with the disjunctive behavioral predicate A and psychological predicate p_2 is coextensive with the disjunctive behavioral predicate B. Suppose further that S_i designates a type of behavior that has sometimes expressed p_1 but not p_2 and at other times expressed p_2 but not p_1. Then, S_i will have to be a disjunct of both A and B. But, the disjuncts of A are severally sufficient conditions for p_1 and the disjuncts of B are severally sufficient conditions of p_2 on the assumption that p_1 and A, and p_2 and B, are respectively coextensive. Hence the theory entails that an organism in S_i is in both p_1 and p_2, which is logically.incompatible with the claim that S_i expresses p_1 (but not p_2) at some times and p_2 (but not p_1) at others. Of course, one could circumvent this objection by including spatiotemporal designators in the specification of the disjuncts mentioned in A and B. But to do so would be totally to abandon the project of expressing psycho-behavioral (or psychophysical) correlations by lawlike biconditionals.

II

It has recently been proposed that these sorts of difficulties can be circumvented, and an adequate theory of the conditions on type identity of psychological states can be formulated, in the following way. Let us assume that any system P to which psychological predicates can be applied has a description as a probabilistic automaton. (A probabilistic automaton is a generalized Turing machine whose machine table includes instructions associated with finite positive probabilities less than or equal to one. For a brief introduction to the notion of a Turing machine, a machine table, and related notions, see Putnam, "Psychological Predicates.") A *description* of P, in the technical sense intended here, is any true statement to the effect that P possesses distinct states S_1, $S_2, \ldots S_n$ which are related to one another and to the outputs and inputs of P by the transition probabilities given in a specified machine table. We will call the states S_1, $S_2, \ldots S_n$ specified by the *description* of an organism, the "machine table states of the organism" relative to that *description*.

It is against the background of the assumption that organisms are describable as probabilistic automata that the

present theory (hereafter "*FSIT*" for "functional state identity theory") seeks to specify conditions upon the type identity of psychological states. In particular, *FSIT* claims that for any organism that satisfies psychological predicates at all, there exists a unique best *description* such that each psychological state of the organism is identical with one of its machine table states relative to that description.

Several remarks about *FSIT* are in order. First, there is an obvious generalization of the notion of a probabilistic automaton in which it is thought of as having a separate input tape on which an "oracle" can print symbols during a computation. *FSIT* presupposes an interpretation of this generalization in which sensory transducers take the place of the "oracle" and in which outputs are thought of as instructions to motor transducers. Such an interpretation must be intended if a *description* of an organism is to provide a model of the mental operations of the organism.

Second, we have presented *FSIT* in the usual way as an *identity* theory:[5] in particular, one which claims that each type of psychological state is identical to (a type of) machine table state. Our aim, however, is to sidestep questions about the identity conditions of abstract objects and discuss only a certain class of biconditionals which type-to-type identity statements entail: that is, statements of the form "O is in such and such a type of psychological state at time t if and only if O is in such and such a type of machine table state at time t."

Third, it is worth insisting that *FSIT* amounts to more than the claim that every organism has a description as a Turing machine or as a probabilistic automaton. For there are a number of respects in which that claim is trivially true; but its truth in these respects does not entail *FSIT*. For example, if we can give a physical characterization of the state of an organism at a time (e.g., in terms of its component elementary particles) and if there is a computable physical state function (whose arguments are the physical state at t_1, the physical inputs between t_1 and t_2, and the value of $t_2 - t_1$; and whose value is the physical state at t_2), then there is a Turing machine capable of simulating the organism (by computing its physical state function) and a corresponding Turing machine description of the organism. But it is not obvious that the states mentioned in this description correspond in any natural way to the psychological states of the organism. Hence it is not obvious that this Turing machine description satisfies the requirements of *FSIT*, and it does not follow that the organism has a unique best *description* of the sort characterized above. Second, as Putnam has pointed out (in conversation), *everything* is describable as a realization of what one might call the "null" Turing machine: that is, a machine which has only one state and stays in it, and emits no output, no matter what the input. (The point is, roughly, that whether a system *P* realizes a Turing machine depends, inter alia, on what counts as a change of state in *P*, and what counts as an output of *P*. If one counts *nothing* as a change of state in *P*, or as an output of *P*, then *P* is a realization of the null Turing machine.) But again, *FSIT* would not be true if the only true *description* of an organism is as a null Turing machine, since *FSIT* requires that the machine table states of an organism correspond one-to-one with its psychological states under its best description.

There are thus two important respects in which *FSIT* involves more than the claim that organisms which satisfy psychological predicates have descriptions. First, *FSIT* claims that such systems have unique best descriptions. Second, *FSIT* claims that the types of machine table states specified by the unique best description of a system are in correspondence with the types of psychological states that the system can be in. It is this

second claim of *FSIT* with which we shall be primarily concerned.

FSIT, unlike either behaviorism or physicalism, is not an ontological theory: that is, it is neutral about what token psychological states *are*, in that as far as *FSIT* is concerned, among the systems to which psychological predicates are applicable (and which therefore have *descriptions*) might be included persons, material objects, souls, and so forth. This last point suggests how *FSIT* might meet certain of the kinds of difficulties we raised against physicalism and behaviorism. Just as *FSIT* abstracts from considerations of the ontological status of the systems which have *descriptions*, so too it abstracts from physical differences between systems which have their *descriptions* in common. As Putnam has remarked, "the *same* Turing machine (from the standpoint of the machine table) may be physically realized in a potential infinity of ways" ("The Mental Life of Some Machines," p. 271), and *FSIT* allows us to state type-identity conditions on psychological states which are neutral as between such different realizations.

Similarly, *FSIT* permits us to state such conditions in a way which abstracts from the variety of behavioral consequences which a psychological state may have. It thereby meets a type of objection which, we supposed above, was fatal to behaviorism.

We remarked that the behaviorist is committed to the view that two organisms are in the same psychological state whenever their behaviors and/or behavioral dispositions are identical; and that this theory is implausible to the extent that the behaviors and the behavioral dispositions of an organism are the effects of *interactions* between its psychological states. But *FSIT* allows us to distinguish between psychological states not only in terms of their behavioral consequences but also in terms of the character of their interconnections. This is because the criterion of

identity for machine table states acknowledges *their relations to one another* as
well as their relations to inputs and outputs. Thus, *FSIT* can cope with the characteristic indirectness of the relation between psychological states and behavior.
Indeed, *FSIT* allows us to see how psychological states which have *no* behavioral
expressions might nevertheless be distinct.

Finally, it may be remarked that
nothing precludes taking at least some of
the transitions specified in a machine table
as corresponding to causal relations in the
system which the table *describes.* In particular, since *FSIT* is compatible with
token physicalism, there is no reason why
it should not acknowledge that token
psychological states may enter into causal
relations. Thus, any advantages which
accrue to causal analyses of the psychological states, or of the relations between
psychological states and behavior, equally
accrue to *FSIT.*[6]

III

In this section we are going to review
a series of arguments which provide one
degree or another of difficulty for the
claim that *FSIT* yields an adequate account of the type-identity conditions for
psychological states. It is our view that,
taken collectively, these arguments are
fairly decisive against the theory of type
identity of psychological states that *FSIT*
proposes. In the final section we will suggest some reasons why the attempt to provide substantive type-identity conditions
on psychological states so often founders.

(1) Any account of type-identity conditions on psychological states that ad-
heres at all closely to our everyday notion
of what types of psychological states there
are will presumably have to draw a distinction between dispositional states[7] (beliefs, desires, inclinations, and so on) and
occurrent states (sensations, thoughts,
feelings, and so on). So far as we can see,
however, *FSIT* has no plausible way of
capturing this distinction short of aban-

doning its fundamental principle that psychological states correspond one-to-one
to machine table states. Suppose, for example, *FSIT* attempts to reconstruct the
distinction between occurrents and dispositions by referring to the distinction between the machine table state that an organism is *in* and all the other states specified by its machine table. Thus, one might
refine *FSIT* to read: for occurrent states,
two organisms are in type-identical psychological states if and only if they are in
the same machine table state; and, for
each dispositional state, there is a machine
table state such that an organism is in the
former if and only if its machine table
contains the latter.

This proposal has serious difficulties.
Every machine table state of an organism
is one which it is possible for the organism
to be in at some time. Hence, if the proposal is right, for an organism to be in a
dispositional state is for it to be possible
for it to be in some "corresponding" occurrent state. But it is hard to see what
sense of "corresponding" could make the
proposal true. Suppose, for example, that
what corresponds to the dispositional
"speaks French" is the occurrent "is speaking French," and what corresponds to the
dispositional "believes that *p*" is the occurrent "is thinking that *p.*" But it is ludi-
crous to suppose that someone believes
that *p* just in case it is possible for him to
think that *p*. Though we do not believe
that there are flying saucers, there are
certainly possible circumstances in which
we would be thinking that there are flying
saucers.

Now, we do not mean to deny that
necessary and sufficient conditions for the
having of dispositional states could be
given by reference to some *abstract* property of the organization of machine tables.
To take a far-fetched example, given a
normal form for descriptions, it might
turn out that an organism believes that
the sun is 93,000,000 miles from the earth
if and only if the first *n* columns in its

machine table have some such abstract property as containing only odd integers. Since saying of a machine that the first n columns . . . and so forth does not ascribe a machine table state to it, psychological states which are analyzed as corresponding to this sort of property would not thereby be described as possible occurrent states.

To take this line, however, would be to abandon a fundamental claim of *FSIT*. For, while this approach is compatible with the view that two organisms have the same psychology if and only if they have the same machine table, it is *not* compatible with the suggestion that two organisms are in the same (dispositional) psychological state if and only if they have a specified state of their machine tables in common. Hence it is incompatible with the view that psychological states are in one-to-one correspondence with machine table states. Moreover, since we have no way of telling what kinds of abstract properties of machine tables might turn out to correspond to psychological states, the present difficulty much reduces the possibility of using *FSIT* to delineate substantive type-identity conditions on psychological states. To say that psychological states correspond to some property or other of machine tables is to say something very much weaker than that psychological states correspond to machine table states. This is a kind of point to which we will return later in the discussion.

There is, of course, at least one other way out of the present difficulty for *FSIT*. It might be suggested that we ought to give up the everyday notion that there are some dispositional states which are not possible occurrent states (for example, to acknowledge an occurrent, though perhaps nonconscious, state of believing that *p*). Clearly, the possibility that we might some day have theoretical grounds for acknowledging the existence of such states cannot be precluded a priori. But we have

no such grounds *now*, and there does seem to us to be a methodological principle of conservatism to the effect that one should resist models which require empirical or conceptual changes that are not independently motivated.

(2) We suggested that *FSIT* allows us to account for the fact that behavior is characteristically the product of interactions between psychological states, and that the existence of such interactions provides a standing source of difficulty for behaviorist theories in so far as they seek to assign characteristic behaviors *severally* to psychological states. It is empirically immensely likely, however, that there are *two* kinds of behaviorally efficacious interactions between psychological states, and *FSIT* provides for a natural model of only one of them.

On one hand, behavior can be the product of a *series* of psychological states, and the *FSIT* account shows us how this could be true, and how some of the states occurring in such a series may not themselves have behavioral expressions. But, on the other hand, behavior can be the result of interactions between *simultaneous* mental states. For example, prima facie, what an organism does at *t* may be a function of what it is feeling at *t* and what it is thinking at *t*. But *FSIT* provides no conceptual machinery for representing this state of affairs. In effect, *FSIT* can provide for the representation of sequential interactions between psychological states, but not for simultaneous interactions. Indeed *FSIT* even fails to account for the fact that an organism can be in more than one occurrent psychological state at a time, since a probabilistic automaton can be in only one machine table state at a time. The upshot of this argument seems to be that if probabilistic automata are to be used as models of an organism, the appropriate model will be a set of intercommunicating automata operating in parallel.

It is again important to keep clear on

what the argument does not show about *FSIT*. We have read *FSIT* as claiming that the psychological states of an organism are in one-to-one correspondence with the machine table states postulated in its best *description*. The present argument suggests that if this claim is to be accepted, then the best *description* of an organism must not represent it as a single probabilistic automaton. If organisms, but not single probabilistic automata, can be in more than one state at a time, then either an organism is not a single probabilistic automaton, or the psychological states of an organism do not correspond to machine table states of single probabilistic automata. (It should be remarked that there is an algorithm which will construct a single automaton equivalent to any given set of parallel automata. It cannot be the case, however, that a set of parallel automata and the equivalent single automaton *both* provide best *descriptions* of an organism.)

These remarks are of some importance since the kind of psychological theory we get on the assumption that organisms are parallel processors will look quite different from the kind we get on the assumption that they are serial processors. Indeed, while the general characteristics of serial processors are relatively well understood, very little is known about the corresponding characteristics of parallel systems.

On the other hand, this argument does not touch the main claim of *FSIT*: even if organisms are in some sense sets of probabilistic automata, it may turn out that each psychological state of an organism corresponds to a machine table state of one or other of the members of the set. In the following arguments, we will assume the serial model for purposes of simplicity and try to show that, even on that assumption, psychological states do not correspond to machine table states.

(3) *FSIT* holds that two organisms are in psychological states of the same type if and only if they are in the same machine table state. But machine table states are identical if and only if they are identically related to other machine table states and to states of the input and output mechanisms. In this sense, the criterion for identity of machine table states is "functional equivalence." Thus *FSIT* claims that type identity of psychological states is also a matter of a certain kind of functional equivalence; psychological states are type identical if and only if they share those properties that must be specified to individuate a machine table state.

But it might plausibly be argued that this way of type-identifying psychological states fails to accommodate a feature of at least some such states that is critical for determining their type: namely, their "qualitative" character. It does not, for example, seem entirely unreasonable to suggest that nothing would be a token of the type "pain state" unless it felt like a pain, and that this would be true even if it were connected to all the other psychological states of the organism in whatever ways pains are. It seems to us that the standard verificationist counterarguments against the view that the "inverted spectrum" hypothesis is conceptually coherent are not persuasive. If this is correct, it looks as though the possibility of qualia inversion poses a serious prima-facie argument against functionalist accounts of the criteria for type identity of psychological states.

It should be noticed, however, that the inverted qualia argument is *only* a prima-facie objection against *FSIT*. In particular, it is available to the proponent of functionalist accounts to meet this objection in either of two ways. On the one hand, he might argue that though inverted qualia, *if they occurred*, would provide counterexamples to his theory, as a matter of nomological fact it is impossible that functionally identical psychological states should be qualitatively distinct: in particular, that anything which altered the qualitative characteristics of a psychological state would alter its functional characteristics. This sort of line may strike one as blatant apriorism, but, in the absence of any relevant empirical data, it might be well to adopt an attitude of wait and see.

There is, moreover, another defense open to the proponent of *FSIT*. He might say that, given two functionally identical psychological states, we would (or perhaps "should") *take* them to be type identical, independent of their qualitative properties: that is, that differences between the qualitative properties of psychological states which do not determine corresponding functional differences are *ipso facto* irrelevant to the goals of theory construction in psychology, and hence should be ignored for purposes of type identification.

To see that this suggestion may be plausible, imagine that it turns out that every person does, in fact, have slightly different qualia (or, better still, grossly different qualia) when in whatever machine table state is alleged to be identical to pain. It seems fairly clear that in this case it might be reasonable to say that the character of an organism's qualia is irrelevant to whether it is in pain or (equivalently) that pains feel quite different to different organisms.

This form of argument may, however, lead to embarrassing consequences. For all that we now know, it may be nomologically possible for two psychological states to be functionally identical (that is, to be identically connected with inputs, outputs, and successor states), even if only one of the states has a qualitative content. In this case, *FSIT* would require us to say that an organism might be in pain even though it is feeling *nothing at all*, and this consequence seems totally unacceptable.

It may be remarked that these "inverted (or absent) qualia" cases in a certain sense pose a deeper problem for *FSIT* than any of the other arguments we shall

be discussing. Our other arguments are, by and large, concerned to show that psychological states cannot be functionally defined in a certain way; namely, by being put in correspondence with machine table states. But though they are incompatible with *FSIT*, they are compatible with functionalism in the broad sense of that doctrine which holds that the type-identity conditions for psychological states refer only to their relations to inputs, outputs, and one another. The present consideration, however, might be taken to show that psychological states cannot be functionally defined *at all* and that they cannot be put into correspondence with *any* properties definable over abstract automata. We will ignore this possibility in what follows, since if psychological states are not functional states at all, the question whether they are machine table states simply does not arise.

(4) We remarked that there are arguments against behaviorism and physicalism which suggest that each proposes constraints upon type-identity conditions on psychological states that are, in one way or another, insufficiently abstract. We will now argue that *FSIT* is susceptible to the same kind of objection.

A machine table specifies a state in terms of a set of instructions which control the behavior of the machine whenever it is in that state. By definition, in the case of a deterministic automaton, such instructions specify, for each state of the machine, an associated output and a successor machine state. Probabilistic automata differ only in that any state may specify a *range* of outputs or of successor states, with an associated probability distribution. In short, two machine table states of a deterministic automaton are distinct if they differ either in their associated outputs or in their associated successor state. Analogously, two machine table states of probabilistic automata differ if they differ in their range of outputs, or in their range of successor states, or in the probability distributions associated with either of these ranges.

If, however, we transfer this convention for distinguishing machine table states to the type identification of psychological states, we get identity conditions which are, as it were, too fine-grained. Thus, for example, if you and I differ *only* in the respect that your most probable response to the pain of stubbing your toe is to say "damn" and mine is to say "darn," it follows that the pain you have when you stub your toe is type-distinct from the pain I have when I stub my toe.

This argument iterates in an embarrassing way. To see this, consider the special case of deterministic automata: x and y are type-distinct machine table states of such an automaton if the immediate successor states of x and y are type-distinct. But the immediate successor states of x and y are type-distinct if *their* immediate successor states are type-distinct. So x and y are type-distinct if the immediate successors of their immediate successors are type-distinct; and so on. Indeed, on the assumption that there is a computational path from every state to every other, any two automata which have less than all their states in common will have none of their states in common. This argument generalizes to probabilistic automata in an obvious way.

It is again important to see what the argument does *not* show. In particular, it does not show that psychological states cannot be type-identified by reference to some sort of *abstract* properties of machine table states. But, as we remarked in our discussion of Argument 1, to say that psychological states correspond to some or other property definable over machine table states is to say much less about the conditions upon the type identity of psychological states than *FSIT* seeks to do. And the present argument *does* seem to show that the conditions used to type-identify machine table states per se cannot be used to type-identify psychological

states. It is presumably this sort of point which Putnam, for example, has in mind when he remarks that "the difficulty of course will be to pass from models of *specific* organisms to a *normal* form for the psychological description of *organisms*" ("Psychological Predicates," p. 43). In short, it may seem at first glance that exploitation of the criteria employed for type-identifying machine table states provides *FSIT* with concepts at precisely the level of abstraction required for type-identifying psychological states. But, in fact, this appears not to be true.

(5) The following argument seems to us to show that the psychological states of organisms cannot be placed in one-to-one correspondence with the machine table states of organisms.

The set of states which constitute the machine table of a probabilistic automaton is, by definition, a list. But the set of mental states of at least some organisms (namely, persons) is, in point of empirical fact, productive. In particular, abstracting from theoretically irrelevant limitations imposed by memory and mortality, there are infinitely many type-distinct, nomologically possible psychological states of any given person. The simplest demonstration that this is true is that, on the assumption that there are infinitely many non-equivalent declarative sentences, one can generate definite descriptions of such states by replacing S with sentences in the schemata A:

A: "the belief (thought, desire, hope, and so forth) that S"

In short, while the set of machine table states of a Turing machine can, by definition, be exhaustively specified by listing them, the set of mental states of a person can at best be specified by finite axiomatization.

It might be maintained against this argument that not more than a finite subset of the definite descriptions generable by substitution in *A* do in fact designate nomologically possible beliefs (desires, hopes, or whatever) and that this is true *not* because of theoretically uninteresting limitations imposed by memory and mortality, but rather because of the existence of psychological laws that limit the set of believable (and so forth) propositions to a finite set. To take a farfetched example, it might be held that if you eliminate all such perhaps unbelievable propositions as "2 + 2 = 17," "2 + 2 = 147," and so forth, the residuum is a finite set.

There is no reason at all to believe that this is true, however, and there are some very persuasive reasons for believing that it is not. For example, the infinite set of descriptions whose members are "the belief that 1 + 1 = 2," "the belief that 2 + 2 = 4," "the belief that 3 + 3 = 6," and so forth would appear to designate a set of possible beliefs of an organism ideally free from limitations on memory; to put it the other way around, the fact that there are arithmetical statements that it is nomologically impossible for any person to believe is a consequence of the character of people's memory, not a consequence of the character of their mental representation of arithmetic.

It should be emphasized, again, that this is intended to be an empirical claim, albeit an overwhelmingly plausible one. It is possible to imagine a creature ideally free from memory limitations whose mental representation of arithmetic nevertheless specifies only a finite set of possible arithmetic beliefs. The present point is that it is vastly unlikely that we are such creatures.

Once again it is important to see what the argument does *not* show. Let us distinguish between the *machine table states* of an automaton, and the *computational states* of an automaton. By the former, we will mean what we have been meaning all along: states specified by columns in its machine table. By the latter we mean any state of the machine which is character-izable in terms of its inputs, outputs, and/or machine table states. In this usage, the predicates "has just run through a computation involving three hundred seventy-two machine table states," or "has just proved Fermat's last theorem," or "has just typed the *i*th symbol in its output vocabulary" all designate possible computational states of machines.

Now, what the present argument seems to show is that the psychological states of an organism cannot be put into correspondence with the machine table states of an automaton. What it of course does *not* show is that the psychological states of an organism cannot be put into correspondence with the *computational* states of an automaton. Indeed, a sufficient condition for the existence of the latter correspondence is that the possible psychological states of an organism should be countable.[8]

(6) We have argued that since the set of machine table states of an automaton is not productive, it cannot be put into correspondence with the psychological states of an organism. We will now argue that even if such a correspondence could be effected, it would necessarily fail to represent essential properties of psychological states. It seems fairly clear that there are structural similarities among at least some psychological states, and that a successful theory of such states must represent and exploit such similarities. For example, there is clearly some theoretically relevant relation between the psychological state that someone is in if he believes that *P* and the psychological state that someone is in if he believes that *P* & *Q*. The present point is simply that representing the psychological states as a list (for example, as a list of machine table states) fails to represent this kind of structural relation. What needs to be said is that believing that *P* is somehow[9] a constituent of believing that *P* & *Q*; but the machine table state model has no conceptual resources for saying that. In particular, the notion

"is a constituent of" is not defined for machine table states.

It might be replied that this sort of argument is not strictly relevant to the claims of *FSIT:* for it is surely possible, in principle, that there should be a one-to-one correspondence between machine table states and psychological states, even though the vocabulary appropriate to the individuation of the former does not capture the structural relations among the latter.

This reply, however, misses the point. To see this, consider the case with sentences. The reason there are structural parallelisms among sentences is that sentences are constructed from a fixed set of vocabulary items by the iterated application of a fixed set of rules, and the theoretical vocabulary required to analyze the ways in which sentences are structurally similar is precisely the vocabulary required to specify the domain of those rules. In particular, structurally similar sentences share either lexical items or paths in their derivations, or both. Thus one explains structural similarities between sentences in the same way that one explains their productivity: namely, by describing them as a generated set rather than a list.

Our point is that the same considerations apply to the set of psychological states of an organism. Almost certainly, they too are, or at least include, a generated set, and their structural similarities correspond, at least in part, to similarities in their derivation; that is, with psychological states as with sentences, the fact that they are productive and the fact that they exhibit internal structure are two aspects of the same phenomenon. If this is true, then a theory which fails to capture the structural relations within and among psychological states is overwhelmingly unlikely to arrive at a *description* adequate for the purposes of theoretical psychology.

This argument, like 5, thus leads to the conclusion that, if we wish to think of the psychology of organisms as represented by automata, then the psychological states of organisms seem to be analogous to the computational states of an automaton rather than to its machine table states.

IV

We have been considering theories in the philosophy of mind which can be construed as attempts to place substantive conditions upon type identity of psychological states. We have argued that none of the major theories currently in the field appears to succeed in this enterprise. It might, therefore, be advisable to reconsider the whole undertaking.

Suppose someone wanted to know what the criteria for type identity of fundamental physical entities are. Perhaps the best one could do by way of answering is to say that two such entities are type-identical if they do not differ with respect to any fundamental physical magnitudes. Thus, as far as we know, the conditions upon type identification of elementary physical particles do not refer to their distance from the North Pole, but do refer to their charge. But notice that this is simply a consequence of the fact that there are no fundamental physical laws which operate on entities as a function of their distance from the North Pole, and there *are* fundamental physical laws which operate on entities as a function of their charge.

One might put it that the basic condition upon type identity in science is that it makes possible the articulation of the domain of laws. This principle holds at every level of scientific description. Thus what is *relevant* to the question whether two entities at a level will be type-distinct is the character of the laws which operate upon entities at that level. But if this is the general case, then it looks as though substantive conditions upon type identity of psychological states will be imposed by reference to the psychological (and perhaps neurological) laws which operate upon those states and in no other way.

In the light of these remarks, we can get a clearer view of what has gone wrong with the kinds of philosophical theories we have been rejecting. For example, one can think of behaviorism as involving an attempt to type-identify psychological states just by reference to whatever laws determine their *behavioral* effects. But this would seem, even prima facie, to be a mistake, since there must be laws which govern the interaction of psychological states and there is no reason to believe (and much reason not to believe) that psychological states which behave uniformly vis-à-vis laws of the first kind characteristically behave uniformly vis-à-vis laws of the second kind.

Analogously, what has gone wrong in the case of physicalism is the assumption that psychological states that are distinct in their behavior vis-à-vis neurological laws are *ipso facto* distinct in their behavior vis-à-vis psychological laws. But, in all probability, distinct neurological states can be functionally identical. That is, satisfaction of the criteria for type-distinctness of neurological states probably does not guarantee satisfaction of the criteria for type-distinctness of psychological states or vice versa.

In short, the fundamental problem with behaviorism and physicalism is that type identity is being determined relative to, at best, a subset of the laws which must be presumed to operate upon psychological states. The only justification for this restriction seems to lie in the reductionist biases of these positions. Once the reductionism has been questioned, we can see that the nomological demands upon type identification for psychological states are likely to be extremely complicated and various. Even what little we already know about psychological laws makes it look implausible that they will acknowledge type boundaries between psychological states at the places where

physicalists or behaviorists want to draw them.

The basic failure of *FSIT* is in certain respects analogous to that of behaviorism and physicalism. Of course, *FSIT* is not reductionist in quite the same way, and in so far as it is a species of functionalism it does invite us to type-identify psychological states by reference to their nomological connections with sensory inputs, behavioral outputs, and with one another. But *FSIT* seeks to impose a further constraint on type identity: namely, that the psychological states of an organism can be placed in correspondence with (indeed, identified with) the machine table states specified by the best *description* of the organism. We have argued that this is in fact a substantive constraint, and one which cannot be satisfied.

What seems to be left of *FSIT* is this. It may be both true and important that organisms are probabilistic automata. But even if it is true and important, the fact that organisms are probabilistic automata seems to have very little or nothing to do with the conditions on type identity of their psychological states.

Notes

1. A number of friends and colleagues have read earlier drafts. We are particularly indebted to Professors Richard Boyd, Donald Davidson, Michael Harnish, and Hilary Putnam for the care with which they read the paper and for suggestions that we found useful.

2. If physicalism is the doctrine that psychological states are physical states, then we get two versions depending whether we take "states" to refer to types or to tokens. The latter construal yields a weaker theory assuming that a token of type x may be identical to a token of type y even though x and y are distinct types. On this assumption, type physicalism clearly entails token physicalism, but not conversely.

The distinction between token identity theories and type identity theories has not been exploited in the case of behavioristic analyses. Unlike either version of physicalism, behaviorism is generally held as a semantic thesis, hence as a theory about logical relations between types. In the present paper, "physicalism" will mean *type* physicalism. When we talk about states, we will specify whether we mean types or tokens only when it is not clear from the context.

3. See Donald Davidson, "Mental Events," in *Fact and Experience*, ed. by Swanson and Foster (Amherst, 1970); Jerry A. Fodor, *Psychological Explanation* (New York, 1968); Hilary Putnam, "Brains and Behavior," in *Analytical Philosophy*, ed. by R. J. Butler (Oxford, 1965); Hilary Putnam, "The Mental Life of Some Machines," in *Modern Materialism: Readings on Mind-Body Identity*, ed. by J. O'Connor (New York, 1966); Hilary Putnam, "Psychological Predicates," in *Art, Mind and Religion*, ed. by Capitan and Merrill (Detroit, 1967).

4. Not all philosophical behaviorists hold this view; philosophical behaviorism may be broadly characterized as the view that for each psychological predicate there is a behavioral predicate to which it bears a "logical relation." (See Fodor, *op. cit.*) Thus the following view qualifies as behaviorist: all ascriptions of psychological predicates entail ascriptions of behavioral predicates, but not conversely. Though this form of behaviorism is not vulnerable to the present argument, the preceding ones are as effective against it as against biconditional forms of behaviorism.

5. Cf. Putnam, "Psychological Predicates" and "On Properties," in *Essays in Honor of C. G. Hempel*, ed. by N. Rescher et al. (New York, 1970).

6. Cf. Donald Davidson, "Actions, Reasons and Causes," *Journal of Philosophy*, 60 (1963), 685-700.

7. We do not intend our use of the traditional "disposition" terminology to commit us to the view that beliefs really are dispositions. (Rather, we would suggest that they are functional states in the broad sense suggested in 3 below.)

8. The claim that organisms are probabilistic automata might be interestingly true even if *FSIT* is false; that is, even if psychological states do not correspond to machine table states. For example, it might turn out that some subset of the psychological states of an organism corresponds to a set of machine table states by which the rest of its psychology is determined. Or it might turn out that what corresponds to each machine table state is a *conjunction* of psychological states . . . , etc. Indeed, though the claim that any organism can be modeled by a probabilistic automaton is not interesting, the claim that for each organism there is a probabilistic automaton which is its *unique best* model *is* interesting. And this latter claim neither entails *FSIT* nor is it by any means obviously true.

In short, there are many ways in which it could turn out that organisms are automata in some sense *more* interesting than the sense in which everything is an automaton under some description. Our present point is that such eventualities, while they would be important, would not provide general conditions upon the type identification of psychological states in the way that *FSIT* attempts to do.

9. Very much "somehow." Obviously, believing p is not a constituent of believing $p \lor q$ in the same way that believing p is a constituent of believing $p \& q$. Equally obviously, there is some relation between believing p and believing $p \lor q$, and a theory of belief will have to say what that relation is.

Functionalism and Qualia

Sydney Shoemaker

1

In their recent paper 'What Psychological States Are Not,' N. J. Block and J. A. Fodor raise a number of objections to the 'functional state identity theory' (FSIT), which says that "for any organism that satisfies psychological predicates at all, there exists a unique best *description* such that each psychological state of the organism is identical with one of its machine states relative to that description."[1] FSIT is a version of 'functionalism', which they characterize as the more general doctrine that "the type-identity conditions for psychological states refer only to their relations to inputs, outputs, and one another."[2] Most of the objections Block and Fodor raise they take to be objections only to FSIT, and not to functionalism more broadly construed. I shall not be concerned with these objections here. But they raise one objection which, they say, "might be taken to show that psychological states cannot be functionally defined *at all* and that they cannot be put into

correspondence with *any* properties definable over abstract automata."[3] Briefly put, the objection is that the way of 'type-identifying' psychological states proposed by FSIT, and by functionalism generally, "fails to accommodate a feature of at least some such states that is critical for determining their type: namely their 'qualitative' character."[4]

Block and Fodor devote only a couple of pages to this objection, and raise it in a fairly tentative way; so it is quite likely that the length of my discussion of it here is disproportionate to the importance they put on it. But they have given a concise and vivid formulation to an objection which is felt, and voiced in conversation, more often than it is expressed in print, and which seems to me to raise fundamental issues. Other philosophers have raised much the same objection by saying that functionalism (or behaviorism, or materialism, or 'causal' theories of the mind—the objection has been made against all of these) cannot account for the 'raw feel' component of mental states, or for their 'internal', or 'phenomenological', character. My primary concern here is not with whether this objection is fatal to FSIT; if I understand that theory correctly, it is sufficiently refuted by the other

From *Philosophical Studies* 27 (1975): 291-315. Reprinted, with revisions by the author, by permission of D. Reidel Publishing Company and the author.

objections Block and Fodor raise against it. But as they characterize functionalism 'in the broad sense', it is, while vague, a view which many philosophers, myself included, find attractive; and it seems to me worth considering whether it can be defended against this objection.

I shall follow Block and Fodor in speaking of mental states (or rather, of some mental states) as having 'qualitative character(s)' or 'qualitative content'. I hope that it will emerge in the ensuing discussion that this does not commit me to anything which a clear headed opponent of 'private objects', or of 'private language', should find objectionable.

2

Block and Fodor develop their objection in two stages. The first of these they call the 'inverted qualia argument', and the second can be called the 'absent qualia argument'.

Because they are unpersuaded by the familiar 'verificationist' arguments against the conceptual coherence of the 'inverted spectrum hypothesis', Block and Fodor are inclined to think that cases of 'inverted qualia' may be possible. They take it that there would be qualia inversion (presumably an extreme case of it) if it were true that "every person does, in fact, have slightly different qualia (or, better still, grossly different qualia) when in whatever machine table state is alleged to be identical to pain."[5] The possibility of this is incompatible with functionalism on the plausible assumption that "nothing would be a token of the type 'pain state' unless it felt like a pain, . . . even if it were connected to all of the other psychological states of the organism in whatever ways pains are."[6]

Block and Fodor do not regard the possibility of qualia inversion as constituting by itself a decisive objection to functionalism, for they think that it may be open to the functionalist to deny the *prima facie* plausible assumption that

pains must be qualitatively similar (and, presumably, the related assumption that anything qualitatively identical to a pain is itself a pain).[7] If qualia inversion actually occurred in the case of pain (i.e., if a state functionally identical to a pain differed from it in qualitative character), then, they say, "it might be reasonable to say that the character of an organism's qualia is irrelevant to whether it is in pain or (equivalently) that pains feel quite different to different organisms."[8] Such a view is not in fact unheard of. According to Don Locke, "A sensation's being a pain sensation is not a matter of how it feels, but a matter of its being of the sort caused by bodily damage and leading to pain behavior."[9] And Alan Donagan has attributed to Wittgenstein the view that "you and I correctly say that we have the same sensation, say toothache, if we both have something frightful that we would naturally express by holding and rubbing our jaws, by certain kinds of grimace, and the like. Whether the internal character of what is expressed in these ways is the same for you as for me is irrelevant to the meaning of the word 'toothache'."[10]

But while Block and Fodor do not dismiss this response to the inverted qualia argument as obviously mistaken, they see it as possibly opening the door to an argument much more damaging to functionalism, namely the *absent* qualia argument. Their thought may be that once it is admitted that a given functional state can exist without having a given 'qualitative content', it will be difficult to deny the possibility that it might exist without having any qualitative content (or character) at all. At any rate, they go on to say that

For all that we know, it may be nomologically possible for two psychological states to be functionally identical (that is, to be identically connected with inputs, outputs, and successor states), even if only one of the states has a qualitative content. In this case, FSIT would require us to say that an organism might be in pain even though it is feeling *nothing at all*, and this consequence seems totally unacceptable.[11]

And if cases of 'absent qualia' are possible, i.e., if a state can be functionally identical to a state having a qualitative character without itself having a qualitative content, then not only FSIT, but also functionalism in the broad sense, would seem to be untenable.

3

If mental states can be alike or different in 'qualitative character', we should be able to speak of a class of states, call them 'qualitative states', whose 'type-identity conditions' could be specified in terms of the notion of qualitative (or 'phenomenological') similarity. For each determinate qualitative character a state can have, there is (i.e., we can define) a determinate qualitative state which a person has just in case he has a state having precisely that qualitative character. For example, there is a qualitative state someone has just in case he has a sensation that feels the way my most recent headache felt. Now, qualitative states will themselves be 'mental' or 'psychological' states. And this calls into question the suggestion by Block and Fodor that a functionalist could deal with the 'inverted qualia argument' by maintaining that "the character of an organism's qualia is irrelevant to whether it is in pain." If mental states include qualitative states, what such a functionalist says about pain could not be said about mental states generally, since it would be self-contradictory to say that the character of an organism's qualia is irrelevant to what qualitative states it has. And of course, if qualitative states themselves could be functionally defined, then the possibility of qualia inversion would pose no difficulty for functionalism, and the functionalist would have no need to make the counterintuitive denial that the charac-

ter of an organism's qualia is relevant to whether it is in pain. But if, as Block and Fodor apparently assume, qualitative states cannot be functionally defined, then there is one class of mental states, namely the qualitative states themselves, that cannot be functionally defined.

This raises questions which I shall return to in later sections, namely (a) in what sense are qualitative states not functionally definable (or, in what sense are they not functionally definable if qualia inversion is possible), and (b) is their being functionally undefinable (in whatever sense they are) seriously damaging to functionalism? As we shall see in the remainder of the present section, this question is also raised by a consideration of the alleged possibility of 'absent qualia'.

We can establish the impossibility of cases of 'absent qualia' if we can show that if a state is functionally identical to a state having qualitative content then it must itself have qualitative content. One might try to do this by construing the notion of functional identity in such a way that qualitative states are included among the 'other psychological states' by relation to which, along with input and output, the 'type-identity' of a given psychological state is to be defined. Thus one might argue that if a given psychological state has a certain qualitative character, this involves its standing in some determinate relationship to some particular qualitative state (namely the qualitative state a person is in just in case he is in a state having that qualitative character), and that any state functionally identical to it must stand in the same relationship to that qualitative state, and so must have the same qualitative character.[12] But this argument is not very convincing. One objection to it is that since qualitative states cannot themselves be functionally defined (assuming the possibility of *inverted* qualia), it is illegitimate to include them among the psychological states by reference to which other psychological states are functionally defined, or in terms of which 'functional identity' is defined. I shall return to this objection later, since it is also a *prima facie* objection against the more plausible argument I shall present next. Another objection is that the relationship which a state has to a qualitative state, in having the 'qualitative character' corresponding to that qualitative state, is not anything like a causal relationship and so is not the sort of relationship in terms of which a psychological state can be functionally defined. But the argument I shall present next is not open to this objection, and does seem to me to show that on any plausible construal of the notion of functional identity a state cannot be functionally identical to a state having qualitative character without itself having qualitative character.

One important way in which pains are related to other psychological states is that they give rise, under appropriate circumstances, to introspective awareness of themselves as having certain qualitative characters, i.e., as feeling certain ways. I shall assume that the meaning of this can be partially unpacked by saying that being in pain typically gives rise, given appropriate circumstances, to what I shall call a 'qualitative belief', i.e., a belief to the effect that one feels a certain way (or, more abstractly, that one is in a state having a certain qualitative character, or, in still other terms, that one has a certain qualitative state). Any state functionally identical to a pain state will share with the pain state not only (1) its tendency to influence overt behavior in certain ways, and (2) its tendency to produce in the person the belief that there is something organically wrong with him (e.g., that he has been cut or burnt), but also (3) its tendency to produce qualitative beliefs in the person, i.e., to make him think that he has a pain having a certain qualitative character (one that he dislikes). According to the 'absent qualia argument', such a state may nevertheless lack qualitative

character, and so fail to be a pain. Let us consider whether this is plausible.

Supposing such cases of 'absent qualia' are possible, how might we detect such a case if it occurred? And with what right does each of us reject the suggestion that perhaps his own case is such a case, and that he himself is devoid of states having qualitative character? Indeed, with what right do we reject the suggestion that perhaps no one ever has any feelings (or other states having qualitative character) at all? It is, of course, a familiar idea that behavior provides inconclusive evidence as to what qualitative character, if any, a man's mental states have. But what usually underlies this is the idea that the man himself has a more 'direct' access to this qualitative character than behavior can possibly provide, namely introspection. And introspection, whatever else it is, is the link between a man's mental states and his beliefs about (or his knowledge or awareness of) those states. So one way of putting our question is to ask whether anything could be evidence (for anyone) that someone was not in pain, given that it follows from the states he is in, plus the psychological laws that are true of him (the laws which describe the relationships of his states to one another and to input and output), that the totality of possible behavioral evidence *plus* the totality of possible introspective evidence points unambiguously to the conclusion that he is in pain? I do not see how anything could be. To be sure, we can imagine (perhaps) that 'cerebroscopes' reveal that the person is not in some neurophysiological state that we ourselves are always in when we are (so we think) in pain. But this simply raises the question, on what basis can we say that *we* have genuine pain (i.e., a state having a qualitative character as well as playing the appropriate functional role in its relationships to input, output, and other psychological states)? Here it seems that if the behavioral and introspective evidence are not enough, nothing could be enough. But if they are enough in the case of us, they are enough in the case of our hypothetical man. In any event, if we are given that a man's state is functionally identical with a state that in us is pain, it is hard to see how a physiological difference between him and us could be any evidence at all that his states lack qualitative character; for if anything can be evidence for us about his psychological state, the evidence that his state is functionally equivalent to ours is *ipso facto* evidence that any physiological difference between us and him is irrelevant to whether, although not to how, the state of pain is realized in him.

To hold that it is logically possible (or, worse, nomologically possible) that a state lacking qualitative character should be functionally identical to a state having qualitative character is to make qualitative character irrelevant both to what we can take ourselves to know in knowing about the mental states of others and also to what we can take ourselves to know in knowing about our own mental states. There could (on this view) be no possible physical effects of any state from which we could argue by an 'inference to the best explanation' that it has qualitative character; for if there were, we could give at least a partial functional characterization of the having of qualitative character by saying that it tends to give rise, in such and such circumstances, to those physical effects, and could not allow that a state lacking qualitative character could be functionally identical to a state having it. And for reasons already given, if cases of 'absent qualia' were possible, qualitative character would be necessarily inaccessible to introspection. If qualitative character were something that is irrelevant in this way to all knowledge of minds, self-knowledge as well as knowledge of others, it would not be at all 'unacceptable', but would instead be just good sense, to deny that pains must have qualitative character. But of course it is absurd to suppose that ordinary people are talking about

something that is in principle unknowable by anyone when they talk about how they feel, or about how things look, smell, sound, etc. to them. (Indeed, just as a causal theory of knowledge would imply that states or features that are independent of the causal powers of the things they characterize would be in principle unknowable, so a causal theory of reference would imply that such states and features are in principle unnamable and inaccessible to reference.) And if, to return to sanity, we take qualitative character to be something that can be known in the ways we take human feelings to be knowable (at a minimum, if it can be known introspectively), then it is not possible, not even logically possible, for a state that lacks qualitative character to be functionally identical to a state that has it.

This is not a 'verificationist' argument. It does not assume any general connection between meaningfulness and verifiability (or knowability). What it does assume is that if there is to be any reason for supposing (as the 'absent qualia argument' does) that it is essential to pain and other mental states that they have 'qualitative character', then we must take 'qualitative character' to refer to something which is knowable in at least some of the ways in which we take pains (our own and those of others) to be knowable. It also assumes that if there could be a feature of some mental state that was entirely independent of the causal powers of the state (i.e., was such that its presence or absence would make no difference to the state's tendencies to bring about other states, and so forth), and so was irrelevant to its 'functional identity', then such a feature would be totally unknowable (if you like, this assumes a causal theory of knowledge).

Against this argument, as against an earlier one, it may be objected that the other psychological states by relation to which (along with inputs and outputs) a given psychological state is functionally defined must not include any states that cannot themselves be functionally defined. For, it may be said, the states I have called 'qualitative beliefs' can no more be functionally defined than can qualitative states themselves. The most important relationship of these states to other states would appear to be their relationship to the qualitative states that characteristically give rise to them, yet (so the argument goes) the latter cannot be functionally defined and so cannot legitimately be referred to in functional definitions of the former. Moreover (remembering that the possibility of cases of *inverted* qualia is not here being questioned), it seems plausible to suppose that if two people differed in the qualitative character of their pains, but in such a way that the difference would not be revealed in any possible behavior, then they would also differ in their qualitative beliefs, and this latter difference too would be such that its existence could not be revealed in any possible behavior. And if this is possible, there seems as much reason to deny that qualitative beliefs are capable of functional definition as there is to deny that qualitative states are capable of functional definition.

This objection does not touch one important point implicit in my argument, namely that we cannot deny, without being committed to an intolerable skepticism about the pains of others, that someone's saying that he feels a sharp pain is good evidence that he has some qualitative state or other, and is so because someone's saying this is, normally, an *effect* of his having a state having qualitative character—and this by itself strongly suggests that if a mental state of one person has qualitative character, and if an otherwise similar state of another person lacks qualitative character, then the states differ in the ways they tend to influence behavior ('output') and hence differ functionally. Still, the possibility of 'inverted qualia' does seem to imply that qualitative states, and hence qualitative beliefs, cannot be functionally

defined. To see whether this is compatible with functionalism, and whether it undercuts the argument given above, we need to consider in what sense it is true that qualitative states (and qualitative beliefs) are not functionally definable, and what limits there are on the ways in which reference to mental states that are not functionally definable can enter into functional definitions of other mental states.

In order to consider these questions I wish to change examples, and shift our consideration from the case of pain to that of visual experience. There are two reasons why such a shift is desirable. First, the possibility of 'spectrum inversion' (one person's experience of colors differing systematically, in its qualitative or phenomenological character, from another person's experience of the same colors) seems to me far less problematical than the possibility of 'qualia inversion' in the case of pain (pain feeling radically different to different persons). Second, and related to this, it is much easier to distinguish seeing blue (for example) from its qualitative character than it is to distinguish pain from its qualitative character, and accordingly much easier to consider how reference to qualitative states might enter into a functional account of seeing colors than it is to consider how reference to such states might enter into a functional account of pain.

4

If I see something, it looks somehow to me, and the way it looks resembles and differs from, in varying degrees and various respects, the ways other things look to me or have looked to me on other occasions. It is because similarities and differences between these 'ways of being appeared to' correlate in systematic ways with similarities and differences between seen objects that we are able to see these objects and the properties of them in virtue of which the similarities and differences obtain.[13] Being appeared to in a certain way, e.g., things looking to one the way things now look to me as I stare out my window, I take to be a qualitative state. So seeing essentially involves the occurrence of qualitative states. Moreover, reference to these qualitative states enters into what looks very much like a functional account of seeing. For it would seem that what it means to say that someone sees something to be blue is something like the following:

S sees something to be blue if and only if (1) S has a repertory of qualitative states which includes a set of states K which are associated with the colors of objects in such a way that (a) visual stimulation by an object of a certain color under 'standard conditions' produces in the person the associated qualitative state, and (b) the degrees of 'qualitative' or 'phenomenological' similarity between the states in K correspond to the degrees of similarity between the associated colors, and (2) person S (a) is at present in the qualitative state associated with the color blue, (b) is so as the result of visual stimulation by something blue and (c) believes, because of (a) and (b), that there is something blue before him.[14]

I must now qualify the assertion that 'being appeared to' in a certain way is a qualitative state. If asked to describe how he is appeared to, or, more naturally, how things look to him, a man might say, among other things, that a certain object looks blue to him, or that it looks to him as if he were seeing something blue, or (if he is a philosopher who speaks the 'language of appearing') that he is 'appeared-blue-to'. And it is natural to make it a condition of someone's being appeared-blue-to that he be in the qualitative state that is, in him at that time, associated with visual stimulation by blue things; that is, it is natural to give an analysis of 'S is appeared-blue-to' which is the same as the above analysis of 'S sees something to be blue' except that clauses (b) and (c) of condition (2) are deleted. But if we do this, then being appeared-blue-to will not

itself be a qualitative state. Or at any rate, this will be so if spectrum inversion is possible. We might sum up the situation by saying that being appeared-blue-to is, on the proposed analysis, a functional state whose functional characterization requires it always to have some qualitative character (or other) but does not require it to have the same qualitative character in different persons (assuming the possibility of intersubjective spectrum inversion) or in the same person at different times (assuming the possibility of intrasubjective spectrum inversion). But this raises again the question of whether qualitative states are themselves functionally definable and, if they are not, whether they can legitimately be referred to in functional characterizations of other mental states.

The expression 'appeared-blue-to' could, I think, have a use in which it would stand for a qualitative state. I could 'fix the reference' of this expression by stipulating that it refers to (or, since it is a predicate rather than a singular term, that it predicates or ascribes) that qualitative state which is at the present time (April, 1974) associated in me with the seeing of blue things.[15] Understanding the expression in this way, if I underwent spectrum inversion tomorrow it would cease to be the case that I am normally appeared-blue-to when I see blue things, and might become the case that I am normally appeared-yellow-to on such occasions.[16] (By contrast, in the 'functional' sense of 'appeared-blue-to' sketched above, it could be true before and after intrasubjective spectrum inversion that I am normally appeared-blue-to when I see blue things, although of course being appeared-blue-to would have the qualitative character at the later time which another visual state, say, being appeared-yellow-to, had at the earlier time.) I do not think that there would be much utility in having expressions that were, in this way, 'rigid designators' (or 'rigid predicators') of visual qualia. On the other hand, I see no reason in principle why we could not have them. But if we did have them, they could not be functionally defined. Such terms would have to be introduced by Kripkean 'reference fixing' or (what is a special case of this) ostensive definition. To be sure, there is the theoretical possibility of giving a verbal definition of one of these expressions by making use of other expressions of the same sort; just as I might define 'blue' by means of a description of the form 'the color that is not yellow, or red, or green . . . etc.', so I might define 'being appeared-blue-to' as equivalent to a description of the form 'the color qualia which is neither being appeared-yellow-to, nor being appeared-red-to, nor being appeared-green-to, . . . etc.' But this is of very little interest, since it is obviously impossible that names (or predicates) for all visual qualia should be defined in this way without circularity. So, assuming that talk of defining functional states is equivalent to talk of defining names or 'rigid designators' for qualitative states, there seems to be a good sense in which qualitative states cannot be functionally defined.

But what seems to force us to this conclusion is the seeming possibility of spectrum inversion. I think that what (if anything) forces us to admit the possibility of spectrum inversion is the seeming conceivability and detectability of *intra*subjective spectrum inversion. And if we reflect on the latter, we will see, I believe, that while we cannot functionally define particular qualitative states, there is a sense in which we can functionally define the *class* of qualitative states—we can functionally define the identity conditions for members of this class, for we can functionally define the relationships of qualitative (phenomenological) similarity and difference. This is what I shall argue in the following section.

5

Taken one way, the claim that spectrum inversion is possible implies a claim that may, for all I know, be empirically false, namely that there is a way of mapping determinate shades of color onto determinate shades of color which is such that (1) every determinate shade (including 'muddy' and unsaturated colors as well as the pure spectral colors) is mapped onto some determinate shade, (2) at least some of the shades are mapped onto shades other than themselves, (3) the mapping preserves, for any normally sighted person, all of the 'distance' and 'betweenness' relationships between the colors (so that if shades *a*, *b* and *c* are mapped onto shades *d*, *e* and *f*, respectively, then a normally sighted person will make the same judgments of comparative similarity about *a* in relation to *b* and *c* as about *d* in relation to *e* and *f*), and (4) the mapping preserves all of our intuitions, except those that are empirically conditioned by knowledge of the mixing properties of pigments and the like, about which shades are 'pure' colors and which have other colors 'in' them (so that, for example, if shades *a* and *b* are mapped onto shades of orange and red, respectively, we will be inclined to say that *a* is less pure than *b* and perhaps that it has *b* in it). But even if our color experience is not in fact such that a mapping of this sort is possible, it seems to me conceivable that it might have been—and that is what matters for our present philosophical purposes.[17] For example, I think we know well enough what it would be like to see the world nonchromatically, i.e., in black, white, and the various shades of grey— for we frequently do see it in this way in photographs, moving pictures, and television. And there is an obvious mapping of the nonchromatic shades onto each other which satisfies the conditions for inversion. In the discussion that follows I shall assume, for convenience, that such a mapping is possible for the full range of colors—but I do not think that anything essential turns on whether this assumption is correct.

Supposing that there is such a mapping (and, a further assumption of convenience, that there is only one), let us call the shade onto which each shade is mapped the 'inverse' of that shade. We will have *inter*subjective spectrum inversion if the way each shade of color looks to one person is the way its inverse looks to another person, or, in other words, if for each shade of color the qualitative state associated in one person with the seeing of that shade is associated in another person with the seeing of the inverse of that shade. And we will have *intra*subjective spectrum inversion if there is a change in the way the various shades of color look to someone, each coming to look the way its inverse previously looked.

What strikes us most about spectrum inversion is that if it can occur *inter*subjectively there would appear to be no way of telling whether the color experience of two persons is the same or whether their color spectra are inverted relative to each other. The systematic difference between experiences in which intersubjective spectrum inversion would consist would of course not be open to anyone's introspection. And there would appear to be no way in which these differences could manifest themselves in behavior—the hypothesis that your spectrum is inverted relative to mine and the hypothesis that our color experience is the same seem to give rise to the same predictions about our behavior. Here, of course, we have in mind the hypothetical case in which the various colors have always looked one way to one person and a different way to another person. And the situation seems

very different when we consider the case of *intra*subjective spectrum inversion. In the first place, it seems that such a change would reveal itself to the introspection, or introspection *cum* memory, of the person in whom it occurred. But if this is so, other persons could learn of it through that person's reports. Moreover, and this is less often noticed, there is non-verbal behavior, as well as verbal behavior, that could indicate such a change. If an animal has been trained to respond in specific ways to objects of certain colors, and then begins, spontaneously, to respond in those ways to things of the inverse colors, and if it shows surprise that its responses are no longer rewarded in the accustomed ways, this will surely be some evidence that it has undergone spectrum inversion. In the case of a person we could have a combination of this sort of evidence and the evidence of the person's testimony.[18]

If we did not think that we could have these kinds of evidence of intrasubjective spectrum inversion, I think we would have no reason at all for thinking that spectrum inversion of any sort, intrasubjective or intersubjective, is even logically possible. To claim that spectrum inversion is possible but that it is undetectable even in the intrasubjective case would be to sever the connection we suppose to hold between qualitative states and introspective awareness of them (between them and the qualitative beliefs to which they give rise), and also their connections to perceptual beliefs about the world and, *via* these beliefs, to behavior. No doubt one could so *define* the term 'qualitative state' as to make it inessential to qualitative states that they have these sorts of connections. But then it would not be in virtue of similarities and differences between 'qualitative states' (in that defined sense) that things look similar and different to people, and the hypothesis that people differ radically in what 'qualitative states' they have when they see things of various colors would be of no philosophical interest, and would not be the 'inverted spectrum hypothesis' as usually understood. Indeed, the supposition that intrasubjective spectrum inversion could occur, but would be undetectable, is incoherent in much the same way as the 'absent qualia hypothesis', i.e., the supposition that states 'functionally identical' to states having qualitative content might themselves lack qualitative content. Neither supposition makes sense unless the crucial notions in them are implicitly defined, or redefined, so as to make the supposition empty or uninteresting.

But what, then, are we supposing about qualitative states, and about the relationships of qualitative or phenomenological similarity and difference between these states, in supposing that intrapersonal spectrum inversion *would* be detectable? In what follows I shall speak of token qualitative states as 'experiences', and will say that experiences are 'co-conscious' if they are conscious to a person at the same time, where an experience counts as conscious to a person when he correctly remembers it as well as when he is actually having it. One thing we are supposing, if we take intrasubjective spectrum inversion to be detectable in the ways I have indicated, is that when experiences are co-conscious the similarities between them tend to give rise to belief in the existence of objective similarities in the physical world, namely similarities between objects in whose perception the experiences occurred, and differences between them tend to give rise to belief in the existence of objective differences in the world. And these beliefs, in turn, give rise (in combination with the person's wants and other mental states) to overt behavior which is appropriate to them. This explains how there can be non-verbal behavior that is evidence of spectrum inversion; the behavior will be the manifestation of mistaken beliefs about things

which result from the fact that in cases of intrasubjective spectrum inversion, things of the same color will produce qualitatively different experiences after the inversion than they did before, while things of each color will produce, after the inversion, experiences qualitatively like those produced by things of a different color before the inversion.

But even if, for some reason, a victim of spectrum inversion were not led to have and act on mistaken beliefs about objective similarities and dissimilarities in this way, we could still have evidence that his spectrum had inverted—for he could tell us that it had. And in supposing that *he* can know of the spectrum inversion in such a case, and so be in a position to inform us of it, we are supposing something further about the relationships of qualitative similarity and difference, namely that when they hold between co-conscious experiences, this tends to give rise to introspective awareness of the holding of these very relationships, i.e., it tends to give rise to correct "qualitative beliefs" to the effect that these relationships hold.

Philosophers who talk of mental states as having behavioral 'criteria' have sometimes said that the criterion of experiences being similar is their subject's sincerely reporting, or being disposed to report, that they are.[19] If we recast this view in functionalist terms, it comes out as the view that what constitutes experiences being qualitatively similar is, in part anyhow, that they give rise, or tend to give rise, to their subject's having a qualitative belief to the effect that such a similarity holds, and, in virtue of this belief, a disposition to make verbal reports to this effect. But as a functional *definition* of qualitative similarity this would of course be circular. If we are trying to explain what it means for experiences to be similar, we cannot take as already understood, and as available for use in our explanation, the notion of believing experiences to be similar.

But no such circularity would be involved in functionally defining the notions of qualitative similarity and difference in terms of the first sort of relationship I mentioned, namely between, on the one hand, a person's experiences being qualitatively similar or different in certain ways, and, on the other, his believing in the existence of certain sorts of objective similarities or differences in the world, and, ultimately, his behaving in certain ways. I believe that a case can be made, although I shall not attempt to make it here, for saying that the tendency of sensory experiences to give rise to introspective awareness of themselves, and of their similarities and differences, is, for creatures having the conceptual capacities of humans, an inevitable by-product of their tendency to give rise to perceptual awareness of objects in the world, and of similarities and differences between these objects. And my suggestion is that what makes a relationship between experiences the relationship of qualitative (phenomenological) similarity is precisely its playing a certain 'functional' role in the perceptual awareness of objective similarities, namely its tending to produce perceptual beliefs to the effect that such similarities hold. Likewise, what makes a relationship between experiences the relationship of qualitative difference is its playing a corresponding role in the perceptual awareness of objective differences.[20]

This suggestion is, of course, vague and sketchy. But all that I have to maintain here is that the claim that we can give a functional account of qualitative similarity and difference along these lines is no less plausible than the claim that such mental states as belief and desire can be functionally defined. For my aim is not the ambitious one of showing that functionalism provides a fully satisfactory philosophy of mind; it is the much more modest one of showing that the fact that some mental states have 'qualitative character' need not pose any special difficul-

ties for a functionalist. And an important step toward showing the latter is to show that the notions of qualitative similarity and difference are as plausible candidates for functional definition as other mental notions. I conceded earlier that there is a sense in which particular qualitative states cannot be functionally defined. But it will be remembered that what distinguishes qualitative states from other sorts of mental states is that their 'type-identity conditions' are to be given in terms of the notion of qualitative similarity. At the beginning of our discussion, specifying identity conditions in such terms seemed to contrast sharply with specifying them in functional terms. But this contrast becomes blurred if, as I have suggested, the notion of qualitative similarity can itself be defined in functional terms. And if the latter is so, and hence the identity conditions for qualitative states can be specified in functional terms, it seems not inappropriate to say, as I did earlier, that while particular qualitative states cannot be functionally defined, the *class* of qualitative states can be functionally defined.

6

Now let us return to the question of whether it is legitimate to make reference to qualitative states in giving functional definitions of other sorts of mental states.

On one construal of it, functionalism in the philosophy of mind is the doctrine that mental, or psychological, terms are, in principle, eliminable in a certain way. If, to simplify matters, we take our mental vocabulary to consist of names for mental states and relationships (rather than predicates ascribing such states and relationships), the claim will be that these names can be treated as synonymous with definite descriptions, each such description being formulable, in principle, without the use of any of the mental vocabulary. Mental states will indeed be quantified over, and in some cases identifyingly referred to, in these definite descriptions;

but when they are, they will be characterized and identified, not in explicitly mentalistic terms, but in terms of their causal and other 'topic neutral' relations to one another and to physical inputs and outputs.[21]

Now what I have already said implies that names of qualitative states (if we had them) could not be defined as equivalent to such definite descriptions—on the assumption, of course, that 'qualia inversion' is possible. If the causal role played by a given qualitative state (in conjunction with other mental states) in mediating connections between input and output could be played by another qualitative state, and if that qualitative state could play a different role, then it is not essential to the state that it plays that causal role and it cannot be part of the meaning, or sense, of a term that rigidly designates it that the state so designated is *the* state that plays such a causal role. Moreover, since such a term could not be eliminated in this way in favor of a definite description, it could not occur within the definite description which functionally defines the name of some other mental state—assuming that the aim of such functionalist definitions is to eliminate mental terminology in favor of physical and topic neutral terminology.

But there is nothing in this to imply that qualitative states cannot be among the states quantified over in the definite descriptions that define other sorts of mental states. And it seems that it would be quantification over such states, rather than reference to particular states of this kind, that would be needed in the defining of other mental states. If spectrum inversion is possible, we do not want to make the occurrence of any particular qualitative state a necessary condition of seeing (or seeming to see) something blue, but we do want to require that at any given time in the history of a person there is some qualitative state or other that is (at

that time) standardly involved in his seeing (or seeming to see) blue things. The specification of the roles of the qualitative states in the seeing of blue things will no doubt invoke the notions of qualitative similarity and difference; but this causes no difficulties for a functionalist if, as I have suggested, these notions can themselves be functionally defined.

There would appear, however, to be some mental states (other than qualitative states) that cannot be functionally defined in the strong sense here under consideration, namely in such a way that there is no essential (uneliminable) use of mental terminology in the *definiens*. For consider the states I have called 'qualitative beliefs', i.e., beliefs about qualitative states and in particular beliefs to the effect that one is (oneself) in a particular qualitative state. Qualitative beliefs can be divided into two groups, those in whose propositional content there is reference to particular qualitative states, and those in whose propositional content there is quantification over qualitative states but no reference to particular qualitative states. So far as I can see, qualitative beliefs of the second sort provide no special difficulties for the functionalist; if other sorts of beliefs can be functionally defined, so can these. But qualitative beliefs of the first sort do seem to resist functional definition. Consider the belief I would express if I said 'I am in the state of being appeared-blue-to', using the phrase 'state of being appeared-blue-to' to rigidly designate a particular qualitative state. If we tried to characterize this state of believing functionally, i.e., in terms of its relationships to other mental states and to input and output, it would seem that we would have to make reference in our characterization to the qualitative state the belief is about—we would have to say that the state of believing that one is appeared-blue-to is typically the result of the state of being appeared-blue-to. If so, it is impossible to define such states (qualitative beliefs of the first sort) without making essential use of mental terms.

But this constitutes no obstacle to our functionally defining other sorts of mental states. For while we may want to include in our functional characterizations of some kinds of mental states that they give rise to qualitative beliefs of the first sort (i.e., those in whose propositional content there is reference to particular qualitative states), this need not involve our making identifying reference to beliefs of this sort in our functional characterizations; all that this need involve is quantifying over such beliefs. Thus, for example, we can build it into our functional characterization of pain that being in pain typically results in some qualitative belief to the ·effect that one has some specific qualitative state, without saying of any specific qualitative state that being in pain tends to give rise to a belief about it. And if quantifying over qualitative states is permissible in giving functional definitions, I see no reason why quantifying over functional beliefs should not be permissible as well.

Now let us return briefly to my argument in section 3 against the possibility of cases of 'absent qualia'. In that argument I pointed out that it is characteristic of pains to give rise to introspective awareness of themselves as having particular qualitative characters, and so to give rise to 'qualitative beliefs', and I used this to argue that any state functionally identical to a state having qualitative character (e.g., a pain) must itself have qualitative character. The objection was raised to this argument that since qualitative beliefs, like qualitative states, cannot be functionally defined, they cannot legitimately enter into a functional account of the 'type-identity conditions' for other mental states. We can now answer this objection. No doubt pains give rise to qualitative beliefs of the sort that (so I am allowing)

cannot be functionally defined, i.e., beliefs to the effect that one is having some specific qualitative state. But they also give rise to beliefs to the effect that one is in pain—and if (as the 'absent qualia argument' apparently assumes) pain is necessarily a state having qualitative character, then the belief that one is in pain presumably involves (at least in the case of a reflective person) the belief that one is in a state having some qualitative character or other. And while the latter belief is a qualitative belief, its propositional content quantifies over qualitative states rather than involving reference to particular qualitative states. No reason has been given why qualitative beliefs of this sort should not be regarded as functionally definable. And if they are functionally definable, there is no reason why the tendency of other states to give rise to such beliefs should not be part of what constitutes the functional identity of those other states. And this is all the argument of section 3 requires.

7

Over the last few decades, much of the controversy in the philosophy of mind has involved a battle between two seemingly conflicting sets of intuitions. On the one hand there is the intuition that mental states are somehow logically, or conceptually, connected with physical states of affairs, in particular the behaviors that are taken to manifest them. This intuition has found expression in a succession of different philosophical positions—logical behaviorism, the 'criteriological' views inspired by Wittgenstein, and, most recently, functional or causal analyses of mental states (these usually being combined with some form of materialism or physicalism).[22] On the other hand there is the intuition that connections between mental states and behavior are, at bottom, contingent; that under the most 'intrinsic' descriptions of mental states, it is a contingent fact that they are related as they are to behavior and to other sorts of physical states. And a common expression of this view has been the claim that spectrum inversion and other sorts of 'qualia inversion' are logically possible; for to say that these are logically possible is apparently to say that what intrinsic, internal character these mental states have, their 'qualitative content', is logically irrelevant to their being related as they are to their bodily causes and behavioral manifestations. I have conceded that there is a substantial element of truth in this view. For I have allowed that spectrum inversion is a possibility, and have allowed that this implies that at least some qualitative states (and qualitative beliefs) cannot be functionally defined. But I believe that there is a substantial element of truth in the other view as well. I think that where the other view —the view that mental states are 'logically' or 'conceptually' connected with behavior—has its greatest plausibility is in its application to such states as desire and belief, and I think that these states do not have 'qualitative character' in the sense that here concerns us, although they may sometimes be accompanied by qualitative states. But as I have tried to show, even qualitative states can be accommodated within the framework of a functional, or causal, analysis of mental states. While it may be of the essence of qualitative states that they are 'ineffable' in the sense that one cannot say in general terms, or at any rate in general terms that do not include names of qualitative states, what it is for a person to be in a particular qualitative state, this does not prevent us from giving a functional account of what it is for a state to be a qualitative state, and of what the identity conditions for qualitative states are. Thus it may be possible to reconcile these firmly entrenched, and seemingly conflicting, intuitions about the contingency or otherwise of relations between mental states and the physical world.

There are a number of issues that would have to be investigated before it could be claimed that this attempted reconciliation is successful. The account of qualitative similarity and difference that I have suggested was tailored to the case of perceptual experiences, and it needs to be considered whether it can be plausibly applied to sensations like pains. What its application to the case of pain may require is the acceptance of the view of pains as somatic sense impressions, i.e., impressions (which need not be veridical) of bodily injuries and the like.[23] Also, this account of qualitative similarity and difference is tailored to the case in which the experiences being compared are experiences of one and the same person, and it needs to be considered whether it gives sense, and the right sort of sense, to intersubjective comparisons of experiences. This would involve, among other things, a consideration of whether it is possible for experiences of different persons to be 'co-conscious' in the sense defined earlier; and I think this reduces to the question of whether it is possible for there to be 'fusion' between persons of the sort envisaged in some recent discussions of personal identity, i.e., a merging of two persons into a single person (or single subject of consciousness) who then remembers, and is able to compare, the experiences the persons had prior to the fusion. (It is worth noting that if fusion is possible, then it is not after all the case that no possible behavior would reveal whether the color experience of two persons was the same or whether their color spectra were inverted relative to each other; for were the persons to fuse, the behavior of the resulting person could presumably settle this question.) But these are all complex issues, and I shall not attempt to discuss them here.[24]

Notes

1. N. J. Block and J. A. Fodor, 'What Psychological States Are Not', *The Philosophical Review* 81 (1972), p. 165.

2. *Op. cit.*, p. 173.

3. *Op. cit.*, pp. 173-174.

4. *Op. cit.*, p. 172.

5. *Op. cit.*, p. 173.

6. *Op. cit.*, p. 172. It is worth noting that this assumption, or one very much like it, plays a crucial role in Saul Kripke's recent arguments against the psychophysical identity theory; Kripke expresses it by saying that pain "is not picked out by one of its accidental properties; rather it is picked out by the property of being pain itself, by its immediate phenomenological quality. Thus pain . . . is not rigidly designated by 'pain' but the reference of the designator is determined by an essential property of the referent"; 'Naming and Necessity', in D. Davidson and H. Harman (eds.) *Semantics of Natural Language* (D. Reidel Publ. Co., Dordrecht-Holland, 1972, p. 340).

7. Block and Fodor mention another way, besides that mentioned in the text, in which a functionalist might try to meet the inverted qualia argument; he might maintain that "though inverted qualia, *if they occurred*, would provide counterexamples to his theory, as a matter of nomological fact it is impossible that functionally identical psychological states should be qualitatively distinct" (p. 172). The thought here must be that the mere logical, or conceptual, possibility of qualia inversion is not incompatible with functionalism. It would seem, however, that if the actual occurrence of inverted qualia would provide counterexamples to functionalism (as the envisioned reply concedes), then the mere logical possibility of inverted qualia is incompatible with functionalism; pain cannot be *identical* with a given functional state if there is a possible world, even a logically but not nomologically possible world, in which the functional state exists without pain existing, or *vice versa*. (On the general claim about identity here being invoked, namely that if *a* and *b* are identical they must be identical in any logically possible world in which either exists, see Kripke's 'Naming and Necessity', already cited, and his 'Identity and Necessity', in Milton K. Munitz, (ed.), *Identity and Individuation*, New York, 1971.)

8. Block and Fodor, *op. cit.*, p. 173.

9. Don Locke, *Myself and Others*, Oxford, 1968, p. 101.

10. Alan Donagan, 'Wittgenstein on Sensations,' in G. Pitcher (ed.), *Wittgenstein: The Philosophical Investigations*, Garden City, New York, 1966.

11. Block and Fodor, *loc. cit.*

12. Just what is the relationship that a state must have to a qualitative state in order to have the qualitative character corresponding to that state? It cannot be, in the cases that concern us, the relationship of identity (that would permit only qualitative states to have qualitative character, and would not permit us to speak of the qualitative character of states whose 'type-identity' conditions are given in functional terms). And presumably it must be something stronger than the relationship 'is accompanied by', or 'is coinstantiated with'. The best I can do is to say that a particular token of a state *S* had the qualitative character corresponding to qualitative state *Q* if on the occasion in question the tokening (instantiation) of *S* essentially involved the tokening (instantiation) of *Q*. Possibly, but I am not sure of this, we could strengthen this, and make it less vague, by saying that on such occasions the token of *S* is a token of *Q*.

13. The 'being appeared to' terminology I take from Roderick Chisholm; see his " 'Appear', 'Take', and 'Evident' ", in R. J. Swartz (ed.), *Perceiving, Sensing and Knowing*, Garden City, New York, 1965, especially p. 480, footnote 6. One is 'appeared to' both in cases of veridical perception and in cases of illusion and hallucination, and can be appeared to in the same ways in all of these sorts of cases. The technical locution 'appeared-blue-to' is used in the text as an abbreviation for the locution 'sees or seems to see something blue' (on a 'nonepistemic' understanding of that locution).

14. As an analysis this will not quite do. I can see something to be blue even though it looks green (i.e., even if my visual qualitative state is that associated with green), if I have been 'tipped off' that in these circumstances blue things look green.

15. I take the notion of 'reference fixing' and the notion of a 'rigid designator' employed below, from Saul Kripke; see his 'Naming and Necessity', pp. 269-275 and *passim*. The use of a definite description 'the *x* such that *Fx*' to 'fix

the reference' of a term T contrasts with defining T as equivalent in meaning to, i.e., as an abbreviation of, the definite description; in the former case, but not in the latter, the statement 'if T exists, then T is the x such that Fx' will be contingently rather than necessarily true. An expression is a rigid designator if it designates the same object in all possible worlds (or in all possible worlds in which it designates anything). According to Kripke, ordinary names are rigid designators, while many definite descriptions are not. When a definite description is used to introduce a name (and hence a rigid designator), it is used to 'fix its reference' rather than to 'define' it or give its 'meaning'.

16. My distinction between the 'functional' sense of 'appeared-blue-to' and a (possible) sense in which it rigidly designates (or, better, rigidly predicates) a qualitative state is similar to Chisholm's distinction between the 'comparative' and 'noncomparative' senses of expressions like 'looks blue'. See his *Perceiving: A Philosophical Study*, Ithaca, 1957, Chapter Four.

17. In a book which came to my attention after this paper was written (*Form and Content*, Oxford, Basil Blackwell, 1973), Bernard Harrison presents empirical evidence against the possibility of what I am calling spectrum inversion. He also tries to show on a priori grounds—and here I find him much less convincing—that "the linguistic and conceptual machinery which governs colour naming works in such a way that any difference in the perceived content of the colour presentations seen by different speakers must show itself in differences in the way in which they apply colour names, or in the privileges of occurrence in sentential contexts which colour names display in their discourse" (p. 133).

18. Sometimes it is suggested that if someone reported having undergone spectrum inversion, the most reasonable thing for us to conclude would be that something had gone awry with his grasp of the color vocabulary. This overlooks the fact that such a report could be backed up by behavioral evidence of a non-verbal sort. And I think we can imagine a series of events that would leave us no alternative but to conclude that spectrum inversion had occurred. Let us represent the color spectrum by a vertical line, and let us, arbitrarily, divide the line into six equal segments, labeling

these from top to bottom with the first six letters of the alphabet. And now consider the case of George. At time t_1 George's color experience, and his use of color words, was perfectly normal. But at time t_2 he tells us that a remarkable change has occurred; while most things look to him just as they used to, or look different only in ways that might be expected (e.g., if there is painting being done), a sizable minority of objects look to him very different than they did before, and he knows, from consulting other persons and from spectroscopic evidence, that in fact these objects have not undergone any significant change in color. George describes the change by saying that if he now looks at what we would regard as a normal spectrum, it looks the way a spectrum would have looked at t_1 if the end segments, A and F, had been interchanged and rotated one hundred and eighty degrees, the positions of the other segments remaining unchanged. According to this, the structure of George's color experience at t_2 is different from its structure at t_1. And since the putative change involves a change in structure, our evidence that it occurred need not be limited to George's testimony. George's claim will be supported by his recognitional and discriminatory behavior if, as we will suppose, he finds it easy to discriminate certain shades of color, for example those on either side of the boundary between segments A and B of the spectrum, which he formerly found it difficult to discriminate (and which the rest of us still find it difficult to discriminate), and sometimes finds it difficult to discriminate between different shades, for example if one is near the bottom boundary of segment A and the other is near the bottom boundary of segment E, which he formerly found it easy to discriminate (and which the rest of us still find it easy to discriminate). To continue the story, at time t_3 George tells us that another such change has occurred and added itself, as it were, to the first one; this time it is as if segments B and E of the spectrum had been interchanged and rotated. Again we can suppose that there is behavioral evidence to substantiate his claim. Finally, at time t_4 he tells us that still another such change has occurred; this time it is as if segments C and D had been interchanged and rotated. And again there is the substantiating behavioral evidence. But at t_4, unlike at t_2 and t_3, George's judgments of color similarity and difference will coincide with ours and with those he made at t_1 (allowing, of course, for whatever objective changes in color may have occurred in the interim); at t_4 the 'structure' of George's color experience will be the same as it was at t_1. Yet George reports that his color experience is systematically different from what it was at t_1; each color looks the way its inverse looked previously. And this claim of George's seems to be supported by the behavioral evidence that supported his claims that there were changes in his color experience between t_1 and t_2, between t_2 and t_3, and between t_3 and t_4; for these partial changes add up to a total spectrum inversion.

19. See, for example, Carl Ginet, "How Words Mean Kinds of Sensations," *The Philosophical Review* 77, 1 (January, 1968), p. 9.

20. Further arguments for this view are presented in my "Phenomenal Similarity," *Critica* 7, 20 (October, 1975), 2-34.

21. This account of what functional definition would amount to, and the elaboration of it that follows, is based loosely on David Lewis' account in 'Psychophysical and Theoretical Identification', *Australasian Journal of Philosophy* 50 (December, 1972), pp. 249-258.

Starting with the 'theory' which consists of the set of 'platitudes' about relations of mental states to one another and to input and output which it is plausible to regard as analytic or quasi-analytic, we can define the mental terms in that theory (supposing them, for simplicity, to be names of mental states) in the following way. We first write the theory as a single conjunctive sentence. We then replace each of the mental terms in the theory with a different variable, forming an open sentence. We then prefix quantifiers which transform the open sentence into the 'modified Ramsey sentence' of the theory, which says (in effect) that there exists a unique n-tuplet of states satisfying the open sentence. We are now in a position to define any of the mental terms that occurred in the original theory. Supposing that T_i is the term we wish to define, and y_i is the variable we replaced it with in forming the modified Ramsey sentence, we can turn the

modified Ramsey sentence into a definite description by (1) adding to the open sentence within the scope of the initial quantifiers the conjunct '$y_i = x$,' where 'x' is a variable that does not occur in the modified Ramsey sentence, and (2) prefixing the whole sentence with a definite description operator binding 'x'. What we then get is something of the form: $(\text{the } x)(E!y_1) \ldots (E!y_i) \ldots (E!y_n)(\ldots \ldots y_i \ldots \ldots \& y_i = x)$. In this description there will occur no mental terms. And we can define T_i as being synonymous with this description. [*Editor's note:* In this anthology, the ordinary "E" is used instead of the backward "E" as the existential quantifier.]

I should emphasize that what I am characterizing here is only one version of functionalism. Many philosophers who would regard themselves as functionalists would disavow any intention of giving, or providing a recipe for giving, any sort of meaning analysis of psychological terms.

22. Some advocates of causal or functional theories of the mind, especially those who would not accept the characterization of functionalism in section 6 and footnote 21, would object to being put in this company. But others have clearly seen their accounts as incorporating what is correct in, or as explaining the intuitions which make plausible, behavioristic and criteriological views. See, for example, David Lewis, *op. cit.*, p. 257, David Armstrong, *A Materialist Theory of the Mind,* London, 1968, p. 92, and Alvin Goldman, *A Theory of Human Action,* Englewood Cliffs, N.J., 1970, p. 112.

23. Such a view has in fact been advanced by D. M. Armstrong and by George Pitcher. See Armstrong, *op. cit.*, p. 313ff., and Pitcher's 'Pain Perception', *The Philosophical Review* 79 (1970), pp. 368-393.

24. I have benefited from discussions on this topic with Jonathan Bennett and Keith Lehrer, and am grateful to Bennett, and to N. J. Block, for criticisms of an earlier version of the paper. The paper was written while I was a Fellow at the Center for Advanced Study in the Behavioral Sciences, in Stanford, California, and I would like to express my gratitude to that institution.

Troubles with Functionalism

Ned Block

1.0 Functionalism, Behaviorism, and Physicalism

The functionalist view of the nature of the mind is now widely accepted.[1] Like behaviorism and physicalism, functionalism seeks to answer the question "What are mental states?" I shall be concerned with identity thesis formulations of functionalism. They say, for example, that pain is a functional state, just as identity thesis formulations of physicalism say that pain is a physical state.

I shall begin by describing functionalism, and sketching the functionalist critique of behaviorism and physicalism. Then I shall argue that the troubles ascribed by functionalism to behaviorism and physicalism infect functionalism as well.

One characterization of functionalism that is probably vague enough to be

From C. W. Savage, ed., *Perception and Cognition. Issues in the Foundations of Psychology, Minnesota Studies in the Philosophy of Science*, vol. 9 (Minneapolis: University of Minnesota Press, 1978), pp. 261–325. Copyright © 1978 by the University of Minnesota. Reprinted, with revisions by the author, by permission of University of Minnesota Press and the author.

accepted by most functionalists is: each type of mental state is a state consisting of a disposition to act in certain ways *and to have certain mental states*, given certain sensory inputs and certain mental states. So put, functionalism can be seen as a new incarnation of behaviorism. Behaviorism identifies mental states with dispositions to act in certain ways in certain input situations. But as critics have pointed out (Chisholm, 1957; Geach, 1957; Putnam, 1963), desire for goal G cannot be identified with, say, the disposition to do A in input circumstances in which A leads to G, since, after all, the agent might not *know* A leads to G and thus might not be disposed to do A. Functionalism replaces behaviorism's "sensory inputs" with "sensory inputs and mental states"; and functionalism replaces behaviorism's "disposition to act" with "disposition to act and have certain mental states." Functionalists want to individuate mental states causally, and since mental states have mental causes and effects as well as sensory causes and behavioral effects, functionalists individuate mental states partly in terms of causal relations to other mental states. One consequence of this difference between functionalism and behaviorism is that there are organisms that according to behaviorism, have mental states but, according to functionalism, do not have mental states.

So, necessary conditions for mentality that are postulated by functionalism are in one respect stronger than those postulated by behaviorism. According to behaviorism, it is necessary and sufficient for desiring that G that a system be characterized by a certain set (perhaps infinite) of input-output relations; that is, according to behaviorism, a system desires that G just in case a certain set of conditionals of the form 'It will emit O given I' are true of it. According to functionalism, however, a system might have these input-output relations, yet not desire that G; for according to functionalism, whether a system desires that G depends on whether it has internal states which have certain causal relations to other internal states (and to inputs and outputs). Since behaviorism makes no such "internal state" requirement, there are possible systems of which behaviorism affirms and functionalism denies that they have mental states.[2] One way of stating this is that, according to functionalism, behaviorism is guilty of *liberalism*—ascribing mental properties to things that do not in fact have them.

Despite the difference just sketched between functionalism and behaviorism, functionalists and behaviorists need not be far apart in spirit.[3] Shoemaker (1975), for example, says, "On one construal of it, functionalism in the philosophy of mind is the doctrine that mental, or psychological, terms are, in principle, eliminable in a certain way" (pp. 306-7). Functionalists have tended to treat the mental-state terms in a functional characterization of a mental state quite differently from the input and output terms. Thus in the simplest Turing-machine version of the theory (Putnam, 1967; Block & Fodor, 1972), mental states are identified with the total Turing-machine states, which are themselves *implicitly* defined by a machine table that explicitly mentions inputs and outputs, described nonmentalistically.

In Lewis's version of functionalism, mental-state terms are defined by means of a modification of Ramsey's method, in a way that eliminates essential use of mental terminology from the definitions but does not eliminate input and output terminology. That is, 'pain' is defined as synonymous with a definite description containing input and output terms but no mental terminology (see Lewis's articles in part three of this volume and "Introduction: What Is Functionalism?").

Furthermore, functionalism in both its machine and nonmachine versions has typically insisted that characterizations of mental states should contain descriptions of inputs and outputs in *physical* language. Armstrong (1968), for example, says,

> We may distinguish between 'physical behaviour', which refers to any merely physical action or passion of the body, and 'behaviour proper' which implies relationship to the mind. . . . Now, if in our formula ["state of the person apt for bringing about a certain sort of behaviour"] 'behaviour' were to mean 'behaviour proper', then we would be giving an account of mental concepts in terms of a concept that already presupposes mentality, which would be circular. So it is clear that in our formula, 'behaviour' must mean 'physical behaviour'. (p. 84)

Therefore, functionalism can be said to "tack down" mental states only at the periphery—i.e., through physical, or at least nonmental, specification of inputs and outputs. One major thesis of this article is that, because of this feature, functionalism fails to avoid the sort of problem for which it rightly condemns behaviorism. Functionalism, too, is guilty of liberalism, for much the same reasons as behaviorism. Unlike behaviorism, however, functionalism can naturally be altered to avoid liberalism—but only at the cost of falling into an equally ignominious failing.

The failing I speak of is the one that functionalism shows *physicalism* to be guilty of. By 'physicalism', I mean the doctrine that pain, for example, is identical to a physical (or physiological) state.[4] As many philosophers have argued (notably Fodor, 1965, and Putnam, 1966; see also Block & Fodor, 1972), if functionalism is true, physicalism is probably false. The point is at its clearest with regard to Turing-machine versions of functionalism. Any given abstract Turing machine can be realized by a wide variety of physical devices; indeed, it is plausible that, given any putative correspondence between a Turing-machine state and a configurational physical (or physiological) state, there will be a possible realization of the Turing machine that will provide a counterexample to that correspondence. (See Kalke, 1969; Gendron, 1971; Mucciolo, 1974, for unconvincing arguments to the contrary; see also Kim, 1972.) Therefore, if pain is a functional state, it cannot, for example, be a brain state, because creatures without brains can realize the same Turing machine as creatures with brains.

I must emphasize that the functionalist argument against physicalism does not appeal merely to the fact that one abstract Turing machine can be realized by systems of different *material composition* (wood, metal, glass, etc.). To argue this way would be like arguing that temperature cannot be a microphysical magnitude because the same temperature can be had by objects with *different* microphysical structures (Kim, 1972). Objects with different microphysical structures, e.g., objects made of wood, metal, glass, etc., can have many interesting microphysical properties in common, such as molecular kinetic energy of the same average value. Rather, the functionalist argument against physicalism is that it is difficult to see how there *could be* a nontrivial first-order (see note 4) physical property in common to all and only the possible physical realizations of a given Turing-machine state. Try to think of a remotely plausible candidate!

At the very least, the onus is on those who think such physical properties are conceivable to show us how to conceive of one.

One way of expressing this point is that, according to functionalism, physicalism is a *chauvinist* theory: it withholds mental properties from systems that in fact have them. In saying mental states are brain states, for example, physicalists unfairly exclude those poor brainless creatures who nonetheless have minds.

A second major point of this paper is that the very argument which functionalism uses to condemn physicalism can be applied equally well against functionalism; indeed, any version of functionalism that avoids liberalism falls, like physicalism, into chauvinism.

This article has three parts. The first argues that functionalism is guilty of liberalism, the second that one way of modifying functionalism to avoid liberalism is to tie it more closely to empirical psychology, and the third that no version of functionalism can avoid both liberalism and chauvinism.

1.1 More about What Functionalism Is

One way of providing some order to the bewildering variety of functionalist theories is to distinguish between those that are couched in terms of a Turing machine and those that are not.

A Turing-machine table lists a finite set of machine-table states, $S_1 \ldots S_n$; inputs, $I_1 \ldots I_m$; and outputs, $O_1 \ldots O_p$. The table specifies a set of conditionals of the form: if the machine is in state S_i and receives input I_j, it emits output O_k and goes into state S_l. That is, given any state and input, the table specifies an output and a next state. Any system with a set of inputs, outputs, and states related in the way specified by the table is described by the table and is a realization of the abstract automaton specified by the table.

To have the power for computing every recursive function, a Turing machine must be able to control its input in certain ways. In standard formulations, the output of a Turing machine is regarded as having two components. It prints a symbol on a tape, then moves the tape, thus bringing a new symbol into the view of the input reader. For the Turing machine to have full power, the tape must be infinite in at least one direction and movable in both directions. If the machine has no control over the tape, it is a "finite transducer," a rather limited Turing machine. Finite transducers need not be regarded as having tape at all. Those who believe that machine functionalism is true must suppose that just what power automaton we are is a substantive empirical question. If we are "full power" Turing machines, the environment must constitute part of the tape.

Machine functionalists generally consider the machine in question as a probabilistic automaton—a machine whose table specifies conditionals of the following form: if the machine is in S_a and receives I_b, it has a probability p_1 of emitting O_1; p_2 of emitting O_2 ... p_k of emitting O_k; r_1 of going into S_1; r_2 of going into S_2 ... r_n of going into S_n. For simplicity, I shall usually consider a deterministic version of the theory.

One very simple version of machine functionalism (Block & Fodor, 1972) states that each system having mental states is described by at least one Turing-machine table of a specifiable sort and that each type of mental state of the system is identical to one of the machine-table states. Consider, for example, the Turing machine described in the accompanying table (cf. Nelson, 1975):

	S_1	S_2
nickel input	Emit no output Go to S_2	Emit a Coke Go to S_1
dime input	Emit a Coke Stay in S_1	Emit a Coke & a nickel Go to S_1

One can get a crude picture of the simple version of machine functionalism by considering the claim that S_1 = dime-desire, and S_2 = nickel-desire. Of course, no functionalist would claim that a Coke machine desires anything. Rather, the simple version of machine functionalism described above makes an analogous claim with respect to a much more complex machine table. Notice that machine functionalism specifies inputs and outputs explicitly, internal states implicitly (Putnam [1967, p. 434] says: "The S_i, to repeat, are specified only *implicitly* by the description, i.e., specified *only* by the set of transition probabilities given in the machine table"). To be described by this machine table, a device must accept nickels and dimes as inputs and dispense nickels and Cokes as outputs. But the states S_1 and S_2 can have virtually any natures, so long as those natures connect the states to each other and to the inputs and outputs specified in the machine table. All we are told about S_1 and S_2 are these relations; thus machine functionalism can be said to reduce mentality to input-output structures. This example should suggest the force of the functionalist argument against physicalism. Try to think of a first-order (see note 4) physical property that can be shared by all (and only) realizations of this machine table!

One can also categorize functionalists in terms of whether they regard functional identities as part of a priori psychology or empirical psychology. (Since this distinction crosscuts the machine/nonmachine distinction, I shall be able to illustrate nonmachine versions of functionalism in what follows.) The a priori functionalists (e.g., Smart, Armstrong, Lewis, Shoemaker) are the heirs of the logical behaviorists. They tend to regard functional analyses as analyses of the meanings of mental terms, whereas the empirical functionalists (e.g., Fodor, Putnam, Harman) regard functional analyses as substantive scientific hypotheses. In what follows, I shall refer to the former view as 'Functionalism' and the latter as 'Psychofunctionalism'. (I shall use 'functionalism' with a lowercase 'f' as neutral between Functionalism and Psychofunctionalism. When distinguishing between Functionalism and Psychofunctionalism, I shall always use capitals.)

Functionalism and Psychofunctionalism and the difference between them can be made clearer in terms of the notion of the Ramsey sentence of a psychological theory. Mental-state terms that appear in a psychological theory can be defined in various ways by means of the Ramsey sentence of the theory (see "Introduction: What is Functionalism?"). All functional-state identity theories (and functional-property identity theories) can be understood as defining a set of functional states (or functional properties) by means of the Ramsey sentence of a psychological theory—with one functional state corresponding to each mental state (or one functional property corresponding to each mental property). The functional state corresponding to pain will be called the 'Ramsey functional correlate' of pain, with respect to the psychological theory. In terms of the notion of a Ramsey functional correlate with respect to a theory, the distinction between Functionalism and Psychofunctionalism can be defined as follows: Functionalism identifies mental state S with S's Ramsey functional correlate with respect to a *common-sense* psychological theory; Psychofunctionalism identifies S with S's Ramsey functional correlate with respect to a *scientific* psychological theory.

This difference between Functionalism and Psychofunctionalism gives rise to a difference in specifying inputs and outputs. Functionalists are restricted to specification of inputs and outputs that are plausibly part of common-sense knowledge; Psychofunctionalists are under no such restriction. Although both groups insist on physical—or at least nonmental

—specification of inputs and outputs, Functionalists require externally observable classifications (e.g., inputs characterized in terms of objects present in the vicinity of the organism, outputs in terms of movements of body parts). Psychofunctionalists, on the other hand, have the option to specify inputs and outputs in terms of internal parameters, e.g., signals in input and output neurons.

The notion of a Ramsey functional correlate can be defined in a variety of ways. For the purposes of this paper, I will adopt the formulation presented in detail in the introduction to part three of this volume (see "Introduction: What Is Functionalism?"). I shall assume that pain is a property, the property ascribed to someone in saying that he has pain. For the purposes of this paper, I ignore differences between the state pain and the property of being in pain.

Let T be a psychological theory of either common-sense or scientific psychology. Reformulate T so that it is a single conjunctive sentence with all mental-state terms as singular terms. E.g., 'is angry' becomes 'has anger'. Suppose that T, so reformulated can be written as

$$T(s_1 \ldots s_n, i_1 \ldots i_k, o_1 \ldots o_m)$$

where s_i, i_i, o_i designate respectively, a mental state, input, and output. T may contain generalizations of the form: being in such and such states, and receiving such and such inputs produces such and such outputs and transitions to such and such states. To get the Ramsey sentence of T, replace the state terms $s_1 \ldots s_n$ (but *not* $i_1 \ldots i_k$, $o_1 \ldots o_m$) by variables, and prefix an existential quantifier for each variable. A singular term designating the Ramsey functional correlate of pain (with respect to T) can be formulated using a property abstraction operator. Let an expression of the form '%xFx' be a singular term meaning the same as an expression of the form 'the property (or attribute) of being an x such that x is F', i.e., 'being F'.[5]

If x_i is the variable that replaced 'pain', the Ramsey functional correlate of pain (with respect to T) is

$$\%yEx_1 \ldots x_n[T(x_1 \ldots x_n, i_1 \ldots i_k,$$
$$o_1 \ldots o_m) \& y \text{ is in } x_i].$$

Notice that this expression contains input and output terms ($i_1 \ldots i_k, o_1 \ldots o_m$), but no mental terms (since they were replaced by variables). Every mental state mentioned in theory T (indeed, every property mentioned in any theory) has a Ramsey functional correlate. Ramsey functional correlates for psychological theories, it should be noted, are defined in terms of inputs and outputs (plus logical terms) alone. It is natural to suppose that the Ramsey functional correlate of a state S is a state that has much in common with S (namely, it shares the *structural* properties specified by T) but is not identical to S. For the Ramsey functional correlate of S (with respect to T) will "include" only those aspects of S that are represented in T. Since no theory can be expected to tell us *everything* about every state it mentions, we would naturally suppose that, in general, S is not identical to its Ramsey functional correlate with respect to T. (An example that illustrates this point with respect to physics is presented below in section 2.0). The bold hypothesis of functionalism is that for at least *some* psychological theory, this natural supposition is false.[6] Functionalism says that pain, for example, *is* its Ramsey functional correlate, at least with respect to some psychological theory; and, furthermore, that this is true not only for pain, but for every mental state. (See the example in "Introduction: What is Functionalism?")[7]

Functional Equivalence

Relations of functional equivalence for all versions of functionalism are relative to specification of inputs and outputs. For both machine and nonmachine versions of functionalism, there are functional-equivalence relations of different strengths. One could regard Turing machines x and y as functionally equivalent (relative to a given specification of inputs and outputs) just in case there is at least one machine table that lists just that set of inputs and outputs and describes both x and y. On the other hand, one could require that *every* machine table that describes x describes y and vice versa—relative to the given specifications of inputs and outputs. One way of being precise—though redundant—is to speak of functional equivalence relative to *both* a given specification of inputs and outputs and a given machine table.

Similar points apply to nonmachine versions of functionalism. One could regard systems x and y as functionally equivalent (relative to a given specification of inputs and outputs) just in case there is at least one psychological theory that adverts to just that set of inputs and outputs and is true of both x and y. Or one might require that all psychological theories with the set of inputs and outputs that are true of x are also true of y. Again, one way of being precise is to relativize to both inputs and outputs and to psychological theory.

In what follows, I shall sometimes speak of x and y as functionally equivalent (with respect to certain inputs and outputs) without specifying a particular psychological theory or Turing-machine table. What I shall mean is that x and y are functionally equivalent (with respect to the given inputs and outputs) with respect to at least one reasonably adequate, true psychological theory (either commonsense or empirical, depending on whether Functionalism or Psychofunctionalism is in question) or with respect to at least one reasonably adequate machine table that describes both x and y. Admittedly, such notions of functional equivalence are quite vague. Unfortunately, I see no way of avoiding this vagueness. Functionalists should be consoled, however, by the fact that their chief rival, physicalism, seems beset by an analogous vagueness. As far as I know, no one has ever come up with a remotely satisfactory way of saying what a physical state or property is without quantifying over unknown, true physical theories (e.g., a physical property is a property expressed by a predicate of some true physical theory); nor has anyone been able to say what it is for x and y to be physical states of the same type without quantifying over reasonably adequate, but unknown, true physical theories (see note 4).

In discussing the various versions of functionalism, I have also been rather vague about what psychology is supposed to be psychology *of*. Presumably, some animals, e.g., dogs, are capable of many of the same mental states as humans, e.g., hunger, thirst, other desires, and some beliefs. Thus, if functionalism is true, we must suppose that there is a psychological theory that applies to people and some animals that says what it is in virtue of which both the animals and the people have beliefs, desires, etc. On the other hand, there are mental states people can have that dogs presumably cannot. Further, there may be mental states that some persons can have but others cannot. Some of us can suffer *weltschmerz*, whereas others, perhaps, cannot. It is possible that there are no basic psychological differences between dogs, persons who can have *weltschmerz*, persons who cannot, etc. Perhaps the gross behavioral differences are due to different values of the same parameters in a single psychological theory that covers all the aforementioned creatures. An analogy: the same theory of nuclear physics covers both reactors and bombs, even though there is a gross difference in their behavior. This is due to different values of a single set of parameters that determine whether or not the reaction is controlled. Perhaps parameters such as information-processing capacity or memory space play the same role in psychology. But this is unlikely for scientific psychology, and it surely is not true for the common-sense psychological theories Functionalism appeals to. Thus, it seems likely that both Functionalism and Psychofunctionalism require psychological theories of different degrees of generality or level of abstraction—one for humans who can have *weltschmerz*, one for all humans, one for dogs and humans, etc. If so, different mental states may be identical to functional states at different abstractness levels. The same point applies to functional-equivalence relations. Two creatures may be functionally equivalent relative to one level of abstractness of psychological theory, but not with respect to another.

The Ramsey functional-correlate characterization of functionalism captures relativities to both abstractness level and input-output specification. According to both Functionalism and Psychofunctionalism, each functional state is identical to its Ramsey functional correlate with respect to a psychological theory. The intended level of abstractness is automatically captured in the level of detail present in the theory. The input and output specifications are just those mentioned. For example, suppose the Ramsey functional correlate of pain with respect to the theory is $\%yEx_1Ex_2$ (x_1 is caused by pin pricks and causes x_2 and screaming & y is in x_1). [*Editor's note:* In this anthology, the ordinary "E" is used instead of the backward "E" as the existential quantifier.] The input and output specifications are 'pin pricks' and 'screaming', and the level of abstractness is determined by those causal relations being the only ones mentioned.

Until Section 3.1, I shall ignore considerations concerning level of abstractness. When I say that two systems are "functionally equivalent," I shall assume that my "reasonable adequacy" condition ensures an appropriate level of concreteness.[8]

If correct, the characterization that I have given of functionalism as being theory relative should be a source of difficulty for the functionalist who is also a realist. Since psychological theories can differ considerably—even if we restrict our attention to true theories—the functionalist would identify pain with one state with respect to one theory and another state with respect to another theory. But how can pain be identical to nonidentical states?[9]

I see only two avenues of escape that have even a modicum of plausibility. One would be to argue that true psychological theories simply do not differ in ways that create embarrassment for realist functionalists. Certain views about the varieties of true psychological theories may be conjoined with views about identity conditions for states in order to argue that the Ramsey functional correlates of pain with respect to the true psychological theories are not different from one another. The second approach is to argue that there is only one true psychological theory (or set of equivalent theories) that provides the *correct* Ramsey functional correlate of pain. According to Lewis (1966, 1972) and Shoemaker (1975), the theory that contains all the truths of meaning analysis of psychological terms has this property. I argue against their claim in Section 1.5.

One final preliminary point: I have given the misleading impression that functionalism identifies *all* mental states with functional states. Such a version of functionalism is obviously far too strong. Let X be a newly created cell-for-cell duplicate of you (which, of course, is functionally equivalent to you). Perhaps you remember being bar-mitzvahed. But X does not remember being bar-mitzvahed, since X never was bar-mitzvahed. Indeed, something can be functionally equivalent to you but fail to know what you know, or [verb], what you [verb], for a wide variety of "success" verbs. Worse still, if Putnam (1975b) is right in saying that "meanings are not in the head," systems functionally equivalent to you may, for

similar reasons, fail to have many of your other propositional attitudes. Suppose you believe water is wet. According to plausible arguments advanced by Putnam and Kripke, a condition for the possibility of your believing water is wet is a certain kind of causal connection between you and water. Your "twin" on Twin Earth, who is connected in a similar way to XYZ rather than H_2O, would not believe water is wet.

If functionalism is to be defended, it must be construed as applying only to a subclass of mental states, those "narrow" mental states such that truth conditions for their application are in some sense "within the person." But even assuming that a notion of narrowness of psychological state can be satisfactorily formulated, the interest of functionalism may be diminished by this restriction. I mention this problem only to set it aside.

I shall take functionalism to be a doctrine about all "narrow" mental states.

1.2 Homunculi-Headed Robots

In this section I shall describe a class of devices that embarrass all versions of functionalism in that they indicate functionalism is guilty of liberalism—classifying systems that lack mentality as having mentality.

Consider the simple version of machine functionalism already described. It says that each system having mental states is described by at least one Turing-machine table of a certain kind, and each mental state of the system is identical to one of the machine-table states specified by the machine table. I shall consider inputs and outputs to be specified by descriptions of neural impulses in sense organs and motor-output neurons. This assumption should not be regarded as restricting what will be said to Psychofunctionalism rather than Functionalism. As already mentioned, every version of functionalism assumes *some* specificiation of inputs and outputs. A Functionalist specification would do as well for the purposes of what follows.

Imagine a body externally like a human body, say yours, but internally quite different. The neurons from sensory organs are connected to a bank of lights in a hollow cavity in the head. A set of buttons connects to the motor-output neurons. Inside the cavity resides a group of little men. Each has a very simple task: to implement a "square" of a reasonably adequate machine table that describes you. On one wall is a bulletin board on which is posted a state card, i.e., a card that bears a symbol designating one of the states specified in the machine table. Here is what the little men do: Suppose the posted card has a 'G' on it. This alerts the little men who implement G squares— 'G-men' they call themselves. Suppose the light representing input I_{17} goes on. One of the G-men has the following as his sole task: when the card reads 'G' and the I_{17} light goes on, he presses output button O_{191} and changes the state card to 'M'. This G-man is called upon to exercise his task only rarely. In spite of the low level of intelligence required of each little man, the system as a whole manages to simulate you because the functional organization they have been trained to realize is yours. A Turing machine can be represented as a finite set of quadruples (or quintuples, if the output is divided into two parts): current state, current input; next state, next output. Each little man has the task corresponding to a single quadruple. Through the efforts of the little men, the system realizes the same (reasonably adequate) machine table as you do and is thus functionally equivalent to you.[10]

I shall describe a version of the homunculi-headed simulation, which is more clearly nomologically possible. How many homunculi are required? Perhaps a billion are enough.

Suppose we convert the government of China to functionalism, and we con-

vince its officials that it would enormously enhance their international prestige to realize a human mind for an hour. We provide each of the billion people in China (I chose China because it has a billion inhabitants) with a specially designed two-way radio that connects them in the appropriate way to other persons and to the artificial body mentioned in the previous example. We replace the little men with a radio transmitter and receiver connected to the input and output neurons. Instead of a bulletin board, we arrange to have letters displayed on a series of satellites placed so that they can be seen from anywhere in China.

The system of a billion people communicating with one another plus satellites plays the role of an external "brain" connected to the artificial body by radio. There is nothing absurd about a person being connected to his brain by radio. Perhaps the day will come when our brains will be periodically removed for cleaning and repairs. Imagine that this is done initially by treating neurons attaching the brain to the body with a chemical that allows them to stretch like rubber bands, thereby assuring that no brain-body connections are disrupted. Soon clever businessmen discover that they can attract more customers by replacing the stretched neurons with radio links so that brains can be cleaned without inconveniencing the customer by immobilizing his body.

It is not at all obvious that the China-body system is physically impossible. It could be functionally equivalent to you for a short time, say an hour.

"But," you may object, "how could something be functionally equivalent to me for *an hour?* Doesn't my functional organization determine, say, how I would react to doing nothing for a week but reading the *Reader's Digest?*" Remember that a machine table specifies a set of conditionals of the form: if the machine is in S_i and receives input I_j, it emits output O_k

and goes into S]. These conditionals are to be understood *subjunctively*. What gives a system a functional organization at a time is not just what it *does* at that time, but also the counterfactuals true of it at that time: what it *would* have done (and what its state transitions would have been) had it had a different input or been in a different state. If it is true of a system at time t that it *would* obey a given machine table no matter which of the states it is in and no matter which of the inputs it receives, then the system is described at t by the machine table (and realizes at t the abstract automaton specified by the table), even if it exists for only an instant. For the hour the Chinese system is "on," it *does* have a set of inputs, outputs, and states of which such subjunctive conditionals are true. This is what makes any computer realize the abstract automaton that it realizes.

Of course, there are signals the system would respond to that you would not respond to, e.g., massive radio interference or a flood of the Yangtze River. Such events might cause a malfunction, scotching the simulation, just as a bomb in a computer can make it fail to realize the machine table it was built to realize. But just as the computer *without* the bomb *can* realize the machine table, the system consisting of the people and artificial body can realize the machine table so long as there are no catastrophic interferences, e.g., floods, etc.

"But," someone may object, "there is a difference between a bomb in a computer and a bomb in the Chinese system, for in the case of the latter (unlike the former), inputs as specified in the machine table can be the cause of the malfunction. Unusual neural activity in the sense organs of residents of Chungking Province caused by a bomb or by a flood of the Yangtze can cause the system to go haywire."

Reply: The person who says what system he or she is talking about gets to say what counts as inputs and outputs. I count as inputs and outputs only neural activity in the artificial body connected by radio to the people of China. Neural signals in the people of Chungking count no more as inputs to this system than input tape jammed by a saboteur between the relay contacts in the innards of a computer count as an input to the computer.

Of course, the object consisting of the people of China + the artificial body has *other* Turing-machine descriptions under which neural signals in the inhabitants of Chungking *would* count as inputs. Such a new system (i.e., the object under such a new Turing-machine description) would not be functionally equivalent to you. Likewise, any commercial computer can be redescribed in a way that allows tape jammed into its innards to count as inputs. In describing an object as a Turing machine, one draws a line between the inside and the outside. (If we count only neural impulses as inputs and outputs, we draw that line inside the body; if we count only peripheral stimulations as inputs and only bodily movements as outputs, we draw that line at the skin.) In describing the Chinese system as a Turing machine, I have drawn the line in such a way that it satisfies a certain type of functional description—one that you *also* satisfy, and one that, according to functionalism, justifies attributions of mentality. Functionalism does not claim that every mental system has a machine table of a sort that justifies attributions of mentality with respect to *every* specification of inputs and outputs, but rather, only with respect to *some* specification.[11]

Objection: The Chinese system would work too slowly. The kind of events and processes with which we normally have contact would pass by far too quickly for the system to detect them. Thus, we would be unable to converse with it, play bridge with it, etc.[12]

Reply: It is hard to see why the system's time scale should matter. What reason is there to believe that *your* mental operations could not be very much slowed down, yet remain mental operations? Is it really contradictory or nonsensical to suppose we could meet a race of intelligent beings with whom we could communicate only by devices such as time-lapse photography? When we observe these creatures, they seem almost inanimate. But when we view the time-lapse movies, we see them conversing with one another. Indeed, we find they are saying that the only way they can make any sense of us is by viewing movies greatly slowed down. To take time scale as all important seems crudely behavioristic. Further, even if the time-scale objection is right, I can elude it by retreating to the point that a homunculi-head that works in normal time is *metaphysically* possible. Metaphysical possibility is all my argument requires. (See Kripke, 1972.)

What makes the homunculi-headed system (count the two systems as variants of a single system) just described a prima facie counterexample to (machine) functionalism is that there is prima facie doubt whether it has any mental states at all—especially whether it has what philosophers have variously called "qualitative states," "raw feels," or "immediate phenomenological qualities." (You ask: What is it that philosophers have called qualitative states? I answer, only half in jest: As Louis Armstrong said when asked what jazz is, "If you got to ask, you ain't never gonna get to know.") In Nagel's terms (1974), there is a prima facie doubt whether there is anything which it is like to be the homunculi-headed system.

The force of the prima facie counterexample can be made clearer as follows: Machine functionalism says that each mental state is identical to a machine-table state. For example, a particular qualitative state, Q, is identical to a machine-table state, S_q. But if there is nothing it is like to be the homunculi-headed system, it cannot be in Q even when it is in S_q.

Thus, if there is prima facie doubt about the homunculi-headed system's mentality, there is prima facie doubt that $Q = S_q$, i.e., doubt that the kind of functionalism under consideration is true.[13] Call this argument the Absent Qualia Argument.

So there is prima facie doubt that machine functionalism is true. So what? After all, prima facie doubt is only prima facie. Indeed, appeals to intuition of this sort are notoriously fallible. I shall not rest on this appeal to intuition. Rather, I shall argue that the intuition that the homunculi-headed simulation described above lacks mentality (or at least qualia) has at least in part a rational basis, and that this rational basis provides a good reason for doubting that Functionalism (and to a lesser degree Psychofunctionalism) is true. I shall consider this line of argument in Section 1.5.[14]

1.3 What If I Turned Out to Have Little Men in My Head?

Before I go any further, I shall briefly discuss a difficulty for my claim that there is prima facie doubt about the qualia of homunculi-headed realizations of human functional organization. It might be objected, "What if *you* turned out to be one?" Let us suppose that, to my surprise, X-rays reveal that inside my head are thousands of tiny, trained fleas, each of which has been taught (perhaps by a joint subcommittee of the American Philosophical Association and the American Psychological Association empowered to investigate absent qualia) to implement a square in the appropriate machine table.

Now there is a crucial issue relevant to this difficulty which philosophers are far from agreeing on (and about which I confess I cannot make up my mind): Do I know on the basis of my "privileged access" that I do not have utterly absent qualia, no matter what turns out to be inside my head? Do I know there is something it is like to be me, even if I am a flea-head? Fortunately, my vacillation on this issue is of no consequence, for either answer is compatible with the Absent Qualia Argument's assumption that there is doubt about the qualia of homunculi-headed folks.

Suppose the answer is no. It is not the case that I know there is something it is like to be me even if I am a flea-head. Then I should admit that my qualia would be in (prima facie) doubt if (God forbid) I turned out to have fleas in my head. Likewise for the qualia of all the other homunculi-headed folk. So far, so good.

Suppose, on the other hand, that my privileged access does give me infallible knowledge that I have qualia. No matter what turns out to be inside my head, my states have qualitative content. There is something it is like to be me. Then if I turn out to have fleas in my head, at least one homunculi-head turns out to have qualia. But this would not challenge my claim that the qualia of homunculi-infested simulations is in doubt. Since I do, in fact, have qualia, supposing I have fleas inside my head is supposing someone with fleas inside his head has qualia. But this supposition that a homunculi-head has qualia is just the sort of supposition my position doubts. Using such an example to argue against my position is like twitting a man who doubts there is a God by asking what he would say if he turned out to *be* God. Both arguments against the doubter beg the question against the doubter by hypothesizing a situation which the doubter admits is logically possible, but doubts is *actual*. A doubt that there is a God entails a doubt that I am God. Similarly, (given that I do have qualia) a doubt that flea-heads have qualia entails a doubt that I am a flea-head.

1.4 Putnam's Proposal

One way functionalists can try to deal with the problem posed by the homunculi-headed counterexamples is by the ad hoc device of stipulating them away. For example, a functionalist might stipulate that two systems cannot be functionally equivalent if one contains parts with functional organizations characteristic of sentient beings and the other does not. In his article hypothesizing that pain is a functional state, Putnam stipulated that "no organism capable of feeling pain possesses a decomposition into parts which separately possess Descriptions" (as the sort of Turing machine which can be in the functional state Putnam identifies with pain). The purpose of this condition is "to rule out such 'organisms' (if they count as such) as swarms of bees as single pain feelers" (Putnam, 1967, pp. 434-435).

One way of filling out Putnam's requirement would be: a pain-feeling organism cannot possess a decomposition into parts *all* of which have a functional organization characteristic of sentient beings. But this would not rule out my homunculi-headed example, since it has nonsentient parts, such as the mechanical body and sense organs. It will not do to go to the opposite extreme and require that *no* proper parts be sentient. Otherwise pregnant women and people with sentient parasites will fail to count as pain-feeling organisms. What seems to be important to examples like the homunculi-headed simulation I have described is that the sentient beings *play a crucial role* in giving the thing its functional organization. This suggests a version of Putnam's proposal which requires that a pain-feeling organism has a certain functional organization and that it has no parts which (1) themselves possess that sort of functional organization and also (2) play a crucial role in giving the whole system its functional organization.

Although this proposal involves the vague notion "crucial role," it is precise enough for us to see it will not do. Suppose there is a part of the universe that contains matter quite different from ours, matter that is infinitely divisible. In this part of the universe, there are intelligent creatures of many sizes, even humanlike creatures much smaller than our elementary particles. In an intergalactic expedition, these people discover the existence of our type of matter. For reasons known only to them, they decide to devote the next few hundred years to creating out of their matter substances with the chemical and physical characteristics (except at the subelementary particle level) of our elements. They build hordes of space ships of different varieties about the sizes of our electrons, protons, and other elementary particles, and fly the ships in such a way as to mimic the behavior of these elementary particles. The ships also contain generators to produce the type of radiation elementary particles give off. Each ship has a staff of experts on the nature of our elementary particles. They do this to produce huge (by our standards) masses of substances with the chemical and physical characteristics of oxygen, carbon, etc. Shortly after they accomplish this, you go off on an expedition to that part of the universe, and discover the "oxygen," "carbon," etc. Unaware of its real nature, you set up a colony, using these "elements" to grow plants for food, provide "air" to breathe, etc. Since one's molecules are constantly being exchanged with the environment, you and other colonizers come (in a period of a few years) to be composed mainly of the "matter" made of the tiny people in space ships. Would you be any less capable of feeling pain, thinking, etc. just because the matter of which you are composed contains (and depends on for its characteristics) beings who themselves have a functional organization characteristic of sentient creatures? I think not. The basic electrochemical mechanisms by which the synapse operates are now fairly well understood. As far as is known, changes that do not affect these electrochemical mechanisms do not affect the operation of the brain, and do not affect mentality. The electrochemical mechanisms in your synapses would be unaffected by the change in your matter.[15]

It is interesting to compare the elementary-particle-people example with the homunculi-headed examples the chapter started with. A natural first guess about the source of our intuition that the initially described homunculi-headed simulations lack mentality is that they have *too much* internal mental structure. The little men may be sometimes bored, sometimes excited. We may even imagine that they deliberate about the best way to realize the given functional organization and make changes intended to give them more leisure time. But the example of the elementary-particle people just described suggests this first guess is wrong. What seems important is *how* the mentality of the parts contributes to the functioning of the whole.

There is one very noticeable difference between the elementary-particle-people example and the earlier homunculus examples. In the former, the change in you as you become homunculus-infested is not one that makes any difference to your psychological processing (i.e., information processing) or neurological processing but only to your microphysics. No techniques proper to human psychology or neurophysiology would reveal any difference in you. However, the homunculi-headed simulations described in the beginning of the chapter are not things to which neurophysiological theories true of us apply, and *if they are construed as Functional* (rather than Psychofunctional) simulations, they need not be things to which psychological (information-processing) theories true of us apply. This difference suggests that our intuitions are in part controlled by the not unreasonable view that our mental states depend on our having the psychology and/or neurophysiology we have. So something that differs markedly from us in both regards (recall that it is a Functional rather than Psychofunctional simulation) should not be assumed to have mentality just on the ground that it is Functionally equivalent to us.[16]

1.5 Is the Prima Facie Doubt Merely Prima Facie?

The Absent Qualia Argument rested on an appeal to the intuition that the homunculi-headed simulations lacked mentality, or at least qualia. I said that this intuition gave rise to prima facie doubt that functionalism is true. But intuitions unsupported by principled argument are hardly to be considered bedrock. Indeed, intuitions incompatible with well-supported theory (e.g., the pre-Copernican intuition that the earth does not move) thankfully soon disappear. Even fields like linguistics whose data consist mainly in intuitions often reject such intuitions as that the following sentences are ungrammatical (on theoretical grounds):

The horse raced past the barn fell.
The boy the girl the cat bit scratched died.

These sentences are in fact grammatical, though hard to process.[17]

Appeal to intuitions when judging possession of mentality, however, is *especially* suspicious. *No* physical mechanism seems very intuitively plausible as a seat of qualia, least of all a *brain*. Is a hunk of quivering gray stuff more intuitively appropriate as a seat of qualia than a covey of little men? If not, perhaps there is a prima facie doubt about the qualia of brain-headed systems too?

However, there is a very important difference between brain-headed and homunculi-headed systems. Since we know that *we are brain-headed systems,* and that *we* have qualia, we know that brain-headed systems can have qualia. So even though we have no theory of qualia which explains how this is *possible,* we have overwhelming reason to disregard whatever prima facie doubt there is about the qualia of brain-headed systems. Of course, this makes my argument partly *empirical* —it depends on knowledge of what makes us tick. But since this is knowledge we in fact possess, dependence on this knowledge should not be regarded as a defect.[18]

There is another difference between us meat-heads and the homunculi-heads: they are systems designed to mimic us, but we are not designed to mimic anything (here I rely on another empirical fact). This fact forestalls any attempt to argue on the basis of an inference to the best explanation for the qualia of homunculi-heads. The best explanation of the homunculi-heads' screams and winces is not their pains, but that they were designed to mimic our screams and winces.

Some people seem to feel that the complex and subtle behavior of the homunculi-heads (behavior just as complex and subtle—even as "sensitive" to features of the environment, human and nonhuman, as your behavior) is itself sufficient reason to disregard the prima facie doubt that homunculi-heads have qualia. But this is just crude behaviorism.

I shall try to convince the reader of this by describing a machine that would act like a mental system in a situation in which only verbal inputs and outputs are involved (a machine that would pass the "Turing Test").

Call a string of sentences whose members, spoken one after another, can be uttered in an hour or less, a speakable string of sentences. A speakable string can contain one very long sentence, or a number of shorter ones. Consider the set of all speakable strings of sentences. Since English has a finite number of words (indeed, a finite number of sound sequences forming possible words short enough to appear in a speakable string), this set has a very large but finite number of members. Consider the subset of the set of all speakable strings of sentences, each of whose member strings can be understood as a conversation in which at least one party is "making sense." Call it the set of smart speakable strings. For example, if we allot each party to a conversation one sentence per "turn," each even-numbered sentence of each string in S would be a sensible contribution to the ongoing discussion. We need not be too restrictive about what is to count as making sense. For example, if sentence 1 is "Let's see you talk nonsense," then sentence 2 could be nonsensical. The set of smart speakable strings is a finite set which could in principle be listed by a very large team working for a long time with a very large grant. Imagine that the smart speakable strings are recorded on tape and deployed by a very simple machine, as follows. An interrogator utters sentence A. The machine searches the set of smart speakable strings, picks out those strings that begin with A, and picks one string at random (or it might pick the first string it finds beginning with A, using a random search). It then produces the second sentence in that string, call it 'B'. The interrogator utters another sentence, call it 'C'. The machine picks a string at random that starts with A, followed by B, followed by C, and utters its fourth sentence, and so on.

Now, if the team has been thorough and imaginative in listing the smart speakable strings, this machine would simulate human conversational abilities. Indeed, if the team did a brilliantly creative job, the machine's conversational abilities might be superhuman (though if it is to "keep up" with current events, the job would have to be redone often). But this machine clearly has no mental states at all. It is just a huge list-searcher plus a tape recorder.

Thus far in this section, I have admitted that the intuition that the homunculi-head lacks qualia is far from decisive, since intuition balks at assigning qualia to any physical mechanism. But I went on to argue that although there is good reason to disregard any intuition that brain-headed systems lack qualia, there is no reason to disregard our intuition that homunculi-headed simulations lack qualia. I now want to argue that the intuition that homunculi-headed simulations lack qualia can be backed up by argument. The rest of this section will be devoted to Functionalism and Functional simulations. The next section will be devoted to parallel considerations with respect to Psychofunctionalism.

Think of the original homunculi-headed example as being designed to be Functionally equivalent to you. Since it need not be Psychofunctionally equivalent to you (see the next section), it need not be something to which any scientific psychological theory true of you applies. Obviously, it would not be something to which neurological theories true of you apply. Now as I pointed out in the last few paragraphs of the last section, it is a highly plausible assumption that mental states are in the domain of psychology and/or neurophysiology, or at least that mentality depends crucially on psychological and/or neurophysiological processes and structures. But since the homunculi-headed Functional simulation of you is markedly unlike you neurophysiologically (insofar as it makes sense to speak of something with no neurons at all being neurophysiologically unlike anything) and since it need not be anything like you psychologically (that is, its information processing need not be remotely like yours), it need not have mentality, even if it is Functionally equivalent to you.[19] My claim is not that every sort of Functional simulation of you must lack qualia. Different causes can have similar effects, so why shouldn't it be possible that mentality can be produced by wildly different sorts of information processing? My point rather is that not every sort of homunculi-headed Functional simulation *need* have qualia. If there is even *one* possible Functional simulation of you that has no qualia, Functionalism is false.

These arguments are not conclusive, but they do throw the onus of argument on Functionalists. Can Functionalists produce *any* minimally decent argument *for* Functionalism? If not, the arguments I have given justify us in rejecting Functionalism.

In sum, I have given two arguments against Functionalism. First, Functionalism has a counterintuitive consequence: that a homunculi-headed Functional simulation of you must have qualia. If there is no reason to disregard this intuition, and in the absence of any good argument *for* Functionalism, we are justified in rejecting Functionalism, at least tentatively. Second, given that mentality depends crucially on psychological and/or neurological processes and structures, and given that a homunculi-headed Functional simulation need not be psychologically or neurophysiologically like us, it would seem that a Functional simulation need not have mentality. Once again, the onus is on the Functionalist to show otherwise.

I shall now discuss what can be said in favor of Functionalism, and in the process sketch additional arguments against the doctrine.

In spite of the widespread belief in forms of Functionalism, I know of only one kind of argument for it in the literature. It is claimed that Functional identities can be shown to be true on the basis of analyses of the meanings of mental terminology. According to this argument, Functional identities are to be justified in the way one might try to justify the claim that the state of being a bachelor is identical to the state of being an unmarried man. A similar argument appeals to commonsense platitudes about mental states instead of truths of meaning. Lewis says that Functional characterizations of mental states are in the province of "common sense psychology—folk science, rather than professional science" (Lewis, 1972, p. 250). (See also Shoemaker, 1975, and Armstrong, 1968. Armstrong equivocates on the analyticity issue. See Armstrong, 1968, pp. 84-85, and p. 90.) And he goes on to insist that Functional characterizations should "include only platitudes which are common knowledge among us —everyone knows them, everyone knows that everyone else knows them, and so on" (Lewis, 1972, p. 256). I shall talk mainly about the "platitude" version of

the argument. The analyticity version is vulnerable to essentially the same considerations, as well as Quinean doubts about analyticity.

Because of the required platitudinous nature of Functional definitions, Functionalism runs into serious difficulties with cases such as paralytics and disembodied brains hooked up to life-support systems. Suppose, for example, that C is a cluster of inputs and mental states which, according to Functionalism, issues in some characteristic behavior, B. We might take C to consist in part in: pain, the desire to be rid of the pain, the belief that an object in front of one is causing the pain, and the belief that the pain can easily be avoided by reverse locomotion. Let B be reverse locomotion. But a paralytic could typically have C without B. It might be objected, "If C typically issues in B, then one of the elements of C would have to be the belief that *B is possible*, but a paralytic would not have this belief." Reply: Imagine a paralytic who does not know he/she is paralyzed and who has the kind of hippocampal lesion that keeps him/her from learning, or imagine a paralytic whose paralysis is *intermittent*. Surely someone in intense pain who believes the only way to avoid intense pain is by reverse locomotion and who believes he or she *might* be capable of reverse locomotion will (other things equal) attempt to locomote in reverse. This is as platitudinous as any of the platitudes in the Functionalist collection. But in the case of an intermittent paralytic, attempts to locomote in reverse might *typically fail*, and, thus, he/she might typically fail to emit B when in C. Indeed, one can imagine that a disease strikes worldwide, resulting in intermittent paralysis of this sort in all of us, so that *none* of us typically emits B in C.

It would seem that such a turn of events would require Functionalists to suppose that some of the mental states which make up C no longer occur. But this seems very implausible.

This objection is further strengthened by attention to brain-in-bottle examples. Recall the example of brains being removed for cleaning and rejuvenation, the connections between one's brain and one's body being maintained by radio while one goes about one's business. The process takes a few days, and when it is completed, the brain is reinserted in the body. Occasionally it may happen that a person's body is destroyed by an accident while the brain is being cleaned and rejuvenated. If hooked up to input sense organs (but not output organs) such a brain would exhibit *none* of the usual platitudinous connections between behavior and clusters of inputs and mental states. If, as seems plausible, such a brain could have almost all the same (narrow) mental states as we have (and since such a state of affairs could become typical), Functionalism is wrong.

It is instructive to compare the way Psychofunctionalism attempts to handle cases like paralysis and brains in bottles. According to Psychofunctionalism, what is to count as a system's inputs and outputs is an empirical question. Counting neural impulses as inputs and outputs would avoid the problems just sketched, since the brains in bottles and paralytics could have the right neural impulses even without bodily movements. Objection: There could be paralysis that affects the nervous system, and thus affects the neural impulses, so the problem which arises for Functionalism arises for Psychofunctionalism as well. Reply: Nervous system diseases can actually *change mentality*, e.g., they can render victims incapable of having pain. So it might actually be true that a widespread nervous system disease that caused intermittent paralysis rendered people incapable of certain mental states.

According to plausible versions of Psychofunctionalism, the job of deciding what neural processes should count as inputs and outputs is in part a matter of deciding *what malfunctions count as changes in mentality and what malfunctions count as changes in peripheral input and output connections.* Psychofunctionalism has a resource that Functionalism does not have, since Psychofunctionalism allows us to *adjust the line we draw between the inside and the outside of the organism so as to avoid problems of the sort discussed.* All versions of Functionalism go wrong in attempting to draw this line on the basis of only common-sense knowledge; "analyticity" versions of Functionalism go especially wrong in attempting to draw the line a priori.

Objection: Sydney Shoemaker suggests (in correspondence) that problems having to do with paralytics, and brains in vats of the sort I mentioned, can be handled using his notion of a "paradigmatically embodied person" (see Shoemaker, 1976). Paradigmatic embodiment involves having functioning sensory apparatus and considerable voluntary control of bodily movements. Shoemaker's suggestion is that we start with a functional characterization of a paradigmatically embodied person, saying, inter alia, what it is for a physical state to realize a given mental state in a paradigmatically embodied person. Then, the functional characterization could be extended to non-paradigmatically embodied persons by saying that a physical structure that is not a part of a paradigmatically embodied person will count as realizing mental states, if, without changing its internal structure and the sorts of relationships that hold between its states, it could be incorporated into a larger physical system that would be the body of a paradigmatically embodied person in which the states in question played the functional roles definitive of mental states of a paradigmatically embodied person. Shoemaker suggests that a brain in a vat can be viewed from this perspective, as a limiting case of an amputee—amputation of everything but the brain. For the brain can (in principle) be incorporated into a system so as to form a paradigmatically embodied person without changing the internal structure and state relations of the brain.

Reply: Shoemaker's suggestion is very promising, but it saves functionalism only by retreating from Functionalism to Psychofunctionalism. Obviously, nothing in prescientific common-sense wisdom about mentality tells us what can or cannot be paradigmatically embodied *without changing its internal structure and state relations* (unless 'state relations' means 'Functional state relations', in which case the question is begged). Indeed, the scientific issues involved in answering this question may well be very similar to the scientific issues involved in the Psychofunctionalist question about the difference between defects in or damage to input-output devices, as opposed to defects in or damage to central mechanisms. That is, the scientific task of drawing the Psychofunctionalist line between the inside and the outside of an organism may be pretty much the same as Shoemaker's task of drawing the line between what can and what cannot be paradigmatically embodied without changing its internal structure and state relations.

I shall briefly raise two additional problems for Functionalism. The first might be called the Problem of Differentiation: there are mental states that are different, but that do not differ with respect to platitudes. Consider different tastes or smells that have typical causes and effects, but whose typical causes and effects are not known or are not known to very many people. For example, tannin in wine produces a particular taste immediately recognizable to wine drinkers. As far as I know, there is no standard name or description (except "tannic") associated with this taste. The causal antecedents and consequents of this taste are not widely known, there are no platitudes about its typical causes and effects. Moreover, there are sensations that not only have no

standard names but whose causes and effects are not yet well understood by anyone. Let A and B be two such (different) sensations. Neither platitudes nor truths of meaning can distinguish between A and B. Since the Functional description of a mental state is determined by the platitudes true of that state, and since A and B do not differ with respect to platitudes, Functionalists would be committed to identifying A and B with the same Functional state, and thus they would be committed to the claim that A = B, which is ex hypothesi false.

A second difficulty for Functionalism is that platitudes are often wrong. Let us call this problem the Problem of Truth. Lewis suggests, by way of dealing with this problem, that we specify the causal relations among mental states, inputs and outputs, not by means of the conjunction of all the platitudes, but rather by "a cluster of them—a disjunction of conjunctions of *most* of them (that way it will not matter if a few are wrong.)" This move may exacerbate the problem of Differentiation, however, since there may be pairs of different mental states that are alike with respect to *most* platitudes.

2.0 Arguments for Psychofunctionalism, and What Is Wrong with Them

I said there is good reason to take seriously our intuition that the homunculi-headed Functional simulations have no mentality. The good reason was that mentality is in the domain of psychology and/or physiology, and the homunculi-headed Functional simulations need not have either psychological (information-processing) or physiological mechanisms anything like ours. But this line will not apply to a homunculi-headed *Psycho*functional simulation. Indeed, there is an excellent reason to disregard any intuition that a homunculi-headed Psychofunctional simulation lacks mentality. Since a Psychofunctional simulation of you would be Psychofunctionally equivalent to you, a reasonably adequate psychological theory true of you would be true of it. Indeed, without changing the homunculi-headed example in any essential way, we could require that *every* reasonably adequate psychological theory true of you be true of it. What better reason could there be to attribute to it whatever mental states are in the domain of psychology? In the face of such a good reason for attributing mental states to it, prima facie doubts about whether it has those aspects of mentality which are in the domain of psychology should be rejected.

I believe this argument shows that a homunculi-headed simulation could have *non*qualitative mental states. However, in the next section I shall describe a Psychofunctional simulation in more detail, arguing that there is nonetheless substantial doubt that it has *qualitative* mental states (i.e., states, that, like pain, involve qualia). So at least with respect to qualitative states, the onus of argument is on Psychofunctionalists. I shall now argue that none of the arguments that have been offered for Psychofunctionalism are any good.

Here is one argument for Psychofunctionalism that is implicit in the literature. It is the business of branches of science to tell us the nature of things in the branches' domains. Mental states are in the domain of psychology, and, hence, it is the business of psychology to tell us what mental states are. Psychological theory can be expected to characterize mental states in terms of the causal relations among mental states, and other mental entities, and among mental entities, inputs, and outputs. But these very causal relations are the ones which constitute the Psychofunctional states that Psychofunctionalism identifies with mental states. So Psychofunctionalism is just the result of applying a plausible conception of science to mentality; Psychofunctionalism is just the doctrine that mental states are the "psychological states" it is the business of psychology to characterize.

That something is seriously amiss with this form of argument can be seen by noting that it would be fallacious if applied to other branches of science.

Consider the analogue of Psychofunctionalism for physics. It says that protonhood, for example, is the property of having certain lawlike relations to certain other physical properties. With respect to current physical theory, protonhood would be identified with a property expressible in terms of the Ramsey sentence of current physical theory (in the manner described above). Now there is an obvious problem with this claim about what it is to be a proton. Namely, this physico-functionalist approach would identify being an anti-proton *with the very same property*. According to current physical theory, protons and anti-protons are "dual" entities: one cannot distinguish the variable which replaced 'protonhood' from the variable that replaced 'anti-protonhood' (in any nontrivial way) in the Ramsey sentence of current physical theory. Yet protons and anti-protons are different types of particles; it is a law of physics that particles annihilate their anti-particles; thus, protons annihilate anti-protons, even though protons get along fine with other protons.[20]

Suppose someone were to argue that 'protonhood = its Ramsey functional correlate with respect to current physical theory' is our best hypothesis as to the nature of protonhood, on the ground that this identification amounts to an application of the doctrine that it is the business of branches of science to tell us the nature of things in their domains. The person would be arguing fallaciously. So why should we suppose that this form of argument is any less fallacious when applied to psychology?

In the preceding few paragraphs I may have given the impression that the analogue of Psychofunctionalism in physics can be used to cast doubt on Psychofunctionalism itself. But there are two important disanalogies between Psychofunctionalism and its physics analogue. First, according to Psychofunctionalism, there is a theoretically principled distinction between, on one hand, the inputs and outputs described explicitly in the Ramsey sentence, and, on the other hand, the internal states and other psychological entities whose names are replaced by variables. But there is no analogous distinction with respect to other branches of science. An observational/theoretical distinction would be analogous if it could be made out, but difficulties in drawing such a distinction are notorious.

Second, and more important, Psychofunctionalism simply need not be regarded as a special case of any general doctrine about the nature of the entities scientific theories are about. Psychofunctionalists can reasonably hold that only *mental* entities—or perhaps only states, events, and their ilk, as opposed to substances like protons—are "constituted" by their causal relations. Of course, if Psychofunctionalists take such a view, they protect Psychofunctionalism from the proton problem at the cost of abandoning the argument that Psychofunctionalism is just the result of applying a plausible conception of science to mentality.

Another argument for Psychofunctionalism (or, less plausibly, for Functionalism) which can be abstracted from the literature is an "inference to the best explanation" argument: "What *else* could mental states be if not Psychofunctional states?" For example, Putnam (1967) hypothesizes that (Psycho)functionalism is true and then argues persuasively that (Psycho)functionalism is a *better* hypothesis than behaviorism or materialism.

But this is a very dubious use of "inference to the best explanation." For what guarantee do we have that *there is* an answer to the question "What are mental states?" of the sort behaviorists, materialists, and functionalists have wanted? Moreover, inference to the best explanation cannot be applied when none of the available explanations is any good. In order for inference to the best explanation to be applicable, two conditions have to be satisfied: we must have reason to believe an explanation is *possible*, and at least one of the available explanations must be *minimally adequate*. Imagine someone arguing for one of the proposed solutions to Newcomb's Problem on the ground that despite its fatal flaw it is the best of the proposed solutions. That would be a joke. But is the argument for functionalism any better? Behaviorism, materialism, and functionalism are not theories of mentality in the way Mendel's theory is a theory of heredity. Behaviorism, materialism, and functionalism (and dualism as well) are attempts to solve a problem: the mind-body problem. Of course, this is a problem which can hardly be guaranteed to have a solution. Further, each of the proposed solutions to the mind-body problem has serious difficulties, difficulties I for one am inclined to regard as fatal.

Why is functionalism so widely accepted, given the dearth of good arguments for it, implicit or explicit? In my view, what has happened is that functionalist doctrines were offered initially as hypotheses. But with the passage of time, plausible-sounding hypotheses with useful features can come to be treated as established facts, even if no good arguments have ever been offered for them.

2.1 Are Qualia Psychofunctional States?

I began this chapter by describing a homunculi-headed device and claiming there is prima facie doubt about whether it has any mental states at all, especially whether it has qualitative mental states like pains, itches, and sensations of red. The special doubt about qualia can perhaps be explicated by thinking about *inverted* qualia rather than *absent* qualia. It makes sense, or seems to make sense, to suppose that objects we both call green look to me the way objects we both call red look to you. It seems that we could be functionally equivalent even though the sensation fire hydrants evoke in you is qualitatively the same as the sensation grass evokes in me. Imagine an inverting lens which when placed in the eye of a subject results in exclamations like "Red things now look the way green things used to look, and vice versa." Imagine further, a pair of identical twins one of whom has the lenses inserted at birth. The twins grow up normally, and at age 21 are functionally equivalent. This situation offers at least some evidence that each's spectrum is inverted relative to the other's. (See Shoemaker, 1975, note 17, for a convincing description of intrapersonal spectrum inversion.) However, it is very hard to see how to make sense of the analogue of spectrum inversion with respect to nonqualitative states. Imagine a pair of persons one of whom believes that p is true and that q is false, while the other believes that q is true and that p is false. Could these persons be functionally equivalent? It is hard to see how they could.[21] Indeed, it is hard to see how two persons could have only this difference in beliefs and yet there be no possible circumstance in which this belief difference would reveal itself in different behavior. Qualia seem to be supervenient on functional organization in a way that beliefs are not (though perhaps not to adherents of Davidsonian Anomalous Monism).

There is another reason to firmly distinguish between qualitative and nonqualitative mental states in talking about functionalist theories: Psychofunctionalism avoids Functionalism's problems with nonqualitative states, e.g., propositional attitudes like beliefs and desires. But Psychofunctionalism may be no more able to handle qualitative states than is Functionalism. The reason is that qualia may well not be in the domain of psychology.

To see this, let us try to imagine what a homunculi-headed realization of human psychology would be like. Current psychological theorizing seems directed toward the description of information-flow relations among psychological mechanisms. The aim seems to be to decompose such mechanisms into psychologically primitive mechanisms, "black boxes" whose internal structure is in the domain of physiology rather than in the domain of psychology. (See Fodor, 1968b, Dennett, 1975, and Cummins, 1975; interesting objections are raised in Nagel, 1969.) For example, a near-primitive mechanism might be one that matches two items in a representational system and determines if they are tokens of the same type. Or the primitive mechanisms might be like those in a digital computer, e.g., they might be (a) *add 1 to a given register*, and (b) *subtract 1 from a given register, or if the register contains 0, go to the nth (indicated) instruction.* (These operations can be combined to accomplish any digital computer operation; see Minsky, 1967, p. 206.) Consider a computer whose machine-language code contains only two instructions corresponding to (a) and (b). If you ask how it multiplies or solves differential equations or makes up payrolls, you can be answered by being shown a program couched in terms of the two machine-language instructions. But if you ask how it adds 1 to a given register, the appropriate answer is given by a wiring diagram, not a program. The machine is hard-wired to add 1. When the instruction corresponding to (a) appears in a certain register, the contents of another register "automatically" change in a certain way. The computational structure of a computer is determined by a set of primitive operations and the ways nonprimitive operations are built up from them. Thus it does not matter to the computational structure of the computer whether the primitive mechanisms are realized by tube circuits, transistor circuits, or relays. Likewise, it does not matter to the psychology of a mental system whether its primitive mechanisms are realized by one or another neurological mechanism. Call a system a "realization of human psychology" if every psychological theory true of us is true of it. Consider a realization of human psychology whose primitive psychological operations are accomplished by little men, in the manner of the homunculi-headed simulations discussed. So, perhaps one little man produces items from a list, one by one, another compares these items with other representations to determine whether they match, etc.

Now there is good reason for supposing this system has some mental states. Propositional attitudes are an example. Perhaps psychological theory will identify remembering that P with having "stored" a sentencelike object which expresses the proposition that P (Fodor, 1975). Then if one of the little men has put a certain sentencelike object in "storage," we may have reason for regarding the system as remembering that P. But unless having qualia is just a matter of having certain information processing (at best a controversial proposal—see later discussion), there is no such theoretical reason for regarding the system as having qualia. In short, there is perhaps as much doubt about the qualia of this homunculi-headed system as there was about the qualia of the homunculi-headed Functional simulation discussed early in the chapter.

But the system we are discussing is ex hypothesi something of which any true psychological theory is true. *So any doubt that it has qualia is a doubt that qualia are in the domain of psychology.*

It may be objected: "The kind of psychology you have in mind is *cognitive* psychology, i.e., psychology of thought processes; and it is no wonder that qualia are not in the domain of *cognitive* psychology!" But I *do not* have cognitive psychology in mind, and if it sounds that way, this is easily explained: nothing we know about the psychological processes underlying our conscious mental life has

anything to do with qualia. What passes for the "psychology" of sensation or pain, for example, is (a) physiology, (b) psychophysics (i.e., study of the mathematical functions relating stimulus variables and sensation variables, e.g., the intensity of sound as a function of the amplitude of the sound waves), or (c) a grabbag of descriptive studies (see Melzack, 1973, Ch. 2). Of these, only psychophysics could be construed as being about qualia per se. And it is obvious that psychophysics touches only the *functional* aspect of sensation, not its qualitative character. Psychophysical experiments done on you would have the same results if done on any system Psychofunctionally equivalent to you, even if it had inverted or absent qualia. If experimental results would be unchanged whether or not the experimental subjects have inverted or absent qualia, they can hardly be expected to cast light on the nature of qualia.

Indeed, on the basis of the kind of conceptual apparatus now available in psychology, I do not see how psychology in anything like its present incarnation *could* explain qualia. We cannot now conceive how psychology could explain qualia, though we *can* conceive how psychology could explain believing, desiring, hoping, etc. (see Fodor, 1975). That something is currently inconceivable is not a good reason to think it is impossible. Concepts could be developed tomorrow that would make what is now inconceivable conceivable. But all we have to go on is what we know, and on the basis of what we have to go on, it looks as if qualia are not in the domain of psychology.

Objection: If the Psychofunctional simulation just described has the same beliefs I have, then among its beliefs will be the belief that it now has a headache (since I now am aware of having a headache). But then you must say that its belief is mistaken—and how can such a belief be mistaken?

Reply: The objection evidently assumes some version of the Incorrigibility Thesis (if x believes he has a pain, it follows that he does have a pain). I believe the Incorrigibility Thesis to be false. But even if it is true, it is a double-edged sword. For one can just as well use it to argue that Psychofunctionalism's difficulties with qualia infect its account of belief too. For if the homunculi-headed simulation is in a state Psychofunctionally equivalent to believing it is in pain, yet has no qualia, and hence no pain, then if the Incorrigibility Thesis is true, it does not believe it is in pain either. But if it is in a state Psychofunctionally equivalent to belief without believing, belief is not a Psychofunctional state.

Objection: At one time it was inconceivable that temperature could be a property of matter, if matter was composed only of particles bouncing about; but it would not have been rational to conclude temperature was not in the domain of physics. Reply: First, what the objection says was inconceivable was probably never inconceivable. When the scientific community could conceive of matter as bouncing particles, it could probably also conceive of heat as something to do with the motion of the particles. Bacon's theory that heat was motion was introduced at the inception of theorizing about heat—a century before Galileo's primitive precursor of a thermometer, and even before distinctions among the temperature of x, the perceived temperature of x, and x's rate of heat conduction were at all clear (Kuhn, 1961). Second, there is quite a difference between saying something is not in the domain of physics and saying something is not in the domain of psychology. Suggesting that temperature phenomena are not in the domain of physics is suggesting that they are not explainable at all.

It is no objection to the suggestion that qualia are not psychological entities that qualia are the very paradigm of something in the domain of psychology. As has often been pointed out, it is in part an empirical question what is in the domain of any particular branch of science. The liquidity of water turns out not to be explainable by chemistry, but rather by subatomic physics. Branches of science have at any given time a set of phenomena they seek to explain. But it can be discovered that some phenomenon which seemed central to a branch of science is actually in the purview of a different branch.

Suppose psychologists discover a *correlation* between qualitative states and certain cognitive processes. Would that be any reason to think the qualitative states are identical to the cognitive states they are correlated with? Certainly not. First, what reason would there be to think this correlation would hold in the homunculi-headed systems that Psychofunctionally simulate us? Second, although a case can be made that certain sorts of general correlations between Fs and Gs provide reason to think F is G, this is only the case when the predicates are predicates of different theories, one of which is reducible to the other. For example, there is a correlation between thermal and electrical conductivity (asserted by the Wiedemann-Franz Law), but it would be silly to suggest that this shows thermal conductivity is electrical conductivity (see Block, 1971, Ch. 3).

I know of only one serious attempt to fit "consciousness" into information-flow psychology: the program in Dennett, 1978. But Dennett fits consciousness into information-flow psychology only by claiming that the contents of consciousness are exhausted by judgments. His view is that to the extent that qualia are not judgments (or beliefs), they are spurious theoretical entities that we postulate to explain why we find ourselves wanting to say all sorts of things about what is going on in our minds.

Dennett's doctrine has the relation to qualia that the U.S. Air Force had to so many Vietnamese villages: he destroys qualia in order to save them. Is it not more reasonable to tentatively hypothesize that qualia are determined by the physiological or physico-chemical nature of our information processing, rather than by the information flow per se?

The Absent Qualia Argument exploits the possibility that the Functional or Psychofunctional state Functionalists or Psychofunctionalists would want to identify with pain can occur without any quale occurring. It also seems to be conceivable that the latter occur without the former. Indeed, there are facts that lend plausibility to this view. After frontal lobotomies, patients typically report that they still have pains, though the pains no longer bother them (Melzack, 1973, p. 95). These patients show all the "sensory" signs of pain (e.g., recognizing pin pricks as sharp), but they often have little or no desire to avoid "painful" stimuli.

One view suggested by these observations is that each pain is actually a *composite* state whose components are a quale and a Functional or Psychofunctional state.[22] Or what amounts to much the same idea, each pain is a quale playing a certain Functional or Psychofunctional role. If this view is right, it helps to explain how people can have believed such different theories of the nature of pain and other sensations: they have emphasized one component at the expense of the other. Proponents of behaviorism and functionalism have had one component in mind; proponents of private ostensive definition have had the other in mind. Both approaches err in trying to give one account of something that has two components of quite different natures.

3.0 Chauvinism vs. Liberalism

It is natural to understand the psychological theories Psychofunctionalism adverts to as theories of *human* psychology. On Psychofunctionalism, so understood, it is logically impossible for a system to have beliefs, desires, etc., except insofar as psychological theories true of us are true of it. Psychofunctionalism (so understood) stipulates that Psychofunctional equivalence to us is necessary for mentality.

But even if Psychofunctional equivalence to us is a condition on our *recognition of mentality*, what reason is there to think it is a condition on mentality itself? Could there not be a wide variety of possible psychological processes that can underlie mentality, of which we instantiate only one type? Suppose we meet Martians and find that they are roughly Functionally (but not Psychofunctionally) equivalent to us. When we get to know Martians, we find them about as different from us as humans we know. We develop extensive cultural and commercial intercourse with them. We study each other's science and philosophy journals, go to each other's movies, read each other's novels, etc. Then Martian and Earthian psychologists compare notes, only to find that in underlying psychology, Martians and Earthians are very different. They soon agree that the difference can be described as follows. Think of humans and Martians as if they were products of conscious design. In any such design project, there will be various options. Some capacities can be built in (innate), others learned. The brain can be designed to accomplish tasks using as much memory capacity as necessary in order to minimize use of computation capacity; or, on the other hand, the designer could choose to conserve memory space and rely mainly on computation capacity. Inferences can be accomplished by systems which use a few axioms and many rules of inference, or, on the other hand, few rules and many axioms. Now imagine that what Martian and Earthian psychologists find when they compare notes is that Martians and Earthians differ as if they were the end products of maximally different design choices (compatible with rough Functional equivalence in adults). Should we reject our assumption that

Martians can enjoy our films, believe their own apparent scientific results, etc.? Should they "reject" their "assumption" that we "enjoy" their novels, "learn" from their textbooks, etc.? Perhaps I have not provided enough information to answer this question. After all, there may be many ways of filling in the description of the Martian-human differences in which it would be reasonable to suppose there simply is no fact of the matter, or even to suppose that the Martians do not deserve mental ascriptions. But surely there are many ways of filling in the description of the Martian-Earthian difference I sketched on which it would be perfectly clear that even if Martians behave differently from us on subtle psychological experiments, they nonetheless think, desire, enjoy, etc. To suppose otherwise would be crude human chauvinism. (Remember theories are chauvinist insofar as they falsely *deny* that systems have mental properties and liberal insofar as they falsely *attribute* mental properties.)

So it seems as if in preferring Psychofunctionalism to Functionalism, we erred in the direction of human chauvinism. For if mental states are Psychofunctional states, and if Martians do not have these Psychofunctional states, then they do not have mental states either. In arguing that the original homunculi-headed simulations (taken as Functional simulations) had no mentality, I appealed, in effect, to the following principle: if the sole reason to think system x has mentality is that x was built to be Functionally equivalent to us, then differences between x and us in underlying information processing and/or neurophysiology are reasons to doubt whether x has mental states. But this principle does not dictate that a system can have mentality only insofar as it is Psychofunctionally equivalent to us. Psychofunctional equivalence to us is a sufficient condition for at least those aspects of mentality in the domain of psychology, but it is not obvious that it is a necessary condition of any aspects of mentality.

An obvious suggestion of a way out of this difficulty is to identify mental states with Psychofunctional states, taking the domain of psychology to include *all creatures with mentality*, including Martians. The suggestion is that we define "Psychofunctionalism" in terms of "universal" or "cross-system" psychology, rather than the human psychology I assumed earlier. Universal psychology, however, is a suspect discipline. For how are we to decide what systems should be included in the *domain* of universal psychology? What systems are the generalizations of universal psychology based on? One possible way of deciding what systems have mentality, and are thus in the domain of universal psychology, would be to use some *other* developed theory of mentality, e.g., behaviorism or Functionalism. But such a procedure would be at least as ill-justified as the other theory used. Further, if Psychofunctionalism must presuppose some other theory of mind, we might just as well accept the other theory of mind instead.

Perhaps universal psychology will avoid this "domain" problem in the same way other branches of science avoid it or seek to avoid it. Other branches of science start with tentative domains based on intuitive and prescientific versions of the concepts the sciences are supposed to explicate. They then attempt to develop natural kinds in a way which allows the formulations of lawlike generalizations which apply to all or most of the entities in the prescientific domains. In the case of many branches of science—including biological and social sciences such as genetics and linguistics—the prescientific domain turned out to be suitable for the articulation of lawlike generalizations.

Now it may be that we shall be able to develop universal psychology in much the same way we develop Earthian psychology. We decide on an intuitive and prescientific basis what creatures to include in its domain, and work to develop natural kinds of psychological theory which apply to all or at least most of them. Perhaps the study of a wide range of organisms found on different worlds will one day lead to theories that determine truth conditions for the attribution of mental states like belief, desire, etc., applicable to systems which are pretheoretically quite different from us. Indeed, such cross-world psychology will no doubt require a whole new range of mentalistic concepts. Perhaps there will be families of concepts corresponding to belief, desire, etc., that is, a family of belieflike concepts, desirelike concepts, etc. If so, the universal psychology we develop shall, no doubt, be somewhat dependent on which new organisms we discover first. Even if universal psychology is in fact possible, however, there will certainly be many possible organisms whose mental status is indeterminate.

On the other hand, it may be that universal psychology is *not* possible. Perhaps life in the universe is such that we shall simply have no basis for reasonable decisions about what systems are in the domain of psychology and what systems are not.[23]

If universal psychology *is* possible, the problem I have been raising vanishes. Universal-Psychofunctionalism avoids the liberalism of Functionalism and the chauvinism of human-Psychofunctionalism. But the question of whether universal psychology is possible is surely one which we have no way of answering now.

In sum, Functionalism is hopelessly liberal (as I argued earlier). Further, Functionalism has a number of other serious difficulties (section 1.5). Psychofunctionalism avoids these difficulties, but Psychofunctionalism is hopelessly chauvinist —*unless* it can be based on universal psychology. However, we cannot suppose universal psychology is possible. My conclusion: we are not justified in holding either of the forms of functionalism.

I shall now summarize the conclusions of the paper so far.

(1) Functionalism dictates that a ho-

munculi-headed simulation of you must have qualia; this is a bizarre conclusion that throws the onus of argument on Functionalists. But the one argument in the literature for Functionalism does not hold water; so Functionalism should be tentatively rejected (section 1.5).

(2) Mentality depends crucially on psychological and/or neurophysiological properties. Since a Functional simulation need not share these properties with us, a Functional simulation need not have mentality. In the absence of an argument for Functionalism, we are justified in rejecting the doctrine.

(3) Point (2) condemns Functionalism; the analogous argument against Psychofunctionalism does not go through, since Psychofunctional simulations do share our psychological processes. But since there is doubt that qualitative states are in the domain of psychology, qualia pose a difficulty for Psychofunctionalism.

(4) None of the arguments in the literature for Psychofunctionalism holds water (section 2.0).

(5) Supporters of functionalism face a dilemma. Functionalism is hopelessly liberal, while Psychofunctionalism is hopelessly chauvinist. Only "universal psychology" can save Psychofunctionalism from chauvinism, and we have no reason to believe that universal psychology is possible (section 3.0).

So what I claim to have shown so far is that Functionalism should be rejected; that Psychofunctionalist accounts of qualia are doubtful; and that Psychofunctionalist accounts of both qualitative and nonqualitative states are at best unjustified.

3.1 The Problem of the Inputs and the Outputs

I have been supposing all along (as Psychofunctionalists often do—see Putnam, 1967) that inputs and outputs can be specified by neural impulse descriptions. But this is a chauvinist claim, since it precludes organisms without neurons (e.g., machines) from having functional descriptions. How can one avoid chauvinism with respect to specification of inputs and outputs? One way would be to characterize the inputs and outputs *only as* inputs and outputs. So the functional description of a person might list outputs by number: output$_1$, output$_2$, . . . Then a system could be functionally equivalent to you if it had a set of states, inputs, and outputs causally related to one another in the way yours are, no matter what the states, inputs, and outputs were like. Indeed, though this approach violates the demand of some functionalists that inputs and outputs be physically specified, other functionalists —those who insist only that input and output descriptions be *nonmental*—may have had something like this in mind. This version of functionalism does not "tack down" functional descriptions at the periphery with relatively specific descriptions of inputs and outputs; rather, this version of functionalism treats inputs and outputs just as all versions of functionalism treat internal states. That is, this version specifies states, inputs, and outputs only by requiring that they *be* states, inputs, and outputs.

The trouble with this version of functionalism is that it is wildly liberal. Economic systems have inputs and outputs, e.g., influx and outflux of credits and debits. And economic systems also have a rich variety of internal states, e.g., having a rate of increase of GNP equal to double the Prime Rate. It does not seem impossible that a wealthy sheik could gain control of the economy of a small country, e.g., Bolivia, and manipulate its financial system to make it functionally equivalent to a person, e.g., himself. If this seems implausible, remember that the economic states, inputs, and outputs designated by the sheik to correspond to his mental states, inputs, and outputs need not be "natural" economic magnitudes. Our hypothetical sheik could pick *any* economic magnitudes at all—e.g., the fifth time derivative of the balance of payments. His

only constraint is that the magnitudes he picks be economic, that their having such and such values be inputs, outputs, and states, and that he be able to set up a financial structure which can be made to fit the intended formal mold. The mapping from psychological magnitudes to economic magnitudes could be as bizarre as the sheik requires.

This version of functionalism is far too liberal and must therefore be rejected. If there are any fixed points when discussing the mind-body problem, one of them is that the economy of Bolivia could not have mental states, no matter how it is distorted by powerful hobbyists. Obviously, we must be more specific in our descriptions of inputs and outputs. The question is: is there a description of inputs and outputs specific enough to avoid liberalism, yet general enough to avoid chauvinism? I doubt that there is.

Every proposal for a description of inputs and outputs I have seen or thought of is guilty of either liberalism or chauvinism. Though this paper has concentrated on liberalism, chauvinism is the more pervasive problem. Consider standard Functional and Psychofunctional descriptions. Functionalists tend to specify inputs and outputs in the manner of behaviorists: outputs in terms of movements of arms and legs, sound emitted and the like; inputs in terms of light and sound falling on the eyes and ears. As I argued earlier, this conception is chauvinist, since it denies mentality to brains in vats and to paralytics. But the chauvinism inherent in Functional descriptions runs deeper. Such descriptions are blatantly *species-specific*. Humans have arms and legs, but snakes do not—and whether or not snakes have mentality, one can easily imagine snake-like creatures that do. Indeed, one can imagine creatures with all manner of input-output devices, e.g., creatures that communicate and manipulate by emitting strong magnetic fields. Of course, one could formulate Functional descriptions for each such species, and somewhere in disjunctive heaven there is a disjunctive description which will handle all species that ever actually exist in the universe (the description may be infinitely long). But even an appeal to such suspicious entities as infinite disjunctions will not bail out Functionalism, since even the amended view will not tell us what there is in common to pain-feeling organisms in virtue of which they all have pain. And it will not allow the ascription of pain to some hypothetical (but nonexistent) pain-feeling creatures. Further, these are just the grounds on which functionalists typically acerbically reject the disjunctive theories sometimes advanced by desperate physicalists. If functionalists suddenly smile on wildly disjunctive states to save themselves from chauvinism, they will have no way of defending themselves from physicalism.

Standard Psychofunctional descriptions of inputs and outputs are also species-specific (e.g., in terms of neural activity) and hence chauvinist as well.

The chauvinism of standard input-output descriptions is not hard to explain. The variety of possible intelligent life is enormous. Given any fairly specific descriptions of inputs and outputs, any high-school-age science-fiction buff will be able to describe a sapient sentient being whose inputs and outputs fail to satisfy that description.

I shall argue that *any physical description* of inputs and outputs (recall that many functionalists have insisted on physical descriptions) yields a version of functionalism that is inevitably chauvinist or liberal. Imagine yourself so badly burned in a fire that your optimal way of communicating with the outside world is via modulations of your EEG pattern in Morse Code. You find that thinking an exciting thought produces a pattern that your audience agrees to interpret as a dot, and a dull thought produces a "dash." Indeed, this fantasy is not so far from real-

ity. According to a recent newspaper article (*Boston Globe*, March 21, 1976), "at UCLA scientists are working on the use of EEG to control machines. . . . A subject puts electrodes on his scalp, and thinks an object through a maze." The "reverse" process is also presumably possible: others communicating with you in Morse Code by producing bursts of electrical activity that affect your brain (e.g., causing a long or short afterimage). Alternatively, if the cerebroscopes that philosophers often fancy become a reality, your thoughts will be readable directly from your brain. Again, the reverse process also seems possible. In these cases, *the brain itself becomes an essential part of one's input and output devices.* This possibility has embarrassing consequences for functionalists. You will recall that functionalists pointed out that physicalism is false because a single mental state can be realized by an indefinitely large variety of physical states that have no necessary and sufficient physical characterization.[24] But if this functionalist point against physicalism is right, *the same point applies to inputs and outputs*, since the physical realization of mental states can serve as an essential part of the input and output devices. That is, on any sense of 'physical' in which the functionalist criticism of physicalism is correct, *there will be no physical characterization that applies to all and only mental systems' inputs and outputs.* Hence, any attempt to formulate a functional description with physical characterizations of inputs and outputs will inevitably either exclude some systems with mentality or include some systems without mentality. Hence, *the kind of functionalism held by virtually all functionalists cannot avoid both chauvinism and liberalism.*

So physical specifications of inputs and outputs will not do. Moreover, mental or "action" terminology (e.g., "punching the offending person") may not be used either, since to use such specifications of inputs or outputs would be to give up the functionalist program of characterizing mentality in nonmental terms. On the other hand, as you will recall, characterizing inputs and outputs simply *as* inputs and outputs is inevitably liberal. I, for one, do not see how there can be a vocabulary for describing inputs and outputs that avoids both liberalism and chauvinism. I do not claim that this is a conclusive argument against functionalism. Rather, like the functionalist argument against physicalism, it is best construed as a burden-of-proof argument. The functionalist says to the physicalist: "It is very hard to see how there could be a single physical characterization of the internal states of all and only creatures with mentality." I say to the functionalist: "It is very hard to see how there could be a single physical characterization of the inputs and outputs of all and only creatures with mentality." In both cases, enough has been said to make it the responsibility of those who think there could be such characterizations to sketch how they could be possible.[25]

Notes

1. See Fodor, 1965, 1968a; Lewis, 1966, 1972; Putnam, 1966, 1967, 1970, 1975a; Armstrong, 1968; Locke, 1968; perhaps Sellars, 1968; perhaps Dennett, 1969, 1978b; Nelson, 1969, 1975 (but see also Nelson, 1976); Pitcher, 1971; Smart, 1971; Block & Fodor, 1972; Harman, 1973; Lycan, 1974; Grice, 1975; Shoemaker, 1975; Wiggins, 1975; Field, 1978.

2. The converse is also true.

3. Indeed, if one defines 'behaviorism' as the view that mental terms can be defined in nonmental terms, then functionalism *is* a version of behaviorism. However, it would be grossly misleading so to define 'behaviorism', for reasons discussed at length in the introduction to this part of the book.

4. State type, not state token. Throughout the chapter, I shall mean by 'physicalism' the doctrine that says each distinct type of mental state is identical to a distinct type of physical state; for example, pain (the univer-

sal) is a physical state. Token physicalism, on the other hand, is the (weaker) doctrine that each particular datable pain is a state of some physical type or other. Functionalism shows that type physicalism is false, but it does not show that token physicalism is false.

By 'physicalism', I mean *first-order* physicalism, the doctrine that, e.g., the property of being in pain is a first-order (in the Russell-Whitehead sense) physical property. (A first-order property is one whose definition does not require quantification over properties; a second-order property is one whose definition requires quantification over first-order properties—and not other properties.) The claim that being in pain is a second-order physical property is actually a (physicalist) form of functionalism. See Putnam, 1970.

'Physical property' could be defined for the purposes of this chapter as a property expressed by a predicate of some true physical theory or, more broadly, by a predicate of some true theory of physiology, biology, chemistry, or physics. Of course, such a definition is unsatisfactory without characterizations of these branches of science (see Hempel, 1970, for further discussion). This problem could be avoided by characterizing 'physical property' as: property expressed by a predicate of some true theory adequate for the explanation of the phenomena of nonliving matter. I believe that the difficulties of this account are about as great as those of the previous account. Briefly, it is conceivable that there are physical laws that "come into play" in brains of a certain size and complexity, but that nonetheless these laws are "translatable" into physical language, and that, so translated, they are clearly physical laws (though irreducible to other physical laws). Arguably, in this situation, physicalism could be true—though not according to the account just mentioned of 'physical property'.

Functionalists who are also physicalists have formulated broadly physicalistic versions of functionalism. As functionalists often point out (Putnam, 1967), it is logically possible for a given abstract functional description to be satisfied by a nonphysical object, e.g., a soul. One can formulate a physicalistic version of functionalism simply by explicitly ruling out this possibility. One such physicalistic version of functionalism is suggested by Putnam

(1970), Field (1978), and Lewis (in conversation): having pain is identified with a second-order physical property, a property that consists of having certain first-order physical properties if certain other first-order physical properties obtain. This doctrine combines functionalism (which can be formulated as the doctrine that having pain is the property of having certain properties if certain other properties obtain) with token physicalism. Of course, the Putnam-Lewis-Field doctrine is *not* a version of (first-order) type physicalism; indeed, the P-L-F doctrine is incompatible with (first-order) type physicalism.

5. Correctly stated: where L is a predicate letter, and v is a variable, let the expression consisting of '%' concatenated with v, then L, then v again be a singular term for the property expressed by Lv.

6. One serious problem for Functionalism is to justify the choice of a unique psychological theory.

7. That example may be somewhat misleading in that it scrimps on causal relations among mental states. It is easy to construct an example which lacks this flaw using the Coke machine described earlier. Let us think of the Coke machine as having two desirelike states, nickel-shmesire and dime-shmesire. The following four sentences describe the causal relations among the Coke machine's mental states, inputs, and outputs:

1. Dime-shmesire + 5¢ input causes nickel-shmesire + (no Coke, 0¢) output.
2. Dime-shmesire + 10¢ input causes dime-shmesire + (Coke, 0¢) output.
3. Nickel-shmesire + 5¢ input causes dime-shmesire + (Coke, 0¢) output.
4. Nickel-shmesire + 10¢ input causes dime-shmesire + (Coke, 5¢) output.

'5¢ input' means that a nickel is put into the machine; '(Coke, 5¢) output' means a Coke and a nickel are emitted by the machine; '+' should be read as 'together with'. T = 1&2&3&4. The Ramsey sentence of T is formed by replacing 'nickel-shmesire' and 'dime-shmesire' with variables and by existentially quantifying. The property of having dime-shmesire is identified with its Ramsey functional correlate, viz.,

$\%zExEy$ [(x + 5¢ input causes y + (no Coke, 0¢) output)

    & (x + 10¢ input causes x + (Coke, 0¢) output)

    & (y + 5¢ input causes x + (Coke, 0¢) output)

    & (y + 10¢ input causes x + (Coke, 5¢) output) & z is in x].

8. I mentioned two respects in which Functionalism and Psychofunctionalism differ. First, Functionalism identifies pain with its Ramsey functional correlate with respect to a common-sense psychological theory, and Psychofunctionalism identifies pain with its Ramsey functional correlate with respect to a scientific psychological theory. Second, Functionalism requires common-sense specification of inputs and outputs, and Psychofunctionalism has the option of using empirical-theory construction in specifying inputs and outputs so as to draw the line between the inside and outside of the organism in a theoretically principled way.

I shall say a bit more about the Psychofunctionalism/Functionalism distinction. According to the preceding characterization, Psychofunctionalism and Functionalism are theory relative. That is, we are told not what pain is, but, rather, what pain is *with respect to this or that theory*. But Psychofunctionalism can be defined as the doctrine that mental states are constituted by causal relations among whatever psychological events, states, processes, and other entities—as well as inputs and outputs—actually obtain in us in whatever ways those entities are actually causally related to one another. Therefore, if current theories of psychological processes are correct in adverting to storage mechanisms, list searchers, item comparators, and so forth, Psychofunctionalism will identify mental states with causal structures that involve storage, comparing, and searching processes as well as inputs, outputs, and other mental states.

Psychofunctional equivalence can be similarly characterized without overt relativizing to theory. Let us distinguish between weak and strong equivalence (Fodor, 1968a). Assume we have agreed on some descriptions of inputs and outputs. I shall say that organisms x and y are weakly or behaviorally equivalent if and only if they have the same output for any input or sequence of inputs. If x and y are weakly equivalent, each is a weak simulation of the other. I shall say x and y are *strongly* equivalent relative to some branch of science if and only if (1) x and y are weakly equivalent, and (2) that branch of science has in its domain processes that mediate inputs and outputs, and x's and y's inputs and outputs are mediated by the same combination of weakly equivalent processes. If x and y are strongly equivalent, they are strong simulations of each other.

We can now give a characterization of a Psychofunctional equivalence relation that is not overtly theory relative. This Psychofunctional equivalence relation is strong equivalence with respect to psychology. (Note that 'psychology' here denotes a branch of science, not a particular theory in that branch.)

This Psychofunctional equivalence relation differs in a number of respects from those described earlier. For example, for the sort of equivalence relation described earlier, equivalent systems need not have any common output if they share a given sequence of inputs. In machine terms, the equivalence relations described earlier require only that equivalent systems have a common machine table (of a certain type); the current equivalence relation requires, in addition, that equivalent systems be in the same state of the machine table. This difference can be eliminated by more complex formulations.

Ignoring differences between Functionalism and Psychofunctionalism in their characterizations of inputs and outputs, we can give a very crude account of the Functionalism/ Psychofunctionalism distinction as follows: Functionalism identifies mental states with causal structures involving conscious mental states, inputs, and outputs; Psychofunctionalism identifies mental states with the same causal structures, elaborated to include causal relations to *unconscious* mental entities as well. That is, the causal relations adverted to by Functionalism are a subset of those adverted to by Psychofunctionalism. Thus, weak or behavioral equivalence, Functional equivalence, and Psychofunctional equivalence form a hierarchy. All Psychofunctionally equivalent systems are Functionally equivalent, and all Functionally equivalent systems are weakly or behaviorally equivalent.

Although the characteristics of Psycho-

functionalism and Psychofunctional equivalence just given are not overtly theory relative, they have the same vagueness problems as the characterizations given earlier. I pointed out that the Ramsey functional-correlate characterizations suffer from vagueness about level of abstractness of psychological theory—e.g., are the psychological theories to cover only humans who are capable of *weltschmerz*, all humans, all mammals, or what? The characterization of Psychofunctionalism just given allows a similar question: what is to count as a psychological entity or process? If the answer is an entity in the domain of some true psychological theory, we have introduced relativity to theory. Similar points apply to the identification of Psychofunctional equivalence, with strong equivalence with respect to psychology.

Appeal to unknown, true psychological theories introduces another kind of vagueness problem. We can allocate current theories among branches of science by appealing to concepts or vocabulary currently distinctive to those branches. But we cannot timelessly distinguish among branches of science by appealing to their distinctive concepts or vocabulary, because we have no idea what concepts and vocabulary the future will bring. If we did know, we would more or less have future theories now. Worse still, branches of science have a habit of coalescing and splitting, so we cannot know whether the science of the future will countenance anything at all like psychology as a branch of science.

One consequence of this vagueness is that no definite answer can be given to the question, Does Psychofunctionalism as I have described it characterize mental states partly in terms of their relations to *neurological* entities? I think the best anyone can say is: at the moment, it seems not. Psychology and neurophysiology seem to be separate branches of science. Of course, it is clear that one must appeal to neurophysiology to explain some psychological phenomena, e.g., how being hit on the head causes loss of language ability. However, it seems as if this should be thought of as "descending" to a lower level in the way evolutionary biology appeals to physics (e.g., cosmic rays hitting genes) to partially explain mutation.

9. The seriousness of this problem may not be obvious to those who think in terms of

Lewis's "functional specification" version of Functionalism. After all, George Washington is both the father of our country *and* the famous cherry-tree chopper. The rub, however, is that no property can be identical both to the property of being the father of our country *and* the property of being the famous cherry-tree chopper. (As I pointed out in the introduction to part three of this book, Lewis's version of Functionalism entails a functional state identity thesis, and the problem just described is a problem for such theses.)

10. The basic idea for this example is due to Putnam (1967). I am indebted to many conversations with Hartry Field on the topic. Putnam's attempt to defend functionalism from the problem posed by such examples is discussed in Section 1.4 of this essay.

11. One potential difficulty for Functionalism is provided by the possibility that one person may have two radically different Functional descriptions of the sort that justify attribution of mentality. In such a case, Functionalists might have to ascribe two radically different systems of belief, desire, etc., to the same person, or suppose that there is no fact of the matter about what the person's propositional attitudes are. Undoubtedly, Functionalists differ greatly on what they make of this possibility, and the differences reflect positions on such issues as indeterminacy of translation.

12. This point has been raised with me by persons too numerous to mention.

13. Shoemaker, 1975, argues (in reply to Block & Fodor, 1972) that absent qualia are logically impossible, that is, that it is logically impossible that two systems be in the same functional state yet one's state have and the other's state lack qualitative content. If Shoemaker is right, it is wrong to doubt whether the homunculi-headed system has qualia. I attempt to show Shoemaker's argument to be fallacious in Block, 1980.

14. The homunculi-headed system is a prima facie counterexample to one version of functionalism. In this note, I shall briefly sketch a few other versions of functionalism and argue that this or similar examples also provide counterexamples to those versions of functionalism. Every version of functionalism I know of seems subject to this type of difficulty. Indeed, this problem seems so close to the core of functionalism that I would be tempted to regard a doctrine not subject to it as ipso facto not a version of functionalism.

The version of functionalism just discussed (mental states are machine-table states) is subject to many obvious difficulties. If state M = state P, then someone has M if and only if he or she has P. But mental and machine-table states fail to satisfy this basic condition, as Fodor and I pointed out (Block & Fodor, 1972).

For example, people are often in more than one psychological state at a time, e.g., believing that P and desiring that G. But a Turing machine can be in only one machine-table state at a time. Lycan (1974) argues against Fodor's and my objection. He says the problem is dissolvable by appeal to the distinction between particular, physical Turing machines and the abstract Turing machine specified by a given description. One abstract machine can be realized by many physical machines, and one physical machine can be the realization of many abstract machines. Lycan says we can identify the n mental states a person happens to be in at one time with machine-table states of n abstract automata that the person simultaneously realizes. But this will not do, for a Functionalist should be able to explain how a number of simultaneous mental states jointly produce an output, e.g., when a belief that action A will yield goal G, plus a desire for G jointly cause A. How could this causal relation be captured if the belief and the desire are identified with states of different abstract automata that the person simultaneously realizes?

The "one-state-at-a-time" problem can be avoided by a natural reformulation of the machine-table state identity theory. Each machine-table state is identified not with a single mental state, but with a conjunction of mental states, e.g., believing that P and hoping that H and desiring that G. . . . Call each of the mental states in such a conjunction the "elements" of the machine-table state. Then, each mental state is identical to the disjunction of the machine-table states of which it is an element. This version of Functionalism is ultimately unsatisfactory, basically because it has no resources for appropriately handling the content relations among mental states, e.g., the relation between the belief that P and the belief that (P or Q).

Fodor and I (1972) raised a number of such criticisms. We concluded that Turing-machine functionalism could probably avoid such difficulties, but only at the cost of weakening the theory considerably. Turing-machine functionalism seemed forced to abandon the idea that mental states could be identified with machine-table states or even states definable in terms of just machine-table states, such as the disjunction of states already suggested. It seemed, rather, that mental states would have to be identified instead with *computational* states of a Turing machine—that is, states definable in terms of mental states *and* states of the tape of a Turing machine.

However, the move from machine-table state functionalism to computational-state functionalism is of no use in avoiding the Absent Qualia Argument. Whatever Turing machine it is whose computational states are supposed to be identical to your mental states will have a homunculi-headed realization of the sort described earlier, i.e., a realization whose mental states are subject to prima facie doubt. Therefore, if a qualitative state, Q, is supposed to be identical to a computational state, C_q, there will be prima facie doubt about whether the homunculi-headed system is in Q even if it is in C_q, and hence prima facie doubt that Q = C_q.

Now let us turn briefly to a version of functionalism that is not framed in terms of the notion of a Turing machine. Like machine functionalists, nonmachine functionalists emphasize that characterizations of mental states can be given in entirely nonmental—indeed, they often say physical—terminology. The Ramsey functional-correlate expression designating pain (section 1.1) contains input and output terms but not mental terms. Thus, nonmachine versions, like machine versions, can be described as "tacking down" mental states only at the periphery. That is, according to both versions of functionalism, something can be functionally equivalent to you if it has a set of states, of whatever nature, that are causally related to one another and to inputs and outputs in the appropriate way.

Without a more precise specification of nonmachine functionalism (e.g., a specification of an actual psychological theory of either the Functionalist or Psychofunctionalist varieties), it would be hard to *prove* that nonma-

chine versions of functionalism are subject to the kind of prima facie counterexample described earlier. But this does seem fairly obviously the case. In this regard, the major difference between machine and nonmachine versions of functionalism is that we cannot assume that the homunculi-headed counterexample for nonmachine functionalism is "discretized" in the way a Turing machine is. In our new homunculi-headed device, we may have to allow for a continuous range of values of input and output parameters, whereas Turing machines have a finite set of inputs and outputs. Further, Turing-machine descriptions assume a fixed time interval, t, such that inputs occur and instructions are executed every t seconds (t = 10 nanoseconds in an IBM 370). Turing machines click, whereas our homunculi-headed device may creep. However, it is not at all obvious that this makes any difference. The input signals in the mechanical body can be changed from on-off lights to continuously varying lights; continuously variable potentiometers can be substituted for the output buttons. We may suppose that each of the little men in the body carries a little book that maps out your functional organization. The little men designate states of themselves and/or their props to correspond to each of your mental states. For example, your being in pain might correspond to a certain little man writing 'pain' on a blackboard. The intensity of the pain might be indicated by the (continuously variable) color of the chalk. Having studied his book, the little man knows what inputs and other mental states cause your pains. He keeps an eye open for the states of his colleagues and the input lights that correspond to those conditions. Little men responsible for simulating states that are contingent on pain keep their eye on the blackboard, taking the appropriate configurations of 'pain' written on the board + input lights and actions of other men as signals to do what they have designated to correspond to states caused by pain. If you, a big man, have an infinite number of possible mental states, the same can be assumed of the little men. Thus, it should be possible for the simulation to have an infinite number of possible "mental" states.

One difference between this simulation and the one described earlier is that these little men need more intelligence to do their jobs.

But that is all to the good as far as the Absent Qualia Argument is concerned. The more intelligence exercised by the little men in simulating you, the less inclined we are to ascribe to the simulation the mental properties they are simulating.

15. Since there is a difference between the role of the little people in producing your functional organization in the situation just described and the role of the homunculi in the homunculi-headed simulations this chapter began with, presumably Putnam's condition could be reformulated to rule out the latter without ruling out the former. But this would be a most ad hoc maneuver. Further, there are other counterexamples which suggest that a successful reformulation is likely to remain elusive.

Careful observation of persons who have had the nerve bundle connecting the two halves of the brain (the *corpus callosum*) severed to prevent the spread of epilepsy, suggest that each half of the brain has the functional organization of a sentient being. The same is suggested by the observation that persons who have had one hemisphere removed or anesthetized remain sentient beings. It was once thought that the right hemisphere had no linguistic capacity, but it is now known that the adult right hemisphere has the vocabulary of a 14-year-old and the syntax of a 5-year-old (*Psychology Today*, 12/75, p. 121). Now the functional organization of each hemisphere is different from the other and from that of a whole human. For one thing, in addition to inputs from the sense organs and outputs to motor neurons, each hemisphere has many input and output connections to the other hemisphere. Nonetheless, each hemisphere may have the functional organization of a sentient being. Perhaps Martians have many more input and output organs than we do. Then each half brain could be functionally like a whole Martian brain. If each of our hemispheres has the functional organization of a sentient being, then a Putnamian proposal would rule us out (except for those of us who have had hemispherectomies) as pain-feeling organisms.

Further, it could turn out that other parts of the body have a functional organization similar to that of some sentient being. For example, perhaps individual neurons have the same functional organization as some species of insect.

(The argument of the last two paragraphs depends on a version of functionalism that construes inputs and outputs as neural impulses. Otherwise, individual neurons could not have the same functional organization as insects. It would be harder to think of such examples if, for instance, inputs were taken to be irradiation of sense organs or the presence of perceivable objects in the "range" of the sense organs.)

16. A further indication that our intuitions are in part governed by the neurophysiological and psychological differences between us and the original homunculi-headed simulation (construed as a Functional simulation) is that intuition seems to founder on an intermediate case: a device that simulates you by having a billion little men each of whom simulates one of your neurons. It would be like you in psychological mechanisms, but not in neurological mechanisms, except at a very abstract level of description.

There are a number of differences between the original homunculi-heads and the elementary-particle-people example. The little elementary-particle people were not described as knowing your functional organization or trying to simulate it, but in the original example, the little men have *as their aim* simulating your functional organization. Perhaps when we know a certain functional organization is intentionally produced, we are thereby inclined to regard the thing's being functionally equivalent to a human as a misleading fact. One could test this by changing the elementary-particle-people example so that the little people have the aim of simulating your functional organization by simulating elementary particles; this change seems to me to make little intuitive difference.

There are obvious differences between the two types of examples. It is *you* in the elementary case and the change is *gradual*; these elements seem obviously misleading. But they can be eliminated without changing the force of the example much. Imagine, for example, that your spouse's parents went on the expedition and that your spouse has been made of the elementary-particle people since birth.

17. Compare the first sentence with 'The fish eaten in Boston stank.' The reason it is

hard to process is that 'raced' is naturally read as active rather than passive. See Fodor, Bever, & Garrett, 1974, p. 360. For a discussion of why the second sentence is grammatical, see Fodor & Garrett, 1967; Bever, 1970; and Fodor, Bever, & Garrett, 1974.

18. We often fail to be able to conceive of how something is possible because we lack the relevant theoretical concepts. For example, before the discovery of the mechanism of genetic duplication, Haldane argued persuasively that no conceivable physical mechanism could do the job. He was right. But instead of urging that scientists should develop ideas that would allow us to conceive of such a physical mechanism, he concluded that a *non*physical mechanism was involved. (I owe the example to Richard Boyd.)

19. This argument backs up the suggestion of the end of the previous section that the "extra" mentality of the little men per se is not the major source of discomfort with the supposition that the homunculi-headed simulation has mentality. The argument now under discussion does not advert at all to the mentality of the homunculi. The argument depends only on the claim that the homunculi-headed Functional simulation need not be either psychologically or neurophysiologically like a human. This point is further strengthened by noticing that it is provable that each homunculus is replaceable by an extremely simple object—a McCullough-Pitts "and" neuron, a device with two inputs and one output that fires just in case the two inputs receive a signal. (The theorem assumes the automaton is a finite automaton and the inputs enter one signal at a time—see Minsky, 1967, p. 45.) So the argument would apply even if the homunculi were replaced by mindless "and" neurons.

20. One could avoid this difficulty by allowing *names* in one's physical theory. For example, one could identify protons as the particles with such and such properties contained in the nuclei of all atoms of the Empire State Building. No such move will save this argument for Psychofunctionalism, however. First, it is contrary to the idea of functionalism, since functionalism purports to identify mental states with abstract causal structures; one of the advantages of functionalism is that it avoids appeal to ostension in definition of mental states. Second, tying Psychofunction-

alism to particular named entities will inevitably result in chauvinism. See Section 3.1.

21. Sylvain Bromberger has pointed out to me that there are counterexamples that exploit spectrum inversion. Suppose a man who has good color vision mistakenly uses 'red' to denote green and 'green' to denote red. That is, he simply confuses the two words. Since his confusion is purely linguistic, though he says of a green thing that it is red, he does not *believe* that it is red, any more than a foreigner who has confused 'ashcan' with 'sandwich' believes people eat ashcans for lunch. Let us say that the person who has confused 'red' and 'green' in this way is a victim of Word Switching.

Now consider a different ailment: having red/green inverting lenses placed in your eyes without your knowledge. Let us say a victim of this ailment is a victim of Stimulus Switching. Like the victim of Word Switching, the victim of Stimulus Switching applies 'red' to green things and vice versa. But the victim of Stimulus Switching *does* have false color beliefs. If you show him a green patch he says *and believes* that it is red.

Now suppose that a victim of Stimulus Switching suddenly becomes a victim of Word Switching as well. (Suppose as well that he is a lifelong resident of a remote Arctic village, and has no standing beliefs to the effect that grass is green, firehydrants are red, and so forth.) He speaks normally, applying 'green' to green patches and 'red' to red patches. Indeed, he is functionally normal. But his *beliefs* are just as abnormal as they were before he became a victim of Word Switching. Before he confused the words 'red' and 'green', he applied 'red' to a green patch, and mistakenly believed the patch to be red. Now he (correctly) says 'red', but his belief is still wrong.

So two people can be functionally the same, yet have incompatible beliefs. Hence, the inverted qualia problem infects belief as well as qualia (though presumably only qualitative belief). This fact should be of concern not only to those who hold functional state identity theories of belief, but also to those who are attracted by Harman-style accounts of meaning as functional role. Our double victim—of Word and Stimulus Switching—is a counterexample to such accounts. For his word 'green' plays the normal role in his reasoning and inference, yet since in saying of something that it "is green," he expresses his belief that it is *red*, he uses 'green' with an abnormal meaning.

22. The quale might be identified with a physico-chemical state. This view would comport with a suggestion Hilary Putnam made in the late '60s in his philosophy of mind seminar. See also Ch. 5 of Gunderson, 1971.

23. To take a very artificial example, suppose we have no way of knowing whether inhabitants of civilizations we discover are the builders of the civilizations or simulations the builders made before departing en masse.

24. Functionalists emphasize that there is no interesting physical condition that is necessary for mentality, because they are interested in refuting the sort of mental-state/brain-state thesis that physicalists have typically proffered. The functionalist point is that no brain state could be necessary for mentality, since a mental system need not even have a brain. Of course, there are *uninteresting* physical necessary conditions for something being a pain, such as being temporally located. What makes such necessary conditions uninteresting is that they are not sufficient.

25. I am indebted to Sylvain Bromberger, Hartry Field, Jerry Fodor, David Hills, Paul Horwich, Bill Lycan, Georges Rey, and David Rosenthal for their detailed comments on one or another earlier draft of this paper. Beginning in the fall of 1975, parts of earlier versions were read at Tufts University, Princeton University, the University of North Carolina at Greensboro, and the State University of New York at Binghamton.

References

Armstrong, D. *A materialist theory of mind.* London: Routledge & Kegan Paul, 1968.

Bever, T. The cognitive basis for linguistic structures. In J. R. Hayes (Ed.), *Cognition and the development of language.* New York: Wiley, 1970.

Block, N. *Physicalism and theoretical identity.* Unpublished doctoral thesis, Harvard University, 1971.

Block, N. Are absent qualia impossible? *Philosophical Review*, 1980, 89(2).

Block, N. & Fodor, J. What psychological states are not. *Philosophical Review*, 1972,

81, 159-81. [Reprinted as chapter 20, this volume.]

Chisholm, Roderick. *Perceiving.* Ithaca: Cornell University Press, 1957.

Cummins, R. Functional analysis. *Journal of Philosophy*, 1975, 72, 741-64. [Reprinted in part as chapter 12, this volume.]

Davidson, D. Mental events. In L. Swanson & J. W. Foster (Eds.), *Experience and theory.* Amherst, University of Massachusetts Press, 1970. [Reprinted as chapter 5, this volume.]

Dennett, D. *Content and consciousness.* London: Routledge & Kegan Paul, 1969.

Dennett, D. Why the law of effect won't go away. *Journal for the Theory of Social Behavior*, 1975, 5, 169-87.

Dennett, D. A cognitive theory of consciousness. *Minnesota studies in the philosophy of science IX.* Minneapolis: University of Minnesota Press, 1978.

Dennett, D. Why a computer can't feel pain. In *Synthese* 1978a, 38, 3.

Dennett, D. *Brainstorms.* Montgomery, Vt.: Bradford, 1978b.

Feldman, F. Kripke's argument against materialism. *Philosophical Studies*, 1973; 416-19.

Field, H. "Mental representation." *Erkenntnis* 1978, 13, 9-61.

Fodor, J. Explanations in psychology. In M. Black (Ed.), *Philosophy in America.* London: Routledge & Kegan Paul, 1965.

Fodor, J. *Psychological explanation.* New York: Random House, 1968a.

Fodor, J. The appeal to tacit knowledge in psychological explanation. *Journal of Philosophy*, 1968b, 65, 627-40.

Fodor, J. Special sciences. *Synthese*, 1974, 28, 97-115. [Reprinted as chapter 6, this volume.]

Fodor, J. *The language of thought.* New York: Crowell, 1975.

Fodor, J., Bever, T., & Garrett, M. *The psychology of language.* New York: McGraw-Hill, 1974.

Fodor, J. & Garrett, M. Some syntactic determinants of sentential complexity. *Perception and Psychophysics*, 1967, 2, 289-96.

Geach, P. *Mental acts.* London: Routledge & Kegan Paul, 1957.

Gendron, B. On the relation of neurological and psychological theories: A critique of the hardware thesis. In R. C. Buck and R. S. Cohen (Eds.), *Boston studies in the philoso-*

phy of science VIII. Dordrecht: Reidel, 1971.

Grice, H. P. Method in philosophical psychology (from the banal to the bizarre). *Proceedings and Addresses of the American Philosophical Association,* 1975.

Gunderson, K. *Mentality and machines.* Garden City: Doubleday Anchor, 1971.

Harman, G. *Thought.* Princeton: Princeton University Press, 1973.

Hempel, C. Reduction: Ontological and linguistic facets. In S. Morgenbesser, P. Suppes & M. White (Eds.), *Essays in honor of Ernest Nagel.* New York: St. Martin's Press, 1970.

Kalke, W. What is wrong with Fodor and Putnam's functionalism? *Nous,* 1969, 3, 83-93.

Kim, J. Phenomenal properties, psychophysical laws, and the identity theory. *The Monist,* 1972, 56(2), 177-92. [Reprinted in part as chapter 19, this volume.]

Kripke, S. Naming and necessity. In D. Davidson & G. Harman (Eds.), *Semantics and natural language.* Dordrecht: Reidel, 1972.

Kuhn, T. The function of measurement in modern physical science. *Isis,* 1961, 52(8), 161-93.

Lewis, D. An argument for the identity theory. *Journal of Philosophy,* 1966, 63, 1. Reprinted (with new footnotes) in D. Rosenthal (Ed.), *Materialism and the mind-body problem.* Englewood Cliffs: Prentice-Hall, 1971.

Lewis, D. Review of *Art, mind and religion. Journal of Philosophy,* 1969, 66, 23-35. [Reprinted in part as chapter 18, this volume.]

Lewis, D. How to define theoretical terms. *Journal of Philosophy* 1970, 67, 427-44.

Lewis, D. Psychophysical and theoretical identifications. *Australasian Journal of Philosophy,* 1972, 50(3), 249-58. [Reprinted as chapter 15, this volume.]

Locke, D. *Myself and others.* Oxford: Oxford University Press, 1968.

Lycan, W. Mental states and Putnam's functionalist hypothesis. *Australasian Journal of Philosophy,* 1974, 52, 48-62.

Melzack, R. *The puzzle of pain.* New York: Basic Books, 1973.

Minsky, M. *Computation.* Englewood Cliffs: Prentice-Hall, 1967.

Mucciolo, L. F. The identity thesis and neuropsychology. *Nous,* 1974, 8, 327-42.

Nagel, T. The boundaries of inner space. *Journal of Philosophy,* 1969, 66, 452-58.

Nagel, T. Armstrong on the mind. *Philosophical Review,* 1970, 79, 394-403.

Nagel, T. Review of Dennett's *Content and consciousness. Journal of Philosophy,* 1972, 50, 220-34.

Nagel, T. What is it like to be a bat? *Philosophical Review,* 1974, 83, 435-50. [Reprinted as chapter 11, this volume.]

Nelson, R. J. Behaviorism is false. *Journal of Philosophy,* 1969, 66, 417-52.

Nelson, R. J. Behaviorism, finite automata & stimulus response theory. *Theory and Decision,* 1975, 6, 249-67.

Nelson, R. J. Mechanism, functionalism, and the identity theory. *Journal of Philosophy,* 1976, 73, 365-86.

Oppenheim, P. and Putnam, H. Unity of science as a working hypothesis. In H. Feigl, M. Scriven & G. Maxwell (Eds.), *Minnesota studies in the philosophy of science II.* Minneapolis: University of Minnesota Press, 1958.

Pitcher, G. *A theory of perception.* Princeton: Princeton University Press, 1971.

Putnam, H. Brains and behavior. 1963. Reprinted as are all Putnam's articles referred to here (except "On properties") in *Mind, language and reality: Philosophical papers,* Vol. 2). London: Cambridge University Press, 1975. [Reprinted as chapter 2, this volume.]

Putnam, H. The mental life of some machines. 1966.

Putnam, H. The nature of mental states (originally published under the title *Psychological Predicates*). 1967. [Reprinted as chapter 17, this volume.]

Putnam, H. On properties. In *Mathematics, matter and method: Philosophical papers,* Vol. 1. London: Cambridge University Press, 1970.

Putnam, H. Philosophy and our mental life. 1975a. [Reprinted as chapter 7, this volume.]

Putnam, H. The meaning of 'meaning'. 1975b.

Rorty, R. Functionalism, machines and incorrigibility. *Journal of Philosophy,* 1972, 69, 203-20.

Scriven, M. *Primary philosophy.* New York: McGraw-Hill, 1966.

Sellars, W. Empiricism and the philosophy of mind. In H. Feigl & M. Scriven (Eds.), *Minnesota studies in philosophy of science I.*

Minneapolis: University of Minnesota Press, 1956.

Sellars, W. *Science and metaphysics.* (Ch. 6). London: Routledge & Kegan Paul, 1968.

Shoemaker, S. Functionalism and qualia. *Philosophical studies,* 1975, 27, 271-315. [Reprinted as chapter 21, this volume.]

Shoemaker, S. Embodiment and behavior. In A. Rorty (Ed.), *The identities of persons.*

Berkeley: University of California Press, 1976.

Shallice, T. Dual functions of consciousness. *Psychological Review,* 1972, 79, 383-93.

Smart, J. J. C. Reports of immediate experience. *Synthese,* 1971, 22, 346-59.

Wiggins, D. Identity, designation, essentialism, and physicalism. *Philosophia,* 1975, 5, 1-30.

Index

Albritton, Rogers, 147n3
Alston, W., 5
Ambiguity, 217, 221
Analytical philosophy, rules of, 223
Analytical strategy, 186-189, 190n8
Animals: pain of, 91, 229, 235; psychological
  states of, 92, 274; consciousness of, 159; color
  and, 259. *See also* Behavior, animal; Brain states
  of animals
Anomaly, 107, 108, 111, 112, 117, 118
Anscombe, G. E. M., 2
Archimedes, 186
Aristotle, 1, 2, 3, 143n6, 171, 177
Armstrong, D. M., 175, 176, 200-206, 219, 271,
  283; on functionalism and physicalism, 177, 179;
  on theory of mind, 180, 217, 269; *A Materialist
  Theory of the Mind*, 197
Artificial intelligence, 5, 94
Automaton, 247, 248, 302n19; Coke machine, 177,
  178; theory of, 189, 231n4; probabilistic, 226-
  228, 240, 243-245, 249, 250n8, 271
Autonomy, 107; of mental life, 134, 139

Bats, 70, 159-168
Bealer, G., 176, 182n
Behavior: animal, 48, 51, 60n1; prediction of, 12,
  44, 45, 48-49, 52; verbal, 48-63, 116, 259
Behaviorism, 11-13, 37-47, 175-176, 179, 250n4;
  logical, 14-22, 24-35; social, 21; linguistic, 48-60;
  definitional, 113; nature of mind and, 193-198,
  201, 206; Rylean, 193-196, 213; pain theory and,
  217; arguments against, 237-240, 241, 245, 249,
  251; functionalism and, 268-270, 296n3
Belief, 6, 113, 247, 302n21; in pain, 213-214; qualitative, 256, 262-263, 264
Beliefs, religious, 137

Block, Ned, 265nn1-8, 11
Boyd, Richard, 6, 172
Brain, 32-34, 94, 136, 142, 200, 204, 296n4; com-
  puters and, 95, 135; process of, and mental
  events, 110, 111; capacity of, 189; physico-
  chemical view of, 191; qualia and, 281; EEG
  patterns of, 295; hemispheres of, 238, 301n15
"Brain spikes," 32-33
Brain states, 74, 111, 168n11, 178-179, 182n9; of
  animals, 228-229, 230, 234; pain and, *see* Pain.
  See also Hypothesis
Brandt, R., 179
Brentano, Franz, 109
Bridge laws, 121-123, 127, 132n5, 207, 235
Brittleness, 193-196

Cannizzaro, Stanislao, 1
Capacities, 186-189, 190n5, 198
Carnap, R., 15, 211, 224
Carnap sentence, 211
Carroll, L., 4
Causal properties, 175
Causal theory of reference, 76, 105
Causality, *see* Causes
Causes, 30, 146n1, 217-222, 285; inner, 37; neural,
  37-38; psychic, 38-39; conceptual, 39; of behav-
  ior, 41-42, 49, 60nn1, 2, 201-206; final, 45-47;
  mental events as, 107-108, 112, 117-118, 160,
  176, 179, 196, 268, 286, 297-298nn7, 8; qualita-
  tive states as, 262
Causey, R., 178, 179
Character, *see* Qualia
Chauvinism, 270, 291-293, 294-296
China, *see* Functionalism
Chisholm, Roderick M., 149, 175, 268
Chomsky, Noam, 2, 13

Church, Alonzo, 231n3
Church-Turing thesis, 172, 181n2
Classification, 105n12
Cluster-concept, 26
Colors, 215n15, 256-260, 264, 265nn13, 14, 266-
    267nn16-18, 302n21
Computational states, 88-89, 92, 96, 247
Computations, 171
Computers, 92-97, 98, 132n6, 135; digital, 4-5,
    288; functionalism and, 171, 172
Concepts, 2, 19, 20, 204, 218, 269; meaning of, 1,
    224; of physics, 15, 18; of pain, 217, 218, 232-
    233
Conditioning, 12, 42-45, 46, 57, 61nn4, 7
Consciousness, 95, 159-161, 168n11, 197-199, 260,
    264
Contingency, 68, 83-84, 144-145, 151-152, 156,
    168n11, 206n2, 264. See also Identity, contin-
    gent
Contingent psychophysical event identity theory,
    148-155
Continuities, 141
Control: of behavior, 41, 61n7; of stimulus, 52-55
Correlationism, mind/behavior, 237
Cummins, Robert, 171, 288

Davidson, Donald, 125, 156, 157, 166, 172, 239
Definition: functional, 211, 263, 264, 267n21
Dennett, Daniel C., 6, 135, 171, 288, 290
Descartes, René, 68, 137, 147n3, 193, 195, 205
Description, 226-227, 248, 279; of behavior, 42,
    46, 50, 55, 57; choice of, 79; of brain, 142; func-
    tional, 232, 294-295, 299n11; of organism, 240-
    241, 242, 244, 251; of color, 258; of mental
    states, 261-262, 263-264, 267n21; of inputs and
    outputs, 295
Determinism, 107, 108
Diagrams, schematic, 187
Diderot, Denis, 137
Differentiation, problem of, 285
Disembodied brain, 283-284
Disembodied mind, 201, 204-205
Disposition, 185-186, 190n5, 193-194, 195-196,
    242, 243, 268; behavior, 175, 229-230
Donagan, Alan, 252
Dualism, 24, 25, 27-28, 38, 72, 91-92, 137; nomo-
    logical, 111, 135; anomalous, 111; psychophysi-
    cal, 122
Dubislav, W., 22
Dworkin, G., 2

Economics, 125, 138, 294; laws of, 124, 132n5, 139
Elevancy, 186, 190n3
Embodiment, paradigmatic, 284-285
Emotions, 2, 5, 22. See also Feeling
Environment, behavior and, 40, 44, 48, 52, 198-
    199, 238
Equipotentiality, neurological, 238
Essence, 69-70
Essential properties, see Properties, essential

Essentialist criticism of materialism, 67-68, 79-80,
    83-85, 97-99, 104
Events, identity theory of, 148-155. See also Men-
    tal events; Physical events
Evolution of organisms, 228, 238
Experiences, 162-165; qualitative states as, 260,
    261, 264
Explanations, 137-138; of behavior, 41; functional,
    171, 185, 188

Facts, knowledge of, 162, 163
Feeling, 254. See also Pain
Feigl, H., 15
Feyerabend, P., 74
Field, Hartry, 6, 297n4, 299n10
Field theory, 31-32
Fodor, Jerry A., 135, 171, 172, 177, 178, 288, 289;
    on behavior, 4; on functionalism, 6, 265n7; on
    physicalism, 179, 270; on functional analysis,
    271
Frank, P., 15
Franklin, Benjamin, 153
Freedom, 107. See also Autonomy
Frege, Gottlob, 75
Freud, Sigmund, 39
Freudian concepts, 38
Functional analysis, 49, 50, 171, 173, 185-190
Functional equivalence, 273-275, 297-298n8
Functional organization of organisms, 227, 229,
    230
Functional relations, 134-135
Functional specification, 191-222
Functional state identity theory, 6, 87-101, 139-
    142, 223-305
Functional states of organisms, 88, 227-233
Functionalism, 6, 87-101, 139-142, 171-184; and
    physicalism, 92-99, 176-181, 218, 227-229, 233,
    234-236, 238-240; and behaviorism, 175-176,
    193-196, 229-230; and qualia, 244-245, 251-264,
    281-291; China counterexample to, 276-277
Fusion of persons, 264

Garfinkel, Alan, 141
Geach, Peter, 102, 175, 268
Gendron, B., 178, 270
Generalization, 114, 118, 124, 130, 131, 138, 292;
    semantic, 58-60, 63n46. See also Statements
Gibson, J. J., 2
Goals, 45-47
God, doubt of, 279
Goldstein, A., 103
Goodman, Nelson, 114
Grammar, 1, 2, 58-60
Gravitation, laws of, 141
Gregory, R. I., 2
Gresham's law, 124

Haddon, W., 306
Haldane, J. S., 95
Hallucination, 28

Harman, Gilbert, 6, 177, 271
Harre, R., 5
Harrison, Bernard, 266n17
Hartman, E., 171
Harvey, William, 192
Heat, 157, 290; definition of, 78, 79, 80, 81; properties of, 144, 145, 146-147n2
Hempel, Carl G., 11, 12
Historical events, 100
Hobbes, Thomas, 192
Homunculi, 275-286, 299-301nn13-16, 302n19
Hume, David, 69, 104n3
Hypothesis, 22n1, 31-33, 259; formation of, 60; empirical, 226; brain-state, 227-228, 232-233; inverted spectrum, 252, 260; scientific, 271

Ideas, 1, 39, 69
Identifications, 207-214, 248
Identity: statements of, 68-69, 72-74, 80-87, 92, 109, 121, 144; contingent, 68, 72, 79, 82-84, 218; mind-body, 86-87, 91, 97, 179; causality and, 112, 117-118; necessity and, 147n3, 148-155; functional, 179-181, 283; synonymy and, 206n4; of properties, 224; species-specific, 235; personal, 264
Identity theory, 79-83, 108, 110-111, 144-157, 182n9, 217, 234-236; functional state (FSIT), 179-180, 181n1, 240-246, 248-249, 250n8, 251, 253, 272; token, 249-250n2; machine-table state, 299n14. See also Type identity of psychological states
Images, 1, 3, 182, 225
Imagination, 161, 166, 168n11
Incorrigibility thesis, 290
Inputs and outputs, 49, 173, 176, 232, 271-273, 275, 293-296, 297n7
Intelligibility, 31
Intentionality, 110. See also Purpose
Intuition, 67-68, 83, 94-95, 98-101, 281
Isomorphism, functional, 134-136

Kalke, W., 178, 270
Kant, Immanuel, 3, 107, 118, 199
Kepler, Johannes, 141, 142
Kim, Jaegwon, 111, 150, 178, 179, 270
Kohlberg, Lawrence, 5
Kripke, Saul A., 206nn2, 4, 265-266n15; "Naming and Necessity," 67, 71, 75-86, 90-92, 94, 97, 99, 103-104, 105n12, 156-157, 167n1, 167-168n11, 265nn7, 8, 15, 278; identity theory and, 148-155; "Identity and Necessity," 265n7
Kuhn, T. S., 1, 104n5, 290

Language, 3, 61n4, 62-63n46, 109, 111-112, 132n10, 248, 261; machine, 5, 88-89, 288; physical, 11, 269, 296n4; of physics, 19, 22n1, 85, 124-125, 131; theory of, 58-60; necessity and, 70-75; conventions of, 71, 74, 76, 77, 78, 103; philosophy of, 103; of science, 123; physicalist, 151. See also Behavior, verbal; Grammar; Meaning; Sentences; Terms

Lashley, Karl S., 58, 60, 125
Law of Effect, 42, 43, 45, 55
Laws, 123, 127-130, 131, 132n4, 138, 141, 186; psychological, 11, 229, 249, 254; of stimulus and response, 52; of behavior, 61n5; causality and, 108, 117-118; psychophysical, 108, 111, 112, 116; of economics, 124, 132n5, 139; of physics, 142; neurophysical, 225; physical, 248, 296n4
Learning, 44, 55, 57, 62n14, 63n48; machine states and, 139, 140
Leibniz, Gottfried Wilhelm von, 157
Lewis, David, 176, 180, 269, 275, 283; on behaviorism, 175, 179, 271; on physicalism, 177, 178, 179, 181
Liberalism, 269, 291-293, 294-296
Linguistics, 281. See also Behaviorism, linguistic; Language
Locke, Don, 252
Locke, John, 69-75, 78, 104nn3, 4, 105n12, 199
Logic and logical analysis, 4, 14-22. See also Behaviorism, logical
Lycan, W., 175, 299n14

Machine table, 173, 178, 182n3, 226-227, 240-249, 273, 276-278
Machine-table states, 178, 182n7, 250n8, 252, 270-271, 278, 299n14
Machines, 92, 139-140, 187, 226-227, 238, 251; functionalism and, 173-175, 177-178, 182n3, 269, 281, 299; mental life of, 230; conversation of, 282. See also Computers; Turing machines
Madman, pain and, 216-222
Martians, 162, 163, 291-292, 301n15; pain and, 216-222
Materialism, 24, 25, 35n2, 67-104, 111, 135, 137, 146; physicalism and, 20, 122, 151; subjectivity and, 160; theory of mind of, 180, 191-206, 251; pain theory and, 217
Mathematical psychology, 5
Meaning, 15, 32, 116; of statements, 16-19, 21, 23n8, 25, 27, 74, 225; change of, 27, 104n11, 225-226; of terms, 69, 70, 72-73, 75, 78, 104n11, 105n12, 208; of names, 75-77
Measurement, 115
Melzack, R., 289, 291
Memory, 247, 291; machine states and, 139, 140
Mental events, 107-118, 165-166. See also Mental phenomena
Mental phenomena: theory of, 67-69, 71, 73-74, 82-83, 85, 86, 157; plasticity and, 88-97, 99; consciousness as, 159; functionalism and, 172, 251-264, 268; psychophysical identifications and, 207-214. See also Brain states; Mind, nature of; Psychofunctionalism
Mental representation, see Representation, mental
Metaphysics, 20, 172
Metzler, J., 3
Mind, nature of, 191-206
Mind-body identity, 86-87, 91, 97, 179
Mind-body problem, 26, 162, 287

Minsky, M., 5, 288

Molecular kinetic energy, 79, 80, 224-225, 229, 235, 270

Molecules, motion of, 99-100, 102, 144, 145, 146n2, 147n3, 157

Monism, 111, 112, 156-157, 288

Mucciolo, L. F., 270

Myth, 213, 215n15

Nagel, Thomas, 5, 6, 159-168, 200-206, 288

Names, 75-78, 261-262, 302n20. *See also* Terms

Nature, concept of, 107

Necessity, 67, 69-81, 85, 86-87, 148-155

Neisser, U., 2

Nelson, R. J., 173, 178

Nervous system, 37-39, 131, 188, 190n6; pain and, 72, 91; plasticity and, 91-92, 96, 100; of animals, 91; consciousness and, 199; physical basis of, 101, 102, 105n15, 178, 235; nature of mind and, 201, 203, 204, 284; psychological states and, 238

Neural correlate, 235-236

Neural processes, 37-38, 41

Neurath, O., 15, 19, 21

Neurological states and events, 126, 131, 179, 249

Neurological structures, 125

Neurophysiology, 201, 204

Newton, Isaac, 1, 141

Number theory, 24-25

Objectivity, 160, 163-164, 166, 167n9

Operants, 50-51, 53, 60n2

O'Shaughnessy, Brian, 186

Pain: meaning of, 26-30, 32-35, 202, 216-222; feeling of, 29, 95, 216, 222, 228, 230, 252; materialist theory of, 68, 70, 72-73, 82-85, 87, 90-93, 96-99, 217, 265nn6, 7; machine states and, 139-140; brain state and, 145-146, 146-147nn1-2, 156-157, 182n9, 223-236, 270; functionalism and, 172, 173-175, 176, 178-181, 227-231, 252-256, 263, 269, 273, 279, 283; belief in, 213-214

Paradigm, 104n5, 284-285

Paralysis, mental states and, 283-284

Particles, 248, 280, 286, 290

Pavlov, Anton, 16, 44

Perception, 1, 3, 107, 108, 162, 177, 260, 261; mental processes and, 198-199, 201-203. *See also* Mental events

Phenomenology, objective, 166

Philosophy, mental life and, 134-142

Physical, definition of term, 168n15

Physical events, 70, 107-108, 109, 110, 165-166, 172

Physical phenomena, 125, 154, 239, 263-264, 270; properties of, 68-69, 73, 79, 81; plasticity and theory of, 87-97, 99-100; pain as, 87, 92

Physical theory, 107, 116, 117-118. *See also* Psychophysics

Physicalism, 14, 18, 20-22, 25, 122, 126, 129; mental events and, 160, 165, 166; pain theory and, 172; functionalism and, 177-181, 182n8, 268-270, 271, 296n4; token, 181; nature of mind and, 191-199; mental states and, 234-236, 237-239, 241-242, 245, 249, 249-250n2; definition of, 296n4

Physics, 1-2, 15-16, 18, 31, 33; language of, 19, 22n1, 85, 124-125, 131; other sciences and, 120-122, 125, 130, 131, 139; laws of, 142

Physiology, behavior and, 41

Piaget, Jean, 5, 13

Plasticity, 87-97, 99, 100

Population, pain and, 219-221

Positivism, 120, 138

Predicate, psychological, 239

Probability: evaluation of, 40; behavioral, 42, 54, 62nn9,15

Production, assembly-line, 186-187

Properties, 149, 150, 154, 166, 179-180, 202, 223-225, 229; essential, 69-70, 71, 77, 79-85, 98-99, 103, 146n1, 147n3; contingent, 69, 144, 145; criterial, 71; compositional, 90; causal, 175; phenomenal, 179; first-order, 182n8; dispositional, 194; mental, 236, 269, 270; physical, 270, 274, 286, 296-297n4; psychological, 293

Propositional attitudes, 149

Propositional event, 153, 154

Psychofunctionalism, 272-275, 282, 284-293, 297-298n8

Psychological states, 91-96, 132n8, 139-140, 142n2, 228-229, 237-249, 250n8, 251-264; functionalism and, 171

Psychometrics, 2

Psychophysics, 2, 34. *See also* Laws, psychophysical

Pucetti, R., 5

Purpose, 45-47, 201-202

Putnam, Hilary, 6, 11, 24-36, 103, 125, 134-143, 223-236, 275; "The Mental Life of Some Machines," 35n2, 227, 229-230; on philosophy of mind, 175, 177-178, 268, 279-281; physicalism and, 179, 270; on terms, 209; "Psychological Predicates," 238, 240, 246; on Turing machine state, 241, 269, 271

Qualia, 6, 244, 245; functionalism and, 251-264, 265n7, 279, 281-283, 286, 291, 299-301n14; psychofunctionalism and, 287-291

Quine, W. V., 75-76

Ramsey sentence formation, 176, 177, 182nn6, 7, 208, 209, 210-211, 232, 267n21, 272-273, 286

Reductionism, 86, 113, 120-131, 132n5, 159, 202, 249; functionalism and, 176-177

Reeves, Alan, 179

Reference, 67

Reflex, conditioned, 44

Reichenbach, H., 22

Reincarnation, 136-137

Reinforcement, 44-46, 49, 50-51, 55-56, 60nn2, 3, 62nn12, 15

Representation, mental, 2-3, 4, 6-7. *See also* Images

Respondents, 50

Response: pain, 27, 29; behavioral, 43-44, 45, 50, 51-57, 61nn4, 5, 63nn46, 48; strength of, 53-55, 56, 62n15; mind and, 200, 212; animal, to color, 259

Response differentiation, 50

Rigid designator, 77-79, 81-82, 84, 86-87, 144-145, 146n2, 152, 182n11, 257-258, 265-266n15; of qualitative states, 262

Robots, 275-278. *See also* Automaton

Rorty, A., 5

Rorty, R., 74

Rule-described action, 1, 4

Rule-governed action, 1, 3-4

Rule-governed reasoning, 5

Rules, *see* Analytical philosophy, rules of; Grammar; Laws

Russell, Bertrand, 24, 25, 75

Ryle, Gilbert, 25, 175, 193, 194; *The Concept of Mind*, 25, 193, 201; behaviorism of, 193-196, 213

Savage, C. W., 2

Savin, Harris, 11-13

Schachter, S., 2

Schlick, M., 15

Science: theory of, 15, 16, 21, 120-131, 296n4; philosophy of, 103; nature of mind and, 191-193

Sciences, special, 120-131

Secord, P., 5

Sellars, W., 177, 213

Sensations, 179, 202, 205, 264, 289; color, 215n15

Sensory organs, 226, 227, 229

Sets, number, 24, 25

Shaffer, J., 74

Shepard, Roger, 3

Shoemaker, Sydney, 175, 176, 271, 283, 288; on philosophy of mind, 6, 177, 269, 275; on paradigmatic embodiment, 284

Simulations: computer, 126; functional, 276, 280, 282-283, 285-286, 289, 290, 292, 293

Singer, J. E., 2

Skinner, B. F., 11-13; *Science and Human Behavior*, 37-47; *Behavior of Organisms*, 52, 55, 60n2, 61n6; *Verbal Behavior*, 48-63

Slote, M., 147n3

Smart, J. J. C., 177, 179, 182n9, 202, 228, 271; "Sensations and Brain Processes," 152; behaviorism and, 175, 176

Social psychology, 5

Solipsism, 168

Solomon, R., 5

Soul, 136, 137, 142

Spectrum inversion, 252, 256, 257, 258, 259-260, 264, 266-267n18, 288, 302n21

Speech, *see* Behavior, verbal; Behaviorism, linguistic

Stalnaker, R., 6

Standards, 31-32, 71

Stimulus, 43-44, 49-57, 60nn2, 3, 61nn4-7, 62nn12, 15,46, 175; pain and, 146-147nn1, 2, 156-157; amusement and, 149, 150, 153, 154; mental states and, 179, 200, 201, 212, 230. *See also* Response

Stimulus Switching, 302n21

Structure, 15, 35, 49, 58; of events, 149, 150, 154

Subjectivity, 160, 162-165, 166, 167n9, 168n14

Symbols, 20, 187

Synonymy, 206n4

Synonymy-classes, 223-224, 231n3

Syntactic structure, 58

Systems, 91, 135, 141-142, 162; mechanical, 95; physical, 95-96, 173, 182; biological, 187, 188; functionalism and, 269, 270, 289, 292; brainheaded, 281

Tarsky, 112

Taylor, Charles, 110

Telepathy, 136

Temperature, concept of, 16-17, 19-20, 215n13, 223-225, 231n3, 290

Terms: natural kind, 69, 71, 78, 105; general, 72; functional, 174; theoretical, 208-213, 214n8, 215n15; mental, 261, 267n21, 269, 272; input and output, 269. *See also* Meaning, of terms

Thalberg, I., 5

Theory, *see* Identifications

Thomas, S., 176, 178, 182n6

Thoughts, spatial location of, 69, 73-74. *See also* Ideas

Token states, 99-101, 157

Transitivity, 115, 207

Turing machines, 4, 135, 159, 172, 182n3, 232, 241, 271, 273, 275-277; states of, 139-140, 173, 177-178, 269-270, 299-301n14; probabilistic automaton and, 226, 240

Type identity of psychological states, 237-238, 242, 244-246, 248, 249; functionalism and, 251, 253

Unconscious, 39

Unified field theory, 31-32

Universal psychology, 292-293

Variables of behavior, 40-42, 48, 54

Verbs, mental, 109

Verification, 33-34, 112

Vienna Circle, 15, 16, 20, 22

Vienna positivists, 25
Vocabulary, *see* Language; Verbs, mental

Waismann, F., 15
Water, identity of, 69, 70, 72, 78-87
Watson, J. B., 188, 193

Whitehead, A. N., 24
Wiedemann-Franz Law, 290
William of Ockham, 3
Wittgenstein, L., 15, 252, 263
Wollheim, R., 2
Word Switching, 302n20